From a Flexible Type System to Metapredicative Wellordering Proofs

Inauguraldissertation
der Philosophisch-naturwissenschaftlichen Fakultät
der Universität Bern

vorgelegt von

Florian Ranzi

aus Italien

Leiter der Arbeit:
Prof. Dr. G. Jäger und Prof. Dr. Th. Strahm
Institut für Informatik und angewandte Mathematik

Von der Philosophisch-naturwissenschaftlichen Fakultät angenommen.

Bern, den 1. Dezember 2015

Der Dekan:
Prof. Dr. G. Colangelo

Acknowledgements

I want to thank Prof. Dr. Gerhard Jäger and Prof. Dr. Thomas Strahm for their guidance, advice, and the optimal working environment they offered. I also want to thank Prof. Dr. Wilfried Buchholz for serving as second examiner and for helping me improve this thesis during my stay as a guest at the University of Munich. The research for this thesis was supported by the Swiss National Science Foundation.

Many thanks go also to the members of the Logic and Theory Group, my friends, and my family: *Liebi Lüt, merssi viumau für die schöni Zyt!—Tusen takk kjære gjøk for at du hjalp meg på mange forskjellige måter!—Caspita, ce l'ho fatta! Grazie mille ai cirilli per il vostro sostegno e grazie anche a quello che bada all'ultima penna del Malcantone.—Ge, oarg! Jetzad kimm i scho z'ruck, i gfrei mi! Dankschee an de Frechbären fürs Woaten.—* ぼちぼち 行こか![1]

[1] *Bochi-bochi iko-ka!*

Contents

Introduction

First-order theories that result from number theory by adding new predicate symbols P and axioms for P are used as a tool to investigate the proof-theoretic strength of various theories (consider for example [BFPS81]). In particular and with focus on the topic of this thesis, predicates $P^{\mathfrak{A}}$ may formalize for each positive arithmetical operator form $\mathfrak{A}(X, x)$ a fixed-point F_Φ of the function $\Phi\colon \mathcal{P}(\mathbb{N}) \to \mathcal{P}(\mathbb{N})$, where Φ is the intended interpretation of $\mathfrak{A}$ and $\mathcal{P}(\mathbb{N})$ is the power set of the natural numbers $\mathbb{N}$ (such functions Φ are also called *operators*, compare [Acz77a] for background information). A famous example of such a formalization is the impredicative theory ID_1 (an arithmetical first-order theory for non-iterated general inductive definitions, see [BFPS81]). ID_1 allows to axiomatize the least fixed-point I_Φ of such Φ by means of axioms for the closure property and the induction principle assigned to $P^{\mathfrak{A}}$; in the context of Φ this can be expressed by

$$\Phi(I_\Phi) \subseteq I_\Phi \tag{Φ-Closure}$$

$$\forall X \subseteq \mathbb{N}\,(\Phi(X) \subseteq X \to I_\Phi \subseteq X) \tag{Φ-Induction}$$

and if considered as a definition of I_Φ, its impredicative characterization becomes apparent by the unrestricted quantification over subsets of $\mathbb{N}$. Furthermore, one can consider just any fixed-point F_Φ, thus described by

$$\Phi(F_\Phi) = F_\Phi \tag{Φ-Fixed-Point}$$

that is a consequence of (Φ-Closure) and (Φ-Induction) in case of F_Φ being I_Φ. For each positive operator form $\mathfrak{A}(X, x)$, let now $P^{\mathfrak{A}}$ be a distinguished new unary relation symbol not in $\mathcal{L}_{\mathsf{PA}}$, i.e., not in the language of Peano arithmetic PA. Then the language obtained by extending $\mathcal{L}_{\mathsf{PA}}$ with such new symbols $P^{\mathfrak{A}}$ is used as the language $\mathcal{L}_{\mathsf{ID}}$ for the theory ID_1 that formalizes (Φ-Induction) by means of the axiom scheme

$$\forall x(\mathfrak{A}(\{z\colon B\}, x) \to B_z(x)) \to \forall x(P^{\mathfrak{A}}(x) \to B_z(x)) \tag{ID}$$

where B can be any $\mathcal{L}_{\mathsf{ID}}$ formula and $B_z(t)$ denotes for any $\mathcal{L}_{\mathsf{PA}}$ term t the substitution of z in B by t; furthermore, $\mathfrak{A}(\{z\colon B\}, x)$ expresses the straight-forward substitution of atomic formulas $t \in X$ in $\mathfrak{A}(X, x)$ by $B_z(t)$.

A theory that formalizes fixed-points over positive arithmetical operator forms $\mathfrak{A}$ is the theory $\widehat{\mathsf{ID}}_1$ that also has $\mathcal{L}_{\mathsf{ID}}$ as its language. $\widehat{\mathsf{ID}}_1$ was introduced in [Acz77b] and further analyzed for the iterated case in [Fef82] and [JKSS99], using predicative methods. While $\widehat{\mathsf{ID}}_1$ has no formalization for (Φ-Induction) at all, a theory that is predicatively reducible and that axiomatizes certain (so-called positive) instances of $\Phi(X) \subseteq X \to I_\Phi \subseteq X$ is the theory ID_1^* that again has $\mathcal{L}_{\mathsf{ID}}$ as its language. ID_1^* has been analyzed in [Pro06] and [AR10], where in particular $|\mathsf{ID}_1^*| = |\widehat{\mathsf{ID}}_1| = \varphi(\varepsilon_0, 0)$ has been shown for the proof-theoretic ordinal of ID_1^*.

Both theories ID_1^* and $\widehat{\mathsf{ID}}_1$ are prominent examples from the realm of metapredicative[2] proof-theory, and they were the starting-point for this thesis in order to analyze new means and theories that reach in proof-theoretic strength to larger[3] ordinals. But the inspiration and motivation to do so came mainly from [Fef92] in case of ID_1^* and from [Lei94] in case of $\widehat{\mathsf{ID}}_1$. This thesis therefore consists of

- an introductory Part I, containing observations on ordinal theoretic concepts and general definitions,
- a main Part II that deals with the concept of *typed induction* as a generalization of *positive induction* from ID_1^*, and
- a Part III that deals with the concept of *stratified induction* as a generalization of the *fixed point* theory $\widehat{\mathsf{ID}}_1$.

It turns out that stratified induction allows for a fine-graded calibration of sub-theories below Γ_0 (the results on ordinals above $\varphi(\varepsilon_0, 0)$ are due to [JP15]) but which is, however, not strong enough to tackle our quest for larger ordinals. Typed induction on the other hand turns out to be a strong version that calibrates with prominent ordinals such as the *small Veblen*

[2]The notion *metapredicativity* is meant in general for the approach to use proof-theoretic methods from the realm of *predicative* proof-theory instead of *impredicative* methods. In particular for wellordering proofs, we aim to avoid the use of so-called collapsing functions. We refer to [Str99] or [JKSS99]. For further reading on *metapredicativity*, we refer to [Jäg05] and [JS05].

[3]The notion *large* is meant from our perspective of metapredicativity, i.e., our focus lies on ordinals that follow in the wake of the Bachmann-Howard ordinal.

ordinal or the *large Veblen ordinal*. We consider the results on typed induction as the main achievement of this thesis because it yields a *positive* result (while stratified induction yields a somewhat negative result as it provides only access to rather small ordinals—but this surely depends on the perspective and the point of interest one has). For this reason, we shall start with typed induction.

About Typed Induction

In [Fef92], S. Feferman introduced a two-sorted quantificational logic and showed that it has the same strength as (Skolem's system of) primitive recursive arithmetic. The characteristics of this two-sorted quantificational logic are that it is an *applicative theory* augmented by type variables as the second sort and with a refined notion of comprehension terms, so-called type and function terms. In particular, this theory embodies a rule $(\mathsf{F}_0\text{-}\mathsf{IR}_N)$ that is called the function-induction rule on N (where N is interpreted as the type for the natural numbers). It was shown to be closed under a strengthening of this rule to *finitary* inductively generated types I, called $(\mathsf{F}_0\text{-}\mathsf{IR}_I)$.

This kind of theory strongly influenced the shape of our applicative theory FIT that we are going to introduce in Part II. Our motivation to examine the theory in [Fef92] was to find a natural theory for carrying out metapredicative wellordering proofs in the spirit of higher type functionals for ordinals. It seemed to provide a suitable environment for doing so. But soon, we realized that aside from this, the theory gave rise to the question of what consequence a function-induction rule for *infinitary* inductively generated types would have on the one side and to the idea of implementing the wellordering proofs through accessible part inductive definitions on the other side (having in mind our desire for metapredicative wellordering proofs). Hence, we tackle this question on infinitary inductively generated types only for inductively generated types that correspond to the (inductively defined) *accessible part* $\mathsf{I}_{\mathbb{P},\mathbb{Q}}$ for a (binary) relation $\mathbb{Q}$ on a domain $\mathbb{P}$. In fact, our methods implicitly suggest that we get the same result for the variant where we allow for general inductively generated types.

FIT stands for "*theory for function(al)s, non-iterated inductive definitions, and types (of level* 1*)*", and it represents the first step for a generalization of the theory in [Fef92] which turns out to have the small Veblen ordinal as measure for its proof-theoretic strength, i.e., $\vartheta\Omega^\omega$ when using the terminology of [RW93]. Theories that have $\vartheta\Omega^\omega$ as proof-theoretic strength are for instance $\Pi^1_2\text{-}\mathsf{BI}_0$ from [RW93] or more recently $\mathsf{RCA}_0 + (\Pi^1_1(\Pi^0_3)\text{-}\mathsf{CA}_0)^-$ from [Jer14]. While these theories are analyzed by *impredicative* proof-theoretic methods, our treatment of FIT uses *metapredicative* methods for the lower bound. For the upper bound, we use an embedding into $\Pi^1_3\text{-}\mathsf{RFN}_0$ and get a desired upper bound result in the realm of metapredicative proof-theory due to D. Probst's *modular ordinal analysis* from [Pro15] that determines by metapredicative methods the proof-theoretic ordinal of various theories with strength below (and reaching to) the Bachmann-Howard ordinal $\vartheta\varepsilon_{\Omega+1}$. One of these theories is Π^1_3-RFN_0 (which is denoted by $\mathsf{p}_3(\mathsf{ACA}_0)$ in [Pro15]) and determined to have the proof-theoretic strength of the small Veblen ordinal. Furthermore, we mention the system $\mathsf{KPi}^0 + (\Pi_3\text{-}\mathsf{Ref})$ from [JS05] which is also related to Π^1_3-RFN_0. In particular, [JS05] explains how the proof-theoretic strength of $\mathsf{KPi}^0 + (\Pi_3\text{-}\mathsf{Ref})$ can be determined to be $\vartheta\Omega^\omega$ by metapredicative methods.

Results on the Theories FIT and TID

We now explain the methods used for the ordinal analysis of FIT. First, we shall consider a canonical implementation of FIT as a subsystem of ID_1 in which metapredicative wellordering proofs can be carried out in a perspicuous way and where the interpretation back into FIT is straightforward. This subsystem of ID_1 is called TID for "*theory of typed (accessible part) inductive definitions (of level* 1)" and essentially arises from ID_1 by restricting to accessible part inductive definitions and adapting the closure axioms, its induction scheme on the natural numbers, and its generalized induction scheme (ID) to (the translation of) the function types of FIT, akin to the restriction of ID_1 to the theory $\mathsf{ID}^*_1\!\restriction$ from [Pro06].

For the (proof-theoretic) upper bound of FIT (and hence for TID), we shall embed it into the system Π^1_3-RFN_0 of second-order arithmetic for Π^1_3 ω-model reflection. In order to obtain the desired upper bound $\vartheta\Omega^\omega$, we shall use the results from [RW93] by impredicative methods, noting that the (meta)predicative treatment from [Pro15] has not been published yet. Figure 1 depicts the abovementioned approaches accordingly. Furthermore, at the end of Chapter 7 we shall give some remarks on the canonical generalization of TID to a theory $\mathsf{TID}^{\mathbf{f}}$ for general typed inductive definitions with the *full* range of positive arithmetical operator forms, leading to the same proof-theoretic strength of TID and $\mathsf{TID}^{\mathbf{f}}$.

Results on the Generalizations TID_n and TID^+_n

The applicative theory FIT from Chapter 5 has the small Veblen ordinal $\vartheta\Omega^\omega$ as its proof-theoretic ordinal. The provided wellordering proof is implemented in an arithmetical theory TID based on accessible part inductive definitions of primitive recursive binary relations and using the *finitary*

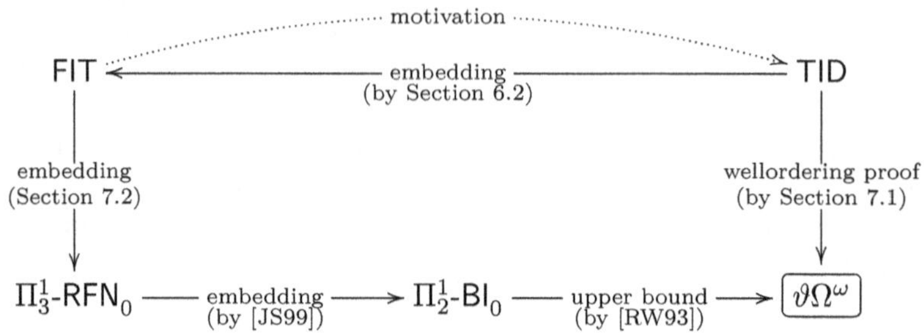

Figure 1.: Strategy to determine the proof-theoretic ordinal $\vartheta\Omega^\omega$ of FIT

Veblen functions as a means to denote ordinals below $\vartheta\Omega^\omega$. We shall generalize TID in Chapter 8 by the theories TID_n and TID_n^+ for each $n \in \mathbb{N}$ where TID_1 essentially corresponds to TID. In particular TID_1^+ and TID_2 are suitable for reusing the wellordering method of TID and generalizing it (by an internalization) to ordinals that are denoted by *Klammersymbols* (as introduced by K. Schütte in [Sch54]), i.e., to ordinals below the large Veblen ordinal $\vartheta\Omega^\Omega$. It turns out that $|\mathsf{TID}_1^+| = \vartheta\Omega^\Omega$ holds.

In order to be able to work more efficiently with Klammersymbols, we shall introduce the notion of a *partition of a Klammersymbol* together with auxiliary notions and operations that allow the manipulation of the represented ordinals in a natural way that is suitable for metapredicative investigations. The benefit of our approach is that we can work directly with the results from [Sch54] and keep the reader focused on the main techniques that are used for the wellordering proof. More precisely, we shall introduce the new notions and operations in such a way that it becomes clear that (apart from the results from [Sch54]) only primitive recursive manipulations of finite strings are needed. The difficulty of this conceptually simple but technically rather complicated section stems merely from our aim to internalize the wellordering proof of TID within the arithmetical theory TID_1^+.

For the upper bound of TID_1^+, we can refer once more to D. Probst's work [Pro15] on modular ordinal analysis of subsystems of second-order arithmetic because we shall show that each arithmetical formula provable in TID_1^+ is also provable in the system $\mathsf{p}_1\mathsf{p}_3(\mathsf{ACA}_0)$ from [Pro15] which formalizes over ACA_0 that each set is contained in a model of Π^1_3-RFN_0. Its strength is the large Veblen ordinal (see [Pro15]).

Conjectures on Further Generalizations TID_n^+ and TID_n

By considering TID_0 as the previously mentioned theory $\mathsf{ID}_1^*\!\restriction$ from [Pro06] and defining TID_0^+ analogously from TID_0 as we defined TID_1^+ from TID_1, we can show upper bound results that suggest generalizations to theories TID_n and TID_n^+ with conjectures as indicated in Table 1 on page 8. This table reads as follows: We use $\Omega(1,\xi) := \Omega^\xi$ and $\Omega(k+1,\xi) := \Omega^{\Omega(k,\xi)}$ for each $k \geq 1$ and each ordinal ξ from [RW93] in order to denote certain ordinals, and we use the following symbols:

✓ marks the treatment in this thesis

"✓" marks a strong conjecture (results of this thesis point to this)

(?) marks a conjecture

The conjectures would not only resonate and calibrate in a nice way with the theories from [Pro15], but they would also identify the *small Veblen ordinal* and the *large Veblen ordinal* as first steps towards a characterization of the notion *metapredicativity* in terms of ordinals such as the notion *impredicativity*[4] is often identified with relying on the ordinal theoretic concepts of *collapsing functions*. The difficulty of further investigating this conjecture is to set up an ordinal notation system that goes beyond the notation system that is based on Klammersymbols and treated in Chapter 8. A promising trail towards an ordinal notation system that is suited to reuse the results from Chapter 7 and Chapter 11 seems to be the concept of *higher type functionals* in the spirit of [Wey76] (see [Buc15] for more details). The theories FIT_n and FIT_n^+ listed in Table 1 on page 8 are not explicitly treated in this thesis but will be mentioned in the conclusion of Part II in Chapter 12.

[4]By impredicativity we mean the notion from the setting of ordinal analysis as used for instance in [BFPS81].

TYPE LEVEL	ORDINAL	UPPER BOUND	LOWER BOUND	REFERENCE SYSTEM FROM [Pro15]	COMMON REFERENCE SYSTEM
TID_0 (FIT_0)	$\vartheta(\Omega\cdot\omega)$ [$\varphi(\omega,0)$]	✓	✓	$\mathsf{p}_2(\mathsf{ACA}_0)$	Σ^1_1-DC_0
TID_0^+ (FIT_0^+)	$\vartheta(\Omega\cdot\Omega)$ [Fef.-Sch. Γ_0]	✓	✓	$\mathsf{p}_1\mathsf{p}_2(\mathsf{ACA}_0)$	ATR_0
TID FIT	$\vartheta\Omega^\omega$ [small Veblen]	✓	✓	$\mathsf{p}_3(\mathsf{ACA}_0)$	Π^1_3-RFN_0
TID_1^+ (FIT_1^+)	$\vartheta\Omega^\Omega$ [large Veblen]	✓	✓	$\mathsf{p}_1\mathsf{p}_3(\mathsf{ACA}_0)$	Π^1_3-RFN_0 $+(\mathsf{BR})$
TID_2 (FIT_2)	$\vartheta\Omega^{\Omega^\omega}$	✓	"✓"	$\mathsf{p}_4(\mathsf{ACA}_0)$	Π^1_4-RFN_0
TID_2^+ (FIT_2^+)	$\vartheta\Omega^{\Omega^\Omega}$	✓	?	$\mathsf{p}_1\mathsf{p}_4(\mathsf{ACA}_0)$	Π^1_4-RFN_0 $+(\mathsf{BR})$
⋮	⋮	⋮	⋮	⋮	⋮
TID_n (FIT_n) for $n \geq 3$	$\vartheta\Omega(n,\omega)$	✓	?	$\mathsf{p}_{n+2}(\mathsf{ACA}_0)$	Π^1_{n+2}-RFN_0
TID_n^+ (FIT_n^+) for $n \geq 3$	$\vartheta\Omega(n,\Omega)$	✓	?	$\mathsf{p}_1\mathsf{p}_{n+2}(\mathsf{ACA}_0)$	Π^1_{n+2}-RFN_0 $+(\mathsf{BR})$
⋮	⋮	⋮	⋮	⋮	⋮
$\mathsf{TID}_{<\omega}$ ($\mathsf{FIT}_{<\omega}$)	$\vartheta\varepsilon_{\Omega+1}$ [Bachm.-How.]	✓	?	$\bigcup_{n\in\mathbb{N}}\mathsf{p}_n(\mathsf{ACA}_0)$	ID_1

Table 1.: Overview of Typed Induction

About Stratified Induction

The aim of Part III is to investigate the proof-theoretic strength of a theory of stratified induction $\mathsf{SID}_{<\omega}$. We remark that this part has been published in an article by Th. Strahm and the author of this thesis (see [RS14]). $\mathsf{SID}_{<\omega}$ has a similar approach as ID_1^*, namely in formalizing certain instances of (Φ-Induction), see page 1, but it is based on the fixed-point theory $\widehat{\mathsf{ID}}_1$. In order to illustrate the differences, we compare the axioms of those two theories in an informal way (precise formulations for $\mathsf{SID}_{<\omega}$ are given in Chapter 13). While $\widehat{\mathsf{ID}}_1$ has no instances of (ID), the theory ID_1^* allows for positive induction (ID^*), i.e., it contains instances of (ID) where B may contain $P^{\mathfrak{A}}$ at most positive. The new theory $\mathsf{SID}_{<\omega}$ that we propose and investigate here is used to express a kind of *stratified induction* (over fixed-points) by admitting indexed copies of the above mentioned symbols $P^{\mathfrak{A}}$, namely by replacing $P^{\mathfrak{A}}$ with infinitely many distinguished new unary relation symbols $P_n^{\mathfrak{A}}$ for $1 \leq n < \omega$ (i.e., $P_1^{\mathfrak{A}}, P_2^{\mathfrak{A}}, \ldots$). Hence, $\mathsf{SID}_{<\omega}$ has a different language than ID_1 and further has stratified induction (over fixed-points) via the following axiom scheme

$$\forall x(\mathfrak{A}(\{z\colon B\}, x) \to B_z(x)) \to \forall x(P_n^{\mathfrak{A}}(x) \to B_z(x)) \qquad (\mathsf{SID})$$

for $1 \leq n < \omega$ and for which B is restricted to be a formula in this new language which may contain relation symbols $P_l^{\mathfrak{B}}$ only if $l < n$ holds (while $\mathfrak{B}$ is some operator form).

Let SID_n denote the restriction of the theory $\mathsf{SID}_{<\omega}$ to formulas that contain at most the symbols $P_l^{\mathfrak{A}}$ with $l \leq n$. The theory SID_0 is just Peano arithmetic PA and the theory SID_1 is essentially a weakening of ID_1^* where (ID^*) is further restricted in B to allow only arithmetical formulas. We will investigate the theories SID_n of *finitely stratified induction* and refer for the next question on the treatment of *transfinitely stratified induction* to [JP15]. We shall show how we can apply the proof-theoretic technique of *asymmetric interpretation* very neatly in order to gain proof-theoretic insight into this concept of stratified induction.

Aiming towards a characterization of $\mathsf{SID}_{<\omega}$, note that it is the same as $\bigcup_{n<\omega} \mathsf{SID}_n$ and that, obviously, SID_n embeds into ID_n^* for any $n < \omega$. So we have for the proof-theoretic ordinal $|\mathsf{SID}_{<\omega}| \leq |\bigcup_{n<\omega} \mathsf{ID}_n^*| = \Gamma_0$, see [Can85]. We show that actually $|\mathsf{SID}_{<\omega}| = |\widehat{\mathsf{ID}}_1|$ holds, and since $\widehat{\mathsf{ID}}_1$

trivially embeds into $\mathsf{SID}_{<\omega}$, it suffices to show that $\varphi(\varepsilon_0, 0) = |\widehat{\mathsf{ID}}_1|$ is an upper bound for $|\mathsf{SID}_{<\omega}|$. The latter is done via an asymmetric interpretation combined with partial cut-elimination. Our approach bears some similarities to D. Leivant's proof-theoretic approach to computational complexity (cf. e.g. [Lei94]) which makes use of ramified theories over (finitary) inductively generated free algebras. Here we treat ramified general inductive definitions over the natural numbers. W. Buchholz's notes [Buc05] contributed to the presentation of the material.

The equality $\varphi(\varepsilon_0, 0) = |\widehat{\mathsf{ID}}_1| = |\mathsf{SID}_n| = |\mathsf{SID}_{<\omega}|$ (with $n < \omega$) established here still leaves the question open concerning the relationship of stratification to iteration. For this, we refer to [JP15] where a generalization of stratification to the transfinite gives an answer. Table 2 captures some aspects of this relationship line by line and we refer again to [JP15] for the meaning and characterization of the last three rows.

STRATIFICATION	ORDINAL	REFERENCE SYSTEM ITERATION
SID_0	ε_0	$\widehat{\mathsf{ID}}_0$
$\mathsf{SID}_{<\omega}$	$\varphi(\varepsilon_0, 0)$	$\widehat{\mathsf{ID}}_1$
$\mathsf{SID}_{<\omega+\omega}$	$\varphi(\varepsilon_{\varepsilon_0}, 0)$	—
$\mathsf{SID}_{<\omega^\omega}$	$\varphi(\varphi(\omega, 0), 0)$	—
$\mathsf{SID}_{<\varepsilon_0}$	$\varphi(\varphi(\varepsilon_0, 0), 0)$	$\widehat{\mathsf{ID}}_2$

Table 2.: Overview of Stratified Induction

Part I.

Ordinals and General Definitions

1. General Definitions

1.1. General Notational Framework

We shall work with three conceptually different kinds of logical frameworks: First in Chapter 5 with the two-sorted theory FIT (where FIT has the language $\mathcal{L}_{\mathsf{FIT}}$) that is an applicative theory enhanced by a type system, then in Chapter 6 and Chapter 13 with the first-order theories TID and $\mathsf{SID}_{<\omega}$, respectively, that are extensions of Peano arithmetic PA (where PA has the language $\mathcal{L}_{\mathsf{PA}}$) by new predicates, and starting from Chapter 7, we shall work with some subsystems of second order arithmetic (with language $\mathcal{L}^2_{\mathsf{PA}}$). Hence, we shall work in this thesis with up to two sorts of (countably many) variables and we use

$a, b, c, d, u, v, w, x, y, z$	as syntactic variables for the first sort,
U, V, W, X, Y, Z	as syntactic variables for the second sort,

and choose

$=, \neg, \rightarrow, \vee, \wedge, \exists, \forall$	as basic logical symbols.

Now, let $\mathcal{L}$ be one of the languages of the abovementioned theories, and assume that the notion of $\mathcal{L}$ terms and $\mathcal{L}$ formulas has been already introduced. In case that $\mathcal{L}$ is clear from the context, we shall sometimes drop the reference to $\mathcal{L}$ by just using the notions term and formula.

- s, t, r shall primarily be used as syntactic variables for $\mathcal{L}$ terms.
- A, B, C, D, E, F shall be used as syntactic variables to denote $\mathcal{L}$ formulas, and we call an atomic $\mathcal{L}$ formula or its negated version a *literal*.
- If an $\mathcal{L}$ formula is introduced as $A(a)$, this means that A denotes this

formula and that the variable a may occur freely in A (i.e., a is not in the scope of any $\forall a$ or $\exists a$ quantification).

- FV(A) denotes the set of free variables of the first sort of A.
- a, b, c, d, u, v, w, shall primarily be used within an $\mathcal{L}$ formula to denote free variables of the first sort.
- k, l, m, n, p, q shall primarily be used as variables in our meta-theory, i.e., as ranging there over the natural numbers.
- Parentheses may be added or dropped in order to make expressions unambiguous or more readable, e.g., we may write a quantification in the form $\exists x A$, $(\exists x) A$, or $\exists x(A)$.
- We often prefer *infix notation* rather than prefix notation when dealing with binary function and relation symbols.
- For $\to$, we follow the usual convention of right-associativity, e.g., $A \to B \to C$ denotes $A \to (B \to C)$. We further write $A \leftrightarrow B$ to denote $(A \to B) \land (B \to A)$. Moreover, $\land$ binds stronger than $\to$.

1.1.1. Vector Notations

If $*$ denotes one of the syntactic variables that will be introduced in the this thesis, then we allow the usual annotations such as $*'$, $\tilde{*}$, or subscripts $*_i$ (for $i \in \mathbb{N}$, i.e., for natural numbers i). With respect to subscripts, we also use the vector notation $\vec{*}$ to denote lists of the form $*_1, \ldots, *_n$ for some $n \in \mathbb{N}$. If we introduce a list as

$$\bar{*}^{(n)}$$

for a particular $n \in \mathbb{N}$ and a syntactic variable $*$, then we mean

$$*_1, \ldots, *_n$$

and we may write $\bar{*}^{(k)}$ for any $k \in \mathbb{N}$ in order to denote $*_1, \ldots, *_{\min(k,n)}$. In some rare cases we may write for specific constants c (e.g., for 0) the expression $\bar{c}^{(n)}$ to denote the list $c, \ldots, c$ of length n, and hence we read $\vec{c}$ analogously. This notation will come in handy in particular when we will be working with ordinal notations that are based on the finitary Veblen functions. If $n = 0$, then $\bar{*}^{(n)}$ and $\vec{*}$ denote the empty list.

Applications of all these notations will be obvious, following common conventions—for instance $\forall \bar{x}^{(3)} A$ shall abbreviate $\forall x_1 \forall x_2 \forall x_3 A$ as usual, and $\forall \vec{x} A$ is just A if $\vec{x}$ is the empty list. Also when writing $f\bar{t}^{(n)}$ for a list of terms $\bar{t}^{(n)}$ and an n-ary function symbol f, it is usually meant to abbreviate $ft_1 \dots t_n$ rather than $ft_1, \dots, t_n$.

1.1.2. Class Terms and Substitution

$\mathcal{L}$ *class terms* are objects of the form

$$\Lambda a.A$$

for any $\mathcal{L}$ formula A and we use $\mathcal{A}, \mathcal{B}, \mathcal{C}, \mathcal{D}$ as syntactic variables for $\mathcal{L}$ class terms. Sometimes, class terms are also called comprehension terms, and we do not use the more common notations $\{a \colon A\}$ or $\lambda a.A$ because these notions are already reserved in our setting of the applicative theory FIT.

Substitution of a variable a in an $\mathcal{L}$ formula A by an $\mathcal{L}$ term t is denoted by $A(t/a)$ and $A_a(t)$, or just by $A(t)$ in case A has been introduced in the form $A(a)$, and as usual we assume (if necessary) an appropriate renaming of bound variables in A to avoid a clash of bound variables. Then for $\mathcal{A}$ being $\Lambda a.A$, we set

$$\mathcal{A}(t) := t \in \mathcal{A} := A(t/a)$$

for any $\mathcal{L}$ term t and we ambiguously write $\mathcal{A} \in \mathcal{L}$ to stress that $\mathcal{A}$ is an $\mathcal{L}$ class term. Moreover, we also extend this to lists of variables $\vec{a} = a_1, \dots, a_n$ and have objects of the form

$$\Lambda a_1. \dots \Lambda a_n.A$$

or $\Lambda \vec{a}.A$ for short with $(\Lambda \vec{a}.A)(\vec{t}) := A(\vec{t}/\vec{a})$ for terms $\vec{t} = t_1, \dots, t_n$ and where $A(\vec{t}/\vec{a})$ is obtained by simultaneously replacing in A all free occurrences of the variables $\vec{a}$ by $\vec{t}$, while a renaming of bound variables may be necessary to avoid a clash of variables. We use $(\Lambda \bar{a}^{(n)}.A)(\bar{t}^{(k)})$ for $k < n$ to denote $(\Lambda a'_{k+1}. \dots \Lambda a'_n.(\Lambda \bar{a}^{(k)}.(A(a'_{k+1}, \dots, a'_n / a_{k+1}, \dots, a_n))(\bar{t}^{(k)})) \dots)$ where $a'_{k+1}, \dots, a'_n$ are fresh variables that do not appear in $\bar{t}^{(k)}$, $\bar{a}^{(n)}$, A.

In case that $\mathcal{L}$ also embodies variables X, Y, Z of the second sort, we mean by *substitution of a variable* X in an $\mathcal{L}$ formula A by an $\mathcal{L}$ class term $\mathcal{B}$ the expression

$$A(\mathcal{B}/X)$$

which is obtained from A by substituting any atomic formula Xt with $\mathcal{B}(t)$ while a renaming of bound variables may be necessary as usual. If A has been introduced in the form $A(X)$, we may also just write $A(\mathcal{B})$ for $A(\mathcal{B}/X)$.

In case R is a unary relation symbol in $\mathcal{L}$ or a second sort variable, we also define

$$A(R/X) := A(\mathcal{B}/X)$$

for $\mathcal{B} := \Lambda a.Ra$. Furthermore, if $\mathcal{A}$ is an $\mathcal{L}$ class term $\Lambda a.A$, then we set

$$\mathcal{A}(\mathcal{B}/X) := \Lambda a.A(\mathcal{B}/X)$$

Accordingly, we let substitution for number variables be defined by $\mathcal{A}_z(t) := \mathcal{A}(t/z) := \Lambda a.A(t/z)$ if a does not occur in t, and otherwise we let $\mathcal{A}_z(t) := \mathcal{A}'_z(t)$ for $\mathcal{A}' := \Lambda b.A(b/a)$ and some b that does not occur in A, t.

1.2. The Base Theory PA of Peano Arithmetic

We introduce basic notions that we are going to use in combination with arithmetical theories.

Definition 1.1. $\mathcal{L}_{\mathsf{PA}}$ is the first-order language of Peano arithmetic with

- just one sort of variables x, referred to as *(number) variables*,
- a unary relation symbol U (without further interpretation and that is needed for proof-theoretic investigations),
- a symbol $=$ for equality,
- function symbols for each primitive recursive function, and for $n \in \mathbb{N}$, we denote by PR^n the collection of those function symbols that have arity n, and

- relation symbols R_f for each function symbol $f \in \mathrm{PR}^n$ with $n \neq 0$, and R_f has the same arity as f.

For the sake of completeness, we provide $\mathrm{PR} := \bigcup_{n \in \mathbb{N}} \mathrm{PR}^n$ via one of the usual formulations by an inductive definition over $n \in \mathbb{N}$ of function symbols, while $\mathbf{0}^n, \mathbf{S}, \mathbf{I}_i^{n+1}$ denote here symbols for the *constant zero function*, the *successor function*, and the *i-th projection function on* $n+1$-*tuple*, respectively, while $\mathbf{C}, \mathbf{R}$ are auxiliary symbols in our meta-theory for expressing *composition* and *primitive recursion*, respectively:

- $\mathbf{0}^n \in \mathrm{PR}^n$, $\mathbf{S} \in \mathrm{PR}^1$, and $\mathbf{I}_i^{n+1} \in \mathrm{PR}^{n+1}$ for each i with $1 \leq i \leq n+1$.
- $(\mathbf{C} f g_1 \ldots g_m) \in \mathrm{PR}^n$ if $f \in \mathrm{PR}^m$, $g_1, \ldots, g_m \in \mathrm{PR}^n$, and $m, n \geq 1$.
- $(\mathbf{R} f g) \in \mathrm{PR}^{n+1}$ if $f \in \mathrm{PR}^n$ and $g \in \mathrm{PR}^{n+2}$.

Remark 1.2. We added relation symbols R_f to $\mathcal{L}_{\mathsf{PA}}$ for technical reasons, namely in order to ease the embedding from TID into FIT in Chapter 6 (cf., Remark 6.12).

Definition 1.3. The language $\mathcal{L}^2_{\mathsf{PA}}$ denotes the extension of $\mathcal{L}_{\mathsf{PA}}$ to the language of second-order arithmetic, i.e., it is $\mathcal{L}_{\mathsf{PA}}$ extended by a second sort of variables X, referred to as *set variables* or just *sets*.

Notation 1.4. We use the following notations for certain symbols of $\mathcal{L}_{\mathsf{PA}}$:

- $0_\mathbb{N}$ and $\mathbf{0}$ denote the constant $\mathbf{0}^0$ for the number zero,
- $+_\mathbb{N}$ denotes the binary function symbol for addition of two natural numbers,
- $<_\mathbb{N}$ denotes the binary less-than relation on the natural numbers, and
- $\dot{-}_\mathbb{N}$ denotes the modified subtraction function on the natural numbers (i.e, if $m <_\mathbb{N} n$ then $m \dot{-}_\mathbb{N} n = 0$ holds).

Further, $1_\mathbb{N}, 2_\mathbb{N}, \ldots$ abbreviate $\mathbf{S0}, \mathbf{S}(\mathbf{S0}), \ldots$ as usual. If the meaning becomes clear from the context, we may drop the subscript $\mathbb{N}$ and just use $0, 1, 2, \ldots, +, <$, and $\dot{-}$ instead. Moreover, $s \leq t$ is used in the obvious way to denote $s < t \vee s = t$.

Definition 1.5. For any $k \in \mathbb{N}$, let $(n_1, \ldots, n_k) \mapsto \langle n_1, \ldots, n_k \rangle$ be any of the usual primitive recursive injective functions $\mathbb{N}^k \to \mathbb{N}$ mapping finite lists of natural numbers of length k into the natural numbers, and let $\langle\rangle_k$ be the corresponding k-ary function symbol in $\mathcal{L}_{\mathsf{PA}}$. Then for any terms $t_1, \ldots, t_k$, we ambiguously write $\langle t_1, \ldots, t_k \rangle$ in order to denote $\langle\rangle_k(t_1, \ldots, t_k)$.

Moreover, we have the usual primitive recursive functions for projection $(m, n) \mapsto (m)_n$, list construction $(m, n) \mapsto \mathrm{cons}(m, n)$, list concatenation $(m, n) \mapsto m{*}n$, and for computing the length $n \mapsto \mathsf{lh}(n)$ of a list, which again we use ambiguously to denote the application of its corresponding function symbol in $\mathcal{L}_{\mathsf{PA}}$ to terms. We also make the following standard properties explicit:

- $\langle n_1, \ldots, n_k \rangle = 0$ if and only if $k = 0$,
- If $n \neq 0$ holds, then there is exactly one $k \neq 0$ and natural numbers $n_1, \ldots, n_k$ such that $n = \langle n_1, \ldots, n_k \rangle$ holds,
- $(n)_i < n$ for each $i < \mathsf{lh}(n)$,
- $\mathsf{lh}(\langle n_1, \ldots, n_k \rangle) = k$,
- $(\langle n_0, \ldots, n_k \rangle)_i = n_i$ for each $0 \leq i \leq k$,
- $\mathrm{cons}(n, \langle n_1, \ldots, n_k \rangle) = \langle n, n_1, \ldots, n_k \rangle$
- $\langle n_1, \ldots, n_k \rangle * \langle m_1, \ldots, m_l \rangle = \langle n_1, \ldots, n_k, m_1, \ldots, m_l \rangle$

Convention 1.6. $\mathcal{L}$ will denote in the following either $\mathcal{L}^2_{\mathsf{PA}}$ or any extension of $\mathcal{L}_{\mathsf{PA}}$ by new relation symbols. We will introduce common notions for such languages $\mathcal{L}$.

Definition 1.7. $\mathcal{L}$ terms s, t, r are defined as usual inductively from function symbols and number variables. Since $\mathcal{L}$ extends $\mathcal{L}_{\mathsf{PA}}$ only by relation symbols or variables of the second sort, all such terms are $\mathcal{L}_{\mathsf{PA}}$ terms. A *constant* is a nullary function symbol. If f is an n-ary function symbol of $\mathcal{L}_{\mathsf{PA}}$ and $\vec{t} = t_1, \ldots, t_n$ is a list of terms, then we set

$$f(\vec{t}) := f(t_1, \ldots, t_n) := f\vec{t} := ft_1 \ldots t_n$$

and this holds analogously for lists introduced by the $\vec{t}^{(n)}$ notation. For closed terms t, we mean by $t^{\mathbb{N}}$ the *numerical value* of t, i.e., the canonical valuation of t in the standard model $\mathbb{N}$.

Definition 1.8. $\mathcal{L}$ *formulas* are defined inductively as usual by use of parentheses and the basic logical symbols and we write ambiguously $A \in \mathcal{L}$ in order to stress that A is an $\mathcal{L}$ formula. For terms s, t, we may sometimes write $s \neq t$ for $\neg(s = t)$. *Atomic* $\mathcal{L}$ *formulas* are equations $s = t$ and all formulas $Rt_1 \ldots t_n$ where $R \in \mathcal{L}$ is an n-ary relation symbol and $t_1, \ldots, t_n$ are terms.

For the case that $\mathcal{L}$ is $\mathcal{L}^2_{\mathsf{PA}}$, then also Xt is an atomic formula for any set variable X and term t. $\mathcal{L}^2_{\mathsf{PA}}$ formulas further allow for *quantification over set variables* and we call an $\mathcal{L}^2_{\mathsf{PA}}$ formula *arithmetical* if it does not contain such a quantification (but set variables may still occur and we sometimes call set variables that occur free in a formula *set parameters* of this formula).

For n-ary relation symbols (or set variables) R of $\mathcal{L}$, a formula A is *positive in* R if it occurs only positively in the usual sense, i.e., no atomic formula of the form $R(t_1, \ldots, t_n)$ occurs negated in the formula which is obtained from A by translating first each subformula of the form $B_1 \to B_2$ to $\neg B_1 \vee B_2$ and where we then move every negation symbol $\neg$ towards atomic formulas, while making use of De Morgan's laws and the law of double negation.[1]

Definition 1.9.

(a) For any language $\mathcal{L}$ that is $\mathcal{L}^2_{\mathsf{PA}}$ or (possibly) extends $\mathcal{L}_{\mathsf{PA}}$ by new relation or function symbols, a standard derivability notion $\vdash$ shall be given that is based on a Hilbert-style deduction system for classical logic with equality axioms (in the first sort). In particular, we assume besides *modus ponens* that we have rules of the form

$$(\forall\text{-intro})\ \frac{A \to B}{A \to \forall x B} \qquad (\exists\text{-intro})\ \frac{B \to A}{\exists x B \to A}$$

for $x \notin \mathrm{FV}(A)$, and we assume in case that $\mathcal{L}$ is $\mathcal{L}^2_{\mathsf{PA}}$ that we have the analogous of these rules for the second sort, too.

(b) Then for any $\mathcal{L}$ formula A, we write $\vdash A$ to denote the derivability of A in this logic. Moreover, if T is a theory (i.e., a collection of non-logical axioms) with language $\mathcal{L}_{\mathsf{T}}$, then writing $\mathsf{T} \vdash A$ for any

[1] Compare this definition of positive formula with the definition of For^+ in the setting of FIT in Chapter 5.

$\mathcal{L}_\mathsf{T}$ formula A denotes the derivability of A from the axioms of T and this logic. For any set of formulas Γ, we write $\vdash \Gamma$ and $\mathsf{T} \vdash \Gamma$ in order to denote that $\vdash A$ and $\mathsf{T} \vdash A$ hold, respectively, for each $A \in \Gamma$. This notion is used analogously also in case that T contains new rules of inference (see for instance TID_n^+ in Chapter 8).

Notation 1.10. For an n-ary relation symbol R with $n \geq 1$ and $\vec{t} = t_1 \dots t_n$, we write $R(\vec{t})$ for $Rt_1 \dots t_n$. and if $n = 1$, we also introduce the following notation:

$$t \in R := Rt \quad \text{and} \quad t \notin R := \neg Rt$$

Then $(\forall x \in R)A$ and $(\exists x \in R)A$ stand for $\forall x(R(x) \to A)$ and $\exists x(R(x) \wedge A)$, respectively. These conventions shall hold analogously also for set variables X. If $\lhd$ is a binary relation symbol, we use expressions $(\forall x \lhd t)A$ and $(\exists x \lhd t)A$ to abbreviate $\forall x(x \lhd t \to A)$ and $\exists x(x \lhd t \wedge A)$, respectively.

Definition 1.11. The first-order theory PA is based on the language $\mathcal{L}_\mathsf{PA}$ and its non-logical axioms are the usual axioms of Peano arithmetic, while for each relation symbol R_f that stems from a function symbol f of arity $n \geq 1$, we have for $\vec{x} = x_1, \dots, x_n$ the axiom $\forall \vec{x}(R_f \vec{x} \leftrightarrow f\vec{x} = 0)$.

In particular for the formulation of PR as presented in Definition 1.1, the non-logical axioms of PA consist of the universal closure of the following formulas where we suppose $A \in \mathcal{L}_\mathsf{PA}$, $(\mathbf{C}fg_1 \dots g_m) \in \mathrm{PR}^n$, and $(\mathbf{R}fg) \in \mathrm{PR}^{n+1}$:

$$\mathbf{S}x \neq 0$$
$$\mathbf{S}x = \mathbf{S}y \to x = y$$
$$\mathbf{0}^n x_1 \dots x_n = 0$$
$$\mathbf{I}_i^n x_1 \dots x_n = x_i$$
$$(\mathbf{C}fg_1 \dots g_m)x_1 \dots x_n = f(g_1 x_1 \dots x_n) \dots (g_m x_1 \dots x_n)$$
$$(\mathbf{R}fg)x_1 \dots x_n 0 = f x_1 \dots x_n$$
$$(\mathbf{R}fg)x_1 \dots x_n(\mathbf{S}y) = g x_1 \dots x_n y((\mathbf{R}fg)x_1 \dots x_n y)$$
$$R_f x_1 \dots x_n \leftrightarrow f x_1 \dots x_n = 0$$
$$A(0/x) \to \forall x(A \to A(\mathbf{S}x/x)) \to \forall x A \qquad \textit{(complete induction)}$$

There is no non-logical axiom for the unary relation symbol U (besides in an instance of complete induction).

Definition 1.12. *(Arithmetical) operator forms* are objects of the form

$$\Lambda X.\mathcal{A}$$

for $\mathcal{L}^2_{\mathsf{PA}}$ class terms of the form $\mathcal{A} = \Lambda x.A$ such that A is an arithmetical formula with X being the *only* set variable that may occur in it (compare also with Section 1.1) and x is the *only* free number variable that may occur in it.[2] Note that the unary relation symbol U may occur in $\mathfrak{A}$. We use $\mathfrak{A}, \mathfrak{B}, \mathfrak{C}, \mathfrak{D}$ as syntactic variables for operator forms. For each $\mathcal{L}$ class terms $\mathcal{B}$, we set

$$(\Lambda X.\mathcal{A})(\mathcal{B}) := \mathcal{A}(\mathcal{B}/X)$$

while note that the expression $\mathcal{A}(\mathcal{B}/X)$ may yield an $\mathcal{L}$ formula here. Moreover, if R is a unary relation symbol in $\mathcal{L}$ or a set variable, then we write $\mathfrak{A}(R)$ to denote $\mathfrak{A}(\Lambda x.Rx)$. *Positive operator forms* are operator forms $\mathfrak{A} := \Lambda X.\Lambda x.A$ such that X occurs only positively in A.

Notation 1.13. We have the following abbreviations for some formulas and operator forms:

- $\mathrm{Cl}_{\mathfrak{A}}(\mathcal{A}) := \forall x(\mathfrak{A}(\mathcal{A}, x) \to \mathcal{A}(x))$ for each operator form $\mathfrak{A}$ and $\mathcal{L}$ class term $\mathcal{A}$.

and for a binary relation symbols $\lhd$ in $\mathcal{L}_{\mathsf{PA}}$ and any class term $\mathcal{A}$, we also have

- $\mathrm{Acc}_{\lhd} := \Lambda X.\Lambda x.\forall y \lhd x(Xy)$,
- $\mathrm{Prog}_{\lhd}(\mathcal{A}) := \mathrm{Cl}_{\lhd}(\mathcal{A}) := \mathrm{Cl}_{\mathrm{Acc}_{\lhd}}(\mathcal{A})$,
- $\mathrm{TI}_{\lhd} := \Lambda X.\Lambda x.(\mathrm{Prog}_{\lhd}(X) \to \forall y \lhd x(Xy))$, and

Note that we shall usually write $\mathrm{Prog}_{\lhd}$ instead of $\mathrm{Cl}_{\lhd}$. If $\lhd$ is clear from the context, we may just write Acc, Cl, Prog, and TI instead of $\mathrm{Acc}_{\lhd}$, $\mathrm{Cl}_{\lhd}$, $\mathrm{Prog}_{\lhd}$, and $\mathrm{TI}_{\lhd}$, respectively.

[2] Recall that $\mathfrak{A} := \Lambda X.\Lambda x.A$ is intended to define an operator $\Phi_{\mathfrak{A}} : \mathcal{P}(\mathbb{N}) \to \mathcal{P}(\mathbb{N})$ where $\mathfrak{A}(X, x)$ corresponds to "$x \in \Phi_{\mathfrak{A}}(X)$" for some interpretation $X \subseteq \mathbb{N}$ and $x \in \mathbb{N}$ of x and X.

2. Ordinal Theoretic Framework

In this chapter, we work in ZFC, i.e., in the broad set-theoretic framework of Zermelo–Fraenkel set theory with the axiom of choice, having the class On of ordinals at hand. The class of limit ordinals is denoted by Lim, while ω denotes the first limit ordinal. Moreover, we write 0 for $\emptyset$, $a <_{\mathrm{On}} b$ (or just $a < b$) for $a \in b$, and $a \leq_{\mathrm{On}} b$ (or just $a \leq b$) for $a \subseteq b$. For $a > 0$, we let Ω_a denote $\aleph_a$, i.e., $\{\Omega_a : a \in \mathrm{On}\}$ is the class of all uncountable initial ordinals, and we write Ω for Ω_1 and Ω_0 for 0. Over ZFC, we have that Ω_{a+1} is regular. A *normal function* is a (with respect to $<$) strictly increasing continuous function $f\colon \mathrm{On} \to \mathrm{On}$. We presuppose a knowledge about this broad set-theoretic framework and shall use commonly used notions and well-known properties of those tacitly, e.g.,

- the notion of *club* classes C with $C \subseteq \mathrm{On}$ and its correspondence to normal functions (i.e., each club class C induces a normal function enum_C that enumerates the elements of C in increasing order),
- the existence of the *derivative* $\mathrm{fix}(f) := \{a \in \mathrm{On} \colon f(a) = a\}$ of a normal function f, being a club class itself,
- *basic ordinal arithmetic* for $a, b \in \mathrm{On}$ with (ordinal) addition $a +_{\mathrm{On}} b$ (or just $a + b$), (ordinal) multiplication $a \cdot_{\mathrm{On}} b$ (or just $a \cdot b$ or ab), (ordinal) exponentiation $\exp_{\mathrm{On}}(a, b)$ (or just a^b), and the Hessenberg sum $a \#_{\mathrm{On}} b$ (or just $a \# b$),
- the usual representation of natural numbers within On as *von Neumann ordinals* $(0)_{\mathrm{On}} := \emptyset$ and $(n+1)_{\mathrm{On}} := \{(n)_{\mathrm{On}}\} \cup (n)_{\mathrm{On}}$ for each $n \in \mathbb{N}$, while we shall from now on identify $(n)_{\mathrm{On}}$ with n for each $n \in \mathbb{N}$.

We refer also to [Buc15] for more details on the relationship between different approaches to ordinal notations. It shall be clear from the context whether $<$ means $<_{\mathbb{N}}$ or $<_{\mathrm{On}}$ (and similar for the other mentioned expressions).

Definition 2.1. Let $\mathbf{P} := \{\omega^a : a \in \mathrm{On}\}$. We call the elements of $\mathbf{P}$ *additive principal numbers.*

Remark 2.2. For $a \in \mathbf{P}$ and $b, c \in \mathrm{On}$ with $b, c < a$, we have $b + c < a$ and $b + a = a$.

2.1. The Finitary Veblen Functions

Definition 2.3. The $n+1$*-ary Veblen function* $\varphi_{n+1} : \mathrm{On}^{n+1} \to \mathrm{On}$ is obtained for each $n \in \mathbb{N}$ from the ω-exponential function and the binary Veblen function φ_2 by generalizing its definition principle, i.e., we let

$$\boxed{\varphi_1(c) := \omega^c}$$

for each $c \in \mathrm{On}$ and define φ_{n+2} for $n \geq 0$ as follows:

- $\varphi_{n+2}(0, \bar{a}^{(n)}, c) := \varphi_{n+1}(\bar{a}^{(n)}, c)$.
- If $a_1, a_k > 0$ holds for some $1 \leq k \leq n+1$ with $a_{k+1} = \cdots = a_{n+1} = 0$, then $\varphi_{n+2}(\bar{a}^{(n+1)}, c)$ denotes the c-th common fixed-point of the functions

  $$x \mapsto \varphi_{n+2}(\bar{a}^{(k-1)}, b, x, \bar{0}^{(n-k+1)})$$

  that are defined on On and for each $b < a_k$.

In particular, we have for the binary Veblen function that $\varphi_2(a, c)$ for $a \in \mathrm{On} \setminus \{0\}$ is the c-th common fixed-point of the functions $x \mapsto \varphi_2(b, x)$ on On and that are given for each $b \in \mathrm{On}$ with $b < a$.

Notation 2.4. We often just use the following abbreviation

$$\boxed{\varphi(a_1, \ldots, a_n) := \varphi_n(a_1, \ldots, a_n)}$$

if the meaning becomes clear from the context.

Remark 2.5. We have that $\varphi(0, 1, 0, 0)$ and $\varphi(1, 0, 0)$ denote the *Feferman-Schütte ordinal* Γ_0 and $\varphi(1, 0)$ denotes the ordinal ε_0.

Lemma 2.6. *Let* $k, l \in \mathbb{N}$ *and* $a_1, \ldots, a_k \in \mathrm{On}$ *be given with* $a_1 \neq 0$ *and* $a_k \neq 0$. *Then*

$$\left(b < a_k \ \ \& \ \ x = \varphi(\bar{a}^{(k)}, \bar{0}^{(l+1)})\right) \implies \varphi(\bar{a}^{(k-1)}, b, \bar{0}^{(i)}, x, \bar{0}^{(j)}) = x$$

holds for every $b, x \in \mathrm{On}$ *and* $i, j \in \mathbb{N}$ *with* $i + j = l$.

Proof. This follows easily from Definition 2.3. □

2.2. Klammersymbols

Definition 2.7. We introduce now the concept of *Klammersymbols*[1] which are a generalization of the finitary Veblen functions to the transfinite by allowing arguments to be indexed by ordinals and which were introduced by K. Schütte in [Sch54].

(a) A *Klammersymbol* κ is an expression of the form

$$\begin{pmatrix} a_0 & \ldots & a_n \\ b_0 & \ldots & b_n \end{pmatrix}$$

for $a_0, \ldots, a_n, b_0, \ldots, b_n \in \mathrm{On}$ and with the condition

$$0 \leq b_0 < \ldots < b_n \tag{2.1}$$

(b) Two Klammersymbols κ_1 and κ_2 are defined to be *equal* in case that κ_1 and κ_2 can be transformed into the same Klammersymbol by adding or dropping of columns of the form $\begin{smallmatrix} 0 \\ b \end{smallmatrix}$. We denote this by

$$\kappa_1 = \kappa_2$$

and we write $\kappa_1 \neq \kappa_1$ in case that κ_1 and κ_2 are not equal. Furthermore, in order to stress that κ_1 and κ_2 are *identical* we write

$$\kappa_1 \equiv \kappa_2$$

More precisely, $\left(\begin{smallmatrix} a_0 & \ldots & a_n \\ b_0 & \ldots & b_n \end{smallmatrix}\right) \equiv \left(\begin{smallmatrix} c_0 & \ldots & c_m \\ d_0 & \ldots & d_n \end{smallmatrix}\right)$ denotes that $m = n$ holds with $a_i = c_i$ and $b_i = d_i$ for all $i \leq n$.

[1]The German word *Klammersymbol* can be translated as "bracket symbol", but the term Klammersymbol is more common in setting of systems of ordinal notations.

(c) Given a normal function $f\colon \mathrm{On} \to \mathrm{On}$ with $f(0) > 0$, the *value* $f(\kappa) := f\kappa$ *of a Klammersymbol* κ *(under* f*)* is defined as follows:

1. If $\kappa \equiv \binom{a_1 \,\cdots\, a_{n+1}}{b_1 \,\cdots\, b_{n+1}}$ and $b_1 \neq 0$ hold, then $f\kappa$ is $f\binom{0\; a_1 \,\cdots\, a_{n+1}}{0\; b_1 \,\cdots\, b_{n+1}}$ and one of the other cases applies.
2. If $\kappa \equiv \binom{c}{0}$ holds, then $f\kappa$ is $f(c)$.
3. If $\kappa \equiv \binom{c\; a_1 \,\cdots\, a_{n+1}}{0\; b_1 \,\cdots\, b_{n+1}}$ and $a_i = 0$ hold for some $i \in \{1, \ldots, n+1\}$, then $f\kappa$ is $f\kappa'$ where κ' is obtained from κ by deleting the column $\begin{smallmatrix}0\\ b_i\end{smallmatrix}$.
4. If $\kappa \equiv \binom{c\; a_1 \,\cdots\, a_{n+1}}{0\; b_1 \,\cdots\, b_{n+1}}$ and $a_i \neq 0$ hold for all $i \in \{1, \ldots, n+1\}$, then $f\kappa$ is the c-th common solution x for the following equations and for all $a' < a_1$ and $b' < b_1$:

$$f\binom{x\;\; a'\;\; a_2 \,\cdots\, a_{n+1}}{b'\;\; b_1\;\; b_2 \,\cdots\, b_{n+1}} = x$$

(d) Given a normal function $f\colon \mathrm{On} \to \mathrm{On}$ such that $f(x) \in \mathrm{Lim}$ holds for all $x \in \mathrm{On}$, the *fixed-point free value* $\overline{f}(\kappa) := \overline{f}\kappa$ *of a Klammersymbol* κ *(under* f*)* is defined as follows (see [Sch54, §3]):

$$\overline{f}\binom{a_0 \,\cdots\, a_n}{b_0 \,\cdots\, b_n} := \begin{cases} f\binom{a_0+1\;\; a_1 \,\cdots\, a_n}{b_0\;\; b_1 \,\cdots\, b_n} & \text{if } a_0 = c + k \text{ holds for some } c \in \mathrm{On} \text{ and } k < \omega \text{ with } f\binom{c\;\; a_1 \,\cdots\, a_n}{b_0\;\; b_1 \,\cdots\, b_n} \in \{c, a_1, \ldots, a_n\} \\ f\binom{a_0\;\; a_1 \,\cdots\, a_n}{b_0\;\; b_1 \,\cdots\, b_n} & \text{otherwise} \end{cases}$$

Remark 2.8. For all Klammersymbols α_1 and α_2, there exist ordinals $a_0, \ldots, a_n$, $b_0, \ldots, b_n$ and ordinals $c_0, \ldots, c_n$ with $c_0 < \ldots < c_n$ such that $\alpha_1 = \binom{a_0 \,\cdots\, a_n}{c_0 \,\cdots\, c_n}$ and $\alpha_2 = \binom{b_0 \,\cdots\, b_n}{c_0 \,\cdots\, c_n}$ hold, simply by adding or removing of columns of the form $\begin{smallmatrix}0\\ c_i\end{smallmatrix}$ where necessary.

Definition 2.9. A *lexicographic order* $<$ on Klammersymbols is defined for Klammersymbols α and β with $\alpha \neq \beta$ as follows:

1. If $\alpha = \binom{a_0 \,\cdots\, a_n}{c_0 \,\cdots\, c_n}$ and $\beta = \binom{b_0 \,\cdots\, b_n}{c_0 \,\cdots\, c_n}$ hold for some $a_0, \ldots, a_n$, $b_0, \ldots, b_n$, $c_0, \ldots, c_n$, and if $i \leq n$ is the *largest* index with $a_i \neq b_i$, then we have $\alpha < \beta$ in case of $a_i < b_i$ and $\beta < \alpha$ otherwise.
2. If $\alpha = \alpha'$, $\beta = \beta'$, and $\alpha < \beta$, then also $\alpha' < \beta'$.

Proposition 2.10.

(a) *The function* $x \mapsto f\binom{1}{x}$ *is normal. In particular, we have* $f\binom{1}{z} = \sup_{x<z} f\binom{1}{x}$ *for each* $z \in \mathrm{Lim}$.

(b) *If* $f(x) \in \mathrm{Lim}$ *holds for all* $x \in \mathrm{Lim}$, *then we have* $\overline{f}\binom{1}{x} = f\binom{1}{x}$ *for each* $x \in \mathrm{On}$.

Proof. Since we assumed $f(0) > 0$ holds, the first claim is immediate from [Sch54, (4.1)–(4.3)]. For the second claim, note in particular that $f\binom{0}{x} = f(0) \neq 0$ for each $x \in \mathrm{On}$ implies by the definition of $\overline{f}\binom{1}{x}$ that $\overline{f}\binom{1}{x} = f\binom{1}{x}$ holds. □

Definition 2.11. Recall that we defined

$$\varphi(x) = \varphi_1(x) = \omega^x$$

in Section 2.1 for all $x \in \mathrm{On}$. We now let

$$\boxed{\varphi_\bullet(x) := \omega^{1+x}}$$

for all $x \in \mathrm{On}$, and further for all $x_1, \ldots, x_n \in \mathrm{On}$, we define

$$\varphi_1 x_n \ldots x_0 := \varphi_1 \begin{pmatrix} x_0 & \cdots & x_n \\ 0 & \cdots & n \end{pmatrix}$$

$$\varphi_\bullet x_n \ldots x_0 := \varphi_\bullet \begin{pmatrix} x_0 & \cdots & x_n \\ 0 & \cdots & n \end{pmatrix}$$

$$\overline{\varphi_\bullet} x_n \ldots x_0 := \overline{\varphi_\bullet} \begin{pmatrix} x_0 & \cdots & x_n \\ 0 & \cdots & n \end{pmatrix}$$

Definition 2.12. The *large Veblen ordinal* $\mathfrak{V}$ is defined as

$$\boxed{\mathfrak{V} := \min\{a \colon a = \varphi_1\tbinom{1}{a}\}}$$

and the *small Veblen ordinal* $\mathfrak{v}$ is defined as

$$\boxed{\mathfrak{v} := \varphi_1\tbinom{1}{\omega}}$$

Convention 2.13.

(a) $f\colon \mathrm{On} \to \mathrm{On}$ shall be for the remainder of Subsection 2.2 any normal function with the property

$$\boxed{f(0) > 0}$$

(b) $a, b, c, d, \ldots$ are primarily used as syntactic variables for On.

(c) $\alpha, \beta, \gamma, \delta, \kappa, \rho, \sigma, \tau, \ldots$ are primarily used as syntactic variables for Klammersymbols.

2.2.1. Recursion Properties

Proposition 2.14. *For each Klammersymbol* $\left(\begin{smallmatrix} a_0 & \cdots & a_n \\ c_0 & \cdots & c_n \end{smallmatrix}\right)$*, we have the following:*

(a) $a_0 \leq f\left(\begin{smallmatrix} a_0 & \cdots & a_n \\ c_0 & \cdots & c_n \end{smallmatrix}\right)$

(b) In case of $a_0 \neq 0$*, we have that* $a_i < f\left(\begin{smallmatrix} a_0 & \cdots & a_n \\ c_0 & \cdots & c_n \end{smallmatrix}\right)$ *holds for all* $i \in \{1, \ldots, n\}$.

In general, we have $a_0, \ldots, a_n \leq f\left(\begin{smallmatrix} a_0 & \cdots & a_n \\ c_0 & \cdots & c_n \end{smallmatrix}\right)$.

Proof. By (3.3) and (6.1) in [Sch54], we have

$$a_0 \leq f\left(\begin{smallmatrix} a_0 & \cdots & a_n \\ c_0 & \cdots & c_n \end{smallmatrix}\right) \tag{2.2}$$

$$a_0 \neq 0 \ \Rightarrow \ a_i < f\left(\begin{smallmatrix} a_0 & \cdots & a_n \\ c_0 & \cdots & c_n \end{smallmatrix}\right) \text{ for all } i \in \{1, \ldots, n\} \tag{2.3}$$

respectively, and the remaining claim follows by induction on n. □

Proposition 2.15. *Let* $\alpha := \left(\begin{smallmatrix} a_1 & \cdots & a_{n+1} \\ c_1 & \cdots & c_{n+1} \end{smallmatrix}\right)$ *be a Klammersymbol. For each Klammersymbol* β *with* $\alpha < \beta$*, the following holds:*

(a) $f\alpha = f\beta$ *holds if and only if* $k \in \{1, \ldots, n+1\}$ *exists such that* $a_k = f\beta$ *and the following holds:*

- $a_i = 0$ *for each* i *with* $1 \leq i < k$*, and*
- $a_i < f\beta$ *for each* i *with* $k < i \leq n+1$.

(b) $f\alpha < f\beta$ *holds if* $a_i < f\beta$ *holds for all* $i \in \{1, \ldots, n+1\}$.

(c) $f\beta < f\alpha$ holds if

- *either $f\beta < a_k$ holds for some $k \in \{1, \dots, n+1\}$, or*
- *$n \geq 1$ and $j, k \in \{1, \dots, n+1\}$ exist such that $j < k$, $a_j \neq 0$, and $a_k = f\beta$.*

Proof. See (7.1)–(7.4) in [Sch54]. Note that the negation of the condition given in (a) yields the conditions stated in (b) and (c). For this, note in particular that $a_k = f\beta$ implies $a_k \neq 0$ and hence if $a_i = 0$ holds for each i with $1 \leq i < k$ and the condition of (a) does not hold, then $k < n+1$ holds and i exists with $a_i \geq f\beta$ and $k < i \leq n+1$, leading to one of the conditions in (c). □

Lemma 2.16. *We have*

$$\varphi_{n+1}(a_1, \dots, a_{n+1}) = \varphi_1\begin{pmatrix} a_{n+1} & a_n & \dots & a_1 \\ 0 & 1 & \dots & n \end{pmatrix}$$

where we denoted with $0, 1, \dots, n$ in the Klammersymbol's second row ambiguously the corresponding finite ordinals.

Proof. If $n = 0$ or $a_1 = \cdots = a_{n+1} = 0$ holds, then the claim is clear. Otherwise, assume $n \neq 0$ and without loss of generality that $a_1 \neq 0$ holds. Further, let $k \in \{1, \dots, n\}$ with $a_k \neq 0$ and $a_{k+1} = \cdots = a_n = 0$. The claim now follows by transfinite induction on a_k since $\varphi(\bar{a}^{(n+1)})$ is the a_{n+1}-th common fixed-point of the functions

$$x \mapsto \varphi(\bar{a}^{(k-1)}, b, x, \bar{0}^{(n-k)})$$

given for each $b < a_k$. Now, we get

$$\begin{aligned}\varphi(\bar{a}^{(k-1)}, b, x, \bar{0}^{(n-k)}) &= f\begin{pmatrix} 0 & \dots & 0 & x & b & a_{k-1} & \dots & a_1 \\ 0 & \dots & n-(k+1) & n-k & n-(k-1) & n-(k-2) & \dots & n \end{pmatrix} \\ &= f\begin{pmatrix} x & b & a_{k-1} & \dots & a_1 \\ n-k & n-(k-1) & n-(k-2) & \dots & n \end{pmatrix}\end{aligned}$$

from the induction hypothesis and for each $x \in \mathrm{On}$. Hence the claim follows from Definition 2.7 and Lemma 2.6. □

Corollary 2.17. *Let $n \geq 1$ and ordinals $a_1, \dots, a_n$ be given, then we have the following:*

(a) $a_i \leq \varphi(\bar{a}^{(n)})$ for all $i \in \{1, \dots, n\}$.

(b) *If* $a_k \neq 0$ *for some* $k \in \{1, \ldots, n\}$, *then* $a_i < \varphi(\bar{a}^{(n)})$ *holds for all* $i \in \{1, \ldots, k-1\}$.

Proof. This follows from Proposition 2.14 and Lemma 2.16. □

Corollary 2.18. *Let* $n \geq 1$ *and ordinals* $a_1, \ldots, a_n, b_1, \ldots, b_n$ *be given. Then* $\varphi(\bar{a}^{(n)}) < \varphi(\bar{b}^{(n)})$ *holds if and only if some* $r \in \{1, \ldots, n\}$ *exists such that* $a_r \neq b_r$ *holds with* $a_i = b_i$ *for all* $i \in \{1, \ldots, r-1\}$, *and such that one of the following holds:*

1. $a_r < b_r$ *and* $a_i < \varphi(\bar{b}^{(n)})$ *for all* $i \in \{r+1, \ldots, n\}$, *or*

2. $b_r < a_r$ *and*
   - *either* $\varphi(\bar{a}^{(n)}) < b_k$ *holds for some* $k \in \{1, \ldots, n\}$, *or*
   - $\varphi(\bar{a}^{(n)}) = b_k$ *and* $b_i \neq 0$ *for some* $i, k \in \{1, \ldots, n\}$ *with* $k < i$.

Proof. This follows immediately from Proposition 2.15 and Lemma 2.16. For the first case $a_r < b_r$, note that $a_i < \varphi(\bar{b}^{(n)})$ holds anyway for $i \in \{1, \ldots, r\}$ by Corollary 2.17: On the one hand, we have $b_r \leq \varphi(\bar{b}^{(n)})$ and so $a_r < \varphi(\bar{b}^{(n)})$, and on the other hand, $a_r < b_r$ also implies $b_r \neq 0$ which by Corollary 2.17.(b) gives $a_i = b_i < \varphi(\bar{b}^{(n)})$ for $i \in \{1, \ldots, r-1\}$. □

Definition 2.19. Let $n \geq 1$.

(a) $a_1, \ldots, a_n$ are in *normal form (w.r.t.* φ_n*)* in case that $a_i < \varphi(\bar{a}^{(n)})$ holds for each $1 \leq i \leq n$, and we denote this by $\mathrm{NF}^{\varphi}_n(\bar{a}^{(n)})$.

(b) $b =_{\mathrm{NF}} \varphi(\bar{a}^{(n)})$ denotes $b = \varphi(\bar{a}^{(n)})$ and $\mathrm{NF}^{\varphi}_n(\bar{a}^{(n)})$.

Lemma 2.20. *Let* $n \geq 1$, $k \in \{1, \ldots, n\}$, *and* $b_1, \ldots, b_n, a_1, \ldots, a_n \in \mathrm{On}$ *be given with* $b_k =_{\mathrm{NF}} \varphi(\bar{a}^{(n)})$ *and* $b_{k+1} = \cdots = b_n = 0$. *Then* $\mathrm{NF}^{\varphi}_n(\bar{b}^{(n)})$ *holds if and only if* $a_r \neq b_r$ *holds for some* $r \in \{1, \ldots, k\}$ *with* $a_i = b_i$ *for all* $i \in \{1, \ldots, r-1\}$ *and one of the following holds:*

1. $a_r < b_r$, *or*

2. $b_r < a_r$ *and for some* $i \in \{1, \ldots, n\}$, *we have* $b_k \leq b_i$.

   (In particular, it suffices here to have $i \in \{r+1, \ldots, k-1\}$*.)*

Proof. Note that we have $b_k \neq 0$ by our assumption $b_k =_{\mathrm{NF}} \varphi(\bar{a}^{(n)})$, and hence by Corollary 2.17 and $\mathrm{NF}^{\varphi}_n(\bar{a}^{(n)})$, we have

$$a_i < b_k \leq \varphi(\bar{b}^{(n)}) \tag{2.4}$$

for all $i \in \{1, \ldots, n\}$ and also $b_i < \varphi(\bar{b}^{(n)})$ for all $i \in \{1, \ldots, k-1\}$. Furthermore, there has to be some $r \in \{1, \ldots, k\}$ such that $a_r \neq b_r$ and $a_i = b_i$ holds for all $i \in \{1, \ldots, r-1\}$ since we have $a_k < b_k$. Recalling the assumption $b_{k+1} = \cdots = b_n = 0$, we thus have that $\mathrm{NF}^{\varphi}_n(\bar{b}^{(n)})$ holds if and only if $b_k < \varphi(\bar{b}^{(n)})$ holds, i.e., $\varphi(\bar{a}^{(n)}) < \varphi(\bar{b}^{(n)})$. By Corollary 2.18 this is equivalent to the following two situations:
1. If $a_r < b_r$: We need $a_i < \varphi(\bar{b}^{(n)})$ for each $i \in \{r+1, \ldots, n\}$. But this holds anyway as we have noted in (2.4).
2. If $a_r > b_r$: We need some $i \in \{1, \ldots, k\}$ such that either $b_i > \varphi(\bar{a}^{(n)}) = b_k$ holds, or otherwise $b_i = \varphi(\bar{a}^{(n)}) = b_k$ holds and there is some $i < j \leq k$ such that $b_j \neq 0$ holds. In both cases, $i = k$ is trivial, moreover recall that $b_k \neq 0$ holds. Hence, $b_k \leq b_i$ for some $i \in \{1, \ldots, n\}$ suffices in this situation. Actually, $i \in \{r+1, \ldots, k-1\}$ is enough since otherwise $b_k \leq b_i$ can never hold: We have that $b_i \leq a_r < \varphi(\bar{a}^{(n)}) = b_k$ holds for all $1 \leq i \leq r$ and that $b_i = 0$ holds for all $k \leq i \leq n$. □

Remark 2.21. In Lemma 2.20, we took the lists of ordinals $a_1, \ldots, a_n$ and $b_1, \ldots, b_n$ to have the same length $n \geq 2$ in order to simplify the formulation and proof of the lemma. Clearly, the lemma holds analogously for lists of ordinals with different length ≥ 2 (just add ordinals of the form 0 to the front of the shorter list to make them the same length).

Proposition 2.22. *Assume that $f(x) \in \mathrm{Lim}$ holds for all $x \in \mathrm{On}$. Then we have for all Klammersymbols $\alpha := \left(\begin{smallmatrix} a_0 & \cdots & a_n \\ c_0 & \cdots & c_n \end{smallmatrix}\right)$ and β the following:*

(a) $\overline{f}\alpha = \overline{f}\beta \iff \alpha = \beta$.

(b) If $\alpha < \beta$ holds, then we have:

(i) $\overline{f}\alpha < \overline{f}\beta \iff a_i < \overline{f}\beta$ *holds for all* $i \leq n$.

(ii) $\overline{f}\beta < \overline{f}\alpha \iff \overline{f}\beta \leq a_j$ *holds for some* $j \leq n$.

Proof. See (8.3) and (8.4) in [Sch54]. □

Proposition 2.23.

(a) $\varphi_1(x) = \varphi_\bullet(x)$ *holds for all* $x \in \mathrm{On}$ *with* $\omega < x$.

(b) *Given* $x_0, \ldots, x_n \in \mathrm{On}$ *such that* $x_j \neq 0$ *holds for some* $1 \leq j \leq n$, *then we have* $\varphi_n(x_n, \ldots, x_1) = \varphi_\bullet x_n \ldots x_1$.

(c) $\varphi_\bullet(x) \in \mathrm{Lim}$ *and* $\overline{\varphi_\bullet}\binom{1}{x} = \varphi_1\binom{1}{x} = \varphi_\bullet\binom{1}{x}$ *hold for all* $x \in \mathrm{On}$.

(d) $\mathfrak{v}$ *is the least ordinal* $a > 0$ *not expressible from ordinals smaller than* a *and by means of* ordinal addition *and the* finitary Veblen functions. *Moreover, the following correspondences hold*

$$\begin{aligned} \omega &= \varphi_2(0,1) = \overline{\varphi_\bullet}00 &&= \overline{\varphi_\bullet}\tbinom{0}{0} \\ \varepsilon_0 &= \varphi_2(1,0) = \overline{\varphi_\bullet}10 &&= \overline{\varphi_\bullet}\tbinom{1}{1} \\ & \quad\ \varphi_2(\omega,0) = \overline{\varphi_\bullet}\omega 0 &&= \overline{\varphi_\bullet}\tbinom{\omega}{1} \\ \Gamma_0 &= \varphi_3(1,0,0) = \overline{\varphi_\bullet}100 &&= \overline{\varphi_\bullet}\tbinom{1}{2} \end{aligned}$$

where for $\vartheta\Omega^\omega$, *we used a notation from [RW93].*

Proof. This follows from the definitions and the previous results. For (d), note that $\varphi_\bullet\omega 0 = \overline{\varphi_\bullet}\omega 0$ holds because of Definition 2.7 and $\omega \neq \varphi_\bullet\binom{\omega}{1}$. □

2.2.2. Klammersymbols as Denotations for Functions

Definition 2.24. For all Klammersymbols $\alpha := \left(\begin{smallmatrix} a_1 & \cdots & a_{n+1} \\ b_1 & \cdots & b_{n+1} \end{smallmatrix}\right)$ and $a \in \mathrm{On}$, we define $\{\alpha\}a \in \mathrm{On}$ as follows:

$$\boxed{\{\alpha\}a := \overline{\varphi_\bullet}\left(\begin{smallmatrix} a & a_1 & \cdots & a_{n+1} \\ 0 & 1+b_1 & \cdots & 1+b_{n+1} \end{smallmatrix}\right)}$$

Corollary 2.25. *For all Klammersymbols* α, β *and all* $a_0, b_0 \in \mathrm{On}$ *we have the following:*

(a) $\{\alpha\}a_0 = \{\beta\}b_0 \iff \alpha = \beta \ \&\ a_0 = b_0$

(b) *If* $\alpha = \beta$ *holds, then we have:* $\{\alpha\}a_0 < \{\beta\}b_0 \iff a_0 < b_0$.

(c) *If* $\alpha < \beta$ *holds and if we let* $\alpha \equiv \left(\begin{smallmatrix} a_1 & \cdots & a_{n+1} \\ c_1 & \cdots & c_{n+1} \end{smallmatrix}\right)$, *then we have:*

  (i) $\{\alpha\}a_0 < \{\beta\}b_0 \iff a_i < \{\beta\}b_0$ *holds for all* $i \leq n+1$.

  (ii) $\{\beta\}b_0 < \{\alpha\}a_0 \iff \{\beta\}b_0 \leq a_j$ *holds for some* $j \leq n+1$.

Proof. This follows from Proposition 2.22. In particular for (b), assuming $\alpha = \beta$ and letting

$$\alpha' := \begin{pmatrix} a_0 & a_1 & \dots & a_{n+1} \\ 0 & 1{+}c_1 & \dots & 1{+}c_{n+1} \end{pmatrix}$$
$$\beta' := \begin{pmatrix} b_0 & a_1 & \dots & a_{n+1} \\ 0 & 1{+}c_1 & \dots & 1{+}c_{n+1} \end{pmatrix}$$

we have the following:

1. If $\{\alpha\}a_0 < \{\beta\}b_0$ holds, then this rewrites to $\overline{\varphi_\bullet}\alpha' < \overline{\varphi_\bullet}\beta'$ and hence by Proposition 2.22.(a), we must have $a_0 \neq b_0$. In particular, we must have $a_0 < b_0$ because otherwise $b_0 < a_0$ implies $\beta' < \alpha'$ and hence we would get by Proposition 2.22.(b).(ii) and due to $\overline{\varphi_\bullet}\alpha' < \overline{\varphi_\bullet}\beta'$ with $\beta' < \alpha'$ that $\overline{\varphi_\bullet}\alpha' \leq b_0$ holds (while note that $a_1, \dots, a_{n+1} < \overline{\varphi_\bullet}\alpha'$ always holds). Since also $a_0 < \overline{\varphi_\bullet}\alpha'$ always hold, we get a contradiction from $b_0 < a_0$.

2. Conversely, if $a_0 < b_0$ holds, then we get also $\{\alpha\}a_0 < \{\beta\}b_0$. □

Corollary 2.26. *We have the following correspondences:*

$$\omega^{1+a} = \{\left(\begin{smallmatrix} 0 \\ 0 \end{smallmatrix}\right)\}a \qquad \varphi_2(\omega, a) = \{\left(\begin{smallmatrix} \omega \\ 0 \end{smallmatrix}\right)\}a$$
$$\varepsilon_a = \{\left(\begin{smallmatrix} 1 \\ 0 \end{smallmatrix}\right)\}a \qquad \Gamma_a = \{\left(\begin{smallmatrix} 1 \\ 1 \end{smallmatrix}\right)\}a$$

Proof. Immediate from Proposition 2.23. □

2.2.3. Representation Properties

Remark 2.27. We have that $\{a\colon a = \varphi_1\left(\begin{smallmatrix} 1 \\ a \end{smallmatrix}\right)\}$ is club and hence non-empty by Proposition 2.10, and we have

$$\begin{aligned} \mathfrak{V} &= \min\{a\colon a = \varphi_\bullet\left(\begin{smallmatrix} 1 \\ a \end{smallmatrix}\right)\} \\ &= \min\{a\colon a = \overline{\varphi_\bullet}\left(\begin{smallmatrix} 1 \\ a \end{smallmatrix}\right)\} \\ &= \min\{a\colon a = \{\left(\begin{smallmatrix} 1 \\ a \end{smallmatrix}\right)\}0\} \end{aligned}$$

by Proposition 2.23, while the last equation is due to the fact that $a \in \mathrm{Lim}$ holds for all a with $a = \varphi_1\left(\begin{smallmatrix} 1 \\ a \end{smallmatrix}\right)$. Moreover, we remark that $\mathfrak{V}$ corresponds to $\vartheta\Omega^\Omega$ from [RW93].

Lemma 2.28. *Let now $c \in \mathrm{On} \setminus \{0\}$ be given with $c < \mathfrak{v}$. Then we have $c = c_1 + \ldots + c_n$ for some $n \geq 1$ with $c \geq c_1 \geq \ldots \geq c_n$ such that*

$$c_i = \varphi_1\left(\begin{smallmatrix} a_{i,1}, & \dots & a_{i,k_i} \\ b_{i,1}, & \dots & b_{i,k_i} \end{smallmatrix}\right)$$

holds for some $k_1, \ldots, k_n \in \mathbb{N}$ and such that $a_{i,j}, b_{i,j} < c_i$ holds for all $1 \leq i \leq n$ and $1 \leq j \leq k_i$. In case of $n > 1$, we further have $c_i < c$ for each $1 \leq i \leq n$.

Proof. Assume $c \neq 0$ and let $c = \omega^{d_1} \cdot m_1 + \ldots + \omega^{d_l} \cdot m_l$ be the Cantor Normal Formal of c at base ω, i.e., we have $0 < m_1, \ldots, m_l < \omega$ and $d_1 > \ldots > d_l$. Due to $m_1, \ldots, m_l < \omega$, we have

$$c = \omega^{e_1} + \ldots + \omega^{e_n}$$

for some $n \geq 1$ with $e_1 \geq \ldots \geq e_n$, while in case of $n > 1$ also $\omega^{e_i} < c$ holds for each $1 \leq i \leq n$. From $c < \mathfrak{v}$ follows $c < \varphi_1\left(\begin{smallmatrix} 1 \\ c \end{smallmatrix}\right)$, we can use [Sch54, (5.1)] in order to get

$$\omega^{e_i} = \varphi_1\left(\begin{smallmatrix} a_{i,1}, & \dots & a_{i,k_i} \\ b_{i,1}, & \dots & b_{i,k_i} \end{smallmatrix}\right)$$

for some $k_i \in \mathbb{N}$ and $a_{i,j}, b_{i,j} < \omega^{e_i}$ for all $1 \leq j \leq k_i$ because $\omega^{e_i} = \varphi_1(e_i)$ holds. This implies the claim with $c_i := \omega^{e_i}$ for $1 \leq j \leq k_i$. □

Proposition 2.29. *Let $c < \mathfrak{V}$ be given, then there exist unique $n \in \mathbb{N}$ and $c_0, \ldots, c_n \in \mathrm{On}$ such that $c = c_n + \ldots + c_0$ holds with*

$$c_0 < \omega$$
$$\omega \leq c_1 \leq \ldots \leq c_n$$

while we have for $n \neq 0$ and each $i \in \{1, \ldots, n\}$ that

$$c_i = \{\left(\begin{smallmatrix} a_1 & \dots & a_{k+1} \\ b_1 & \dots & b_{k+1} \end{smallmatrix}\right)\}a_0 \leq c$$

holds for some $k \in \mathbb{N}$ and $a_0, \ldots, a_{k+1}, b_1, \ldots, b_{k+1} < c_i$.

Proof. In case of $c < \omega$, we can take $n := 0$ and $c_0 := c$. Assume now $c \geq \omega$ and let $c = \omega^{d_l} \cdot e_l + \ldots + \omega^{d_0} \cdot e_0$ be the Cantor Normal Formal of c at base ω, i.e., we have $0 < e_0, \ldots, e_l < \omega$ and $0 \leq d_0 < \ldots < d_l \leq c$. Due to $e_0, \ldots, e_l < \omega$, we have $c = (\omega^{f_n} + \ldots + \omega^{f_1}) + c_0$ for some $c_0 < \omega$

and some $n \in \mathbb{N}$ with $0 < f_1 \leq \ldots \leq f_n$. Furthermore, we have for each $i \in \{1, \ldots, n\}$ that $\omega^{f_i} = \varphi_\bullet(g_i)$ holds for some $g_i \leq f_i$ (more precisely, in case of $f_i < \omega$ we have $f_i = f_i' + 1$ and can take $g_i := f_i'$, while otherwise we take $g_i := f_i$). We have $\varphi_\bullet(g_i) < \{(\,{}^{\;1}_{\varphi_\bullet(g_i)}\,)\}0$ since $\omega^{f_i} \leq c < \mathfrak{V}$ holds, and hence we can set $c_i := \omega^{f_i}$ and use Corollary 2.31 in order to get the claim. □

Proposition 2.30. *Assume that $f(x) \in \mathrm{Lim}$ holds for all $x \in \mathrm{On}$ and let $c \in \mathrm{On}$ be such that $c < f(\,{}^1_c\,)$ and $c = f(d)$ hold for some $d \in \mathrm{On}$. Then there exist $n \in \mathbb{N}$ and $a_0, \ldots, a_n, b_0, \ldots, b_n < c$ such that $c = \overline{f}\left(\begin{smallmatrix} a_0 & \cdots & a_n \\ b_0 & \cdots & b_n \end{smallmatrix}\right)$ holds.*

Proof. See (8.1) in [Sch54]. □

Corollary 2.31. *Let $c \in \mathrm{On}$ be such that $c < \{(\,{}^1_c\,)\}0$ holds with $c = \varphi_\bullet(d)$ for some $d \in \mathrm{On}$. Then there exist $n \in \mathbb{N}$ and $a_0, \ldots, a_{n+1}, b_1, \ldots, b_{n+1} < c$ such that we have*

$$c = \{\left(\begin{smallmatrix} a_1 & \cdots & a_{n+1} \\ b_1 & \cdots & b_{n+1} \end{smallmatrix}\right)\}a_0$$

Proof. This follows from Proposition 2.30. □

2.3. The ϑ-function

See [RW93] and [Buc15] for more details.

Definition 2.32 ([RW93, 1.]). Sets of ordinals $C(\alpha, \beta)$, $C_n(\alpha, \beta)$, and ordinals $\vartheta\alpha$ are defined by main recursion on $\alpha < \varepsilon_{\Omega+1}$ and subsidiary recursion on $n < \omega$ (for $\beta < \Omega$) as follows:

1. $\{0, \Omega\} \cup \beta \subseteq C_n(\alpha, \beta)$,
2. $(\gamma, \delta \in C_n(\alpha, \beta) \;\&\; \xi =_{\mathrm{NF}} \omega^\gamma + \delta) \implies \xi \in C_{n+1}(\alpha, \beta)$,
3. $\delta \in C_n(\alpha, \beta) \cap \alpha \implies \vartheta\delta \in C_{n+1}(\alpha, \beta)$,
4. $C(\alpha, \beta) := \bigcup\{C_n(\alpha, \beta) \colon n < \omega\}$,
5. $\vartheta\alpha := \min\{\xi < \Omega \colon C(\alpha, \xi) \cap \Omega \subseteq \xi \wedge \alpha \in C(\alpha, \xi)\}$.

where we used $\xi =_{\mathrm{NF}} \omega^\gamma + \delta$ to denote that $\xi = \omega^\gamma + \delta$ holds such that either $\delta = 0$ and $\gamma < \xi$ hold, or such that $\delta = \omega^{\delta_1} + \ldots + \omega^{\delta_k}$ holds with $\gamma \geq \delta_1 \geq \ldots \geq \delta_k$ and $k \geq 1$.

Notation 2.33. As it is given in [RW93], we introduce also the following notation $\Omega(n, x)$ for all $n \geq 1$ and all $x \in \mathrm{On}$:

$$\Omega(1, x) := \Omega^x$$
$$\Omega(n+1, x) := \Omega^{\Omega(n,x)}$$

In contrast to [RW93], we extend this notion also to $n = 0$ as follows:

$$\Omega(0, x) := \Omega \cdot x$$

Proposition 2.34. *We have* $\vartheta\Omega^\omega = \varphi_1\binom{1}{\omega} = \{\binom{1}{\omega}\}0 = \mathfrak{v}$.

Proof. This is due to [Sch92]. See also [Buc15] and note Subsection 2.2.2. □

Remark 2.35. We remark that for the Buchholz ψ-functions from [BS88] or the Feferman-Aczel θ-functions from [Bri75], we have the correspondence $\vartheta\Omega^\omega = \psi_0\Omega^{\Omega^\omega} = \theta\Omega^\omega 0$. See also the last paragraph in [Rat92].

2.4. Cherry-Picking from [Sch92] and [Buc15]: $\vartheta\tilde{\alpha} = \overline{\varphi_{\mathbf{E}}}\alpha$

We give some remarks on the correspondence of the ϑ-function for arguments smaller than Ω^Ω and the ordinals obtained via the concept of Klammersymbols. We shall get to a generalized form of Proposition 2.34, i.e., to the core result of [Sch92]. It has been rephrased in [Buc15], while considering a more complex setting that compares many other ordinal-theoretic approaches for describing ordinals around the Bachmann-Howard ordinal.

In this small section, we focus on certain results of [Buc15] that provide the correspondence of the ϑ-function to Klammersymbols. First, we note that Klammersymbols represent in a straight-forward way ordinals smaller than Ω^{Ω}. Namely, if α is a Klammersymbol such that

$$\alpha \equiv \begin{pmatrix} a_0 & \dots & a_n \\ b_0 & \dots & b_n \end{pmatrix}$$

holds with $0 < a_i < \Omega$ for each $i \leq n$ and $b_0 < \ldots < b_n < \Omega$, then

$$\tilde{\alpha} := \Omega^{b_n} a_n + \ldots + \Omega^{b_0} a_0$$

is an ordinal such that $\tilde{\alpha} < \Omega^{\Omega}$ holds and which is in Cantor Normal Formal (at base Ω). Letting $\varphi_{\mathbf{E}}$ denote the function $x \mapsto \varepsilon_x$ on On, we obtain

$$\vartheta\tilde{\alpha} = \overline{\varphi_{\mathbf{E}}}\alpha \tag{$*$}$$

We refer to the paragraph "Note on Klammersymbols" in [Buc15] for this result. Furthermore, we get

$$\begin{aligned} \vartheta(\Omega \cdot \omega) &= \overline{\varphi_{\mathbf{E}}}\binom{\omega}{1} && (2.5) \\ &= \varphi_{\mathbf{E}}\binom{\omega}{1} && (2.6) \\ &= \varphi_{\mathbf{P}}\binom{\omega}{1} && (2.7) \\ &= \varphi(\omega, 0) && (2.8) \end{aligned}$$

where we let $\varphi_{\mathbf{E}}(x) := \varepsilon_x$ and $\varphi_{\mathbf{P}}(x) := \omega^x$ (i.e., $\varphi_{\mathbf{P}}$ is φ_1 from Section 2.1) and where (2.5) is due to ($*$) (or [Sch92]), (2.6) is due to Definition 2.7, (2.7) is due to the fact that $\varphi_{\mathbf{E}}\binom{n}{1} = \varphi_{\mathbf{P}}\binom{n+1}{1}$ holds for $n < \omega$, and (2.8) is essentially due to Lemma 2.16. Similarly, we have

$$\vartheta(\Omega \cdot \Omega) = \varphi_1 100 = \Gamma_0$$

2.5. Proof-Theoretic Ordinal

Following [Poh09, page 100], we define for every theory T whose language $\mathcal{L}_{\mathsf{T}}$ includes the language of arithmetic (possibly via an interpretation[2]) the *proof-theoretic ordinal* $|\mathsf{T}|$ *of* T to be the ordinal

$$\sup\{\mathrm{otyp}(\prec) : (\prec \text{ is a primitive recursive linear order}) \ \& \ \mathsf{T} \vdash \mathrm{TI}(\prec, \mathsf{U})\}$$

where $\mathrm{otyp}(\prec)$ denotes the order type of $\prec$, U shall be the special unary relation from Definition 1.1, and $\mathrm{TI}(\prec, \mathsf{U})$ abbreviates

$$\mathrm{Prog}_{\prec}(\mathsf{U}) \rightarrow \forall x \in \mathsf{field}(\prec)(x \in \mathsf{U})$$

and where $\mathrm{Prog}_{\prec}(\mathsf{U})$ is defined according to Notation 1.13. This means that $|\mathsf{T}|$ denotes the supremum of the order types of primitive recursive linear orderings $\prec$ that can be proven in T to be wellfounded (noting that $\mathrm{TI}_{\prec}(\mathsf{U})$ corresponds to the Π^1_1-statement "$\forall X(\mathrm{TI}_{\prec}(X))$").

In particular, this means that for determining a *lower bound* a of $|\mathsf{T}|$, it suffices to set up first an ordinal notation system $(\mathrm{OT}, \prec)$ that corresponds to a, e.g., as we shall do in Chapter 3 or Chapter 4, and then prove that

$$\mathsf{T} \vdash \mathrm{TI}_{\prec}(\mathsf{U}, \mathfrak{b})$$

holds for all $\mathfrak{b} \in \mathrm{OT}$ and where $\mathrm{TI}_{\prec}(\mathsf{U}, \mathfrak{b})$ is according to Notation 1.13. Furthermore, for determining an *upper bound* a of $|\mathsf{T}|$, it suffices to embed T into another theory T' for which it is known to fulfill $|\mathsf{T}'| \leq a$. In particular, it already suffices here to show that each arithmetical formula that is provable in T can be proven in T' because $\mathrm{TI}(\mathsf{U}, \mathfrak{b})$ is arithmetical. Compare this with Chapter 9.

[2]As it is the case with $\mathcal{L}_{\mathsf{FIT}}$, see also Section 6.2. This thesis investigates only theories that comprise the language of arithmetic (directly or via an interpretation).

3. Ordinal Notations for the Small Veblen Ordinal

In order to determine the lower bound for the proof-theoretic ordinal of both FIT and TID, we shall carry out wellordering proofs within TID in Chapter 7. We therefore need a framework for ordinals and ordinal notations which we shall introduce in the following sections. We rely on the literature for most of the preparatory work that is needed to formulate the ordinals that are involved here and try to explain only as much as to make this chapter sufficiently self-contained.

3.1. The Ordinal Notation System $(\mathrm{OT}, \prec)$

For carrying out the wellordering proofs in TID, we shall fix a primitive recursive notation system $(\mathrm{OT}, \prec)$ for ordinals below the small Veblen ordinal. It is based on Lemma 2.20 (essentially on (7.1)–(7.4) in [Sch54]). The representation of the following material was inspired by [Buc05]. The properties of $(\mathrm{OT}, \prec)$ can be formalized and established within PA.

Definition 3.1. Using the coding machinery from Definition 1.5, we set:

$$\phi\bar{a}^{(n+1)} := \phi a_1 \dots a_{n+1} := \phi(a_1, \dots, a_{n+1}) := \langle 1, a_1, \dots, a_{n+1} \rangle$$

$$\tilde{1} := \phi 0 \qquad a \oplus b := \begin{cases} a & \text{if } b = 0 \\ \langle 2, a, b \rangle & \text{otherwise} \end{cases}$$

$$\begin{aligned} \mathrm{PT}_+ &:= \{\phi\bar{a}^{(n+1)} \colon a_1 \neq 0 \ \& \ a_1, \dots, a_{n+1} \in \mathbb{N}\} \\ &= \{a \colon \mathsf{lh}(a) \geq 2 \wedge (a)_0 = 1 \wedge (a)_1 \neq 0\} \\ \mathrm{PT} &:= \mathrm{PT}_+ \cup \{\tilde{1}\} \end{aligned}$$

$$\mathsf{hd}(a) := \begin{cases} a & \text{if } a \in \mathrm{PT} \\ (a)_1 & \text{otherwise} \end{cases} \qquad \mathsf{tl}(a) := \begin{cases} 0 & \text{if } a \in \mathrm{PT} \\ (a)_2 & \text{otherwise} \end{cases}$$

Definition 3.2. Moreover, for any binary relation $\lhd$ on $\mathbb{N}$, we define the *(length-sensitive) lexicographic order* $\lhd_{\mathbf{lex}}$ *with respect to* $\lhd$ recursively as follows. $a \lhd_{\mathbf{lex}} b$ holds for any $a, b \in \mathbb{N}$ if and only if:

1. $\mathsf{lh}(a) < \mathsf{lh}(b)$ holds, or
2. $\mathsf{lh}(a) = \mathsf{lh}(b)$ holds and there is some $k < \mathsf{lh}(a)$ with $(a)_k \lhd (b)_k$ such that $(a)_i = (b)_i$ holds for all $i < k$.

Example 3.3. Note that $\langle 1, 2 \rangle <_{\mathbf{lex}} \langle 1, 1, 3 \rangle$ holds but not $\langle 1, 1, 3 \rangle <_{\mathbf{lex}} \langle 1, 2 \rangle$ and that $\langle 1, 2 \rangle$ corresponds to $\langle 0, 1, 2 \rangle$ here. If we have $a < b$, then $\langle a, a \rangle <_{\mathbf{lex}} \langle a, b \rangle$ holds but not $\langle b, a \rangle <_{\mathbf{lex}} \langle a, b \rangle$. Note that $\lhd_{\mathbf{lex}}$ is primitive recursive if $\lhd$ is.

Definition 3.4. Motivated by Corollary 2.18 and Lemma 2.20, we now define *simultaneously* the primitive recursive set OT of ordinal notations and the binary primitive recursive relation $\prec$ on OT. We have $c \in \mathrm{OT}$ if and only if one of the following cases holds:

1. $c = 0$ or $c = \tilde{1}$ holds.
2. $c \in \mathrm{PT}_+$ holds with $c = \phi\bar{a}^{(m+1)}\bar{0}^{(k)}$ for some $a_1, \ldots, a_{m+1} \in \mathrm{OT}$ such that $a_{m+1} \neq 0$ and one of the following cases holds:
   (i) $a_{m+1} \notin \mathrm{PT}_+$,
   (ii) $a_{m+1} \in \mathrm{PT}_+$ and $a_{m+1} \prec_{\mathbf{lex}} c$, or
   (iii) $a_{m+1} \in \mathrm{PT}_+$, $c \prec_{\mathbf{lex}} a_{m+1}$ and $a_{m+1} \preceq a_j$ holds for some $1 \leq j \leq m$.
3. $c = a \oplus b$ holds for some $a, b \in \mathrm{OT}$ and such that $a \in \mathrm{PT}$, $b \neq 0$, and $\mathsf{hd}(b) \preceq a$ hold.

With $a \preceq b$, we abbreviate in general $a \prec b \vee (a = b \wedge a \in \mathrm{OT} \wedge b \in \mathrm{OT})$. Now, $a \prec b$ holds if and only if $a, b \in \mathrm{OT}$ and one of the following cases hold:

1. $a = 0$ and $b \neq 0$ hold.
2. $a = \tilde{1}$, $b \neq 0$, and $b \neq \tilde{1}$ hold.
3. $a \in \mathrm{PT}_+$ and $b \in \mathrm{PT}_+$ hold with $a = \phi\bar{a}^{(m+1)}\bar{0}^{(k)}$ and $b = \phi\bar{b}^{(n+1)}\bar{0}^{(l)}$ such that $a_{m+1}, b_{n+1} \neq 0$ and one of the following cases hold:

(i) $a \prec_{\mathbf{lex}} b$ and $a_i \prec b$ for all $1 \leq i \leq m+1$, or

(ii) $b \prec_{\mathbf{lex}} a$ and $a \prec b_{n+1}$ or $a \preceq b_j$ for some $1 \leq j \leq n$.

4. $a = a_1 \oplus a_2$, $b = b_1 \oplus b_2$, and $a_1, b_1 \in \mathrm{PT}$ hold with $a_2 \neq 0$ or $b_2 \neq 0$ such that one of the following cases holds:

   (i) $a_1 \prec b_1$ or

   (ii) $a_1 = b_1$ and $a_2 \prec b_2$.

We use common abbreviations in combination with these notions, e.g., $a \not\prec b$ abbreviates $\neg(a \prec b)$, $(\forall x \preceq t)A$ abbreviates $\forall x(x \preceq t \to A)$, and analogously $(\exists x \preceq t)A$ abbreviates $\exists x(x \preceq t \wedge A)$.

Remark 3.5.

(a) For $a \in \mathrm{OT}$, we have that $\phi a \prec_{\mathbf{lex}} a$ is impossible since in Definition 3.4, in order to have $\phi \bar{a}^{(m+1)} \bar{0}^{(k)} \in \mathrm{OT}$ for $m = 0$, there are no a_j with $1 \leq j \leq m$.

So $\phi a \in \mathrm{OT}$ holds if and only if $a \notin \mathrm{PT}_+$ or $a \in \mathrm{PT}_+$ with $a \prec_{\mathbf{lex}} \phi a$ holds, i.e., $a = \phi b$ with $b \prec a$. Correspondingly, $\phi a \notin \mathrm{OT}$ holds if and only if $a_1 \in \mathrm{PT}_+$ and $\phi a \prec_{\mathbf{lex}} a$ hold, i.e., $a = \phi \bar{b}^{(n+2)}$ for some $n \geq 0$.

(b) Note that due to the definition of OT, for each $a \in \mathrm{OT}$ with $a \neq 0$ there are unique $a_1, a_2 \in \mathrm{OT}$ such that $a = a_1 \oplus a_2$ and $a_1 \in \mathrm{PT}$ hold: Either $a \in \mathrm{PT}$ and we have $a = a \oplus 0$, or $a = \langle 2, a_1, a_2 \rangle = a_1 \oplus a_2$ and $a_1 \in \mathrm{PT}$ holds.

(c) When we write $a = a_1 \oplus a_2$ for $a \in \mathrm{OT}$, then we usually mean that $a_1 \in \mathrm{PT}$ holds. Nevertheless, we shall often stress that $a_1 \in \mathrm{PT}$ holds in order to avoid confusion. Note for example that with $a_1 := \phi 0 \oplus \phi 0$, we have $a_1 \oplus 0 = a_1 \in \mathrm{OT}$ by the definition of $\oplus$ but we also have $a_1 \notin \mathrm{PT}$.

(d) Let $a = \phi \bar{a}^{(m+1)} \bar{0}^{(k)}$ and $b = b_1 \oplus b_2$ with $b_2 \neq 0$, then we obviously have $a_1, \ldots, a_{m+1} <_{\mathbb{N}} a$ and $b_1, b_2 <_{\mathbb{N}} b$. Moreover $a \neq 0$ and $b \neq 0$ hold.

Theorem 3.6. (OT, $\prec$) *and* $(\mathrm{PT}_{\mathrm{OT}}, \prec_{\mathbf{lex}})$ *are strict total orders, where we let here* $\mathrm{PT}_{\mathrm{OT}} := \{\phi \bar{a}^{(n+1)} \in \mathrm{PT} \colon a_1, \ldots, a_{n+1} \in \mathrm{OT}\}$.

Proof. By a straightforward but long and cumbersome induction on the build-up of OT, see A.1 in the appendix for details. □

Remark 3.7. We include the proof of the following lemma in order to make the reader more familiar with $(\mathrm{OT}, \prec)$.

Lemma 3.8. *Let* $a \in \mathrm{OT}$.

(a) *If* $a = a_1 \oplus a_2$ *with* $a_1 \in \mathrm{PT}$ *and* $a_2 \neq 0$, *then* $a_1, a_2 \prec a$.

(b) *If* $a = \phi\bar{a}^{(m+1)}\bar{0}^{(k)}$ *with* $a_{m+1} \neq 0$, *then* $a_i \prec a$ *for each* $1 \leq i \leq m+1$.

Proof. For (a), we have $0 \prec a_2$, hence we get $a_1 = a_1 \oplus 0 \prec a_1 \oplus a_2 = a$. We show $a_2 \prec a$ by induction on a_2: Since $a_2 \neq 0$ holds, we have $b_1, b_2 \in \mathrm{OT}$ such that $a_2 = b_1 \oplus b_2$ and $b_1 \in \mathrm{PT}$ hold (cf. Remark 3.5). Due to $a \in \mathrm{OT}$ and $a = a_1 \oplus a_2$, we have $b_1 = \mathsf{hd}(a_2) \preceq a_1$ by definition of OT. If $b_2 = 0$, then we have $a_2 = b_1 \preceq a_1$, and since we have already shown $a_1 \prec a$, we get $a_2 \prec a$ by transitivity. If $b_2 \neq 0$, we get $b_2 \prec a_2$ by the induction hypothesis on a_2 (note that $a_2 <_{\mathbb{N}} a$ holds), and with $b_1 \preceq a_1$, we have $a_2 = b_1 \oplus b_2 \prec a_1 \oplus a_2 = a$.

For (b), we proceed by a (main) induction on $a \in \mathrm{OT}$, assuming $a = \phi\bar{a}^{(m+1)}\bar{0}^{(k)}$ with $a_{m+1} \neq 0$. As an auxiliary statement, we show for all $b \in \mathbb{N}$:

$$\left.\begin{array}{l}\text{If } b \preceq a_j \text{ and } b \leq_{\mathbb{N}} a_j \text{ hold for some } 1 \leq j \leq m+1,\\ \text{then } b \prec a \text{ holds.}\end{array}\right\} \qquad (*)$$

This implies the main claim by taking $b \in \{a_1, \ldots, a_{m+1}\}$. We prove $(*)$ by a side induction b.

<u>**1.**</u> $b = 0$: $b \prec a$ holds trivially, since $a \neq 0$.

<u>**2.**</u> $b = \tilde{1}$: We have $a \in \mathrm{PT}_+$, hence $a \neq 0$ and $a \neq \tilde{1}$, yielding $b \prec a$ immediately by the definition of $\prec$.

<u>**3.**</u> $b \in \mathrm{PT}_+$ with $b = \phi\bar{b}^{(n+1)}\bar{0}^{(l)}$ and $b_{n+1} \neq 0$: By $b \leq_{\mathbb{N}} a_j <_{\mathbb{N}} a$ and the main induction hypothesis, we get $b_1, \ldots, b_{n+1} \prec b$, and hence by $b \preceq a_j$ and transitivity of $\prec$ we get also

$$b_1, \ldots, b_{n+1} \prec a_j \qquad (3.1)$$

Further, we have $b_1, \ldots, b_{n+1} <_{\mathbb{N}} b$, and we get from (3.1) and the side induction hypothesis

$$b_1, \ldots, b_{n+1} \prec a \tag{3.2}$$

We consider the following cases:
3.1. $b \prec_{\mathbf{lex}} a$: By (3.2) and the definition of $\prec$, we get $b \prec a$.
3.2. $a \prec_{\mathbf{lex}} b$: We consider the following cases.
3.2.1. $b \preceq a_k$ for some $1 \le k \le m$: By definition, we get $b \prec a$.
3.2.2. $a_i \prec b$ for all $1 \le i \le m$: Hence $b \preceq a_{m+1}$ must hold because our assumption from the premiss of $(*)$ now implies $j = m + 1$. If $b = a_{m+1}$, then we have $a_{m+1} = b \in \mathrm{PT}_+$ and $a \prec_{\mathbf{lex}} b = a_{m+1}$, hence with $a \in \mathrm{OT}$ and the definition of OT, we get $b = a_{m+1} \preceq a_k$ for some $1 \le k \le m$. But this contradicts our assumption that $a_i \prec b$ holds for all $1 \le i \le m$. Hence $b \prec a_{m+1}$ holds and we get $b \prec a$ by definition of $\prec$.
4. $b = b_1 \oplus b_2$ with $b_1 \in \mathrm{PT}$ and $b_2 \neq 0$. Then $b_1 \prec b$ holds by (a), and since we have $b_1 <_{\mathbb{N}} b$, we get by the side induction hypothesis that $b_1 \prec a$ holds, hence we get $b = b_1 \oplus b_2 \prec a \oplus 0 = a$ due to $a \in \mathrm{PT}$. □

3.2. Ordinal Arithmetic within $(\mathrm{OT}, \prec)$

We point out that the following definitions and properties can be formalized and established within PA.

Definition 3.9. In order to simulate ordinal addition and the finitary Veblen functions within OT, we introduce the following primitive recursive functions on natural numbers:

(a) For each $a, b \in \mathbb{N}$, we define

$$a \tilde{+} b := \begin{cases} a & \text{if } a \in \mathrm{OT} \text{ and } b = 0 \\ b & \text{if } a = 0 \text{ and } b \in \mathrm{OT} \setminus \{0\} \\ \mathsf{hd}(a) \oplus (\mathsf{tl}(a) \tilde{+} b) & \text{if } a, b \in \mathrm{OT} \setminus \{0\} \text{ and} \\ & \quad \mathsf{hd}(b) \preceq \mathsf{hd}(a) \\ b & \text{if } a, b \in \mathrm{OT} \setminus \{0\} \text{ and} \\ & \quad \mathsf{hd}(a) \prec \mathsf{hd}(b) \\ 0 \oplus \tilde{1} & \text{otherwise, i.e.,} \\ & \quad \text{if } a \notin \mathrm{OT} \text{ or } b \notin \mathrm{OT} \end{cases}$$

(b) For each $n \in \mathbb{N}$ and $\bar{a}^{(n+1)} \in \mathbb{N}$, we define:

$$\tilde{\varphi}_{n+1}(\bar{a}^{(n+1)}) := \begin{cases} \phi\bar{a}^{(n+1)} & \text{if } \phi\bar{a}^{(n+1)} \in \mathrm{OT} \\ \mathrm{cr}(\langle\bar{a}^{(n+1)}\rangle) & \text{if } \phi\bar{a}^{(n+1)} \notin \mathrm{OT}, \\ & \quad a_1, \ldots, a_{n+1} \in \mathrm{OT}, \\ & \quad \text{and } a_1 \neq 0 \\ \tilde{\varphi}_n(a_2, \ldots, a_{n+1}) & \text{if } \phi\bar{a}^{(n+1)} \notin \mathrm{OT}, \\ & \quad a_1, \ldots, a_{n+1} \in \mathrm{OT}, \\ & \quad \text{and } a_1 = 0 \\ 0 \oplus \tilde{1} & \text{otherwise, i.e.,} \\ & \quad \text{if } a_j \notin \mathrm{OT} \text{ holds} \\ & \quad \text{for some } 1 \leq j \leq n+1 \end{cases}$$

and

$$\mathrm{cr}(\langle\bar{a}^{(n)}\rangle) := \begin{cases} 0 & \text{if } n = 0 \\ \mathrm{cr}(\langle\bar{a}^{(n-1)}\rangle) & \text{if } n \neq 0 \text{ and } a_n = 0 \\ a_n & \text{otherwise} \end{cases}$$

and since the index $n+1$ will be clear from the context, we also just write $\tilde{\varphi}(a_1, \ldots, a_{n+1})$ in order to denote $\tilde{\varphi}_{n+1}(a_1, \ldots, a_{n+1})$.

Remark 3.10. Note that $n \neq 0$ holds in the third clause of the definition of $\tilde{\varphi}_{n+1}(\bar{a}^{(n+1)})$. Furthermore, the naming of $\mathrm{cr}\colon \mathbb{N} \to \mathbb{N}$ is motivated from the intention of returning a fixed-point of $\tilde{\varphi}_{n+1}$ and that fixed-points $\beta = \varphi(\alpha, \beta)$ of the binary Veblen function are sometimes called *critical* in the literature.

Definition 3.11. We further introduce the following notations for every $a, x \in \mathbb{N}$:

$$\tilde{\omega}^a := \tilde{\varphi}(a) \quad \tilde{\varepsilon}_a := \tilde{\varphi}(\tilde{1}, a) \quad a \mathbin{\tilde{\cdot}} x := \begin{cases} 0 & \text{if } x = 0 \\ a \oplus (a \mathbin{\tilde{\cdot}} x_0) & \text{if } x = x_0 +_{\mathbb{N}} 1 \end{cases}$$

$$\tilde{\omega} := \tilde{\omega}^{\tilde{1}} (= \phi(\phi 0)) \quad \tilde{\omega}_x(a) := \begin{cases} a & \text{if } x = 0 \\ \tilde{\omega}^{\tilde{\omega}_{x_0}(a)} & \text{if } x = x_0 +_{\mathbb{N}} 1 \end{cases}$$

Definition 3.12.

$$\text{last}(a) := \begin{cases} \text{last}(a_2) & \text{if } a = a_1 \oplus a_2 \text{ and } a_2 \neq 0 \\ a & \text{otherwise} \end{cases}$$

$$\text{Lim} := \{a \in \text{OT}\colon a \neq 0 \wedge \text{last}(a) \neq \tilde{1}\} \qquad \text{Suc} := \{a \in \text{OT}\colon \text{last}(a) = \tilde{1}\}$$

Elements of Lim are called *limits* and elements of Suc are called *successors.*

Lemma 3.13. *Let* $a, b, a_1, \dots, a_{n+1}, x \in \mathbb{N}$*, then we have:*

(a) $a \,\tilde{\cdot}\, 0 \in \text{OT}$.

(b) $a \,\tilde{\cdot}\, (x +_{\mathbb{N}} 1) \in \text{OT} \iff a \in \text{OT}$.

(c) $\tilde{\varphi}(\bar{a}^{(n+1)}) \in \text{OT} \iff a_1, \dots, a_{n+1} \in \text{OT}$.

(d) $\tilde{\omega}_x(a) \in \text{OT} \iff a \in \text{OT}$.

(e) $a \,\tilde{+}\, b \in \text{OT} \iff a, b \in \text{OT}$.

Proof. (a), (b), (c), and (d) follow easily from the definitions (noting that $0 \oplus \tilde{1} \notin \text{OT}$ holds). For (e), the only nontrivial case is if we have

$$a, b \in \text{OT} \setminus \{0\} \;\;\&\;\; \mathsf{hd}(b) \preceq \mathsf{hd}(a) \tag{3.3}$$

Then we have to show

$$\mathsf{hd}(a) \oplus (\mathsf{tl}(a) \,\tilde{+}\, b) \in \text{OT}$$

and we do this by induction on a. Furthermore, we let

$$c := \mathsf{tl}(a) \,\tilde{+}\, b$$

<u>1.</u> If $a \in \text{PT}$: We have $\mathsf{hd}(a) = a$, $\mathsf{tl}(a) = 0$, and that $0 \,\tilde{+}\, b = b$ holds. So, we get $a \,\tilde{+}\, b = a \oplus (0 \,\tilde{+}\, b) = a \oplus b$ and we are done because of $a \in \text{PT}$ and (3.3).
<u>2.</u> If $a \notin \text{PT}$: Note that we get $\mathsf{tl}(a) = (a)_2 <_{\mathbb{N}} a$ because we assumed $a \neq 0$ in (3.3), hence we get $c \in \text{OT}$ by the induction hypothesis. Since $a \in \text{OT} \setminus \{0\}$ holds, we have $a = \mathsf{hd}(a) \oplus \mathsf{tl}(a)$ where $\mathsf{hd}(a) \in \text{PT} \cap \text{OT}$, $\mathsf{tl}(a) \neq 0$, and

$$\mathsf{hd}(\mathsf{tl}(a)) \preceq \mathsf{hd}(a) \tag{3.4}$$

hold. The claim $\mathsf{hd}(a) \oplus c \in \mathrm{OT}$ follows now from $\mathsf{hd}(c) \preceq \mathsf{hd}(a)$ which we get from the definition of $\tilde{+}$ in $c = \mathsf{tl}(a) \tilde{+} b$ and by recalling that we assumed $b \neq 0$ in (3.3): Either $c = b$ holds, and we can use the assumption $\mathsf{hd}(b) \preceq \mathsf{hd}(a)$ from (3.3), or we have $c = \mathsf{hd}(\mathsf{tl}(a)) \oplus (\mathsf{tl}(\mathsf{tl}(a)) \tilde{+} b)$ and $\mathsf{hd}(c) = \mathsf{hd}(\mathsf{tl}(a))$, and hence get $\mathsf{hd}(c) \preceq \mathsf{hd}(a)$ by (3.4). □

Remark 3.14. The following properties reflect common properties from the context of ordinal arithmetic (and we follow essentially [Buc05]).

Lemma 3.15. *Let* $a, b, c \in \mathrm{OT}$.

(a) $(a \oplus b \in \mathrm{OT}$ *and* $c \preceq b) \implies a \tilde{+} c = a \oplus c$.

(b) $a \tilde{+} (b \tilde{+} c) = (a \tilde{+} b) \tilde{+} c$.

(c) $b \prec c \implies a \tilde{+} b \prec a \tilde{+} c$.

(d) $a \preceq c \implies c = a \tilde{+} d$ *for some* $d \in \mathrm{OT}$.

(e) $(a \preceq c$ *and* $c \prec a \tilde{+} b) \implies c = a \tilde{+} d$ *for some* $d \in \mathrm{OT}$ *with* $d \prec b$.

(f) $a, b \preceq a \tilde{+} b$.

(g) $a \preceq c \implies a \tilde{+} b \preceq c \tilde{+} b$.

(h) $(a \neq 0$ *or* $b \neq 0) \implies a \tilde{+} b \neq 0$.

(i) $a \prec b \tilde{+} \tilde{1} \implies a \preceq b$.

(j) $a \in \mathrm{Lim} \iff (a \in \mathrm{PT}_+$ *or* $a = a_1 \oplus a_2$ *with* $a_2 \in \mathrm{Lim})$

(k) $(a \in \mathrm{Lim}$ *and* $b \prec a) \implies b \tilde{+} \tilde{1} \prec a$.

(l) $a \in \mathrm{Suc} \implies (a \notin \mathrm{PT}_+$ *and* $a = d \tilde{+} \tilde{1}$ *for some* $d \in \mathrm{OT}$ *with* $d \prec a$ *and* $d <_{\mathbb{N}} a)$.

Proof. Mostly by induction on the build-up of $a, b, c \in \mathrm{OT}$, see A.2 in the appendix for details. □

Remark 3.16. Every ordinal notation $d \in \mathrm{OT}$ mentioned in Lemma 3.15 can be computed primitive recursively from the given context.

Lemma 3.17. *For every* $k, m \in \mathbb{N}$ *and* $a_1, \ldots, a_{m+1} \in \mathrm{OT}$*, we have the following:*

(a) $\phi\bar{a}^{(m+1)} \in \mathrm{OT}$
$\Longrightarrow \tilde{\varphi}(\bar{a}^{(m+1)}) = \phi\bar{a}^{(m+1)}$.

(b) $\tilde{\varphi}(\bar{0}^{(k)}, \bar{a}^{(m+1)}) = \tilde{\varphi}(\bar{a}^{(m+1)})$.

(c) $\tilde{\varphi}(\bar{0}^{(k)}) = \tilde{1} \in \mathrm{PT}$.

(d) $(a_1 \neq 0 \;\&\; a_{m+1} \neq 0 \;\&\; \phi\bar{a}^{(m+1)}\bar{0}^{(k)} \notin \mathrm{OT})$
$\Longrightarrow \tilde{\varphi}(\bar{a}^{(m+1)}, \bar{0}^{(k)}) = a_{m+1} \;\&\; a_{m+1} \in \mathrm{PT}_+ \;\&\; \phi\bar{a}^{(m+1)}\bar{0}^{(k)} \prec_{\mathbf{lex}} a_{m+1}$.

(e) $a_j \neq 0$ *for some* $1 \leq j \leq m+1$
$\Longrightarrow \tilde{\varphi}(\bar{a}^{(m+1)}) \in \mathrm{PT}_+$.

(f) $(a_1 \neq 0 \;\&\; a_{m+1} \notin \mathrm{PT}_+ \cup \{0\})$
$\Longrightarrow \tilde{\varphi}(\bar{a}^{(m+1)}, \bar{0}^{(k)}) = \phi\bar{a}^{(m+1)}\bar{0}^{(k)}$.

(g) $a_1, \ldots, a_m \prec \tilde{\varphi}(\bar{a}^{(m+1)}, \bar{0}^{(k)})$.

Proof. (a), (b), and (c) are immediate from the definition of $\tilde{\varphi}$.

For (d), we let $a_1 \neq 0$ and $\phi\bar{a}^{(n+1)} \notin \mathrm{OT}$. Further let k be such that $a_k \neq 0$ and $a_i = 0$ for all $k < i \leq n+1$. Since $a_1 \neq 0$ holds, this k exists. By definition of $\tilde{\varphi}$, we get $\tilde{\varphi}(\bar{a}^{(n+1)}) = \mathrm{cr}(\langle\bar{a}^{(n+1)}\rangle) = a_k$. Since $\phi\bar{a}^{(n+1)} \notin \mathrm{OT}$ hols, this implies $a_k \in \mathrm{PT}_+$.

For (e), we can assume without loss of generality that $a_1 \neq 0$ holds (due to (b)). Then either $\phi\bar{a}^{(m+1)} \in \mathrm{OT} \cap \mathrm{PT}_+$ holds and we can use (a), or otherwise we can use (d).

For (f), we use the definition of OT together with (a), noting that $a_1 \neq 0$ and $a_{m+1} \notin \mathrm{PT}_+ \cup \{0\}$ imply $\phi\bar{a}^{(m+1)}\bar{0}^{(k)} \in \mathrm{OT}$.

For (g), we can assume without loss of generality and due to (b) that also $a_1 \neq 0$ holds. In case of $\phi\bar{a}^{(m+1)}\bar{0}^{(k)} \in \mathrm{OT}$, we get the claim from Lemma 3.8 together with (a). Otherwise, we have $\tilde{\varphi}(\bar{a}^{(m+1)}, \bar{0}^{(k)}) = \mathrm{cr}(\langle\bar{a}^{(m+1)}, \bar{a}^{(k)}\rangle) = a_j$ for some $1 \leq j \leq m+1$ and $a_i = 0$ for all $j < i \leq m+1$ and we have $k \leq j$. By the definition of OT, this means that $a_j \in \mathrm{PT}_+$ must hold but not $a_j \prec_{\mathbf{lex}} \phi\bar{a}^{(m+1)}\bar{0}^{(k)}$. Since $a_j \neq \phi\bar{a}^{(m+1)}\bar{0}^{(k)} (= \langle 1, \bar{a}^{(m+1)}, \bar{0}^{(k)}\rangle)$ holds, we get $\phi\bar{a}^{(m+1)}\bar{0}^{(k)} \prec_{\mathbf{lex}} a_j$ from totality of $\prec_{\mathbf{lex}}$ which means that $a_i \prec a_j = \tilde{\varphi}(\bar{a}^{(m+1)}, \bar{0}^{(k)})$ must hold for all $1 \leq i < j$ since $\phi\bar{a}^{(m+1)}\bar{0}^{(k)} \notin \mathrm{OT}$. □

3.3. Semantics of $(\mathrm{OT}, \prec)$

Definition 3.18.

(a) $f_\omega(\gamma) := \omega^\gamma$ for all $\gamma \in \mathrm{On}$.

(b) $\nu_n := f_\omega\binom{1}{n}$ for each $n < \omega$.

Lemma 3.19.

(a) $\sup_{n<\omega} \nu_n = \vartheta\Omega^\omega$.

(b) $\nu_n < \nu_{n+1}$ *for all* $n \in \mathbb{N}$.

(c) $\gamma < \vartheta\Omega^\omega \implies \nu_n \leq \gamma < \nu_{n+1}$ *for some* $n \in \mathbb{N}$.

Proof. (a) and (b) follow directly from Propositions 2.10 and 2.34. For (c), note that the claim is obvious if $\gamma = 0$, so assume $\gamma \geq 1 = f_\omega\binom{1}{0}$. Now, recall that for any normal function $g\colon \mathrm{On} \to \mathrm{On}$ and every $\gamma \in \mathrm{On}$ with $\gamma \geq g(0)$ there is a unique $\alpha \in \mathrm{On}$ such that

$$g(\alpha) \leq \gamma < g(\alpha + 1)$$

holds. Then Proposition 2.10 yields that $g\colon \mathrm{On} \to \mathrm{On}, \xi \mapsto f_\omega\binom{1}{\xi}$ is a normal function, and we are done. □

Definition 3.20. We define $\mathrm{o}(a) \in \mathrm{On}$ and $|a|_\prec \in \mathrm{On}$ for each $a \in \mathrm{OT}$ recursively as follows:

$$\mathrm{o}(a) := \begin{cases} 0 & \text{if } a = 0 \\ \mathrm{o}(a_1) + \mathrm{o}(a_2) & \text{if } a = a_1 \oplus a_2 \text{ with } a_2 \neq 0 \\ \varphi(\mathrm{o}(a_1), \ldots, \mathrm{o}(a_n)) & \text{if } a = \phi a_1 \ldots a_n \text{ with } n \geq 1 \end{cases}$$
$$|a|_\prec := \sup\{|b|_\prec + 1 \colon b \prec a\}$$

where 1 denotes the first non-zero ordinal in the definition of $|a|_\prec$.

Lemma 3.21. *Let* $a, b \in \mathrm{OT}$.

(a) $\mathrm{o}(a) \in \mathrm{On}$ & $(a \in \mathrm{PT} \implies \mathrm{o}(a) \in \mathbf{P})$.

(b) $a \prec b \iff \mathrm{o}(a) < \mathrm{o}(b)$.

(c) $\mathrm{o}(a \tilde{+} b) = \mathrm{o}(a) + \mathrm{o}(b)$

(d) $\mathrm{o}(a) < \vartheta\Omega^\omega$.

(e) $\gamma < \vartheta\Omega^\omega \implies \mathrm{o}(c) = \gamma$ *for some* $c \in \mathrm{OT}$.

Proof. See A.4 in the appendix. The proof uses essentially Lemma 3.19, Definition 3.4, and the results from Chapter 2, more precisely: Lemma 2.28, Proposition 2.15, Lemma 2.16, Corollary 2.18, Lemma 2.20, and Proposition 2.34. □

Theorem 3.22.

(a) *With* $a \mapsto \mathrm{o}(a)$, *we have an order isomorphism between* $(\mathrm{OT}, \prec)$ *and* $(\vartheta\Omega^\omega, <)$.

(b) $|a|_\prec = \mathrm{o}(a)$ *for each* $a \in \mathrm{OT}$.

Proof. For (a): This follows from Lemma 3.21. For (b): From (a), we get that $(\{z \in \mathrm{OT}\colon x \prec a\}, \prec)$ is isomorphic to $(\mathrm{o}(a), <)$ and this yields the claim. □

3.4. Fundamental Sequences

Definition 3.23. *Fundamental sequences* for limit notations $d \in \mathrm{Lim}$ are defined within PA by means of a binary primitive recursive function L whose defining equations are described as follows, where d, x range over natural numbers and where we write $d[x]$ in order to denote $L(d, x)$.

- If $d = 0$ or $d \notin \mathrm{OT}$, then
$$d[x] := 0$$
- If $d \in \mathrm{Suc}$ with $d = d_0 \tilde{+} \tilde{1}$, then
$$d[x] := d_0$$
- If $d \in \mathrm{Lim}$ and $d = a \oplus b$ with $a \in \mathrm{OT}$ and $b \in \mathrm{Lim}$, then
$$d[x] := a \tilde{+} b[x]$$

- If $d \in \mathrm{Lim}$ and $d = \phi a$ with $a \neq 0$, then

$$d[x] := \begin{cases} \tilde{\omega}^{a_0} \tilde{\cdot} (x +_{\mathbb{N}} 1) & \text{if } a = a_0 \tilde{+} \tilde{1} \\ \tilde{\omega}^{a[x]} & \text{otherwise} \end{cases}$$

- If $d \in \mathrm{Lim}$ with $d = \phi \bar{a}^{(m)} b \bar{0}^{(k)} c$ for some $\bar{a}^{(m)}, b, c \in \mathrm{OT}$ with $b \neq 0$ and $m, k \in \mathbb{N}$, then

$$d[0] := \begin{cases} \tilde{\varphi}(\bar{a}^{(m)}, b, \bar{0}^{(k)}, c[0]) & \text{if } c \in \mathrm{Lim} \\ \tilde{\varphi}(\bar{a}^{(m)}, b[0], \bar{0}^{(k+1)}) & \text{if } c = 0 \text{ and } b \in \mathrm{Lim} \\ \tilde{1} & \text{if } c = 0 \text{ and } b \in \mathrm{Suc} \\ \tilde{\varphi}(\bar{a}^{(m)}, b, \bar{0}^{(k)}, c[0]) \tilde{+} \tilde{1} & \text{otherwise, i.e., if } c \in \mathrm{Suc} \end{cases}$$

$$d[x +_{\mathbb{N}} 1] := \begin{cases} \tilde{\varphi}(\bar{a}^{(m)}, b, \bar{0}^{(k)}, c[x +_{\mathbb{N}} 1]) & \text{if } c \in \mathrm{Lim} \\ \tilde{\varphi}(\bar{a}^{(m)}, b[x +_{\mathbb{N}} 1], \bar{0}^{(k+1)}) & \text{if } c = 0 \text{ and } b \in \mathrm{Lim} \\ \tilde{\varphi}(\bar{a}^{(m)}, b[x], d[x], \bar{0}^{(k)}) & \text{otherwise, i.e., } c \in \mathrm{Suc} \\ & \quad \text{or } (c = 0 \text{ and } b \in \mathrm{Suc}) \end{cases}$$

  Note that $m \neq 0$ implies that $a_1 \neq 0$ holds.

Remark 3.24. Given $d = \phi \bar{a}^{(m+1)} \bar{0}^{(k)} \in \mathrm{OT}$ with $a_{m+1} \in \mathrm{Lim}$, we cannot expect that $\phi \bar{a}^{(m)} b \bar{0}^{(k)} \in \mathrm{OT}$ holds for every $b \prec a_{m+1}$. In particular, we cannot expect $\phi \bar{a}^{(m)} (a_{m+1}[x]) \bar{0}^{(k)} \in \mathrm{OT}$ to hold for any x. Take for instance $d := \phi a$ with $a := \phi \tilde{\varepsilon}_0 \tilde{1}$. Since $a \in \mathrm{Lim}$ holds, we have $d[x] = \tilde{\varphi}(a[x])$ with $a[x] = \tilde{\omega}^{\tilde{\varepsilon}_0} \tilde{\cdot} (x +_{\mathbb{N}} 1) = \tilde{\varepsilon}_0 \tilde{\cdot} (x +_{\mathbb{N}} 1)$. Hence, we have $\phi(a[0]) = \phi(\tilde{\varepsilon}_0) = \phi(\phi \tilde{1} 0) \notin \mathrm{OT}$ because of $\phi(\phi \tilde{1} 0) \prec_{\mathbf{lex}} \phi \tilde{1} 0$ and the definition of OT, and hence $(\tilde{\varphi}(a))[x] = \tilde{\varphi}(a[x]) \neq \phi(a[x])$ holds.

Theorem 3.25.

(a) $\mathsf{PA} \vdash \forall d, x (d \in \mathrm{Suc} \to d[x] \prec d)$.

(b) $\mathsf{PA} \vdash \forall d, x (d \in \mathrm{Lim} \to (0 \prec d[x] \wedge d[x] \prec d[x +_{\mathbb{N}} 1] \wedge d[x] \prec d))$.

Proof. See A.5 in the appendix. □

Corollary 3.26. PA *proves for each* $d \in \mathrm{Lim}$ *with* $d = \phi\bar{a}^{(m)}b\bar{0}^{(k)}c$ *and* $b \neq 0$ *the following:*

$$
\begin{aligned}
&c \in \mathrm{Suc} \vee (c = 0 \wedge b \in \mathrm{Suc}) \\
&\to \forall x \Big(d[x +_{\mathbb{N}} 1] = \tilde{\varphi}(\bar{a}^{(m)}, b[x], d[x], \bar{0}^{(k)}) \\
&\qquad = \begin{cases} \phi(d[x])\bar{0}^{(k)} & \text{if } m = 0 \text{ and } b = \tilde{1} \\ \phi\bar{a}^{(m)}(b[x])(d[x])\bar{0}^{(k)} & \text{otherwise} \end{cases} \Big)
\end{aligned}
$$

Proof. Theorem 3.25 implies $d[x] \prec d[x +_{\mathbb{N}} 1]$ and $d[x] \neq 0$, hence the claim follows with Lemma 3.17. □

Theorem 3.27. $\mathsf{PA} \vdash \forall d, d_0(d \in \mathrm{Lim} \wedge d_0 \prec d \to \exists x(d_0 \prec d[x]))$.

Proof. See A.6 in the appendix. □

Example 3.28. $\mathsf{PA} \vdash \forall a\big(a \prec \tilde{\varepsilon}_0 \to \exists x(a \prec \tilde{\omega}_x(\tilde{1}))\big)$.

Proof. Since $\tilde{\varepsilon}_b = \tilde{\varphi}(\tilde{1}, b)$ holds for any $b \in \mathrm{OT}$, we have

$$
\begin{aligned}
\tilde{\varepsilon}_0[0] &= (\phi\tilde{1}0)[0] & \qquad \tilde{\varepsilon}_0[x +_{\mathbb{N}} 1] &= (\phi\tilde{1}0)[x +_{\mathbb{N}} 1] \\
&= \tilde{1} & &= \tilde{\varphi}(0, \tilde{\varepsilon}_0[x]) = \tilde{\omega}^{\tilde{\varepsilon}_0[x]}
\end{aligned}
$$

and obtain $\tilde{\varepsilon}_0[x] = \tilde{\omega}_x(\tilde{1})$ by induction on x. Then Theorem 3.25 and Theorem 3.27 yield the claim. □

Corollary 3.29. *Let* $k, m \in \mathbb{N}$. PA *proves that for every* $\bar{a}^{(m)}, b, d_0 \in \mathrm{OT}$ *with*

$$d_0 \prec \tilde{\varphi}(\bar{a}^{(m+1)}, \bar{0}^{(k)}, b)$$

the following holds:

(a) $b \in \mathrm{Lim} \to \exists x\big(d_0 \prec \tilde{\varphi}(\bar{a}^{(m+1)}, \bar{0}^{(k)}, b[x])\big)$.

(b) $(b \notin \mathrm{Lim} \wedge a_1 = 0 \wedge \ldots \wedge a_{m+1} = 0) \to \exists x\big(d_0 \prec \tilde{\omega}^{b[x]} \mathbin{\tilde{\cdot}} (x +_{\mathbb{N}} 1)\big)$.

(c) $(b = 0 \wedge a_{m+1} \in \mathrm{Lim}) \to \exists x\big(d_0 \prec \tilde{\varphi}(\bar{a}^{(m)}, a_{m+1}[x], \bar{0}^{(k+1)})\big)$.

Proof. Let $d := \tilde{\varphi}(\bar{a}^{(m+1)}, \bar{0}^{(k)}, b)$. In case of $d = \phi\bar{a}^{(m+1)}\bar{0}^{(k)}b$, the claims follow from Theorem 3.27. Now, assuming $d \neq \phi\bar{a}^{(m+1)}\bar{0}^{(k)}b$, we have the following cases:
<u>1.</u> If $a_i = 0$ holds for all $1 \leq i \leq m+1$:
<u>1.1.</u> If $\phi b \notin \mathrm{OT}$: Then $d = \tilde{\omega}^b = b$ holds with $b \in \mathrm{PT}_+$, i.e., $b \in \mathrm{Lim}$. From $d_0 \prec d = b$, we get x with $d_0 \prec b[x]$ by Theorem 3.27. The claim hence follows from $b[x] \preceq \tilde{\omega}^{b[x]} = \tilde{\varphi}(\bar{a}^{(m+1)}, \bar{0}^{(k)}, b[x])$ with Lemma 3.17.
<u>1.2.</u> If $\phi b \in \mathrm{OT}$: Then $d = \phi b$ and assuming $d_0 \prec d$, we get x with $d_0 \prec d[x]$ by Theorem 3.27.
<u>1.2.1.</u> If $b \in \mathrm{Lim}$: We get $d[x] = \tilde{\omega}^{b[x]} = \tilde{\varphi}(\bar{a}^{(m+1)}, \bar{0}^{(k)}, b[x])$.
<u>1.2.2.</u> Otherwise: We only need to consider the case where $b \in \mathrm{Suc}$ holds. Let $b = b_0 \tilde{+} \tilde{1}$ for some b_0 (and which we can compute from b). Then we get $d[x] = \tilde{\omega}^{b_0} \tilde{\cdot} (x +_{\mathbb{N}} 1)$ and are done since $b[x] = b_0$.
<u>2.</u> Otherwise: Then there is some $1 \leq l \leq m+1$ such that $a_l \neq 0$ and $a_1 = \ldots = a_{l-1} = 0$ hold, and we have $d = \tilde{\varphi}(a_l, \ldots, a_{m+1}, \bar{0}^{(k)}, b)$.
<u>2.1.</u> If $\phi a_l \ldots a_{m+1}\bar{0}^{(k)}b \notin \mathrm{OT}$:
<u>2.1.1.</u> If $b = 0$: This means, we only have to show (c) and we therefore assume now also $a_{m+1} \in \mathrm{Lim}$. Then we must have $a_{m+1} \in \mathrm{PT}_+$ and $d = \tilde{\varphi}(a_l, \ldots, a_{m+1}, \bar{0}^{(k)}, b) = a_{m+1}$, hence we have $d[x] = a_{m+1}[x]$ for all x, and $d_0 \prec d$ implies $d_0 \prec a_{m+1}[x] \preceq \tilde{\varphi}(\bar{a}^{(m)}, a_{m+1}[x], \bar{0}^{(k+1)})$ for some x, using Lemma 3.17.
<u>2.1.2.</u> Otherwise: Then we get $d = \tilde{\varphi}(a_l, \ldots, a_{m+1}, \bar{0}^{(k)}, b) = b$ with $b \in \mathrm{PT}_+$, i.e., $b \in \mathrm{Lim}$. We have $d[x] = b[x]$, so $d_0 \prec b[x] \preceq \tilde{\varphi}(\bar{a}^{(m+1)}, \bar{0}^{(k)}, b)$ holds again by Lemma 3.17.
<u>2.2.</u> If $\phi a_l \ldots a_{m+1}\bar{0}^{(k)}b \in \mathrm{OT}$: Then $d = \phi a_l \ldots a_{m+1}\bar{0}^{(k)}b$ holds and by Theorem 3.27, we get $d_0 \prec d[x]$ for some x.
<u>2.2.1.</u> If $b \in \mathrm{Lim}$: $d[x] = \tilde{\varphi}(a_l, \ldots, a_{m+1}, \bar{0}^{(k)}, b[x]) = \tilde{\varphi}(\bar{a}^{(m+1)}, \bar{0}^{(k)}, b[x])$ holds by Definition 3.23.
<u>2.2.2.</u> Otherwise: Then we only need to consider the case where $b = 0$ and $a_{m+1} \in \mathrm{Lim}$ holds. We get $d[x] = \tilde{\varphi}(a_l, \ldots, a_m, a_{m+1}[x], \bar{0}^{(k+1)}) = \tilde{\varphi}(\bar{a}^{(m)}, a_{m+1}[x], \bar{0}^{(k+1)})$ by Definition 3.23. □

4. Ordinal Notations for the Large Veblen Ordinal

In Chapter 8, we shall carry out wellordering proofs that rely on a simplified representation of Klammersymbols and that we shall introduce in the following chapter in order to work more efficiently with Klammersymbols.

This means that we shall introduce further below the notion of a *partition* of a Klammersymbol together with auxiliary notions and operations that allow the manipulation of the represented ordinals in a natural and suitable way for the proofs of Chapter 8. The benefit of our approach is that we can work directly with the results from [Sch54], not having to introduce a completely new concept for establishing a suitable ordinal notation system, hence keeping the reader focused on the main techniques that are used for the wellordering proof. More precisely, we shall introduce the new notions and operations in such a way that it becomes clear that (apart from the results from [Sch54]) only primitive recursive manipulations of finite strings are needed. The difficulty of the following chapter comes from our aim in Chapter 11 to internalize some methods from Chapter 7 within the arithmetical theory TID_1^+ from Chapter 8.

We do not explicitly introduce the underlying ordinal notation system because similar work has been already done in the context of finitary Veblen functions in Chapter 3 which gives the information needed to deal with Klammersymbols in general. Hence, we shall presuppose that an underlying ordinal notation system $(\mathrm{OT}(\boldsymbol{L}_0), \prec)$ is given that can be formalized already in a system like PA. In particular, $\mathrm{OT}(\boldsymbol{L}_0)$ is motivated by Proposition 2.29 and shall be built up inductively from

1. codes for *finite ordinals*,

2. codes for *ordinal addition*, and

3. codes $\overline{\varphi_{\bullet}}\alpha$ for the *fixed-point free value of $\varphi_{\bullet}$ applied to Klammersymbols.*

4.1. Towards an Ordinal Notation System $\mathrm{OT}(\boldsymbol{K}\!\restriction)$

Definition 4.1. $(\mathrm{OT}(\boldsymbol{K}\!\restriction), \prec)$ is the primitive recursive ordinal notation system defined by simultaneous induction in the following way:

- $\prec \subseteq \mathrm{OT}(\boldsymbol{K}\!\restriction) \times \mathrm{OT}(\boldsymbol{K}\!\restriction)$ shall be defined according to Corollary 2.25 and the usual properties of ordinal addition. We write $a \preceq b$ in order to abbreviate

$$a \prec b \vee (a = b \wedge a \in \mathrm{OT}(\boldsymbol{K}\!\restriction))$$

- $\boldsymbol{K}\!\restriction \subseteq \mathbb{N}$ shall be built up from (codes for) expressions of the form $\left(\begin{smallmatrix} a_0 & \dots & a_n \\ b_0 & \dots & b_n \end{smallmatrix}\right)$ such that we have

$$\begin{aligned} & a_0, b_0, \dots, b_n \in \mathrm{OT}(\boldsymbol{K}\!\restriction) \\ & a_1, \dots, a_n \in \mathrm{OT}(\boldsymbol{K}\!\restriction) \setminus \{0\} \\ & b_0 \prec \dots \prec b_n \end{aligned}$$

- $\mathrm{OT}(\boldsymbol{K}\!\restriction) \subseteq \mathbb{N}$ shall be defined according to Proposition 2.29, where in particular it shall consist of the following kinds of codes:
  1. $\underline{0} := 0$ and $\underline{n} := \langle 0, n \rangle$ denoting codes for the *zero ordinal* and the *finite successor ordinals* for each $n \in \mathbb{N} \setminus \{0\}$.
  2. $\{\alpha\}a := \langle 1, \alpha, a \rangle$ denoting codes for *Klammersymbol-function application* for each $\alpha \in \boldsymbol{K}\!\restriction$ and $a \in \mathrm{OT}(\boldsymbol{K}\!\restriction)$.
  3. Finite lists

     $$\{\alpha_0\}a_0 \oplus \dots \oplus \{\alpha_m\}a_m \oplus b := \langle 2, \{\alpha_0\}a_0, \dots, \{\alpha_m\}a_m, b \rangle$$

     such that

     - $\{\alpha_{i+1}\}a_{i+1} \preceq \{\alpha_i\}a_i$ holds for each $i <_{\mathbb{N}} m$ and
     - b is either of the form $\underline{n}$ with $n \neq 0$ or b is of the form $\{\beta\}b$ with $\{\beta\}b \preceq \{\alpha_m\}a_m$,

     denoting codes for expressions that respect Proposition 2.29 for $\alpha_0, \dots, \alpha_m \in \boldsymbol{K}\!\restriction$ and $n \in \mathbb{N}$.

  We let $a_0 \oplus \dots \oplus a_n$ denote a_0 in case of $n = 0$.

Remark 4.2. We did not give an exact definition of $(\mathrm{OT}(\boldsymbol{K}\!\restriction), \prec)$ because it is not crucial for our investigations on TID_1^+ and TID_2 in Chapter 6. More precisely, we actually only need the exact definition of $(\mathrm{OT}(\boldsymbol{K}\!\restriction), \prec)$ in order to verify on the one hand the above properties and on the other hand that $(\mathrm{OT}(\boldsymbol{K}\!\restriction), \prec)$ is primitive recursive with $\prec$ being a *strict total order*. In particular the proof of the latter would be technically cumbersome and is similar to the proofs for the ordinal notation system given in the context of finitary Veblen functions (see Chapter 3).

4.2. Extending $\mathrm{OT}(\boldsymbol{K}\!\restriction)$ to $\mathrm{OT}(\boldsymbol{K})$ with an Equivalence Relation

We introduce an extension $(\mathrm{OT}(\boldsymbol{K}), \prec)$ of $(\mathrm{OT}(\boldsymbol{K}\!\restriction), \prec)$ in order to conceptually identify $(\mathrm{OT}(\boldsymbol{K}\!\restriction), \prec)$ and $(\mathfrak{V}, <)$.

Definition 4.3. Let $\boldsymbol{K}$, $=_{\boldsymbol{K}}$, and $(\mathrm{OT}(\boldsymbol{K}), \prec_{\mathrm{OT}(\boldsymbol{K})})$ be defined simultaneously and inductively, having the following properties:

1. $\boldsymbol{K}$ shall be the primitive recursive set of *general (codes of) Klammersymbols (over* $\mathrm{OT}(\boldsymbol{K}\!\restriction)$*)* that consists of all expressions $\binom{a_0\ \cdots\ a_n}{b_0\ \cdots\ b_n}$ with $a_0, \ldots, a_n, b_0, \ldots, b_n \in \mathrm{OT}(\boldsymbol{K})$ and $b_0 \prec_{\mathrm{OT}(\boldsymbol{K})} \cdots \prec_{\mathrm{OT}(\boldsymbol{K})} b_n$.

2. $=_{\boldsymbol{K}}$ and $\prec_{\mathbf{lex}}$ shall be the primitive recursive *equivalence relation* on $\boldsymbol{K}$ and the primitive recursive *lexicographic order* on $\boldsymbol{K}$, respectively, that is analog to the corresponding notions of Section 2.2. To stress that $\alpha, \beta \in \boldsymbol{K}$ denote the same (code of a) Klammersymbol, we write $\alpha \equiv \beta$.

3. $(\mathrm{OT}(\boldsymbol{K}), \prec_{\mathrm{OT}(\boldsymbol{K})})$ shall be defined analogously to Definition 4.1 such that $\mathrm{OT}(\boldsymbol{K})$ contains all expressions $\{\alpha\}a$ with $\alpha \in \boldsymbol{K}$ and $a \in \mathrm{OT}(\boldsymbol{K})$. Moreover, we also have an equivalence relation $=_{\mathrm{OT}(\boldsymbol{K})}$ on $\mathrm{OT}(\boldsymbol{K})$ that is based on the equivalence relation $=_{\boldsymbol{K}}$ on $\boldsymbol{K}$, hence $\prec$ is extended to $\prec_{\mathrm{OT}(\boldsymbol{K})}$ over $\mathrm{OT}(\boldsymbol{K})$ according to this equivalence. To stress that $a, b \in \mathrm{OT}(\boldsymbol{K})$ denote (as codes) the same natural numbers, we write $a \equiv b$.

We write form now on simply $\prec$ instead of $\prec_{\mathrm{OT}(\boldsymbol{K})}$.

Definition 4.4.

- $\tilde{+}$ shall be the primitive recursive binary function on $\mathrm{OT}(\boldsymbol{K})$, denoting *ordinal addition.* In particular, the following shall hold:

$$\begin{aligned}&\{\alpha_0\}a_0 \oplus \ldots \oplus \{\alpha_m\}a_m \oplus b \in \mathrm{OT}(\boldsymbol{K})\\ &\quad\Longrightarrow\ \{\alpha_0\}a_0 \tilde{+} \ldots \tilde{+} \{\alpha_m\}a_m \oplus b = \{\alpha_0\}a_0 \oplus \ldots \oplus \{\alpha_m\}a_m \oplus b\end{aligned}$$

- $\mathrm{Suc} := \{a \in \mathrm{OT}(\boldsymbol{K})\colon a = \{\alpha_0\}a_0 \oplus \ldots \oplus \{\alpha_m\}a_m \oplus \underline{n} \ \ \&\ \ n \neq 0\}$ defines the set of *successors (in* $\mathrm{OT}(\boldsymbol{K})$*).* In particular, we have $a \in \mathrm{Suc}$ if and only if $a = a_0 \tilde{+} \underline{1}$ holds for some $a_0 \in \mathrm{OT}(\boldsymbol{K})$.

- $\mathrm{Lim} := \mathrm{OT}(\boldsymbol{K}) \setminus (\mathrm{Suc} \cup \{\underline{0}\})$ defines the set of *limits (in* $\mathrm{OT}(\boldsymbol{K})$*).*

Definition 4.5. We write $\alpha =_{\mathrm{NF}(\boldsymbol{K}\restriction)} \beta$ in order to denote for $\alpha, \beta \in \boldsymbol{K}$ that $\alpha =_{\boldsymbol{K}} \beta$ holds with $\beta \in \boldsymbol{K}\restriction$.

Lemma 4.6. *For each $\alpha \in \boldsymbol{K}$ there is a unique $\beta \in \boldsymbol{K}\restriction$ such that $\alpha =_{\mathrm{NF}(\boldsymbol{K}\restriction)} \beta$ holds. In particular, β can be computed primitive recursively from α.*

Proof. This follows easily by induction on the build-up of $\alpha \in \boldsymbol{K}$. If not already $\alpha \in \boldsymbol{K}\restriction$ holds, then delete first each row of the form ${0 \atop a}$ and obtain a Klammersymbol α' with $\alpha =_{\boldsymbol{K}} \alpha'$. Then proceed with each component of α' and rewrite each Klammersymbol that occurs there. □

Notation 4.7.

(a) For each $n \in \mathbb{N}$, we simply write n instead of $\underline{n}$ if the meaning is clear from the context.

(b) Motivated by Proposition 2.23.(d) and Corollary 2.26, we introduce the following notations for each $a \in \mathrm{OT}(\boldsymbol{K})$:

$$\underline{\omega}^a := \begin{cases}\underline{1} & \text{if } a = \underline{0}\\ \{\left(\begin{smallmatrix}\underline{0}\\ \underline{0}\end{smallmatrix}\right)\}\underline{n_0} & \text{if } a = \underline{n_0 +_{\mathbb{N}} 1}\\ \{\left(\begin{smallmatrix}\underline{0}\\ \underline{0}\end{smallmatrix}\right)\}a & \text{otherwise}\end{cases} \qquad \begin{aligned}\underline{\varepsilon}_a &:= \{\left(\begin{smallmatrix}\underline{1}\\ \underline{0}\end{smallmatrix}\right)\}\underline{0}\\ \underline{\varphi_{\bullet}\omega}a &:= \{\left(\begin{smallmatrix}\underline{\omega}\\ \underline{0}\end{smallmatrix}\right)\}a\\ \underline{\Gamma}_a &:= \{\left(\begin{smallmatrix}\underline{1}\\ \underline{1}\end{smallmatrix}\right)\}a\end{aligned}$$

$$\underline{\omega} := \underline{\omega}^{\underline{1}} = \{\left(\begin{smallmatrix}\underline{0}\\ \underline{0}\end{smallmatrix}\right)\}\underline{0} \qquad\qquad \underline{\vartheta\Omega^\omega} := \{\left(\begin{smallmatrix}\underline{1}\\ \underline{\omega}\end{smallmatrix}\right)\}\underline{0}$$

and shall write ω, ω^a, ε_a, $\varphi_{\bullet}\omega a$, Γ_a, and $\vartheta\Omega^\omega$ for $\underline{\omega}$, $\underline{\omega}^a$, $\underline{\varepsilon}_a$, $\underline{\varphi\omega a}$, $\underline{\Gamma}_a$, and $\underline{\vartheta\Omega^\omega}$, respectively.

(c) n may be used from now on also for $\underline{n}$ (besides $n_{\mathbb{N}}$), and it shall be clear from the context which of those is meant. Moreover, we may also write $a + b$ to denote $a \tilde{+} b$ (besides $a +_{\mathbb{N}} b$), but we shall make only rare use of this abbreviation and prefer writing $a \tilde{+} b$ explicitly instead.

(d) $a \preceq b$ is used in the obvious way to abbreviate $a \prec b \vee a =_{\mathrm{OT}(\boldsymbol{K})} b$, and analogously, $\alpha \preceq_{\mathsf{lex}} \beta$ is used to abbreviate $\alpha \prec_{\mathsf{lex}} \beta \vee \alpha =_{\boldsymbol{K}} \beta$.

4.3. Primitive Recursive Properties of $\mathrm{OT}(\boldsymbol{K})$

It is more or less clear that $(\mathrm{OT}(\boldsymbol{K}), \prec)$ and the results of Section 4.2 can be formalized and proven within PA, given the assumptions that we made and the definitions that we introduced. Based on this and the results of Subsection 2.2.2, we shall list now straight-forward properties and that are needed for the wellordering proofs for TID_1^+ and TID_2.

- Motivated by Corollary 2.31, compound codes shall be built up from smaller components (w.r.t. $\prec$ and $<_{\mathbb{N}}$):

$$b := a_0 \oplus \ldots \oplus a_{m+1} \in \mathrm{OT}(\boldsymbol{K}) \implies \begin{cases} a_0, \ldots, a_{m+1} \prec b \\ a_0, \ldots, a_{m+1} <_{\mathbb{N}} b \end{cases}$$

$$c := \{\left(\begin{smallmatrix} a_0 & \cdots & a_n \\ b_0 & \cdots & b_n \end{smallmatrix}\right)\}c_0 \in \mathrm{OT}(\boldsymbol{K}) \implies \begin{cases} c_0, a_0, \ldots, a_n, b_0, \ldots, b_n \prec c \\ c_0, a_0, \ldots, a_n, b_0, \ldots, b_n <_{\mathbb{N}} c \end{cases}$$

- Motivated by Corollary 2.25, we assume for $\alpha, \beta \in \boldsymbol{K}$ with $\alpha := \left(\begin{smallmatrix} a_1 & \cdots & a_{n+1} \\ c_1 & \cdots & c_{n+1} \end{smallmatrix}\right)$, $\beta := \left(\begin{smallmatrix} b_1 & \cdots & b_{m+1} \\ d_1 & \cdots & d_{m+1} \end{smallmatrix}\right)$, and $a_0, b_0 \in \mathrm{OT}(\boldsymbol{K})$ that $\{\alpha\}a_0 \prec \{\beta\}b_0$ holds if and only if one of the following holds:
  1. $\alpha =_{\boldsymbol{K}} \beta$ holds with $a_0 \prec b_0$.
  2. $\alpha \prec_{\mathsf{lex}} \beta$ holds with $a_i \prec \{\beta\}b_0$ for all $i \leq n$, or
  3. $\beta \prec_{\mathsf{lex}} \alpha$ holds with $\{\alpha\}a_0 \preceq b_j$ for some $j \leq m$.
- If $a \prec \{\left(\begin{smallmatrix} 0 \\ 0 \end{smallmatrix}\right)\}0$ holds, then already $a \prec \underline{n}$ holds for some $n \in \mathbb{N}$.

- If $a \in \mathrm{Lim}$ and $c \prec \{\alpha\}a$ hold for some $\alpha \in \boldsymbol{K}$, then already $c \prec \{\alpha\}a_0$ holds for some $a_0 \prec a$.
- If $b \in \mathrm{Lim}$ and $c \prec \{\left(\begin{smallmatrix}1\\b\end{smallmatrix}\right)\}0$ hold, then already $c \prec \{\left(\begin{smallmatrix}1\\b_0\end{smallmatrix}\right)\}0$ holds for some $b_0 \prec b$.
- For each $a, b, c \in \mathrm{OT}(\boldsymbol{K})$, we have that $c \prec a \tilde{+} b$ implies either $a \prec b$ or that some $d \in \mathrm{OT}(\boldsymbol{K})$ exists with $d \prec c$ such that $c = a \tilde{+} d$ holds.
- Klammersymbols can be coded as finite lists of pairs, therefore we can assume that $a_0, \ldots, a_n, b_0, \ldots, b_n <_{\mathbb{N}} \alpha$ holds for each (thus encoded) Klammersymbol $\alpha := \left(\begin{smallmatrix}a_0 & \cdots & a_n\\ b_0 & \cdots & b_n\end{smallmatrix}\right)$.

4.4. Partitioning via Labeled Klammersymbols yielding $\mathrm{OT}(\boldsymbol{L}_0)$

This section singles out two primitive recursive subsets $\boldsymbol{S}$ and $\boldsymbol{L}$ from $\boldsymbol{K}$ that consist of so-called *simple* and *labeled* Klammersymbols. These turn out to be technically more amenable from a formal standpoint and sufficient for denoting ordinals below $\mathfrak{V}$, hence leading to an alternative representation

$$\mathrm{OT} := \mathrm{OT}(\boldsymbol{L}_0)$$

of $\mathrm{OT}(\boldsymbol{K})$. In particular and building on $\boldsymbol{S}$, we introduce for each $\alpha \in \boldsymbol{K}$ a Klammersymbol $\beta \in \boldsymbol{K}$ which we call the *partition of* α. Then, expressions of the form $\{\beta\}b$ occur in $\mathrm{OT}(\boldsymbol{L}_0)$ only if β is such a partition and $b \in \mathrm{OT}(\boldsymbol{L}_0)$ holds.

Definition 4.8. $\mathbb{L}(\boldsymbol{K}) := \{a \in \mathrm{OT}(\boldsymbol{K})\colon a = 0 \;\text{ or }\; a \in \mathrm{Lim}\}$ defines the collection of *labels* of $\mathrm{OT}(\boldsymbol{K})$.

Definition 4.9. For each $a \in \mathrm{OT}(\boldsymbol{K})$, we define the following notions.

(a) The *label* $a{\Downarrow} \in \mathbb{L}(\boldsymbol{K})$ *of* a is defined as

$$a{\Downarrow} := \begin{cases} 0 & \text{if } a \text{ is of the form } \underline{n} \\ a_1 \oplus \ldots \oplus a_m & \text{if } a \text{ is of the form } a_1 \oplus \ldots \oplus a_m \oplus \underline{n} \\ a & \text{otherwise (i.e., } a \in \mathrm{Lim}) \end{cases}$$

(b) The *successor length* $\mathsf{lh}_{\mathsf{Suc}}(a) \in \mathrm{OT}(\boldsymbol{K})$ *of* a is defined as

$$\mathsf{lh}_{\mathsf{Suc}}(a) := \begin{cases} \underline{n} & \text{if } a \text{ is of the form } a_1 \oplus \ldots \oplus a_m \oplus \underline{n} \\ 0 & \text{otherwise} \end{cases}$$

Definition 4.10. For each $b, a_0, \ldots, a_n \in \mathrm{OT}(\boldsymbol{K})$, we define

$$\frac{\quad}{b} := \binom{0}{0}$$

$$\frac{a_0,\ldots,a_n}{b} := \begin{cases} \frac{a_0,\ldots,a_{n-1}}{b} & \text{if } a_n = 0 \\ \begin{pmatrix} a_0 & a_1 & \ldots & a_n \\ b & b\tilde{+}\underline{1} & \ldots & b\tilde{+}\underline{n} \end{pmatrix} & \text{otherwise} \end{cases}$$

$$\triangleright\!\frac{\langle a_0,\ldots,a_{n-1}\rangle}{b}\!\triangleleft := \frac{a_0,\ldots,a_{n-1}}{b}$$

and for $\alpha := \begin{pmatrix} a_0 & \ldots & a_n \\ b_0 & \ldots & b_n \end{pmatrix} \in \boldsymbol{K}$ and $\beta := \begin{pmatrix} c_0 & \ldots & c_m \\ d_0 & \ldots & d_m \end{pmatrix} \in \boldsymbol{K}$, we further define

$$\alpha *_{\boldsymbol{K}} \beta := \begin{cases} \beta & \text{if } \alpha = \frac{0}{0} \\ \alpha & \text{if } \alpha \neq \frac{0}{0},\ m = 0, \text{ and } d_0 \prec b_n \\ \begin{pmatrix} a_0 & \ldots & a_n\tilde{+}c_0 \\ b_0 & \ldots & b_n \end{pmatrix} & \text{if } \alpha \neq \frac{0}{0},\ m = 0, \text{ and } d_0 = b_n \\ \begin{pmatrix} a_0 & \ldots & a_n & c_0 \\ b_0 & \ldots & b_n & d_0 \end{pmatrix} & \text{if } \alpha \neq \frac{0}{0},\ m = 0, \text{ and } b_n \prec d_0 \\ \left(\alpha *_{\boldsymbol{K}} \binom{a_0}{b_0}\right) *_{\boldsymbol{K}} \begin{pmatrix} c_1 & \ldots & c_m \\ d_1 & \ldots & d_m \end{pmatrix} & \text{otherwise, i.e.,} \\ & \quad \alpha \neq \frac{0}{0} \text{ and } m > 0 \end{cases}$$

Notation 4.11. We write ambiguously $\alpha * \beta$ for $\alpha *_{\boldsymbol{K}} \beta$ if the meaning is clear from the context. Moreover, we let

$$\alpha_1 * \ldots * \alpha_n := \begin{cases} \frac{0}{0} & \text{if } n = 0 \\ (\alpha_1 * \ldots * \alpha_{n-1}) * \alpha_n & \text{otherwise} \end{cases}$$

for each $\alpha_0, \ldots, \alpha_n \in \boldsymbol{K}$.

Definition 4.12. Let $\alpha \in \boldsymbol{K}$ be given with $\alpha \neq \frac{0}{0}$.

(a) $\boldsymbol{S} := \{\frac{a_0,\ldots,a_n}{b} \in \boldsymbol{K} \colon b \in \mathbb{L}(\boldsymbol{K}) \ \& \ a_n \neq 0\}$ and we say that α is *simple* in case that $\alpha \in \boldsymbol{S}$ holds. In particular, this means $\frac{0}{0} \notin \boldsymbol{S}$.

Moreover, we let

$$\boldsymbol{S}^b := \{\alpha \in \boldsymbol{S} \colon \alpha \equiv \tfrac{a_0,\ldots,a_n}{b} \text{ for some } a_0,\ldots,a_n\}$$
$$\boldsymbol{S}^{\prec b} := \{\alpha \colon \alpha \in \boldsymbol{S}^{b_0} \text{ for some } b_0 \prec b\}$$
$$\boldsymbol{S}^{\preceq b} := \boldsymbol{S}^{\prec b} \cup \boldsymbol{S}^b$$

and

$$\boldsymbol{S}_0 := \boldsymbol{S} \cup \{\tfrac{0}{0}\} \qquad \boldsymbol{S}_0^{\prec b} := \boldsymbol{S}^{\prec b} \cup \{\tfrac{0}{0}\}$$
$$\boldsymbol{S}_0^b := \boldsymbol{S}^b \cup \{\tfrac{0}{0}\} \qquad \boldsymbol{S}_0^{\preceq b} := \boldsymbol{S}^{\preceq b} \cup \{\tfrac{0}{0}\}$$

We say for $\alpha \in \boldsymbol{S}^b$ that α *is simple with label* b.

(b) $\boldsymbol{L} := \{\alpha_0 * \ldots * \alpha_m \in \boldsymbol{K} \colon \alpha_i \in \boldsymbol{S}^{b_i} \text{ for } i \leq m \text{ with } b_0 \prec \ldots \prec b_m\}$ and we say that $\alpha \in \boldsymbol{L}$ is *labeled*. In particular, this means $\frac{0}{0} \notin \boldsymbol{L}$. Moreover, we let

$$\boldsymbol{L}^b := \{\alpha * \sigma \in \boldsymbol{L} \colon \sigma \in \boldsymbol{S}^b\}$$
$$\boldsymbol{L}^{\prec b} := \{\alpha * \sigma \in \boldsymbol{L} \colon \sigma \in \boldsymbol{S}^{\prec b}\}$$
$$\boldsymbol{L}^{\preceq b} := \boldsymbol{L}^{\prec b} \cup \boldsymbol{L}^b$$

and

$$\boldsymbol{L}_0 := \boldsymbol{L} \cup \{\tfrac{0}{0}\} \qquad \boldsymbol{L}_0^{\prec b} := \boldsymbol{L}^{\prec b} \cup \{\tfrac{0}{0}\}$$
$$\boldsymbol{L}_0^b := \boldsymbol{L}^b \cup \{\tfrac{0}{0}\} \qquad \boldsymbol{L}_0^{\preceq b} := \boldsymbol{L}^{\preceq b} \cup \{\tfrac{0}{0}\}$$

We say for $\alpha \in \boldsymbol{L}^b$ that α *has label* b.

Definition 4.13.

(a) $\mathrm{OT}(\boldsymbol{L}_0)$ shall be the restriction of $\mathrm{OT}(\boldsymbol{K})$ that consists of all such $a \in \mathrm{OT}(\boldsymbol{K})$ such that $\alpha \in \boldsymbol{L}_0$ holds for every Klammersymbol α that occurs in a. In particular, this implies hereditarily that also $\beta \in \boldsymbol{L}_0$ holds for all Klammersymbols β that occur in α.

(b) $\mathbb{L}(\boldsymbol{L}_0)$ is then just $\mathbb{L}(\boldsymbol{K}) \cap \mathrm{OT}(\boldsymbol{L}_0)$.

Definition 4.14. Let $\alpha \in \boldsymbol{K}$ be given with $\alpha \neq \frac{0}{0}$. Moreover, let $\beta, \gamma, \alpha_0, \ldots, \alpha_m \in \boldsymbol{K}$ be given.

(a) $\alpha =_{\mathrm{NF}(\boldsymbol{S})} \beta * \gamma$ denotes that we have

1. $\alpha = \beta * \gamma$ with $\beta \in \boldsymbol{S}$ and
2. $\gamma \in \boldsymbol{L}_0$ such that we have $\beta \in \boldsymbol{S}^{\prec b_0 \Downarrow}$ in case of $\gamma \neq \frac{0}{0}$ and $\gamma \equiv \left(\begin{smallmatrix} a_0 & \ldots & a_n \\ b_0 & \ldots & b_n \end{smallmatrix}\right)$.

We call $\beta * \gamma$ the *simple normal form of* α.

(b) $\alpha =_{\mathrm{NF}(\boldsymbol{L})} \alpha_0 * \ldots * \alpha_m$ denotes that we have

1. $\alpha = \alpha_0 * \ldots * \alpha_m$ and
2. $b_0, \ldots, b_m \in \mathbb{L}(\boldsymbol{K})$ exist with $b_0 \prec \ldots \prec b_m$ and such that $\alpha_i \in \boldsymbol{S}^{b_i}$ holds for each $i \leq m$.

We call $\alpha_0 * \ldots * \alpha_m$ the *partition of* α (or also the *labeled normal form of* α).[1]

Remark 4.15. We defined $=_{\mathrm{NF}(\boldsymbol{S})}$ and $=_{\mathrm{NF}(\boldsymbol{L})}$ by using the equivalence relation $=$ and not the notion of identity $\equiv$. Note that $\alpha =_{\mathrm{NF}(\boldsymbol{S})} \beta * \frac{0}{0}$ implies $\beta \in \boldsymbol{S}$ and $\alpha = \beta$ but we have not necessarily $\alpha \in \boldsymbol{S}$.

Example 4.16. For $\alpha := \left(\begin{smallmatrix} 1 & 3 & 2 & 1 & 2 \\ 0 & 2 & 4 & \omega \tilde{+} 1 & \omega \tilde{+} \omega \end{smallmatrix}\right)$, we get

$$\alpha = \left(\begin{smallmatrix} 1 & 0 & 3 & 0 & 2 & 0 & 1 & 2 \\ 0 & 1 & 2 & 3 & 4 & \omega & \omega \tilde{+} 1 & \omega \tilde{+} \omega \end{smallmatrix}\right)$$

Now, we have $\alpha =_{\mathrm{NF}(\boldsymbol{L})} \frac{1,0,3,0,2}{0} * \frac{0,1}{\omega} * \frac{2}{\omega \tilde{+} \omega}$ because of

$$\begin{aligned} \frac{1,0,3,0,2}{0} * \frac{0,1}{\omega} * \frac{2}{\omega \tilde{+} \omega} &\equiv \left(\begin{smallmatrix} 1 & 0 & 3 & 0 & 2 \\ 0 & 1 & 2 & 3 & 4 \end{smallmatrix}\right) * \left(\begin{smallmatrix} 0 & 1 \\ \omega & \omega \tilde{+} 1 \end{smallmatrix}\right) * \left(\begin{smallmatrix} 2 \\ \omega \tilde{+} \omega \end{smallmatrix}\right) \\ &= \left(\begin{smallmatrix} 1 & 3 & 2 & 1 & 2 \\ 0 & 2 & 4 & \omega \tilde{+} 1 & \omega \tilde{+} \omega \end{smallmatrix}\right) \end{aligned}$$

and $0 \prec \omega \prec \omega \tilde{+} \omega$. We have $\alpha =_{\mathrm{NF}(\boldsymbol{S})} \beta * \gamma$ for $\beta := \frac{1,0,3,0,2}{0}$ and $\gamma := \left(\begin{smallmatrix} 0 & 1 & 2 \\ \omega & \omega \tilde{+} 1 & \omega \tilde{+} \omega \end{smallmatrix}\right)$. Moreover, we have $\beta =_{\mathrm{NF}(\boldsymbol{L})} \beta * \frac{0}{0}$ and $\beta =_{\mathrm{NF}(\boldsymbol{S})} \beta * \frac{0}{0}$.

[1] Note in particular that $\alpha_0 * \ldots * \alpha_m \in \boldsymbol{L}$ holds.

Theorem 4.17. *Let $\alpha \in \boldsymbol{K}$ be given with $\alpha \neq \frac{0}{0}$.*

(a) α has a unique partition, *i.e., there exist unique $\alpha_0, \ldots, \alpha_m$ and $b_0, \ldots, b_m \in \mathbb{L}(\boldsymbol{L}_0)$ with $b_0 \prec \ldots \prec b_m$ such that we have*

$$\alpha =_{\mathrm{NF}(\boldsymbol{L})} \alpha_0 * \ldots * \alpha_m \ \ \& \ \ \alpha_i \in \boldsymbol{S}^{b_i} \text{ for all } i \leq m$$

(b) α can be uniquely written in simple normal form, *i.e., there exist unique β, γ such that we have*

$$\alpha =_{\mathrm{NF}(\boldsymbol{S})} \beta * \gamma$$

In particular, the simple normal form and the partition of α can be computed primitive recursively from α.

Proof. Note that (b) is a direct consequence of (a) and note for the followin that we used only primitive recursive operations. For (a), let $\alpha \in \boldsymbol{K}$ be given with $\alpha \neq \frac{0}{0}$. We can write α as $\left(\begin{smallmatrix} a_0 & \cdots & a_n \\ d_0 & \cdots & d_n \end{smallmatrix}\right)$ with $a_i \neq 0$ for each $i \leq n$. We proceed by a induction on n.

<u>**1.**</u> $n = 0$: We have $\alpha \equiv \left(\begin{smallmatrix} a_0 \\ d_0 \end{smallmatrix}\right)$, so we can set $m := 0$ and $\alpha_0 := \frac{\bar{0}^{(k)}, a_0}{b_0} \in \boldsymbol{S}$ where we let $b_0 := d_0{\Downarrow}$ and $k := \mathsf{lh}_{\mathsf{Suc}}(d_0)$, while noting that we have

$$\frac{\bar{0}^{(k)}, a_0}{b_0} \equiv \begin{cases} \left(\begin{smallmatrix} a_0 \\ b_0 \end{smallmatrix}\right) & \text{if } k = 0 \\ \left(\begin{smallmatrix} 0 & \cdots & 0 & a_0 \\ b_0 \tilde{+} \underline{0} & \cdots & b_0 \tilde{+} \underline{k-1} & d_0 \end{smallmatrix}\right) & \text{otherwise} \end{cases}$$

<u>**2.**</u> $n \neq 0$: We get by the induction hypothesis some unique $m_0 \in \mathbb{N}$, some unique $b_0, \ldots, b_{m_0} \in \mathbb{L}(\boldsymbol{L}_0)$ with $b_0 \prec \ldots \prec b_{m_0}$, and some unique $\alpha'_0, \ldots, \alpha'_{m_0}$ such that

$$\left(\begin{smallmatrix} a_0 & \cdots & a_{n-1} \\ d_0 & \cdots & d_{n-1} \end{smallmatrix}\right) =_{\mathrm{NF}(\boldsymbol{L})} \alpha'_0 * \ldots * \alpha'_{m_0} \ \ \& \ \ \alpha'_i \in \boldsymbol{S}^{b_i} \text{ for all } i \leq m$$

holds. Analogously to the base case $n = 0$, we get $\alpha' := \frac{\bar{0}^{(k)}, a_n}{b} \in \boldsymbol{S}^b$ for $b := d_n{\Downarrow}$ and some (unique) $k \in \mathbb{N}$. In case of $b_{n-1} \prec b$, we can set $m := m_0 + 1$, $\alpha_m := \alpha'$, and $\alpha_i := \alpha'_i$ for all $i \leq m_0$. Otherwise, we have $b = b_{n-1}$ and can then set $m := m_0$, $\alpha_m := \alpha'_{m_0} * \alpha'$, and $\alpha_i := \alpha'_i$ for all $i < m_0$. □

Corollary 4.18. *For each $a \in \mathrm{OT}(\boldsymbol{K})$ there exists some unique $a' \in \mathrm{OT}(\boldsymbol{L}_0)$ such that $a =_{\mathrm{OT}(\boldsymbol{K})} a'$ holds.*

Proof. This follow by induction on the build-up of $a \in \mathrm{OT}(\boldsymbol{K})$ and using Theorem 4.17. □

Convention 4.19. A consequence of Theorem 4.17 and Corollary 4.18 is that we can define an alternative representation $\mathrm{OT}(\boldsymbol{L}_0)$ of $\mathrm{OT}(\boldsymbol{K})$ as remarked in the beginning of this section, and we can work with $(\mathrm{OT}(\boldsymbol{L}_0), \prec)$ from now on. In this sense, we change terminology as follows:

- The notion *Klammersymbol* refers to elements of $\boldsymbol{L}_0$, i.e., either $\frac{0}{0}$ or a labeled Klammersymbol. Moreover, we use $\alpha, \beta, \gamma, \delta, \ldots$ as syntactic variables for Klammersymbols.
- $(\mathrm{OT}, \prec)$ shall denote $(\mathrm{OT}(\boldsymbol{L}_0), \prec)$ and we use $a, b, c, d, \ldots$ as syntactic variables for elements of OT.
- $\mathbb{L}$ shall denote $\mathbb{L}(\boldsymbol{L}_0)$.

4.5. Motivation and Interpretation

The motivation for $\{\alpha\}a$ is that α can be seen as the *name* of a function

$$a \mapsto \{\alpha\}a$$

on ordinals. Moreover and without going into further details, we point out that Klammersymbols and ordinals below Ω^Ω have a natural correspondence if interpreting OT as the set Ω of *countable ordinals.* Since each Klammersymbol distinct from $\binom{0}{0}$ can be written in the form $\binom{a_0 \, \cdots \, a_n}{b_0 \, \cdots \, b_n}$ such that $0 \leq b_0 < \ldots < b_n$ and $a_0, \ldots, a_n \neq 0$ hold, we get for

$$\Omega^{b_n} a_n + \ldots + \Omega^{b_0} a_0$$

that this expression is in Cantor normal form with base Ω and an ordinal distinct from 0, i.e., we get a representation of $\binom{a_0 \, \cdots \, a_n}{b_0 \, \cdots \, b_n} \neq \binom{0}{0}$ in $\Omega^\Omega \setminus \{0\}$. Compare this with the notation $\{\Omega^{b_n} a_n + \ldots + \Omega^{b_0} a_0\}a$ from [Buc15].

4.6. Primitive Recursive Operations on Labeled Klammersymbols

Definition 4.20. For each $\alpha \in \boldsymbol{L}$, there exist by Theorem 4.17 unique $m, n \in \mathbb{N}$, $a_0, \ldots, a_n \in \mathrm{OT}$, $b \in \mathbb{L}$, and $\alpha_1, \ldots, \alpha_m \in \boldsymbol{L}$ such that

$$\alpha =_{\mathrm{NF}(\boldsymbol{L})} \tfrac{a_0, \ldots, a_n}{b} * \alpha_1 * \ldots * \alpha_m$$

holds, and therefore we define the following notions

$$\mathsf{lh}_{\boldsymbol{L}}(\alpha) := m$$

$$\mathsf{hd}_{\boldsymbol{L}}(\alpha) := \tfrac{a_0, \ldots, a_n}{b} \qquad \mathsf{tl}_{\boldsymbol{L}}(\alpha) := \begin{cases} \alpha_1 * \ldots * \alpha_m & \text{if } m \neq 0 \\ \frac{0}{0} & \text{otherwise} \end{cases}$$

Furthermore, we define

$$\mathsf{c}(\alpha) := \langle a_0, \ldots, a_n \rangle \qquad \mathsf{e}(\alpha) := b$$

$$\mathsf{lh}_{\boldsymbol{S}}(\alpha) := n \qquad \mathsf{hd}_{\boldsymbol{S}}(\alpha) := a_n \qquad \mathsf{tl}_{\boldsymbol{S}}(\alpha) := \begin{cases} \langle a_0, \ldots, a_{n-1} \rangle & \text{if } n \neq 0 \\ \langle\rangle & \text{otherwise} \end{cases}$$

where $\mathsf{c}(\alpha)$ defines the *(simple) coefficients of* α and $\mathsf{e}(\alpha)$ the *(simple) label of* α (or also called *(simple) exponent of* α). Finally, we extend these definitions to $\boldsymbol{L}_0$ by setting

$$\mathsf{c}(\tfrac{0}{0}) := \langle 0 \rangle \qquad \mathsf{e}(\tfrac{0}{0}) := \mathsf{hd}_{\boldsymbol{S}}(\tfrac{0}{0}) := 0 \qquad \mathsf{tl}_{\boldsymbol{S}}(\tfrac{0}{0}) := \langle\rangle$$

$$\mathsf{lh}_{\boldsymbol{L}}(\tfrac{0}{0}) := \mathsf{lh}_{\boldsymbol{S}}(\tfrac{0}{0}) := 0 \qquad \mathsf{hd}_{\boldsymbol{L}}(\tfrac{0}{0}) := \mathsf{tl}_{\boldsymbol{L}}(\tfrac{0}{0}) := \tfrac{0}{0}$$

Definition 4.21. The *base* $\alpha\Downarrow$ *of* α for each $\alpha \in \boldsymbol{L}_0$ is defined as

$$\alpha\Downarrow := \begin{cases} \frac{1}{\mathsf{e}(\alpha)} * \mathsf{tl}_{\boldsymbol{L}}(\alpha) & \text{if } \mathsf{e}(\alpha) \neq 0 \\ \mathsf{tl}_{\boldsymbol{L}}(\alpha) & \text{otherwise} \end{cases}$$

Remark 4.22. For each $a \in \mathrm{OT}$ and $\alpha \in \boldsymbol{L}_0$, we have the following properties.

(a) $a = a\Downarrow \tilde{+} \mathsf{lh}_{\mathrm{Suc}}(a)$.

(b) $\alpha \equiv \mathsf{hd}_{\boldsymbol{L}}(\alpha) * \mathsf{tl}_{\boldsymbol{L}}(\alpha)$ holds. $\alpha \neq \frac{0}{0}$ implies $\alpha =_{\mathrm{NF}(\boldsymbol{S})} \mathsf{hd}_{\boldsymbol{L}}(\alpha) * \mathsf{tl}_{\boldsymbol{L}}(\alpha)$.

(c) $\mathsf{hd}_{\boldsymbol{L}}(\alpha) \equiv \triangleright\frac{\mathsf{c}(\alpha)}{\mathsf{e}(\alpha)}\triangleleft \equiv \triangleright\frac{\mathsf{tl}_{\boldsymbol{S}}(\alpha) * \langle \mathsf{hd}_{\boldsymbol{S}}(\alpha)\rangle}{\mathsf{e}(\alpha)}\triangleleft$ where $*$ denotes finite list concatenation (see Definition 1.5).

(d) $\mathsf{lh}(\mathsf{c}(\alpha)) = \mathsf{lh}_{\boldsymbol{S}}(\alpha) +_{\mathbb{N}} 1$.

Definition 4.23. For each $\alpha \in \boldsymbol{L}_0$, we define the *$k$-th element* $\mathsf{p}(\alpha, k)$ *of the partition of* α as follows:

$$\mathsf{p}(\alpha, k) := \begin{cases} \mathsf{hd}_{\boldsymbol{L}}(\alpha) & \text{if } k = 0 \\ \mathsf{p}(\mathsf{tl}_{\boldsymbol{L}}(\alpha), k \dot{-} 1) & \text{otherwise} \end{cases}$$

Definition 4.24. For each $\alpha \in \boldsymbol{L}_0$ and $k \in \mathbb{N}$, we define the *k-th exponent* $\mathsf{e}(\alpha, k) \in \mathrm{OT}$ *of* α, the *k-th coefficient* $\mathsf{c}(\alpha, k) \in \mathrm{OT}$ *of* α, the *k-th* ***S****-cropped Klammersymbol* $\alpha|_k^{\boldsymbol{S}}$ *of* α, and the *k-th* ***L****-cropped Klammersymbol* $\alpha|_k^{\boldsymbol{L}}$ *of* α as follows:

$$\mathsf{e}(\alpha, k) := \mathsf{e}(\alpha) \tilde{+} \underline{k} \qquad \mathsf{c}(\alpha, k) := \begin{cases} (\mathsf{c}(\alpha))_k & \text{if } k \leq \mathsf{lh}_{\boldsymbol{S}}(\alpha) \\ 0 & \text{otherwise} \end{cases}$$

$$\alpha|_k^{\boldsymbol{S}} := \begin{cases} \frac{\bar{0}^{(k+1)}, \mathsf{c}(\alpha, k+1), \ldots, \mathsf{c}(\alpha, \mathsf{lh}_{\boldsymbol{S}}(\alpha))}{b} * \mathsf{tl}_{\boldsymbol{L}}(\alpha) & \text{if } k < \mathsf{lh}_{\boldsymbol{S}}(\alpha) \\ \mathsf{tl}_{\boldsymbol{L}}(\alpha) & \text{otherwise} \end{cases}$$

$$\alpha|_k^{\boldsymbol{L}} := \begin{cases} \mathsf{p}(\alpha, k) * \ldots * \mathsf{p}(\alpha, \mathsf{lh}_{\boldsymbol{L}}(\alpha)) & \text{if } k \leq \mathsf{lh}_{\boldsymbol{L}}(\alpha) \\ \frac{0}{0} & \text{otherwise} \end{cases}$$

Further, we let $\alpha * \beta|_k^{\boldsymbol{S}} := \alpha * (\beta|_k^{\boldsymbol{S}})$ and $\alpha * \beta|_k^{\boldsymbol{L}} := \alpha * (\beta|_k^{\boldsymbol{L}})$.

Lemma 4.25. *For each $\alpha \in \boldsymbol{L}_0$ and $k \in \mathbb{N}$, the following holds.*

(a) $\mathsf{e}(\alpha, k), \mathsf{c}(\alpha, k) \in \mathrm{OT}$.

(b) $\mathsf{p}(\alpha, k), \alpha|_k^{\boldsymbol{S}}, \alpha|_k^{\boldsymbol{L}} \in \boldsymbol{L}_0$.

(c) $\alpha \equiv \mathsf{p}(\alpha, 0) * \ldots * \mathsf{p}(\alpha, \mathsf{lh}_{\boldsymbol{L}}(\alpha))$ *and* $\mathsf{p}(\alpha, k) \equiv \frac{0}{0}$ *for each* $k > \mathsf{lh}_{\boldsymbol{S}}(\alpha)$. *We have* $\alpha =_{\mathrm{NF}(\boldsymbol{L})} \mathsf{p}(\alpha, 0) * \ldots * \mathsf{p}(\alpha, \mathsf{lh}_{\boldsymbol{L}}(\alpha))$ *in case of* $\alpha \neq \frac{0}{0}$.

Proof. This is immediate from the definitions. □

Part II.

Typed Induction

5. FIT for Functions, Inductive Definitions, and Types

5.1. Basic Language of FIT

The full language of FIT will be defined in Section 5.2. Here, we shall introduce a basic language that is needed for the applicative part of FIT.

Definition 5.1. The *basic language* of FIT is built-up on two sorts of variables, while first sort variables are called *individual variables* and second sort variables are called *type variables.* The basic language further consists of the following symbols.

(a) *Constants of the first sort:*

$\mathsf{k}, \mathsf{s}, \mathsf{p}, \mathsf{p}_0, \mathsf{p}_1, 0, \mathsf{s_N}, \mathsf{p_N}, \mathsf{d_N}$ (denoting the usual applicative constants)

(b) *Constants of the second sort:*

N (denoting the natural numbers)

$\overline{\mathsf{N}}$ (denoting the complement of the natural numbers)

U (without further interpretation[1])

(c) *Relation symbols of the first sort:*

$=$ (denoting equality on individual terms[2])

$\downarrow$ (denoting definedness for individual terms)

(d) *Further symbols:*

$\cdot$ (denoting a binary function symbol for first sort term application)

$\in$ (denoting a binary relation symbol between individual terms and types[3])

[1] It is needed for proof-theoretic investigations.
[2] Individual terms will be defined in Definition 5.2.
[3] Types will be defined in Definition 5.5.

Definition 5.2. *Individual terms* s, t, r are defined inductively from individual variables and constants by use of the binary function symbol $\cdot$ as usual.

Definition 5.3. The following notions and abbreviations will serve as basic applicative tools.

(a) $t' := \mathsf{s_N} t$ and $1 := 0'$.

(b) *Term application on n inputs* is defined recursively on $n \geq 0$:

$$st_1 \ldots t_n := s(t_1, \ldots, t_n) := \begin{cases} s & \text{if } n = 0 \\ (s \cdot t_1)t_2 \ldots t_n & \text{if } n > 0 \end{cases}$$

(c) *General n-tupling* is defined recursively on $n \geq 0$:

$$\langle s_0, \ldots, s_{n-1} \rangle^{\mathsf{FIT}} := \begin{cases} 0 & \text{if } n = 0 \\ \mathsf{p} s_0 \langle s_1, \ldots, s_{n-1} \rangle^{\mathsf{FIT}} & \text{if } n > 0 \end{cases}$$

Write shall write $\langle s_0, \ldots, s_{n-1} \rangle$ for $\langle s_0, \ldots, s_{n-1} \rangle^{\mathsf{FIT}}$ if the meaning is clear from the context.

(d) The *n-th projection* is defined recursively on $n \geq 0$:

$$(s)_n^{\mathsf{FIT}} := \begin{cases} \mathsf{p_0} s & \text{if } n = 0 \\ (\mathsf{p_1} s)_{n-1}^{\mathsf{FIT}} & \text{if } n > 0 \end{cases}$$

Write shall write $(s)_n$ for $(s)_n^{\mathsf{FIT}}$ if the meaning is clear from the context.

(e) *Lambda abstraction of a variable x* on a term t is defined recursively on the build-up of t:

$$\lambda x.t := \begin{cases} \mathsf{skk} & \text{if } t \text{ is } x \\ \mathsf{k}t & \text{if } t \text{ is a constant or} \\ & \quad \text{a variable that is different from } x \\ \mathsf{s}(\lambda x.t_1)(\lambda x.t_2) & \text{if } t \text{ is } t_1 t_2 \end{cases}$$

while note that $\lambda x.t$ does not contain the variable x. In general, *lambda abstraction of a list of variables* $\vec{x} = x_1, \ldots, x_n$ over a term t is defined recursively on $n \geq 0$:

$$\lambda \vec{x}.t := \begin{cases} t & \text{if } n = 0 \\ \lambda x_1.(\lambda x_2 \ldots x_n.t) & \text{if } n > 0 \end{cases}$$

Remark 5.4. $\langle\rangle$ appears for instance in the proof of Lemma 6.15.

5.2. Full Language of FIT

Definition 5.5. The language $\mathcal{L}_{\mathsf{FIT}}$ is defined simultaneously and inductively with the notions for *formulas* (For), *positive formulas* (For^+), *types* (Ty), *restricted types* ($\mathrm{Ty}{\restriction}$), and *terms of the second sort*:

(a) $\mathcal{L}_{\mathsf{FIT}}$ extends the basic language from Definition 5.1 by new (syntactically different) kinds of *terms of the second sort*

$$\{x \colon A\} \qquad \text{and} \qquad \mathsf{I}_{\mathbb{P},\mathbb{Q}}$$

demanding here $A \in \mathrm{For}^+$ and $\mathbb{P}, \mathbb{Q} \in \mathrm{Ty}{\restriction}$.

(b) For denotes the collection of *formulas* A, B, C, D, which consists of the expressions

$$t \in \mathbb{P} \quad t \in \mathsf{U} \quad t{\downarrow} \quad s = t$$
$$\neg A \quad A \to B \quad A \vee B \quad A \wedge B \quad \exists x A \quad \forall x A \quad \exists X A \quad \forall X A$$

and we demand here $\mathbb{P} \in \mathrm{Ty}$. We sometimes write $A \in \mathcal{L}_{\mathsf{FIT}}$ ambiguously for $A \in \mathrm{For}$.

(c) For^+ denotes the collection of *positive (elementary) formulas*, i.e., formulas $A \in \mathrm{For}$ such that

- quantifications of type variables do not occur and
- expressions of the form $t \in \mathbb{P}$ for types $\mathbb{P} \in \mathrm{Ty}$ occur at most positively[4]

[4]Positive is meant in the usual way: $t \in \mathbb{P}$ is called *positive* in $A \in \mathrm{For}$ if it does not

(d) Ty denotes the collection of *types* $\mathbb{P}, \mathbb{Q}, \mathbb{R}$ (also called *positive types*), i.e., expressions of the form

$$X, Y, Z, \ldots \text{ (i.e., type variables)}$$
$$\mathsf{N} \quad \overline{\mathsf{N}} \quad \{x\colon A\} \quad \mathsf{I}_{\mathbb{P},\mathbb{Q}}$$

demanding here $A \in \text{For}^+$ and $\mathbb{P}, \mathbb{Q} \in \text{Ty}\restriction$. Note that U itself is not treated as a type.

(e) $\text{Ty}\restriction$ denotes the collection of *restricted types*, i.e., types such that
- no type variables and
- no expressions of the form $\mathsf{I}_{\mathbb{P},\mathbb{Q}}$ occur

Definition 5.6. Let $\twoheadrightarrow$ be a new distinguished symbol. The collection FT of *function types* $\mathbb{F}, \mathbb{G}, \mathbb{H}$ is defined inductively to consist of expressions of the form

$$\mathbb{P} \qquad \text{and} \qquad \mathbb{P} \twoheadrightarrow \mathbb{F}$$

for any $\mathbb{P} \in \text{Ty}$ and $\mathbb{F} \in \text{FT}$. Note that function types are defined as objects in the meta-language.

We can write any $\mathbb{F} \in \text{FT}$ in the form $(\mathbb{P}_1 \twoheadrightarrow (\ldots(\mathbb{P}_{n-1} \twoheadrightarrow \mathbb{P}_n)\ldots))$, and we allow to simplify this notation to $\mathbb{P}_1 \twoheadrightarrow \ldots \mathbb{P}_{n-1} \twoheadrightarrow \mathbb{P}_n$ by following the convention of right-associativity for $\twoheadrightarrow$.

Remark 5.7. We did not define U to be a type because we can use $\{x\colon x \in \mathsf{U}\}$ in order to get $t \in \mathsf{U}$, while noting $\{x\colon x \in \mathsf{U}\}$ is a type because $x \in \mathsf{U}$ is in For^+. Moreover, any type $\mathbb{P}$ in any formula appears only in the form $t \in \mathbb{P}$. More precisely, from the definition of FIT below, it is clear that $t \in \mathsf{U}$ is equivalent over FIT to $t \in \{x\colon x \in \mathsf{U}\}$ for every individual term t (by making use of (CA^+) and the defined axioms from Definitions 5.11 and 5.12).

Definition 5.8 (Free variables and substitution)**.** The notion of $\text{FV}(A)$ is extended to the notion of atomic formulas $t \in \mathbb{P}$ for $\mathbb{P} \in \text{Ty}$ by defining recursively on the build-up of types and formulas:

occur in negated form $\neg(t \in \mathbb{P})$ in A', while A' shall be the translation of A where first each subformula of the form $B_1 \to B_2$ is transformed to $\neg B_1 \vee B_2$ and where we then move the negation symbol $\neg$ next to atomic formulas, while making use of De Morgan's laws and the law of double negation.

- $\mathrm{FV}(t \in \mathbb{P}) := \mathrm{FV}(t) \cup \mathrm{FV}(\mathbb{P})$ and

- $\mathrm{FV}(\mathbb{P}) := \begin{cases} \mathrm{FV}(A) \setminus \{x\} & \text{if } \mathbb{P} \text{ is } \{x\colon A\} \\ \mathrm{FV}(\mathbb{P}') \cup \mathrm{FV}(\mathbb{Q}') & \text{if } \mathbb{P} \text{ is } \mathsf{I}_{\mathbb{P}',\mathbb{Q}'} \\ \emptyset & \text{otherwise} \end{cases}$

With this extension explained, the *substitution of individual and type variables* is defined as in Section 1.1.

Notation 5.9. We have the following abbreviations for some formulas and types:

- $s \simeq t$ is $(s{\downarrow} \vee t{\downarrow}) \to s = t$.
- $s \neq t$ is $s{\downarrow} \wedge t{\downarrow} \wedge \neg(s = t)$.
- $t \in \mathbb{P} \twoheadrightarrow \mathbb{F}$ is recursively $\forall x(x \in \mathbb{P} \to tx \in \mathbb{F})$.
- $\mathsf{N}^{n+1} \twoheadrightarrow \mathbb{F}$ is recursively $\mathsf{N} \twoheadrightarrow (\mathsf{N}^n \twoheadrightarrow \mathbb{F})$ where $\mathsf{N}^0 \twoheadrightarrow \mathbb{F}$ is $\mathbb{F}$.
- $t \notin \mathbb{F}$ is $\neg(t \in \mathbb{F})$.
- $(\exists x \in \mathbb{F})B$ is $\exists x(x \in \mathbb{F} \wedge B)$.
- $(\forall x \in \mathbb{F})B$ is $\forall x(x \in \mathbb{F} \to B)$.
- $\mathrm{Cl}_{\mathbb{P},\mathbb{Q}}(\mathcal{A})$ is $\forall x\big((x \in \mathbb{P} \wedge (\forall y \in \mathbb{P})(\langle y, x\rangle \in \mathbb{Q} \to \mathcal{A}(y))) \to \mathcal{A}(x)\big)$.

  We assume as usual for such notational abbreviations that x, y are supposed to not occur in $\mathcal{A}$, $\mathbb{P}$, and $\mathbb{Q}$. This shall hold analogously for similar such abbreviations for formulas.

- $A(\mathbb{F}/X)$ for the formula obtained by substituting any occurrence of $t \in X$ in A by $t \in \mathbb{F}$.

Remark 5.10.

(a) We chose $\mathrm{Cl}_{\mathbb{P},\mathbb{Q}}(\mathcal{A})$ to be defined with a conjunction rather than a chain of implications such as in $\forall x\big(x \in \mathbb{P} \to (\forall y \in \mathbb{P})(\langle y, x\rangle \in \mathbb{Q} \to \mathcal{A}(y)) \to \mathcal{A}(x)\big)$ which is logically equivalent to $\mathrm{Cl}_{\mathbb{P},\mathbb{Q}}(\mathcal{A})$. The reason for this is of syntactical nature, allowing for a simplified representation in Section 7.2 (cf., Remark 7.40).

(b) Note that function types are not necessarily part of the language $\mathcal{L}_{\mathsf{FIT}}$: We defined expressions of the form $\mathbb{P} \twoheadrightarrow \mathbb{F}$ from outside and in our meta-language, using the delimiter $\twoheadrightarrow$. Within $\mathcal{L}_{\mathsf{FIT}}$ formulas, these new expressions will only occur in the form $t \in \mathbb{P} \twoheadrightarrow \mathbb{F}$, i.e., as $\mathcal{L}_{\mathsf{FIT}}$ formulas.

Alternatively and in order to make function types first-class members of $\mathcal{L}_{\mathsf{FIT}}$, we could have introduced a more general form of type (called *general type* as in [Fef92]), allowing for expressions $\{x\colon A\}$ for any $A \in \mathrm{For}$ and thus abbreviate $\mathbb{P} \twoheadrightarrow \mathbb{F}$ by $\{x\colon (\forall y \in \mathbb{P})(xy \in \mathbb{F})\}$ where x, y are any distinct individual variables that do not occur in $\mathbb{P}$ or $\mathbb{F}$, and then we would need to strengthen the comprehension scheme to allow for general types. This alternative approach does not change anything in the result because the comprehension scheme can be reduced to the variant we have here (this has been also done in [Fef92]).

(c) We used the restriction to $\mathrm{Ty}{\restriction}$ in the definition of $\mathsf{I}_{\mathbb{P},\mathbb{Q}} \in \mathrm{Ty}$ in order to account for a non-iterated inductive definition.

5.3. The Theory FIT

Definition 5.11. The logic of FIT is a two-sorted logic whose first-order part (i.e., for individual variables) is based on the *classical logic of partial terms* LPT due to Beeson [Bee85]:

- **Propositional axioms and rules.** The usual propositional axioms and rules, based on some sound Hilbert calculus for classical propositional logic.
- **Quantificational logic for the first sort.** For A being an $\mathcal{L}_{\mathsf{FIT}}$ formula and t an individual term, we have

$$(\forall x A \land t{\downarrow}) \to A(t/x)$$
$$(A(t/x) \land t{\downarrow}) \to \exists x A$$

and for A, B being $\mathcal{L}_{\mathsf{FIT}}$ formulas and $x \notin \mathrm{FV}(A)$, we have the following figures:

$$\frac{A \to B}{A \to \forall x B} \qquad \frac{B \to A}{\exists x B \to A}$$

- **Quantificational logic for the second sort.** For A, B being $\mathcal{L}_{\mathsf{FIT}}$ formulas and $\mathbb{P}$ a type, we have

$$\forall X A \to A(\mathbb{P}/X)$$
$$A(\mathbb{P}/X) \to \exists X A$$

and for A, B being $\mathcal{L}_{\mathsf{FIT}}$ formulas and X not occurring free in A, we have the following figures:

$$\frac{A \to B}{A \to \forall X B} \qquad \frac{B \to A}{\exists X B \to A}$$

- **Equality axioms.**

$$x = x$$
$$(x_1 = y_1 \wedge \ldots \wedge x_n = y_n \wedge A) \to (\ldots (A(y_1/x_1)) \ldots (y_n/x_n))$$

- **Definedness axioms.** For all constants c of the first sort of $\mathcal{L}_{\mathsf{FIT}}$, we have

$$c{\downarrow} \wedge x{\downarrow}$$
$$(st){\downarrow} \to (s{\downarrow} \wedge t{\downarrow})$$
$$s = t \to (s{\downarrow} \wedge t{\downarrow})$$

and for every type $\mathbb{P}$ and individual term t, we have

$$t \in \mathbb{P} \to t{\downarrow}$$
$$t \in \mathsf{U} \to t{\downarrow}$$

Writing $\vdash A$ for any $\mathcal{L}_{\mathsf{FIT}}$ formula A denotes the derivability of A in the logic of FIT.

Definition 5.12. FIT is the two-sorted applicative theory based on the logic of partial terms LPT (and on [Fef92]). Its non-logical axioms are as follows:

I. Applicative axioms.

I.1. Partial combinatory algebra.

$$\mathsf{k}xy = x$$
$$\mathsf{s}xy{\downarrow} \wedge \mathsf{s}xyz \simeq (xz)(yz)$$

I.2. Pairing and projection.

$$\mathsf{p}_0(\mathsf{p}xy) = x \wedge \mathsf{p}_1(\mathsf{p}xy) = y$$

I.3. Definition by numerical cases.

$$x \in \mathsf{N} \wedge y \in \mathsf{N} \wedge x = y \to \mathsf{d}_{\mathsf{N}} z_1 z_2 xy = z_1$$
$$x \in \mathsf{N} \wedge y \in \mathsf{N} \wedge x \neq y \to \mathsf{d}_{\mathsf{N}} z_1 z_2 xy = z_2$$

I.4. Axioms about N and $\overline{\mathsf{N}}$.

$$0 \in \mathsf{N} \wedge (x \in \mathsf{N} \to x' \in \mathsf{N})$$
$$x \in \mathsf{N} \to (x' \neq 0 \wedge \mathsf{p}_{\mathsf{N}}(x') = x)$$
$$(x \in \mathsf{N} \wedge x \neq 0) \to (\mathsf{p}_{\mathsf{N}}x \in \mathsf{N} \wedge (\mathsf{p}_{\mathsf{N}}x)' = x)$$
$$x \in \overline{\mathsf{N}} \leftrightarrow x \notin \mathsf{N}$$

II. Induction on N for $\mathbb{F} \in \mathrm{FT}$.

$$(\text{FT-}\mathsf{Ind}) \qquad t0 \in \mathbb{F} \wedge (\forall x \in \mathsf{N})(tx \in \mathbb{F} \to tx' \in \mathbb{F}) \to t \in (\mathsf{N} \twoheadrightarrow \mathbb{F})$$

III. Positive comprehension for $A \in \mathrm{For}^+$.

$$(\mathsf{CA}^+) \qquad y \in \{x \colon A\} \leftrightarrow A(y/x)$$

IV. Axioms about $\mathsf{I}_{\mathbb{P},\mathbb{Q}}$ for $\mathbb{F} \in \mathrm{FT}$ and $\mathbb{P}, \mathbb{Q} \in \mathrm{Ty}\restriction$.

(FT-CI)	$\mathrm{Cl}_{\mathbb{P},\mathbb{Q}}(\Lambda z.z \in \mathsf{I}_{\mathbb{P},\mathbb{Q}})$
(FT-ID)	$\mathrm{Cl}_{\mathbb{P},\mathbb{Q}}(\Lambda z.tz \in \mathbb{F}) \to t \in (\mathsf{I}_{\mathbb{P},\mathbb{Q}} \twoheadrightarrow \mathbb{F})$

Writing $\mathsf{FIT} \vdash A$ for any $\mathcal{L}_{\mathsf{FIT}}$ formula A denotes the derivability of A from these axioms in the logic of FIT given in Definition 5.11.

Lemma 5.13 (Basic applicative tools).

(a) Lambda abstraction: For all $\mathcal{L}_{\mathsf{FIT}}$ terms t, s and $\vec{s} = s_1, \ldots, s_n$, and all individual variables y and $\vec{x} = x_1, \ldots, x_n$ with $y \notin \{x_1, \ldots, x_n\}$, we have the following:

1. $\mathsf{FIT} \vdash (\lambda\vec{x}.t)\downarrow \wedge (\lambda\vec{x}.t)\vec{x} \simeq t$.
2. $\mathsf{FIT} \vdash (s_1\downarrow \wedge \ldots \wedge s_n\downarrow) \to (\lambda\vec{x}.t)\vec{s} \simeq t(\vec{s}/\vec{x})$.
3. $\mathsf{FIT} \vdash (\lambda\vec{x}.t)(s/y)x \simeq (\lambda\vec{x}.t(s/y))x$.

(b) Fixed-point: There exists a closed term fix *such that* $\mathsf{FIT} \vdash \mathsf{fix}y\downarrow \wedge \mathsf{fix}yx \simeq y(\mathsf{fix}y)x$ *holds for all number variables* x, y.

(c) Pairs and tupling: For all $\mathcal{L}_{\mathsf{FIT}}$ variables $x_0, \ldots, x_n$ and each $0 \le i \le n$, we have $\mathsf{FIT} \vdash (s_0\downarrow \wedge \ldots \wedge s_n\downarrow) \to (\langle s_0, \ldots, s_n\rangle)_i = s_i$.

Proof. The applicative part of FIT corresponds to the standard axioms and constants that appear in applicative theories. For details on (a) and (b), we refer to [FJS]. For (c), we argue by induction on n and show at the same time that $s\downarrow$ holds. Let $s := \langle s_0, \ldots, s_n\rangle$, i.e., $\mathsf{p}s_0(\mathsf{p}s_1(\ldots(\mathsf{p}s_n0))\ldots)$. Further, assume $s_0\downarrow \wedge \ldots \wedge s_n\downarrow$. In case of $n = 0$, we have that s is $\mathsf{p}s_00$ and then $0\downarrow$ and $s_0\downarrow$ imply $\mathsf{FIT} \vdash \mathsf{p}_0(s) = s_0$ since we can use LPT together with **I.2.** from Definition 5.12. Hence, we are done since $(s)_0$ equals $\mathsf{p}_0 s$. Note that the definedness axioms yield $s\downarrow$ from $\mathsf{FIT} \vdash \mathsf{p}_0(s) = s_0$. For $n \neq 0$, we can argue analogously to get $s\downarrow$ by using instead of $0\downarrow$ the induction hypothesis $s'\downarrow$ for $s' := (\mathsf{p}s_1(\ldots(\mathsf{p}s_n0))\ldots)$, namely we have that s is $\mathsf{p}_0 s'$. So $\mathsf{FIT} \vdash \mathsf{p}_0(s) = s_0$ holds and we get the claim for $i = 0$, and $\mathsf{FIT} \vdash \mathsf{p}_1(s) = s'$ holds, so we get $\mathsf{FIT} \vdash (s)_i = s_i$ also for $1 \le i \le n$ while noting that then $(s)_i$ equals $(\mathsf{p}_1(s))_{i-1}$: The induction hypothesis for s' yields $\mathsf{FIT} \vdash (s')_{i-1} = s_i$ and the equality axioms yield $\mathsf{FIT} \vdash (\mathsf{p}_1(s))_{i-1} = (s')_{i-1}$, so we get the claim. □

5.4. Informal Interpretation of FIT

Since FIT directly evolved from Feferman's theory $\mathrm{QL}(\mathsf{F_0}\text{-}\mathsf{IR}_N)$, we refer for a thorough motivation and informal interpretation of FIT to [Fef92, sections 2 and 5]. Moreover, the special constant U can be interpreted as a subset of the natural numbers, having no further interpretation. It is needed for proof-theoretic investigations.

6. TID for Typed Inductive Definitions

FIT is a natural theory for specifying the behaviour of an applicative term t by use of types, say by a function type $\mathbb{P}_1 \twoheadrightarrow \ldots \twoheadrightarrow \mathbb{P}_{n+1}$ that conists of types. For checking this behaviour, we have the axiom schemes (FT-Ind) and (FT-ID) at hand. The latter allows the discussion of the behaviour of an operation t that acts on the inductively defined accessible part of a given binary relation (e.g., if $\mathbb{P}_1$ is $\mathsf{I}_{\mathbb{P},\mathbb{Q}}$ in the example above). This gives an idea for the following definition of the theory TID for typed inductive definitions as a subtheory of ID_1.

6.1. The Accessible Part Theory TID

Definition 6.1.

(a) For each operator form $\mathfrak{A}$, let $P_{\mathfrak{A}}$ denote a new unary relation symbol not in $\mathcal{L}_{\mathsf{PA}}$. Then, $P_{\lhd}$ abbreviates $P_{\mathrm{Acc}_{\lhd}}$ for any binary relation symbol $\lhd$ in $\mathcal{L}_{\mathsf{PA}}$.

(b) The language of TID is defined as

$$\mathcal{L}_{\mathsf{TID}} := \mathcal{L}_{\mathsf{PA}} \cup \{P_{\lhd} : \lhd \text{ is a binary relation symbol in } \mathcal{L}_{\mathsf{PA}}\}$$

Definition 6.2 (Pos_0 and $\mathrm{Pos}_1(a)$). We first set

$$\mathrm{Pos}_0 := \{A \in \mathcal{L}_{\mathsf{TID}} : P_{\lhd} \text{ occurs at most positively in } A \text{ for any binary relation symbol } \lhd \text{ in } \mathcal{L}_{\mathsf{PA}}\}$$

and then define $\mathrm{Pos}_1(a)$ for any number variable a as the collection of $\mathcal{L}_{\mathsf{TID}}$ formulas A such that one of the following cases holds:[1]

[1]This is motivated by FT from the setting of FIT.

- $A \in \mathrm{Pos}_0$
- $A = \forall\vec{x}(B_1 \to B_2)$ with
  - $a \notin \mathrm{FV}(B_1)$,
  - $B_1, B_2 \in \mathrm{Pos}_0$, and
  - $\vec{x}$ being a (possibly empty) list of variables.

Definition 6.3 (Neg_0)**.** Let $\mathrm{Neg}_0 := \{A \in \mathcal{L}_{\mathsf{TID}} \colon \neg A \in \mathrm{Pos}_0\}$.

Notation 6.4. We write $\Lambda a.A \in \mathrm{Pos}_1$ in order to denote $A \in \mathrm{Pos}_1(a)$.

Example 6.5. Let f be some binary function symbol in $\mathcal{L}_{\mathsf{PA}}$ and a a number variable. Then $\mathrm{Pos}_1(a)$ contains the formula $A := \forall y(P_\triangleleft y \to \forall x \triangleleft a(P_\triangleleft fxy))$ and we have $\Lambda a.A \in \mathrm{Pos}_1$.

Definition 6.6 (TID)**.** TID is the theory that arises from the axioms of Peano arithmetic PA without complete induction by adding the following axioms and axiom schemes

(Ind) $\mathcal{B}(0) \wedge \forall x(\mathcal{B}(x) \to \mathcal{B}(\mathbf{S}x)) \to \forall x\mathcal{B}(x)$
for $\mathcal{B} \in \mathrm{Pos}_1$

(CI) $\mathrm{Prog}_\triangleleft(P_\triangleleft)$ (i.e., $\forall x(\mathrm{Acc}_\triangleleft(P_\triangleleft, x) \to P_\triangleleft x)$)
for $\triangleleft$ being a binary relation symbol in $\mathcal{L}_{\mathsf{PA}}$

(TID) $\mathrm{Prog}_\triangleleft(\mathcal{B}) \to \forall x(P_\triangleleft x \to \mathcal{B}(x))$
for $\mathcal{B} \in \mathrm{Pos}_1$ and $\triangleleft$ being a binary relation symbol in $\mathcal{L}_{\mathsf{PA}}$

where (CI) is called *closure* and (TID) is called *typed inductive definition.*

Remark 6.7. For any binary relation symbol $\triangleleft$ in $\mathcal{L}_{\mathsf{PA}}$, we may identify (CI) with a fixed-point principle

$$\text{(FP)} \qquad \forall x(P_\triangleleft x \leftrightarrow \mathrm{Acc}_\triangleleft(P_\triangleleft, x))$$

and therefore we will sometimes use (CI) to ambiguously mean (FP).

Abbreviating $P_\triangleleft$ by P and $\mathrm{Acc}_\triangleleft$ by Acc, we explain how (FP) follows from TID: We get $\forall x(Px \to \mathrm{Acc}(P, x))$ by (TID) with $\mathcal{B} := \Lambda a.\mathrm{Acc}(P, a)$, first because $\mathrm{Acc}(P, a)$ equals $\forall y(y \triangleleft a \to Py)$ which is in $\mathrm{Pos}_0(a)$, and second because $\forall x(\mathrm{Acc}(\mathcal{B}, x) \to \mathcal{B}(x))$ holds by using (CI) and that Acc is a positive operator form.

Remark 6.8. We can use instead of (Ind) also the following course-of-value variant of complete induction for Pos_1 formulas, i.e., we have

$$\forall x(\forall x_0 <_{\mathbb{N}} x\mathcal{B}(x_0) \to \mathcal{B}(x)) \to \forall x\mathcal{B}(x)$$

as an induction principle for all $\mathcal{B} \in \text{Pos}_1$. In the following, we shall make use of this variant without mentioning it explicitly.

6.2. Embedding TID into FIT

Definition 6.9. For each $f \in \text{PR}^n$ and $n \in \mathbb{N}$, we define an $\mathcal{L}_{\mathsf{FIT}}$ term pr_f recursively on the build-up of f (and where we let $\vec{x} = x_1, \ldots, x_n$):

$$\begin{array}{ll} \lambda\vec{x}.0 & \text{if } f = \mathbf{0}^n \\ \mathsf{s}_{\mathsf{N}} & \text{if } f = \mathbf{S} \\ \lambda\vec{x}.x_i & \text{if } f = \mathbf{I}^n_i \\ \lambda\vec{x}.\mathsf{pr}_g(\mathsf{pr}_{h_1}\vec{x})\ldots(\mathsf{pr}_{h_m}\vec{x}) & \text{if } f = (\mathbf{C}gh_1\ldots h_m) \\ \lambda\vec{x}.\mathsf{fix}(t_{g,h}\vec{x}^{(n-1)})x_n & \text{if } f = (\mathbf{R}gh) \end{array}$$

where

$$t_{g,h} := \begin{cases} \lambda\vec{x}^{(n-1)}h_0x_n. \\ \mathsf{d}_{\mathsf{N}}\mathsf{pr}_g(\lambda\vec{z}^{(n-1)}.\mathsf{pr}_h\vec{z}^{(n-1)}(\mathsf{p}_{\mathsf{N}}x_n)(h_0\vec{z}^{(n-1)}(\mathsf{p}_{\mathsf{N}}x_n)))0x_n\vec{x}^{(n-1)} \end{cases}$$

and fix is the closed term given in Lemma 5.13.(b).

Theorem 6.10. *For each n-ary function symbol $f \in \mathcal{L}_{\mathsf{PA}}$, we have the following.*

(a) FIT *proves the reformulation of every defining equation of f from Definition 1.11 with respect to pr_f, while interpreting number variables x as individual variables x with $x \in \mathsf{N}$.*

(b) $\mathsf{FIT} \vdash \mathsf{pr}_f \in \mathsf{N}^n \twoheadrightarrow \mathsf{N}$.

Proof. It is straight-forward to verify (a) and (b) by induction on the build-up of $f \in \text{PR}^n$, given the translation from Definition 6.9 and by making use of the induction principle (FT-Ind).

In order to make this a bit clearer, we consider for instance the case that f is $(\mathbf{R}gh)$. Then $n > 0$ holds with $g \in \mathrm{PR}^{n-1}, h \in \mathrm{PR}^{n+1}$, so we can assume that (a) and (b) holds for g, h. Further, pr_f is $\lambda \vec{x}.\mathsf{fix}(t_{g,h}\bar{x}^{(n-1)})x_n$ for

$$t_{g,h} := \lambda \bar{x}^{(n-1)} h_0 x_n . \mathsf{d_N} \mathsf{pr}_g s_{x_n} 0 x_n \bar{x}^{(n-1)}$$

while we let

$$s_r := \left(\lambda \bar{z}^{(n-1)}.\mathsf{pr}_h \bar{z}^{(n-1)}(\mathsf{p_N} r)((\mathrm{fix}(t_{g,h}\bar{x}^{(n-1)}))\bar{z}^{(n-1)}(\mathsf{p_N} r))\right)$$

here for any term r. In order to show (a) for f, we have to verify the following reformulation of the defining equations for f from Definition 1.11 with respect to pr_f. We assume $x_1 \in \mathsf{N} \wedge \ldots \wedge x_{n-1} \in \mathsf{N}$ and show first

$$\mathsf{pr}_f \bar{x}^{(n-1)} 0 = \mathsf{pr}_g \bar{x}^{(n-1)} \qquad (*)$$

Noting

$$\mathsf{pr}_f \bar{x}^{(n-1)} 0 \simeq (t_{g,h}\bar{x}^{(n-1)})0$$
$$(t_{g,h}\bar{x}^{(n-1)})0 \simeq (t_{g,h}\bar{x}^{(n-1)})(\mathrm{fix}(t_{g,h}\bar{x}^{(n-1)}))0$$

we get from the definition of $t_{g,h}$ and since $\simeq$ is transitive that

$$\mathsf{pr}_f \bar{x}^{(n-1)} 0 \simeq \mathsf{d_N} \mathsf{pr}_g s_0 0 0 \bar{x}^{(n-1)}$$

holds. Now, since we have that $s_0{\downarrow}$ because of Lemma 5.13 (while in case of $n = 1$, use that $(\mathrm{fix}(t_{g,h}\bar{x}^{(n-1)})){\downarrow}$ holds in s_0), we get

$$\mathsf{d_N} \mathsf{pr}_g s_0 0 0 \bar{x}^{(n-1)} = \mathsf{pr}_g \bar{x}^{(n-1)}$$

and hence $(*)$. Next, we show

$$\mathsf{pr}_f \bar{x}^{(n-1)}(\mathsf{s_N} y) = \mathsf{pr}_h \bar{x}^{(n-1)} y (\mathsf{pr}_f \bar{x}^{(n-1)} y) \qquad (**)$$

As before when showing $(*)$, we get

$$\mathsf{pr}_f \bar{x}^{(n-1)}(\mathsf{s_N} y) \simeq \mathsf{d_N} \mathsf{pr}_g s_{\mathsf{s_N} y} 0 (\mathsf{s_N} y) \bar{x}^{(n-1)}$$

and due to Lemma 5.13 and since $\mathsf{s_N}y \neq 0$ holds, we get

$$\mathsf{d_N}\mathsf{pr}_g s_{\mathsf{s_N}y} 0(\mathsf{s_N}y)\bar{x}^{(n-1)}$$
$$= s_{\mathsf{s_N}y}\bar{x}^{(n-1)}$$
$$= \mathsf{pr}_h\bar{x}^{(n-1)}(\mathsf{p_N}(\mathsf{s_N}y))((\mathrm{fix}(t_{g,h}\bar{x}^{(n-1)}))\bar{x}^{(n-1)}(\mathsf{p_N}(\mathsf{s_N}y)))$$

and hence $(**)$ from the axioms on $\mathsf{p_N}$, and $(\mathrm{fix}(t_{g,h}\bar{x}^{(n-1)})) = \mathsf{pr}_f\bar{x}^{(n-1)}$ holds due to Lemma 5.13.(a) and $(\mathrm{fix}(t_{g,h}\bar{x}^{(n-1)}))\downarrow$, while the latter holds due to Lemma 5.13.(b).

For (b), we can use (FT-Ind) with $\mathbb{F} := \mathsf{N}$ and $t := \mathsf{pr}_f\bar{x}^{(n-1)}$ and get $t \in \mathsf{N} \twoheadrightarrow \mathsf{N}$. For $t0 \in \mathbb{N}$, we use $(*)$ and the induction hypothesis on g with our assumptions $x_i \in \mathsf{N}$ for all $1 \leq i \leq n-1$. Given $y \in \mathsf{N}$ and $ty \in \mathsf{N}$, we get $t(\mathsf{s_N}y) \in \mathsf{N}$. □

Definition 6.11. Based on the translation given in Definition 6.9, we define for each $\mathcal{L}_{\mathsf{PA}}$ term t the translation $t^\bullet$ to an $\mathcal{L}_{\mathsf{FIT}}$ term recursively on the build-up of t:

x	if t is a variable x
pr_c	if t is a constant c
$\mathsf{pr}_f t_1^\bullet \dots t_n^\bullet$	if t is of the form $ft_1 \dots t_n$ with $f \in \mathrm{PR}^n$ and $n \geq 1$

The translation on terms is now extended to $\mathcal{L}_{\mathsf{TID}}$ formulas A. We define the $\mathcal{L}_{\mathsf{FIT}}$ formula $A^\bullet$ recursively on the build-up of an $\mathcal{L}_{\mathsf{TID}}$ formula A:

$s^\bullet = t^\bullet$	if A is of the form $s = t$
$\mathsf{pr}_f t_1^\bullet \dots t_n^\bullet = 0$	if A is of the form $R_f t_1 \dots t_n$
$t^\bullet \in \mathsf{U}$	if A is of the form $\mathsf{U}t$
$t^\bullet \in \mathsf{I}_{\mathsf{N},\mathbb{Q}_\lhd}$	if A is of the form $P_\lhd t$ and where $\mathbb{Q}_\lhd := \{\langle x, y\rangle \colon (x \lhd y)^\bullet\}$
$\neg(B^\bullet)$	if A is of the form $\neg B$
$B^\bullet \circ C^\bullet$	if A is of the form $B \circ C$ for $\circ \in \{\wedge, \vee, \rightarrow\}$
$\forall x(x \in \overline{\mathsf{N}} \vee B^\bullet)$	if A is of the form $\forall xB$ (see also Remark 6.12)
$\exists x(x \in \mathsf{N} \wedge B^\bullet)$	if A is of the form $\exists xB$

The expression $\{\langle x, y\rangle \colon (x \lhd y)^\bullet\}$ is a short-hand notation for the expression

$$\{z\colon z = \langle (z)_0, (z)_1\rangle \wedge (x \lhd y)^\bullet((z)_0/x, (z)_1)/y\}$$

i.e., for $\{z\colon z = \langle (z)_0, (z)_1\rangle \wedge R_f(z)_0(z)_1\}$ where f is such that R_f is $\lhd$.

Remark 6.12.

(a) It can be readily checked that $A^\bullet$ is indeed a $\mathcal{L}_{\mathsf{FIT}}$ formula. Moreover, A and $A^\bullet$ have the same free variables. In particular, note that $(x \lhd y)^\bullet((z)_0/x, (z)_1)/y\}$ contains only z as a free variable.

(b) We will use the expression $\mathbb{Q}_\lhd$ without further mentioning in order to denote the type that we introduced in the definition of $(P_\lhd t)^\bullet$. Recall also that $(x \lhd y)^\bullet$ equals $\mathsf{pr}_f xy = 0$ for some binary function symbol $f \in \mathcal{L}_{\mathsf{PA}}$ because the binary relation symbol $\lhd \in \mathcal{L}_{\mathsf{PA}}$ is of the form R_f for such an f.

Lemma 6.13.

(a) For each $A \in \mathrm{Pos}_0$ there is a formula $A' \in \mathrm{For}^+$ with $\mathrm{FV}(A^\bullet) = \mathrm{FV}(A')$ and such that $\mathsf{FIT} \vdash A^\bullet \leftrightarrow A'$ holds.

(b) For each $A \in \mathrm{Neg}_0$, there is a formula $A' \in \mathrm{For}^+$ with $\mathrm{FV}(A^\bullet) = \mathrm{FV}(A')$ and such that $\mathsf{FIT} \vdash A^\bullet \leftrightarrow \neg A'$ holds.

Proof. By simultaneous induction on the build-up of A.
1. A is an atomic formula: Then $A \notin \mathrm{Neg}_0$ and $A \in \mathrm{Pos}_0$. Now $A^\bullet \in \mathrm{For}^+$ follows by definition and we can take $A' := A^\bullet$.
2. $A = \forall x B$: We have $A^\bullet = \forall x(x \in \overline{\mathsf{N}} \vee B^\bullet)$.
2.1. $A \in \mathrm{Pos}_0$: Then $B \in \mathrm{Pos}_0$ holds and by the induction hypothesis there is some $B' \in \mathrm{For}^+$ such that $\mathsf{FIT} \vdash B^\bullet \leftrightarrow B'$ and $\mathrm{FV}(B^\bullet) = \mathrm{FV}(B')$ holds. We can set $A' := \forall x(x \in \overline{\mathsf{N}} \vee B')$ and get $A' \in \mathrm{For}^+$ and the claim follows.
2.2. $A \in \mathrm{Neg}_0$: Then $B \in \mathrm{Neg}_0$ holds and by the induction hypothesis there is some $B' \in \mathrm{For}^+$ such that $\mathsf{FIT} \vdash B^\bullet \leftrightarrow \neg B'$ and $\mathrm{FV}(B^\bullet) = \mathrm{FV}(B')$ holds. We can set $A' := \exists x(x \in \mathsf{N} \wedge B')$, so we get $A' \in \mathrm{For}^+$ and that $\neg A'$ is equivalent to $\forall x(\neg(x \in \mathsf{N}) \vee \neg B')$. Over FIT, this is equivalent to $A^\bullet$, while recalling that we have $\mathsf{FIT} \vdash \neg(x \in \mathsf{N}) \leftrightarrow x \in \overline{\mathsf{N}}$.
3. $A = \exists x B$: As before.

4. $A = B \circ C$ with $\circ \in \{\wedge, \vee\}$: This case is easy because we have $A^\bullet = B^\bullet \circ C^\bullet$.
5. $A = \neg B$:
5.1. $A \in \mathrm{Pos}_0$: Then $B \in \mathrm{Neg}_0$ and by the induction hypothesis, we get $\mathsf{FIT} \vdash B^\bullet \leftrightarrow \neg B'$ for some $B' \in \mathrm{For}^+$ and $\mathrm{FV}(B^\bullet) = \mathrm{FV}(B')$ holds. Since $A^\bullet = \neg B^\bullet$ holds, we get $\mathsf{FIT} \vdash A^\bullet \leftrightarrow \neg\neg B' \leftrightarrow B'$ and then the claim follows for $A' = B'$.
5.2. $A \in \mathrm{Neg}_0$: Then $B \in \mathrm{Pos}_0$ and by the induction hypothesis, we get $\mathsf{FIT} \vdash B^\bullet \leftrightarrow B'$ for some $B' \in \mathrm{For}^+$ and $\mathrm{FV}(B^\bullet) = \mathrm{FV}(B')$ holds. Since $A^\bullet = \neg B^\bullet$, we get $\mathsf{FIT} \vdash A^\bullet \leftrightarrow \neg B'$ and then the claim follows for $A' = \neg B'$.
6. $A = B \to C$: We have $A^\bullet = B^\bullet \to C^\bullet$ which is equivalent to $A_0 := \neg B^\bullet \vee C^\bullet$ and $\mathrm{FV}(A_0) = \mathrm{FV}(A^\bullet)$ holds.
6.1. $A \in \mathrm{Pos}_0$: Then $B \in \mathrm{Neg}_0$ and $C \in \mathrm{Pos}_0$, so $\mathsf{FIT} \vdash B^\bullet \leftrightarrow \neg B'$ for some $B' \in \mathrm{For}^+$ and $\mathsf{FIT} \vdash C^\bullet \leftrightarrow C'$ for some $C' \in \mathrm{For}^+$. We can set $A' := B' \vee C'$ and get $A' \in \mathrm{For}^+$ and $\mathsf{FIT} \vdash A^\bullet \leftrightarrow A_0 \leftrightarrow (\neg\neg B' \vee C') \leftrightarrow A'$ and then the claim follows.
6.2. $A \in \mathrm{Neg}_0$: Then $B \in \mathrm{Pos}_0$ and $C \in \mathrm{Neg}_0$, so $\mathsf{FIT} \vdash B^\bullet \leftrightarrow B'$ for some $B' \in \mathrm{For}^+$ and $\mathsf{FIT} \vdash C^\bullet \leftrightarrow \neg C'$ for some $C' \in \mathrm{For}^+$. We can set $A' := B' \wedge C'$ and get $A' \in \mathrm{For}^+$ and $\mathsf{FIT} \vdash A^\bullet \leftrightarrow A_0 \leftrightarrow \neg A'$ and then the claim follows. □

Definition 6.14. For every $A \in \mathcal{L}_{\mathsf{TID}}$, we define

$$A^\bullet_{\mathsf{N}} := \begin{cases} A^\bullet & \text{if } \mathrm{FV}(A) = \emptyset \\ x_1 \in \mathsf{N} \to \ldots \to x_n \in \mathsf{N} \to A^\bullet & \text{if } \mathrm{FV}(A) = \{x_1, \ldots, x_n\} \\ & \quad \text{for some } n \neq 0 \end{cases}$$

Lemma 6.15. *For each $B \in \mathrm{Pos}_1(a)$, there is an $\mathcal{L}_{\mathsf{FIT}}$-term t and a function type $\mathbb{F} \in \mathrm{FT}$ such that*

$$\mathsf{FIT} \vdash \forall x(tx \in \mathbb{F} \leftrightarrow B^\bullet(x/a))$$

holds.

Proof. We distinguish the following cases on $B \in \mathrm{Pos}_1(a)$:
1. If $B \in \mathrm{Pos}_0$, then Lemma 6.13 provides some $B' \in \mathrm{For}^+$ such that $\mathsf{FIT} \vdash B^\bullet \leftrightarrow B'$ holds, so for $\mathbb{F} := \{a\colon B'\}$ we have $\mathbb{F} \in \mathrm{FT}$. Moreover, with $t := \lambda x.x$, we get the claim.

2. If B is of the form $\forall\vec{y}(B_1 \to B_2)$ with $a \notin \mathrm{FV}(B_1)$, $\vec{y} = y_1, \ldots, y_n$, and $B_1, B_2 \in \mathrm{Pos}_0$, we first get $B_1', B_2' \in \mathrm{For}^+$ from Lemma 6.13 such that

$$B_i^\bullet \leftrightarrow B_i' \;\&\; \mathrm{FV}(B_i^\bullet) = \mathrm{FV}(B_i') \qquad (i = 1, 2)$$

and then we set

$$\begin{aligned}
\mathbb{Q}_1 &:= \{z \colon z = \langle (z)_0, \ldots, (z)_{n-1} \rangle \wedge B_1'((z)_0/y_1, \ldots, (z)_{n-1}/y_n)\} \\
\mathbb{Q}_2 &:= \{z \colon z = \langle (z)_0, \ldots, (z)_n \rangle \wedge B_2'((z)_n/a, (z)_0/y_1, \ldots, (z)_{n-1}/y_n)\} \\
\mathbb{F} &:= \mathbb{Q}_1 \twoheadrightarrow \mathbb{Q}_2 \\
t &:= \lambda x, z.\langle x, (z)_0, \ldots, (z)_{n-1} \rangle
\end{aligned}$$

Obviously $\mathbb{F} \in \mathrm{FT}$ holds and then similar as in [Fef92, 6.3], we have over FIT and for any x

$$\begin{aligned}
tx \in \mathbb{F} &\leftrightarrow \forall z(z \in \mathbb{Q}_1 \to txz \in \mathbb{Q}_2) \\
&\leftrightarrow \forall\vec{y}(B_1^\bullet \to tx\langle y_1, \ldots, y_n \rangle \in \mathbb{Q}_2) \\
&\leftrightarrow \forall\vec{y}(B_1^\bullet \to \langle x, y_1, \ldots, y_n \rangle \in \mathbb{Q}_2) \\
&\leftrightarrow \forall\vec{y}(B_1^\bullet \to B_2^\bullet(x/a)) \\
&\leftrightarrow B^\bullet(x/a)
\end{aligned}$$

which gives us the claim. Note that $n = 0$ is possible, so $\forall\vec{y}(B_1^\bullet \to tx\langle y_1, \ldots, y_n \rangle \in \mathbb{Q}_2)$ denotes then $B_1^\bullet \to (tx\langle\rangle \in \mathbb{Q}_2)$. □

Theorem 6.16. FIT *proves every translation* $A^\bullet$ *of an instance* A *of axioms* (Ind), (Cl), *and* (TID) *from* TID_1. *More precisely, if* A *is an instance of* (Ind), (Cl), *or* (TID), *then we have* $\mathsf{FIT} \vdash A^\bullet$.

Proof. Let A be an instance of (Ind), (Cl), or (TID). We have to show $\mathsf{FIT} \vdash A^\bullet$.

1. For (Cl): If $A = \mathrm{Prog}_\lhd(P_\lhd)$ holds for some $\lhd$, then we have that $A^\bullet$ is logically equivalent over FIT to $\mathrm{Cl}_{\mathsf{N},\mathbb{Q}_\lhd}(\Lambda z.z \in \mathsf{I}_{\mathsf{N},\mathbb{Q}_\lhd})$, and this is an instance of (FT-Cl). More precisely, we have over FIT:

$$
\begin{aligned}
&(\mathrm{Prog}_{\lhd}(P_{\lhd}))^{\bullet} \\
&\leftrightarrow (\forall x(\mathrm{Acc}_{\lhd}(P_{\lhd}, x) \to P_{\lhd}x))^{\bullet} \\
&\leftrightarrow \forall x(x \in \overline{\mathsf{N}} \vee ((\mathrm{Acc}_{\lhd}(P_{\lhd}, x))^{\bullet} \to x \in \mathsf{I}_{\mathsf{N},\mathbb{Q}_{\lhd}})) \\
&\leftrightarrow \forall x(x \in \overline{\mathsf{N}} \vee (\forall y(y \in \overline{\mathsf{N}} \vee ((y \lhd x)^{\bullet} \to y \in \mathsf{I}_{\mathsf{N},\mathbb{Q}_{\lhd}})) \to x \in \mathsf{I}_{\mathsf{N},\mathbb{Q}_{\lhd}})) \\
&\leftrightarrow \forall x(x \in \overline{\mathsf{N}} \vee (\forall y(y \in \overline{\mathsf{N}} \vee (\langle y, x\rangle \in \mathbb{Q}_{\lhd} \to y \in \mathsf{I}_{\mathsf{N},\mathbb{Q}_{\lhd}})) \to x \in \mathsf{I}_{\mathsf{N},\mathbb{Q}_{\lhd}})) \\
&\leftrightarrow (\forall x \in \mathsf{N})((\forall y \in \mathsf{N})(\langle y, x\rangle \in \mathbb{Q}_{\lhd} \to y \in \mathsf{I}_{\mathsf{N},\mathbb{Q}_{\lhd}}) \to x \in \mathsf{I}_{\mathsf{N},\mathbb{Q}_{\lhd}}) \\
&\leftrightarrow \mathrm{Cl}_{\mathsf{N},\mathbb{Q}_{\lhd}}(\Lambda z.z \in \mathsf{I}_{\mathsf{N},\mathbb{Q}_{\lhd}})
\end{aligned}
$$

2. For (Ind) and (TID): Let $B \in \mathrm{Pos}_1(a)$ be arbitrary. By Lemma 6.15 some $\mathcal{L}_{\mathsf{FIT}}$-term t and function type $\mathbb{F} \in \mathrm{FT}$ exist such that we have

$$\mathsf{FIT} \vdash \forall x(tx \in \mathbb{F} \leftrightarrow B^{\bullet}(x/a)) \tag{6.1}$$

2.1. If $A = \mathcal{B}(0) \wedge \forall x(\mathcal{B}(x) \to \mathcal{B}(\mathbf{S}x)) \to \forall x\mathcal{B}(x)$ holds for $\mathcal{B} = \Lambda a.B$: We note that for $B_1 := B(a/\mathbf{S}a)$ one can prove (by induction on the build-up of B) that $B_1^{\bullet}$ is $B^{\bullet}(a/\mathsf{s}_{\mathsf{N}}a)$. So, with $\mathcal{B}(\mathbf{S}x)^{\bullet}$ being $(B(a/\mathbf{S}x))^{\bullet}$ this becomes $(B_1(x))^{\bullet}$, i.e., we get $B_1^{\bullet}(a/x)$ and hence $(B^{\bullet}(a/\mathsf{s}_{\mathsf{N}}a))(a/x)$. So, we obtain that $\mathcal{B}(\mathbf{S}x)^{\bullet}$ is $B^{\bullet}(a/\mathsf{s}_{\mathsf{N}}x)$, while note that for any $B' \in \mathcal{L}_{\mathsf{TID}}$, we have that B' and $B'^{\bullet}$ share the same first-order variables. For proving $A^{\bullet}$, we can therefore assume that

$$B^{\bullet}(0/a) \tag{6.2}$$

$$\forall x(x \in \overline{\mathsf{N}} \vee (B^{\bullet}(x/a) \to B^{\bullet}(\mathsf{s}_{\mathsf{N}}x/a))) \tag{6.3}$$

holds, and we have to show $\forall x(x \in \overline{\mathsf{N}} \vee B^{\bullet}(x/a))$, while this is equivalent to $t \in \mathsf{N} \twoheadrightarrow \mathbb{F}$ due to (6.1). Now we can directly apply (FT-Ind) because (6.2) is equivalent to $t0 \in \mathbb{F}$ and (6.3) is equivalent to $(\forall x \in \mathsf{N})(tx \in \mathbb{F} \to t(\mathsf{s}_{\mathsf{N}}) \in \mathbb{F})$.

2.2. If $A = \mathrm{Prog}_{\lhd}(\mathcal{B}) \to \forall x(P_{\lhd}x \to \mathcal{B}(x))$ holds for $\mathcal{B} = \Lambda a.B$: With

$$(\mathrm{Prog}_{\lhd}(\mathcal{B}))^{\bullet} = (\forall x \in \mathsf{N})(\forall y \in \mathsf{N})\begin{pmatrix} \langle y, x\rangle \in \mathbb{Q}_{\lhd} \\ \to (\mathcal{B}(y))^{\bullet} \\ \to (\mathcal{B}(x))^{\bullet} \end{pmatrix} \tag{6.4}$$

we get that FIT proves the following:

$$\left.\begin{aligned}&(\mathrm{Prog}_{\lhd}(\mathcal{B}))^{\bullet}\\&\leftrightarrow (\forall x \in \mathsf{N})(\forall y \in \mathsf{N})(\langle y, x\rangle \in \mathbb{Q}_{\lhd} \to ty \in \mathbb{F} \to tx \in \mathbb{F})\\&\leftrightarrow \mathrm{Cl}_{\mathsf{N},\mathbb{Q}_{\lhd}}(\Lambda z.tz \in \mathbb{F})\end{aligned}\right\} \tag{6.5}$$

This accumulates in the provability of $A^{\bullet}$. Namely, assume $(\mathrm{Prog}_{\lhd}(\mathcal{B}))^{\bullet}$ and get $t \in (\mathsf{I}_{\mathsf{N},\mathbb{Q}_{\lhd}} \twoheadrightarrow \mathbb{F})$ from (6.5) and (FT-ID), hence (6.1) yields

$$\begin{aligned}\forall x(x \in \mathsf{I}_{\mathsf{N},\mathbb{Q}_{\lhd}} \to tx \in \mathbb{F}) &\leftrightarrow \forall x(x \in \mathsf{I}_{\mathsf{N},\mathbb{Q}_{\lhd}} \to B^{\bullet}(x/a))\\&\to (\forall x \in \mathsf{N})(x \in \mathsf{I}_{\mathsf{N},\mathbb{Q}_{\lhd}} \to B^{\bullet}(x/a))\end{aligned}$$

Now, we are done because $(\forall x(P_{\lhd}x \to \mathcal{B}(x)))^{\bullet}$ is $(\forall x \in \mathsf{N})(x \in \mathsf{I}_{\mathsf{N},\mathbb{Q}_{\lhd}} \to B^{\bullet}(x/a))$. □

Corollary 6.17 (Embedding TID into FIT). *Let* $A \in \mathcal{L}_{\mathsf{TID}}$ *with* $\mathrm{FV}(A) = \{x_1, \ldots, x_n\}$. *Then we have*

$$\mathsf{TID} \vdash A \implies \mathsf{FIT} \vdash A^{\bullet}_{\mathsf{N}}$$

Proof. The claim follows essentially from Theorems 6.10 and 6.16. In particular, we remark that for FIT, the propositional logical rules and axioms and the quantificational logic for individual variables correspond (under the translation of Definition 6.11) to first-order predicate logic in the setting of TID. □

7. The Small Veblen Ordinal $\vartheta\Omega^\omega$ measures FIT and TID

7.1. Lower Bound $\vartheta\Omega^\omega$ for FIT and TID

This section provides a lower bound for the proof-theoretic ordinal of the theory TID by means of wellordering proofs. Hence, together with the embedding of TID into FIT from Section 6.2, we automatically get a lower bound for FIT as well. We based the following proofs on the fundamental sequences from Section 3.4 in order to make the present section depend less on the implementation of the ordinal notation system $(\mathrm{OT}, \prec)$. The fundamental sequences are motivated by and can be understood from an intuitive set-theoretic view-point, without relying too much on intrinsic properties of the ordinal notation system $(\mathrm{OT}, \prec)$ that we introduced in Section 3.1. However, the cost of having a more accessible approach to the wellordering proofs is that we had to verify the fundamental sequences' adequate behaviour in the background (cf., Sections 3.2 and 3.4).

We remark that an alternative approach would be to implement the following proofs directly in the setting of ϕ and the ordinal notation system $(\mathrm{OT}, \prec)$, allowing us to avoid the introduction of $\tilde{\varphi}$ and the proof of its adequate behaviour. In this case, it would be technically more sensible to work with fixed-point free variants $\overline{\varphi}_{n+1}$ of the finitary Veblen functions and base $(\mathrm{OT}, \prec)$ on those (see also [Sch54, §3]). We did not choose this approach for the sake of a better motivation and understanding of the wellordering proof.

Notation 7.1. In this section, we work within TID and fix the following notational conventions:

(a) The notion *ordinal* denotes terms that are given according to the ordinal notation system $(\mathrm{OT}, \prec)$.

(b) Small black letters $\mathfrak{a}, \mathfrak{b}, \mathfrak{c}, \mathfrak{d}, \ldots$ denote explicit terms for ordinal notations in sense of OT and which are given externally in the metatheory.

(c) P denotes $P_\prec$, and analogously Acc, Prog, and TI denote $\mathrm{Acc}_\prec$, $\mathrm{Prog}_\prec$, and $\mathrm{TI}_\prec$, respectively.

(d) $\mathcal{L}\text{-TI}(\prec\mathfrak{a}) := \{\mathrm{TI}(\mathcal{A}, \mathfrak{b})\colon \mathcal{A} \in \mathcal{L} \ \& \ \mathfrak{b} \prec \mathfrak{a}\}$ for $\mathcal{L}$ being $\mathcal{L}_{\mathsf{PA}}$ or $\mathcal{L}_{\mathsf{TID}}$.

(e) Moreover and in case it is clear from the context, we shall also use the following notations:

- $1, \omega^a, \omega, \varepsilon_0, a \cdot n$ denote $\tilde{1}, \tilde{\omega}^a, \tilde{\omega}, \tilde{\varepsilon}_0, a \tilde{\cdot} n$, respectively.
- $\varphi(a_1, \ldots, a_{n+1})$ and $\varphi a_1 \ldots a_{n+1}$ denote $\tilde{\varphi}(a_1, \ldots, a_{n+1})$. (Recall in particular that $\varphi(a_1) = \omega^{a_1}$ holds.)
- $a + b$ denotes $a \tilde{+} b$ whenever it appears in a formula.[1]

Proposition 7.2.

(a) $\mathsf{TID} \vdash \forall x(x \notin \mathrm{OT} \to Px)$.

(b) $\mathsf{TID} \vdash \forall x(Px \to \mathrm{TI}(\mathcal{A}, x))$ *for all* $\mathcal{A} \in \mathcal{L}_{\mathsf{PA}}$.

(c) $\mathsf{TID} \vdash \mathrm{TI}(\mathcal{A}, \mathfrak{a})$ *holds for each* $\mathfrak{a} \prec \omega$ *and* $\mathcal{A} \in \mathcal{L}_{\mathsf{TID}}$.

Proof (Sketch). (a) holds immediately by (CI), using that $a \notin \mathrm{OT}$ implies $b \not\prec a$ for all b. For (b), assume Pa, $\mathrm{Prog}(\mathcal{A})$, and $b \prec a$. We get Pb by (FP) from Remark 6.7, and since $\mathcal{A} \in \mathrm{Pos}_1$ holds, we then get $\mathcal{A}(b)$ by (TID). For (c), note that we can show $\mathrm{TI}(\mathcal{A}, \mathfrak{n}_k)$ for all $k \in \mathbb{N}$ by (meta-)induction on k and where we set $\mathfrak{n}_0 := 0$ and $\mathfrak{n}_{m+1} := \mathfrak{n}_m \tilde{+} \tilde{1}$ for each $m \in \mathbb{N}$. ☐

Remark 7.3. Dropping the restriction on the induction formula used in (Ind) yields $\mathsf{TID} \vdash \mathrm{TI}(\mathcal{A}, \mathfrak{a})$ for each $\mathfrak{a} \prec \varepsilon_0$ and $\mathcal{A} \in \mathcal{L}_{\mathsf{TID}}$. This is because TID would extend PA in this case with complete induction for the full language $\mathcal{L}_{\mathsf{TID}}$, so by following the usual wellordering proofs for PA and adapted to the representation of ordinals below ε_0 as given here (e.g., by using Example 3.28), we could derive every formula from $\mathcal{L}_{\mathsf{TID}}\text{-TI}(\prec\varepsilon_0)$ in TID.[2]

[1] In this context, we shall take care to use $+_{\mathbb{N}}$ instead of $+$ in order to rule out confusion with $\tilde{+}$, though it shall always be clear from the context which of $+_{\mathbb{N}}$ and $\tilde{+}$ is meant when writing $+$.

[2] See also Section 11.5 where we make use of this property.

Remark 7.4. Due to Proposition 7.2.(a), we can assume from now on without loss of generality that $a \in \mathrm{OT}$ holds whenever we try to show Pa for some a within TID. In particular, if we aim to prove $P(a+b)$ or $P\varphi(\bar{a}^{(n)})$ for some $a, b, a_1, \ldots, a_n$ (with $n \geq 1$), we shall tacitly assume that $a + b \in \mathrm{OT}$ and $\varphi(\bar{a}^{(n)}) \in \mathrm{OT}$ hold, respectively. Then Lemma 3.13 yields also $a, b, a_1, \ldots, a_n \in \mathrm{OT}$. Recall that this holds similarly if we have assumptions of the form $c \prec a + b$ or $c \prec \varphi(\bar{a}^{(n)})$ because this implies $a + b \in \mathrm{OT}$ and $\varphi(\bar{a}^{(n)}) \in \mathrm{OT}$, respectively, by the definition of $\prec$.

Lemma 7.5. $\mathsf{TID} \vdash \forall x, y(Px \land Py \to P(x+y))$.

Proof. Assume a_1, a_2 with Pa_1 and Pa_2, so we have to show $P(a_1 + a_2)$. By showing $\mathrm{Prog}(\mathcal{B})$ for $\mathcal{B} := \Lambda b.P(a_1 + b)$, we can use (TID) together with Pa_2 to get the claim. Now, $\mathrm{Prog}(\mathcal{B})$ is $\forall z(\mathrm{Acc}(\mathcal{B}, z) \to \mathcal{B}(z))$, so assume c and $\mathrm{Acc}(\mathcal{B}, c)$, i.e., $\forall z \prec c(P(a_1 + z))$. Due to (CI), it suffices to show $(\forall z \prec a_1 + c)(Pz)$. Let now $d \prec a_1 + c$. Then Lemma 3.15 yields either $d \prec a_1$, and we can then use (FP) on assumption Pa_1 to get Pd, or we have $a_1 \preceq d \prec a_1 + c$. In the latter case, we have $d = a_1 + c_0$ for some $c_0 \prec c$, so our assumptions yield the claim. □

7.1.1. The Simple Case for the Binary Veblen Function

This subsection treats the case for the binary Veblen function separately in order to give a more transparent proof that avoids the technicalities that appear in the treatment of the general case in Subsection 7.1.2 (e.g., we shall later formulate auxiliary class terms of the form Small_n^k for $1 \leq k \leq n$).

Lemma 7.6. $\mathsf{TID} \vdash \forall x, y(Px \land Py \to P\varphi(x, y))$.

Proof. Note that $P0$ and hence $P1$ hold due to (CI). Now, we assume a_1, a_2 with Pa_1, Pa_2. We use the class term

$$\mathcal{B} := \Lambda a.\forall y(Py \to P\varphi(a, y))$$

with $\mathcal{B} \in \mathrm{Pos}_1$ and show $\mathrm{Prog}(\mathcal{B})$. Then we can use (TID) with Pa_1 and Pa_2. Now, in order to bring the proof of this lemma closer to the proof of Theorem 7.15 that deals with the general case of a finitary Veblen function, we note that $\mathrm{Prog}(\mathcal{B})$ is

$$\forall z(\forall x \prec z(\mathcal{B}(x)) \to \mathcal{B}(z))$$

Now, using the class term

$$\mathcal{A}_2^1 := \Lambda a.\forall y(Py \to \forall x \prec a(P\varphi(x,y)))$$

and that $\mathcal{A}_2^1(a)$ is logically equivalent to $\forall x \prec a(\mathcal{B}(x))$, we get that $\mathrm{Prog}(\mathcal{B})$ is logically equivalent to

$$\forall z(\mathcal{A}_2^1(z) \to \mathcal{B}(z)) \tag{$*$}$$

So, it rests to show $(*)$. For proving this, assume a with

$$\mathcal{A}_2^1(a) \tag{7.1}$$

and show $\mathcal{B}(a)$, while for proving $\mathcal{B}(a)$, assume b with

$$Pb \tag{7.2}$$

and show $P\varphi(a,b)$. Once more, we can use (TID), namely with

$$\mathcal{A}_2^2 := \Lambda d.P\varphi(a,d)$$

on (7.2) since $\mathcal{A}_2^2 \in \mathrm{Pos}_1$ holds, while we have to show $\mathrm{Prog}(\mathcal{A}_2^2)$.[3] Now, for proving $\mathrm{Prog}(\mathcal{A}_2^2)$, we assume d and z with

$$\forall z_0 \prec d(\mathcal{A}_2^2(z_0)) \quad \Big(\text{i.e., } \forall z_0 \prec d(P\varphi(a,z_0))\Big) \tag{7.3}$$

$$z \prec \varphi(a,d) \tag{7.4}$$

and show Pz. This yields $P\varphi(a,d)$ by (CI) because z is arbitrary. We consider now the following case distinction.
<u>1.</u> If $d \in \mathrm{Lim}$: We get that $z \prec \varphi(a,d[x])$ holds for some x by Corollary 3.29. Since we have $d[x] \prec d$ by Theorem 3.25, we get $P\varphi(a,d[x])$ by (7.3), implying Pz by (FP).
<u>2.</u> If $d \notin \mathrm{Lim}$:

[3] Noting our current assumption (7.1) and our current goal, we remark that we actually show

$$\mathcal{A}_2^1(a) \to \mathrm{Prog}(\mathcal{A}_2^2)$$

which is a special case of Theorem 7.12, and also note that $\mathcal{A}_2^1 \in \mathrm{Pos}_1$ holds with $\mathcal{A}_2^1 \notin \mathrm{Pos}_0$, while we have $\mathcal{A}_2^2 \in \mathrm{Pos}_0$.

<u>**2.1.**</u> If $a = 0$: Since $d \notin \mathrm{Lim}$ holds, we get $z \prec t(x)$ for some x by Corollary 3.29, where we let

$$t(x) := \omega^{d[x]} \cdot (x +_{\mathbb{N}} 1)$$

We show $\forall x(P(t(x)))$ by induction on x and note that (Ind) is applicable here because of $\Lambda x.P(t(x)) \in \mathrm{Pos}_1$. For $x = 0$, we can argue as for the case $d \in \mathrm{Lim}$ and get $P(\omega^{d[0]})$. For $x = x_0 +_{\mathbb{N}} 1$, the claim follows from $P(t(0))$, the induction hypothesis, and Lemma 7.5, noting that $d[0] = d[x_0]$ holds by definition and because of $d \notin \mathrm{Lim}$.
<u>**2.2.**</u> If $a \in \mathrm{Lim}$ and $d = 0$: We have by Corollary 3.29 that $z \prec \varphi(a[x], 0)$ holds for some x. Since we have $a[x] \prec a$ by Theorem 3.25, we get $P\varphi(a[x], 0)$ with (7.1).
<u>**2.3.**</u> Otherwise, i.e., either $d = 0$ with $a \in \mathrm{Suc}$ or $d \in \mathrm{Suc}$ with $a \neq 0$: Letting $t := \tilde{\varphi}(a, d)$, we have by Theorem 3.27 some x such that $z \prec t[x]$ holds. Proving

$$\forall x(P(t[x]))$$

by induction on x suffices now. Note again that (Ind) is applicable because we have $\Lambda x.P(t[x]) \in \mathrm{Pos}_1$, and note for the following computations of $t[x]$ also that we have $\varphi(a, d) = \phi a d$ by Lemma 3.17.
<u>**2.3.1.**</u> If $x = 0$: If $d = 0$ holds, then we have $t[0] = 1$ and are done since we have $P1$. If $d \in \mathrm{Suc}$ holds with $d = d_0 + 1$, then we have $t[0] = \varphi(a, d_0) + 1$, and since $d_0 \prec d$ holds, we get $P(t[0])$ from (7.3) and Lemma 7.5 by using $P1$.
<u>**2.3.2.**</u> If $x = x_0 +_{\mathbb{N}} 1$: We have $t[x_0 +_{\mathbb{N}} 1] = \varphi(a[x_0], t[x_0])$, so the claim follows with $a[x_0] \prec a$ from Theorem 3.25, the induction hypothesis $P(t[x_0])$, and (7.1). ☐

Corollary 7.7. TID $\vdash P\varphi(\mathfrak{a}, 0)$ *holds for each* $\mathfrak{a} \prec \omega$.

Proof. The claim is a direct consequence of Lemma 7.6. Note hereby that for $\mathfrak{a} \prec \omega$, we get $P\mathfrak{a}$ from Proposition 7.2.(c): We get $\forall x \prec \mathfrak{a}(Px)$ from $\mathrm{TI}(\Lambda a.Pa, \mathfrak{a})$ and closure (Cl), hence $P\mathfrak{a}$ by (FP). ☐

Remark 7.8. We proved Lemma 7.6 by applying (TID) to a class term $\mathcal{B}$ in Pos_1 that is not in Pos_0. Though, in order to show $\mathrm{Prog}(\mathcal{B})$ in the proof of Lemma 7.6, we can work with a (weaker) subtheory TID_0 of TID that we shall define in Chapter 8. It can be obtained from TID by restricting (the instances of) the axiom schemes (TID) and (Ind) to class terms that are in Pos_0 (rather than Pos_1). The theory TID_0 is the restriction of the theory $\mathsf{ID}_1^*\restriction$ to accessible part positive operator forms, i.e., to the language $\mathcal{L}_{\mathsf{TID}}$, while $\mathsf{ID}_1^*\restriction$ is a subtheory of ID_1 for positive induction and with the same restriction for complete induction. The proof-theoretic ordinal of $\mathsf{ID}_1^*\restriction$ is $\varphi(\omega, 0)$. See for instance [Pro06], and note furthermore Remark 7.14 below.

7.1.2. The General Case for the Finitary Veblen Functions

Remark 7.9. Recall from Chapter 3 that the expression $\varphi(\bar{a}^{(n+1)})$, i.e., $\tilde{\varphi}(\bar{a}^{(n+1)})$, is also defined in case of $n = 0$. We then have $\varphi(a_1) = \omega^{a_1}$.

Definition 7.10. For $k, n \in \mathbb{N}$ with $1 \leq k < n$, we define

$$\begin{aligned}
\mathrm{Small}_n^k &:= \Lambda\bar{a}^{(k)}.\forall y(Py \rightarrow \forall x \prec a_k(P\varphi(\bar{a}^{(k-1)}, x, y, \bar{0}^{(n-k-1)}))) \\
\mathrm{Hyp}_n^k &:= \Lambda\bar{a}^{(k)}.\mathrm{Small}_n^1(a_1) \wedge \ldots \wedge \mathrm{Small}_n^k(\bar{a}^{(k)}) \\
\mathrm{Hyp}_n^0 &:= (0 = 0)
\end{aligned}$$

Lemma 7.11. *For $k, n \in \mathbb{N}$ and variables $a_1, \ldots, a_{n-1}$, the following holds:*

(a) $(\Lambda a.P(\varphi(\bar{a}^{(n-1)}, a))) \in \mathrm{Pos}_0$ *for* $1 \leq n$.

(b) $(\Lambda a.\mathrm{Small}_n^k(\bar{a}^{(k-1)}, a)) \in \mathrm{Pos}_1$ *for* $1 \leq k < n$.

Proof. (a) is obvious. For (b), note in the definition of $\mathrm{Small}_n^k(\bar{a}^{(k-1)}, a)$ that Py and $\forall x(x \prec a \rightarrow P\varphi(\bar{a}^{(k-1)}, x, y, \bar{0}^{(n-k-1)}))$ are in Pos_0. Furthermore, Py does not contain a as a free variable, so we get indeed that $\forall y(Py \rightarrow \forall x \prec a(P\varphi(\bar{a}^{(k-1)}, x, y, \bar{0}^{(n-k-1)})))$ is in $\mathrm{Pos}_1(a)$. □

Theorem 7.12. *For $n \in \mathbb{N}$ with $n \geq 1$, we have*

$$\mathsf{TID} \vdash \forall\bar{a}^{(n-1)}\big(\mathrm{Hyp}_n^{n-1}(\bar{a}^{(n-1)}) \rightarrow \mathrm{Prog}(\Lambda a.P\varphi(\bar{a}^{(n-1)}, a))\big)$$

Proof. Let $n \geq 1$ and $\bar{a}^{(n-1)}$ be given with

$$\mathrm{Hyp}_n^{n-1}(\bar{a}^{(n-1)}) \tag{7.5}$$

In order to show $\text{Prog}(\Lambda a.P\varphi(\bar{a}^{(n-1)}, a))$, assume a and d such that

$$\forall x \prec a(P\varphi(\bar{a}^{(n-1)}, x)) \tag{7.6}$$

$$d \prec \varphi(\bar{a}^{(n-1)}, a) \tag{7.7}$$

hold and show Pd. This would yield $P\varphi(\bar{a}^{(n-1)}, a)$ by (CI) because d is arbitrary.

1. If $n = 1$ or $a_1 = \ldots = a_{n-1} = 0$ hold: We can proceed as in Lemma 7.6 since we have $\varphi(\bar{a}^{(n-1)}, a) = \varphi(a) = \omega^a$.
2. Otherwise: We can assume now that some $1 \le l \le n-1$ exists with

$$a_l \neq 0 \;\; \& \;\; a_{l+1} = \ldots = a_{n-1} = 0$$

i.e., that we have $\varphi(\bar{a}^{(n-1)}, a) = \varphi(\bar{a}^{(l)}, \bar{0}^{(n-l-1)}, a)$ with $a_l \neq 0$. Furthermore, (7.5) yields

$$\text{Small}_n^1(a_1) \wedge \ldots \wedge \text{Small}_n^{n-1}(\bar{a}^{(n-1)}) \tag{7.8}$$

Consider now the following case distinction and note that $P0$ and hence $P1$ hold due to (CI).
2.1. If $a \in \text{Lim}$: We get that $d \prec \varphi(\bar{a}^{(n-1)}, a[x])$ holds for some x by Corollary 3.29 and (7.7). Since we have $a[x] \prec a$ by Theorem 3.25, we get $P\varphi(\bar{a}^{(n-1)}, a[x])$ by (7.6) which implies Pd by (FP).
2.2. If $a \notin \text{Lim}$:
2.2.1. If $a_l \in \text{Lim}$ and $a = 0$: By Corollary 3.29, we have some x such that $z \prec \varphi(\bar{a}^{(l-1)}, a_l[x], \bar{0}^{(n-l)})$ holds. Since we have $a_l[x] \prec a_l$ by Theorem 3.25, we get $P\varphi(\bar{a}^{(l-1)}, a_l[x], \bar{0}^{(n-l)})$ with $\text{Small}_n^l(\bar{a}^{(l)})$ from (7.8).
2.2.2. Otherwise, i.e., either $a = 0$ with $a_l \in \text{Suc}$ or $a \in \text{Suc}$ with $a_l \neq 0$: In this situation, Lemma 3.17 implies $\varphi(\bar{a}^{(l)}, \bar{0}^{(n-l)}) = \phi a_p \ldots a_l \bar{0}^{(n-l-1)} a$ for some $1 \le p \le l$ where $a_1, \ldots, a_p = 0$ holds. In order to simplify notation and without loss of generality, we shall assume $p = 1$, noting that the following argument works for the general case as well. Letting

$$t := \phi \bar{a}^{(l)} \bar{0}^{(n-l-1)} a \tag{7.9}$$

we have by Theorem 3.27 some x such that $z \prec t[x]$ holds. Proving

$$\forall x(P(t[x]))$$

by induction on x suffices now. (Ind) is applicable because $\Lambda x.P(t[x]) \in$ Pos_1 holds.
2.2.2.1. If $x = 0$: For $a = 0$, we have $t[0] = 1$ and are done since we have $P1$. If $a \in \mathrm{Suc}$ holds with $a = a_0 + 1$, then we have $t[0] = \varphi(\bar{a}^{(n-1)}, a_0) + 1$ due to the form of t in (7.9) and the definition of $t[0]$. Since $a_0 \prec a$ holds, we get $P(t[0])$ from (7.6) and Lemma 7.5 by using $P1$.
2.2.2.2. If $x = x_0 +_{\mathbb{N}} 1$: We get $t[x_0 +_{\mathbb{N}} 1] = \varphi(\bar{a}^{(l-1)}, a_l[x_0], t[x_0], \bar{0}^{(n-l)})$, so the claim follows with $a_l[x_0] \prec a_l$ from Theorem 3.25, the induction hypothesis $P(t[x_0])$, and $\mathrm{Small}^l_n(\bar{a}^{(l)})$ from (7.8). □

Corollary 7.13. *For* $n \in \mathbb{N}$ *with* $n \geq 1$, *we have*

$$\mathsf{TID} \vdash \forall \bar{a}^{(n)} (\mathrm{Hyp}^{n-1}_n(\bar{a}^{(n-1)}) \wedge Pa_n \to P\varphi(\bar{a}^{(n)}))$$

Proof. Immediate from Theorem 7.12 by using (TID) and Lemma 7.11.(a). □

Remark 7.14. Note that we did not invoke (TID) in the proof of Theorem 7.12, so this result holds also for the restriction TID_0 of TID that we mentioned in Remark 7.8. Clearly, our proof of Theorem 7.12 does not work directly within PA because we invoked (CI) and (FP).

Theorem 7.15. *For* $k, n \in \mathbb{N}$ *with* $1 \leq k < n$, *we have*

$$\mathsf{TID} \vdash \forall \bar{a}^{(k-1)} (\mathrm{Hyp}^{k-1}_n(\bar{a}^{(k-1)}) \to \mathrm{Prog}(\Lambda a.\mathrm{Small}^k_n(\bar{a}^{(k-1)}, a)))$$

Proof. We fix $n \geq 1$ and argue by induction on $n - k$ for $1 \leq k < n$. Let $\bar{a}^{(k-1)}$ be given with

$$\mathrm{Hyp}^{k-1}_n(\bar{a}^{(k-1)}) \tag{7.10}$$

and where (7.10) just gives us the formula $0 = 0$ in case of $k = 1$. In order to show $\mathrm{Prog}(\Lambda a.\mathrm{Small}^k_n(\bar{a}^{(k-1)}, a))$, assume a, a_k, a_{k+1} with

$$\forall x \prec a(\mathrm{Small}^k_n(\bar{a}^{(k-1)}, x)) \tag{7.11}$$

$$Pa_{k+1} \tag{7.12}$$

$$a_k \prec a \tag{7.13}$$

and in case we have $k \neq n-1$, further let

$$a_i := 0$$

for each $k < i \leq n$. We have to show $P(\varphi(\bar{a}^{(k+1)}, \bar{0}^{(n-k-1)}))$, i.e.,

$$P(\varphi(\bar{a}^{(n)})) \tag{$*$}$$

From (7.13) and (7.11), we get

$$\mathrm{Small}_n^k(\bar{a}^{(k-1)}, a_k) \tag{7.14}$$

and hence

$$\mathrm{Hyp}_n^k(\bar{a}^{(k)}) \tag{7.15}$$

with (7.10). From (7.12) and $P0$, we get

$$Pa_{k+1} \wedge \ldots \wedge Pa_n \tag{7.16}$$

We show by a side induction on i that the following holds:

$$1 \leq i < n \implies \mathrm{Hyp}_n^i(\bar{a}^{(i)}) \tag{$**$}$$

From $(**)$ with $i := n-1$ and Pa_n from (7.16), we then get $(*)$ by Corollary 7.13. For the proof of $(**)$, we note that the claim follows in case of $1 \leq i \leq k$ from (7.15). If we have $k < i < n$, then we can use the side induction hypothesis and get

$$\mathrm{Hyp}_n^{i-1}(\bar{a}^{(i-1)}) \tag{7.17}$$

This and the main induction hypothesis yield $\mathrm{Prog}(\Lambda a.\mathrm{Small}_n^i(\bar{a}^{(i-1)}, a))$ and hence we get $\forall a(Pa \to \mathrm{Small}_n^i(\bar{a}^{(i-1)}, a))$ by (TID), while noting here Lemma 7.11.(b). Now, $\mathrm{Small}_n^i(\bar{a}^{(i)})$ follows from (7.16) and the current case $k < i < n$. Hence, we get $\mathrm{Hyp}_n^i(\bar{a}^{(i)})$ by (7.17). □

Corollary 7.16. *For $k, n \in \mathbb{N}$ with $1 \leq k < n$, we have*

$$\mathsf{TID} \vdash \forall \bar{a}^{(k)}(\mathrm{Hyp}_n^{k-1}(\bar{a}^{(k-1)}) \wedge Pa_k \to \mathrm{Hyp}_n^k(\bar{a}^{(k)}))$$

Proof. From $\mathrm{Hyp}_n^{k-1}(\bar{a}^{(k-1)}) \wedge Pa_k$, we get $\mathrm{Small}_n^k(\bar{a}^{(k)})$ by Theorem 7.15 and (TID), while noting Lemma 7.11.(b). Hence, we get $\mathrm{Hyp}_n^k(\bar{a}^{(k)})$. □

Theorem 7.17. *For each* $n \geq 1$, *we have*

$$\mathsf{TID} \vdash \forall \bar{a}^{(n)} (\textstyle\bigwedge_{i=1}^n Pa_i \to P\varphi(\bar{a}^{(n)}))$$

Proof. Let $n \geq 1$ and assume $\bar{a}^{(n)}$ with $\bigwedge_{i=1}^n Pa_i$. We trivially get

$$\mathrm{Hyp}_n^0(\bar{a}^{(0)}) \wedge \textstyle\bigwedge_{i=1}^n Pa_i \tag{7.18}$$

due to the definition of Hyp_n^0. We now show by induction on $k \in \mathbb{N}$ that the following holds:

$$0 \leq k < n \implies \mathrm{Hyp}_n^k(\bar{a}^{(k)}) \wedge \textstyle\bigwedge_{i=k+1}^n Pa_i \tag{$*$}$$

Then the claim $P\varphi(\bar{a}^{(n)})$ follows from Corollary 7.13 and $(*)$ with $k := n-1$. We show now $(*)$ and assume $0 \leq k < n$:
1. $k = 0$: This is (7.18).
2. $0 < k \leq n$: The induction hypothesis yields $\mathrm{Hyp}_n^{k-1}(\bar{a}^{(k-1)}) \wedge \bigwedge_{i=k}^n Pa_i$ and hence the claim $(*)$ due to Corollary 7.16. □

Corollary 7.18 (Lower bound of TID)**.** *For each* $\mathcal{A} \in \mathcal{L}_{\mathsf{PA}}$ *and* $\mathfrak{a} \in \mathrm{OT}$, *we have*

$$\mathsf{TID} \vdash \mathrm{TI}(\mathcal{A}, \mathfrak{a})$$

Proof. By induction on the build-up of $\mathfrak{a} \in \mathrm{OT}$. We can use Lemma 7.5 and Theorem 7.17 together with Proposition 7.2.(b). □

Remark 7.19. Similar to Remark 7.8, we shall give an informal and intuitive explanation why Corollary 7.18 is the best we can expect from TID. The method used in the proof of Theorem 7.15 relied on an *external* representation of the finite list of arguments that the finitary Veblen function is applied to. This is made apparent by the use of the syntactic variable n in Definition 7.10 to denote the arity of a Veblen function. In particular, induction in the meta-theory has been applied to cope with arbitrary but finite lists of arguments. The proof of Theorem 7.15 is designed for the theory TID, and in order to use it to get beyond the small Veblen ordinal, for instance by working with infinitary Veblen functions or Klammersymbols, we would need to *internalize the proof* and deal with non-standard argument positions (for which we do not have a denotation in the meta-theory). The next section shall provide the formal explanation why the small Veblen ordinal is the upper bound of TID.

Remark 7.20. Concluding and with regard to the theory TID_0 that we mentioned in Remark 7.8, we point out that $P\varphi(\mathfrak{a},0)$ for $\mathfrak{a} \prec \omega$ is the best we can expect from TID_0 even though Corollary 7.7 would yield $\mathsf{TID}_0 \vdash \mathcal{L}_{\mathsf{TID}}\text{-TI}(\prec\varphi(\omega,0))$. An intuitive approach to an explanation why this method does not push further when used with $\mathcal{L}_{\mathsf{TID}}\text{-TI}(\prec\varphi(\omega,0))$ is the following property:

$$a \prec \omega \;\;\&\;\; b \prec \varphi(\omega,0) \;\Rightarrow\; \varphi(a,b) \prec \varphi(a,\varphi(\omega,0)) = \varphi(\omega,0) \qquad (\#)$$

Note that if we want to use $\mathcal{L}_{\mathsf{TID}}\text{-TI}(\prec\varphi(\omega,0))$ to prove Corollary 7.7 with $\mathfrak{a} = \omega$, then the induction hypothesis yields only $\forall x(Px \to P(\varphi(\mathfrak{a}_0,x)))$ for $\mathfrak{a}_0 \prec \omega$. Since we can so far provide Pa only for $a \prec \varphi(\omega,0)$, the property (#) prevents us from reaching $\varphi(\omega,0)$.

Note also that (CI) can neither be used to get $P\varphi(\omega,0)$ because we did not show "$\mathsf{TID}_0 \vdash \forall x \prec \omega(P\varphi(x,0))$", namely we showed the statement "$\mathsf{TID}_0 \vdash P(\varphi(\mathfrak{a},0))$" only externally from the perspective of our meta-theory and for $\mathfrak{a} \prec \omega$ with $\mathfrak{a}$ being a numeral whose index ranges over the meta-theory's universe, hence neglecting instances that are non-standard from the perspective of TID_0.

We refer to Section 7.2 that provides (together with the embedding of TID into FIT from Chapter 6) a justification for the above assertions. Now, we shall turn to the general part of the wellordering proofs for TID.

7.2. Upper Bound $\vartheta\Omega^\omega$ for FIT and TID

For determining the upper bound of FIT, we apply one result from [JS99] that relates over ACA_0 the scheme (Π^1_3-RFN) of ω-model reflection for Π^1_3 formulas to the scheme (Π^1_2-BI) of bar induction for Π^1_2 formulas, and one result of [RW93] that determines the proof-theoretic ordinal of $\Pi^1_2\text{-}\mathsf{BI}_0$ to be the small Veblen ordinal $\vartheta\Omega^\omega$. Then an embedding of FIT into the second order theory $\Pi^1_3\text{-}\mathsf{RFN}_0$ of ω-model reflection for Π^1_3 formulas suffices to get the desired upper bound result for FIT. Moreover and due to Section 6.2, this also provides an upper bound for TID. In particular, we shall exploit the Π^1_1 definability of a least fixed-point. A similar approach has been taken in [AR10] and [Pro06] for the treatment of the theories $\Pi^1_2\text{-}\mathsf{RFN}_0$ and ID^*_1 (a subsystem of ID_1 that allows only positive induction for the predicates $P_\mathfrak{A}$ that are assigned to each positive operator form $\mathfrak{A}$). Below, we shall provide an upper bound for FIT by embedding it directly into $\Pi^1_3\text{-}\mathsf{RFN}_0$. We remark that if we were to investigate only the subtheory TID of ID_1, we could have embedded it directly into $\Pi^1_3\text{-}\mathsf{RFN}_0$ (rather than taking the detour via FIT as figure 1 from the introduction on page 6 suggests). Furthermore, we recall that D. Probst's *modular ordinal analysis* from [Pro15] determines the proof-theoretic ordinal of $\Pi^1_3\text{-}\mathsf{RFN}_0$ to be the small Veblen ordinal by *metapredicative* methods.

7.2.1. Subsystems of Second Order Arithmetic

We shall introduce here subsystems of second order arithmetic, and we formulate them in the language $\mathcal{L}^2_{\mathsf{PA}}$ that we defined in Section 1.2. In particular, recall that $\mathcal{L}^2_{\mathsf{PA}}$ formulas allow for quantification over set variables X. The following definitions are taken to some extent from [JS99] and [Sim09], respectively, and we refer to these sources for more details on subsystems of second order arithmetic and in particular to the underlying two-sorted logic.

Definition 7.21. We use the following standard abbreviations

$$
\begin{aligned}
(X)_t &:= \Lambda a.\langle t, a\rangle \in X \\
(QY \mathrel{\dot\in} X)A &:= (Qy)A((X)_y/Y) && \text{(where } Q \in \{\forall, \exists\}) \\
Y \mathrel{\dot\in} X &:= (\exists Z \mathrel{\dot\in} X)(Z = Y) && \text{(i.e., } Y \mathrel{\dot\in} X \text{ is } \exists z((X)_z = Y))
\end{aligned}
$$

and we define the relativization A^X of a formula A to a set variable X inductively as follows:

A	if A is an atomic formula
$\neg(A_0^X)$	if A is $\neg A_0$
$A_0^X \circ A_1^X$	if A is $A_0 \circ A_1$ and $\circ \in \{\vee, \wedge, \rightarrow\}$
$(Qx)A_0^X$	if A is $(Qx)A_0$ and $Q \in \{\exists, \forall\}$
$(QY \dot{\in} X)A_0^X$	if A is $(QX)A_0$ and $Q \in \{\exists, \forall\}$

As usual, we assume tacitly a renaming of bound variables in order to avoid a clash of variables. Note that set variables occur at most free in A^X, i.e., A^X is arithmetical.

Notation 7.22. We also write

$$X \models A$$

in order to denote A^X.

Definition 7.23 (Usual hierarchies of formulas).

(a) Π^1_0 *(or also* Σ^1_0*) formulas* are called those formulas A that are arithmetical, i.e., $\mathcal{L}^2_{\mathsf{PA}}$ formulas without quantifications over set variables. We denote this also by writing $A \in \Pi^1_0$ or $A \in \Sigma^1_0$.

(b) Π^1_{n+1} *formulas* are called those formulas which are of the form

$$\forall X_1 \exists X_2 \ldots (Q_{n+1} X_{n+1})A$$

for some $A \in \Pi^1_0$, and where Q_{n+1} is $\exists$ for even n and Q_{n+1} is $\forall$ otherwise. We denote this also by writing $A \in \Pi^1_n$.

(c) Σ^1_{n+1} *formulas* are all those formulas which are of the form $\exists X A$ with $A \in \Pi^1_n$. We denote this also by writing $A \in \Sigma^1_n$.

Definition 7.24. The two-sorted theory ACA_0 is based on the language $\mathcal{L}^2_{\mathsf{PA}}$. Its axioms are the axioms of PA without complete induction, and where the equality axioms (for the first sort) hold for the language $\mathcal{L}^2_{\mathsf{PA}}$. Moreover, ACA_0 consists of the following principles:

- *Set induction:*

$$\forall X((0 \in X \land \forall x(x \in X \to \mathbf{S}x \in X)) \to \forall x(x \in X))$$

- *Arithmetical comprehension:*

$$(\mathsf{ACA}) \quad \exists X \forall x(x \in X \leftrightarrow A)$$

for each $A \in \Pi^1_0$ that does not contain X (though it might contain free occurrences of other set variables).

Proposition 7.25. ACA_0 *is finitely axiomatizable by a* Π^1_2*-sentence* $\mathrm{F}_{\mathsf{ACA}}$.

Proof. See for instance [Sim09, Lemma VIII.1.5]. □

Definition 7.26. We define the following principles:

- Σ^1_1 *axiom of choice:*

$$(\Sigma^1_1\text{-}\mathsf{AC}) \quad \forall x \exists X A \to \exists Y \forall x(A((Y)_x/X))$$

for each $A \in \Sigma^1_1$.

- Σ^1_1 *axiom of dependent choice:*

$$(\Sigma^1_1\text{-}\mathsf{DC}) \quad \begin{cases} \forall x \forall X \exists Y A \\ \to \forall U \exists Z((Z)_0 = U \land \forall x(A((Z)_x/X, (Z)_{x+1}/Y))) \end{cases}$$

for each $A \in \Sigma^1_1$.

- Π^1_n *ω-model reflection* for $n \in \mathbb{N}$:

$$(\Pi^1_n\text{-}\mathsf{RFN}) \quad \begin{cases} \forall U_1, \ldots, U_k \\ (A \to \exists X(A^X \land \mathrm{F}^X_{\mathsf{ACA}} \land U_1 \dot{\in} X \land \ldots \land U_k \dot{\in} X)) \end{cases}$$

for each $A \in \Pi^1_n$ with at most $U_1, \ldots, U_k$ occurring as free set variables in A (and where $\mathrm{F}_{\mathsf{ACA}}$ is taken from Proposition 7.25).

- Π^1_n *bar induction* for $n \in \mathbb{N}$:

$$(\Pi^1_n\text{-}\mathsf{BI}) \quad \forall X(\mathrm{WO}(X) \to \mathrm{TI}_X(\Lambda a.A))$$

for each $A \in \Pi^1_n$ and where we let

$$\begin{aligned} \mathrm{WO}(X) &:= \mathrm{LO}(X) \wedge \mathrm{WF}(X) \\ \mathrm{WF}(X) &:= \forall Y(\mathrm{TI}_X(Y)) \\ \mathrm{TI}_X(\Lambda a.A) &:= \mathrm{PROG}(X, \Lambda a.A) \to \forall x A(x/a) \\ \mathrm{PROG}(X, \Lambda a.A) &:= \forall x(\forall y(\langle y, x\rangle \in X \to A(y/a)) \to A(x/a)) \end{aligned}$$

and where $\mathrm{LO}(X)$ denotes the usual arithmetical formula that expresses that X encodes a binary relation that is a linear ordering.

The theories $\Sigma^1_1\text{-}\mathsf{AC}_0$, $\Sigma^1_1\text{-}\mathsf{DC}_0$, $\Pi^1_n\text{-}\mathsf{RFN}_0$, and $\Pi^1_n\text{-}\mathsf{BI}_0$ are defined by extending ACA_0 with the axiom scheme (Σ^1_1-AC), (Σ^1_1-DC), (Π^1_n-RFN), and (Π^1_n-BI), respectively.

Remark 7.27. We added the definition for (Π^1_n-BI) for the sake of completeness but we shall not need to use it directly in the following.

7.2.2. Upper Bound Results from the Literature

Theorem 7.28 ([RW93])**.** $|\Pi^1_{n+2}\text{-}\mathsf{BI}_0| = \vartheta\Omega(n+1, \omega)$ *holds for all* $n \in \mathbb{N}$.

Theorem 7.29 ([JS99])**.** (Π^1_{n+1}-BI) *and* (Π^1_{n+2}-RFN) *are equivalent over* ACA_0 *for all* $n \in \mathbb{N}$.

Theorem 7.30 ([Sim09])**.** *Over* ACA_0, *we have*

(a) (Π^1_n-RFN) *implies* (Π^1_k-RFN) *for* $k \le n$.

(b) (Π^1_2-RFN) *is equivalent to* (Σ^1_1-DC).

(c) (Σ^1_1-DC) *implies* (Σ^1_1-AC).

Corollary 7.31. (Π^1_{n+2}-RFN) *implies* (Σ^1_1-AC) *over* ACA_0 *for all* $n \in \mathbb{N}$.

Theorem 7.32 ([Can86])**.** $|\Sigma^1_1\text{-}\mathsf{DC}_0| = \varphi(\omega, 0)$.

Corollary 7.33. $|\Pi^1_{n+2}\text{-}\mathsf{RFN}_0| = \vartheta\Omega(n, \omega)$ *holds for all* $n \in \mathbb{N}$.

Proof. For $n \ge 1$, this is immediate from Theorem 7.28 and Theorem 7.29. For $n = 0$, use also Theorem 7.32 and that $\vartheta\Omega(0, \omega) = \vartheta(\Omega \cdot \omega) = \varphi(\omega, 0)$ holds by Section 2.4. □

7.2.3. Some Syntactical Properties of $\mathcal{L}^2_{\mathsf{PA}}$ Formulas

Definition 7.34 (Refined hierarchies of formulas). Let T be some theory of $\mathcal{L}^2_{\mathsf{PA}}$ as introduced in Subsection 7.2.1, e.g., $\mathsf{T} = \mathsf{ACA}_0$ or $\mathsf{T} = \Sigma^1_1\text{-}\mathsf{AC}_0$.

(a) Π^1_n *formulas over* T are all $A \in \mathcal{L}^2_{\mathsf{PA}}$ that are provably equivalent over T to some formula $A' \in \Pi^1_n$.

(b) $A \in \Pi^1_n(\mathsf{T})$ denotes that A is an Π^1_n formula over T.

Remark 7.35. In case that $A \in \Pi^1_n(\mathsf{T})$ is given for some theory T of $\mathcal{L}^2_{\mathsf{PA}}$ and we consider some $A' \in \Pi^1_n$ that is provably equivalent over T to A, then we can assume that A and A' have the same free variables, and we shall tacitly do so from now on. Moreover, if $\mathsf{T}_1, \mathsf{T}_2$ are theories of $\mathcal{L}^2_{\mathsf{PA}}$ as introduced in Subsection 7.2.1 such that T_2 comprises T_1, then obviously $A \in \Pi_n(\mathsf{T}_1)$ implies $A \in \Pi_n(\mathsf{T}_2)$.

Proposition 7.36. *Let* $k, n \in \mathbb{N}$ *and* $\mathsf{T} \in \{\mathsf{ACA}_0, \Sigma^1_1\text{-}\mathsf{AC}_0\}$. *Then we have the following.*

(a) $(A \in \Pi^1_k(\mathsf{T}) \ \& \ k < n) \implies (A \in \Pi^1_n(\mathsf{T}) \ \& \ \neg A \in \Pi^1_n(\mathsf{T}))$.

(b) $\Pi^1_n(\mathsf{T})$ *is closed under conjunction, disjunction, and universal quantification for number variables, i.e., we have*

$$A, B \in \Pi^1_n(\mathsf{T}) \implies A \circ B \in \Pi^1_n(\mathsf{T}) \quad \textit{where } \circ \in \{\wedge, \vee\}$$
$$A \in \Pi^1_n(\mathsf{T}) \implies \forall x A \in \Pi^1_n(\mathsf{T})$$

(c) $\Pi^1_{n+1}(\mathsf{T})$ *is closed under universal quantification for set variables, i.e., we have*

$$A \in \Pi^1_{n+1}(\mathsf{T}) \implies \forall X A \in \Pi^1_{n+1}(\mathsf{T})$$

Proof. (a) is obvious. For (b), note that the case $n = 0$ is obvious. Now, we show (b) and (c) simultaneously for $n + 1$ by induction $n \in \mathbb{N}$ and a case distinction on the build-up of the formula C given in the right-hand sides of the claims.

We shall provide formulas $C'(W) \in \Sigma^1_n$ such that $\mathsf{T} \vdash C \leftrightarrow \forall X C'(X)$ holds. Note that for each $A \in \Pi^1_{n+1}(\mathsf{T})$, there exist some $A'(U) \in \Sigma^1_n$ and $A''(U) \in \Pi^1_n$ such that the following holds:

$$\left.\begin{array}{l} \mathsf{T} \vdash A \leftrightarrow \forall Y A'(Y) \\ \mathsf{T} \vdash A'(U) \leftrightarrow \neg A''(U) \end{array}\right\} \qquad (*)$$

Hence, the induction hypothesis may be used in combination with A''.

1. For *conjunction* $C = A \wedge B$: We have $A, B \in \Pi^1_{n+1}(\mathsf{T})$. So, let $A'(U), B'(V) \in \Sigma^1_{n+1}$ and $A''(U), B''(V) \in \Pi^1_{n+1}$ be given for A and B, respectively, with properties as indicated by $(*)$. Given any set variable W, we also have $A''((W)_0), B''((W)_1) \in \Pi^1_{n+1}$. Therefore, the induction hypothesis yields some $C''(W) \in \Pi^1_n$ such that

$$\mathsf{T} \vdash C''(W) \leftrightarrow \big(A''((W)_0) \vee B''((W)_1)\big)$$

holds. Since $\neg C''(W)$ is logically equivalent to some formula $C'(W) \in \Sigma^1_n$, we get eventually $\mathsf{T} \vdash C \leftrightarrow \forall X C'(X)$ by making use of (ACA). Note that we have

$$\mathsf{T} \vdash C'(W) \leftrightarrow \neg(A''((W)_0) \vee B''((W)_1)) \leftrightarrow A'((W)_0) \wedge B'((W)_1)$$

2. For *disjunction* $C = A \vee B$, the proof is similar as for conjunction.
3. For *universal quantification (for numbers)* $C = \forall x A$: Let $A'(U, u) \in \Sigma^1_n$ and $A''(U, u) \in \Pi^1_n$ be given for A with properties as indicated by $(*)$. With

$$B(W) := \exists x(x \in (W)_0) \rightarrow \exists y(y \in (W)_0 \wedge A'((W)_1, y))$$

we have $\mathsf{T} \vdash \forall x \forall X A'(X, x) \leftrightarrow \forall Y B(Y)$ due to the following:

For "$\rightarrow$", assume $\forall x \forall X A'(X, x)$ and let Y be given with $\exists x(x \in (Y)_0)$. Furthermore, note that for any z, we have that $z \in (Y)_1$ is the arithmetical formula $\langle 1, z\rangle \in Y$, so we have $\mathsf{ACA}_0 \vdash \exists X \forall z(z \in X \leftrightarrow z \in (Y)_1)$. So, given such an X and given x with $x \in (Y)_0$, we get eventually $A'(X, x)$ from the assumption $\forall x \forall X A'(X, x)$, and hence $\exists y(y \in (Y)_0 \wedge A'((Y)_1, y))$.

For "$\leftarrow$", assume $\forall Y B(Y)$ and let x and X be given. With $D := ((z)_0 = 0 \wedge (z)_1 = x) \vee ((z)_0 = 1 \wedge (z)_1 \in X)$, we have $D \in \Pi^1_0$, and hence $\mathsf{ACA}_0 \vdash \exists Y \forall z(z \in Y \leftrightarrow D)$. Given such an Y, we get $B(Y)$ from the assumption $\forall Y B(Y)$, and due to $x \in (Y)_0$, we further get $\exists y(y \in (Y)_0 \wedge A'((Y)_1, y))$. Since we have $z \in (Y)_0 \leftrightarrow z = x$ and $z \in (Y)_1 \leftrightarrow z \in X$ for each z, we get $A'(X, x)$.

Turning now to the proof of the main claim, we let

$$B'(W) := \exists x(x \in (W)_0) \wedge \forall y(\neg(y \in (W)_0) \vee A''((W)_1, y))$$

and note that $B(W)$ is equivalent to $\neg B'(W)$. Since $\exists x(x \in (W)_0) \in \Pi^1_0$ and $\neg(y \in (W)_0) \in \Pi^1_0$ hold, we have $B'(W) \in \Pi^1_n(\mathsf{T})$ by the induction hypothesis for A'', i.e., there is some $C''(W) \in \Pi^1_n$ such that

$$\mathsf{T} \vdash C''(W) \leftrightarrow B'(W)$$

holds. Since $\neg C''(W)$ is logically equivalent to some formula $C'(W) \in \Sigma^1_n$, we finally get

$$\mathsf{T} \vdash C \leftrightarrow \forall x \forall X A'(X, x) \leftrightarrow \forall X B(X) \leftrightarrow \forall X \neg C''(X) \leftrightarrow \forall X C'(X)$$

4. For *universal quantification (for sets)* $C = \forall X A(X/V)$: Let $A'(U, V) \in \Sigma^1_n(\mathsf{T})$ and $A''(U, V) \in \Pi^1_n(\mathsf{T})$ be given for $A(V)$ with properties as indicated by $(*)$. Letting $C'(W) := A'((W)_0, (W)_1)$ yields $C'(W) \in \Sigma^1_n$ and we get $\mathsf{T} \vdash C \leftrightarrow \forall X C'(X)$ by making use of (ACA). □

Corollary 7.37. *Let* $k, n \in \mathbb{N}$ *and* $\mathsf{T} \in \{\mathsf{ACA}_0, \Sigma^1_1\text{-}\mathsf{AC}_0\}$. *Then we have*

$$\begin{aligned}&(A_0, \ldots, A_k \in \Pi^1_n(\mathsf{T}) \ \ \& \ \ B \in \Pi^1_{n+1}(\mathsf{T}))\\ &\quad\Longrightarrow \forall \vec{x}(A_0 \to \ldots \to A_k \to B) \in \Pi^1_{n+1}(\mathsf{T})\end{aligned}$$

Proof. Immediate by Proposition 7.36 and induction on $k \in \mathbb{N}$, while noting that $A_k \in \Pi^1_n(\mathsf{T})$ implies $\neg A_k \in \Pi^1_{n+1}(\mathsf{T})$, and that $A_k \to B$ is equivalent to $\neg A_k \vee B$. □

7.2.4. Embedding FIT into Π^1_3-RFN$_0$

In order to interpret within Π^1_3-RFN$_0$ the applicative part of FIT, i.e., **I.** in Definition 5.12, we shall first implement the so-called *canonical model* $\mathfrak{PR}$ for this applicative part. It is built upon ordinary recursion theory and by using indices of *partial recursive* functions for interpreting the function symbol $\cdot$ of $\mathcal{L}_{\mathsf{FIT}}$. For a thorough introduction to this construction and a more detailed treatment of the following (in a slightly different setting), we refer to [FJS]. Without going into detail, we let $\mathbf{T}$ be the ternary, primitive recursive relation $\mathbf{T}$ according to Kleene's Normal Form Theorem, and let $\mathbf{U}$ be the corresponding unary primitive recursive (result-extracting) function, and in the sense that $\exists x(\mathbf{T}(e, \langle n_1, \dots, n_k\rangle, x) \wedge \mathbf{U}(x) = m)$ for $e, k, m, n_1, \dots, n_k \in \mathbb{N}$ corresponds to the expression $\{e\}(n_1, \dots, n_k) \simeq m$ in the usual sense that $\{e\}$ denotes the partial recursive function indexed by the number e. Furthermore, let $\sqcap^1_1(x, y)$ with $x \neq y$ denote a universal Π^1_1 formula for Π^1_1 formulas that have one free variable, i.e., we have $\sqcap^1_1(x, y) \in \Pi^1_1$ and for each $\mathcal{L}^2_{\mathsf{PA}}$ formula $A \in \Pi^1_1$ with $\mathrm{FV}(A) = \{y\}$, we have that $\exists x \forall y(\sqcap^1_1(x, y) \leftrightarrow A)$ holds over ACA_0.[4]

Definition 7.38 (Interpretation of $\mathcal{L}_{\mathsf{FIT}}$ into $\mathcal{L}^2_{\mathsf{PA}}$)**.** In the abovementioned setting, we let $\mathbf{T}$ and $\mathbf{U}$ also denote the corresponding relation and function symbols in $\mathcal{L}_{\mathsf{PA}}$, and then we set

$$(\{a\}(b) \simeq c) := \exists x(\mathbf{T}(a, b, x) \wedge \mathbf{U}(x) = c)$$

Next, we assume an assignment of the constants k, s of $\mathcal{L}_{\mathsf{FIT}}$ to numerals $\mathsf{k}^\star, \mathsf{s}^\star$ that have corresponding properties over ACA_0 as described by the axiom group **I.1.** in definition 5.12. For the remaining constants $\mathsf{p}, \mathsf{p}_0, \mathsf{p}_1, 0, \mathsf{s}_\mathsf{N}, \mathsf{p}_\mathsf{N}, \mathsf{d}_\mathsf{N}$ of $\mathcal{L}_{\mathsf{FIT}}$, we set $\mathsf{p}^\star$ to be the numeral of the (primitive recursive) function $(m, n) \mapsto \langle m, n\rangle$; $\mathsf{p}^\star_i$ to be the numeral of $m \mapsto (m)_i$ for $i = 0, 1$; $0^\star$ to be 0; $\mathsf{s}^\star_\mathsf{N}$ to be the numeral of $m \mapsto m + 1$; $\mathsf{p}^\star_\mathsf{N}$ to be the numeral of $m \mapsto m \dot{-} 1$; and $\mathsf{d}^\star_\mathsf{N}$ to be the numeral of the case distinction function, mapping (k, l, m) to l if $k = 0$, otherwise to m. See also [FJS].

The translation $\mathrm{V}^\star_t(x)$ of a $\mathcal{L}_{\mathsf{FIT}}$ term t into the language of $\mathcal{L}_{\mathsf{PA}}$ is defined for variables $x \notin \mathrm{FV}(t)$ as follows:

$t = x$	if t is a variable
$t^\star = x$	if t is a constant
$\exists y, z(\mathrm{V}^\star_r(y) \wedge \mathrm{V}^\star_s(z) \wedge \{y\}(z) \simeq x)$	if t is of the form rs

and for each $\mathcal{L}_{\mathsf{FIT}}$ formula A, we let the $\mathcal{L}^2_{\mathsf{PA}}$ formula $A^\star$ be defined recursively on the build-up of A as follows for every $x \notin \mathrm{FV}(A)$ (while we shall provide the case where A is $t \in \mathsf{I}_{\mathbb{P},\mathbb{Q}}$ in ($\star$-$\mathsf{I}_{\mathbb{P},\mathbb{Q}}$) below):

[4] Bear in mind that this universal Π^1_1 formula shall include the unary relation symbol U of $\mathcal{L}_{\mathsf{PA}}$ as a parameter.

$\exists x(\mathrm{V}^\star_s(x) \wedge \mathrm{V}^\star_t(x))$	if A is of the form $s = t$
$\exists x(\mathrm{V}^\star_t(x))$	if A is of the form $t{\downarrow}$ or $t \in \mathsf{N}$
$\exists x(\mathrm{V}^\star_t(x) \wedge x \in \mathsf{U})$	if A is of the form $t \in \mathsf{U}$
$\mathrm{V}^\star_t(0) \wedge \neg\mathrm{V}^\star_t(0)$	if A is of the form $t \in \overline{\mathsf{N}}$ (see Lemma 7.39)
$\exists x(\mathrm{V}^\star_t(x) \wedge x \in X)$	if A is of the form $t \in X$
$\exists x(\mathrm{V}^\star_t(x) \wedge B^\star(z/x))$	if A is of the form $t \in \{z\colon B\}$ for $B \in \mathrm{For}^+$
$\neg(B^\star)$	if A is of the form $\neg B$
$B^\star \circ C^\star$	if A is of the form $B \circ C$ for $\circ \in \{\wedge, \vee, \rightarrow\}$
$QzB^\star$	if A is of the form QzB for $Q \in \{\forall, \exists\}$
$Qz(B^\star((\Lambda a.\Pi^1_1(z,a))/X))$	if A is of the form QXB for $Q \in \{\forall, \exists\}$

and for the case that A is of the form $t \in \mathsf{I}_{\mathbb{P},\mathbb{Q}}$, we introduce first the following positive operator form (for any $\mathbb{P}, \mathbb{Q} \in \mathrm{Ty}{\restriction}$)

$$\mathrm{Acc}^\star_{\mathbb{P},\mathbb{Q}} := \Lambda X \Lambda x.(x \in \mathbb{P})^\star \wedge \forall y((y \in \mathbb{P})^\star \rightarrow (\langle y, x\rangle \in \mathbb{Q})^\star \rightarrow y \in X)$$

and note that $\mathbb{P}, \mathbb{Q}$ do not contain expressions of the form $\mathsf{I}_{\mathbb{P}',\mathbb{Q}'}$. Eventually, we set

$$(t \in \mathsf{I}_{\mathbb{P},\mathbb{Q}})^\star := \forall X(\forall x(\mathrm{Acc}^\star_{\mathbb{P},\mathbb{Q}}(X,x) \rightarrow x \in X) \rightarrow (t \in X)^\star) \qquad (\star\text{-}\mathsf{I}_{\mathbb{P},\mathbb{Q}})$$

Furthermore, we tacitly assume in the definition of the translation $A^\star$ as usual a renaming of bound variables in order to avoid a clash of variables. Note also that the translation is meant to interpret type variables as Π^1_1 definable sets and that $\mathsf{I}_{\mathbb{P},\mathbb{Q}} \in \mathrm{Ty}$ implies that $\mathbb{P}, \mathbb{Q}$ do not contain type variables (since $\mathbb{P}, \mathbb{Q} \in \mathrm{Ty}{\restriction}$).

Lemma 7.39. *Let* $A \in \mathcal{L}_{\mathsf{FIT}}$, *then* $A^\star$ *and* A *have the same free variables.*

Proof. This is clear from the definition of $A^\star$, while note that it is due to this lemma that we defined $(t \in \overline{\mathsf{N}})^\star$ as $\mathrm{V}^\star_t(0) \wedge \neg\mathrm{V}^\star_t(0)$ instead as $\neg(0 = 0)$. □

Remark 7.40. For any $\mathbb{F} \in \mathrm{FT}$, consider the $\mathcal{L}^2_{\mathsf{PA}}$ class term $\mathcal{A} := \Lambda z.(tz \in \mathbb{F})^\star$. In order to make later arguments more readable, we shall make the translation of the $\mathcal{L}_{\mathsf{FIT}}$ formula $\mathrm{Cl}_{\mathbb{P},\mathbb{Q}}(\Lambda z.tz \in \mathbb{F})$ more explicit (cf., Notation 5.9):

$$\left.\begin{aligned}&(\mathrm{Cl}_{\mathbb{P},\mathbb{Q}}(\Lambda z.tz \in \mathbb{F}))^\star\\&= \begin{pmatrix}\forall x(x \in \mathbb{P} \wedge (\forall y \in \mathbb{P})(\langle y,x\rangle \in \mathbb{Q} \to ty \in \mathbb{F}))\\ \to tx \in \mathbb{F}\end{pmatrix}^\star\\&= \forall x(\mathrm{Acc}^\star_{\mathbb{P},\mathbb{Q}}(\mathcal{A},x) \to \mathcal{A}(x))\end{aligned}\right\} \qquad (\star\text{-}\mathrm{Cl}_{\mathbb{P},\mathbb{Q}})$$

As mentioned in Remark 5.10, we defined $\mathrm{Cl}_{\mathbb{P},\mathbb{Q}}(\Lambda z.tz \in \mathbb{F})$ in Chapter 5 in order to have the above representation that allows to use $\mathrm{Acc}^\star_{\mathbb{P},\mathbb{Q}}$ in a intuitive way. This correspondence would appear as directly as here in case we would have defined $\mathrm{Cl}_{\mathbb{P},\mathbb{Q}}(\Lambda z.tz \in \mathbb{F})$ for instance as

$$\forall x(x \in \mathbb{P} \to (\forall y \in \mathbb{P})(\langle y,x\rangle \in \mathbb{Q} \to ty \in \mathbb{F})) \to tx \in \mathbb{F}$$

Lemma 7.41. *Let $n \geq 0$. For each $\mathcal{L}_{\mathsf{FIT}}$ term t and each $\mathcal{L}_{\mathsf{PA}}$ term r, the following holds.*

(a) $\mathrm{V}^\star_t(x) \in \Pi^1_0$.

(b) $(t \in X)^\star \in \Pi^1_0 \ \& \ \big(\mathbb{P} \in \mathrm{Ty}{\restriction} \implies (t \in \mathbb{P})^\star \in \Pi^1_0\big)$.

(c) For $\mathsf{T} \in \{\mathsf{ACA}_0, \Sigma^1_1\text{-}\mathsf{AC}_0\}$, $\mathcal{B} := \Lambda a.B(a)$ *with* $B \in \mathcal{L}^2_{\mathsf{PA}}$, *and* $\mathbb{P},\mathbb{Q} \in \mathrm{Ty}{\restriction}$, *we have:*

$$B \in \Pi^1_n(\mathsf{T}) \implies \mathrm{Acc}^\star_{\mathbb{P},\mathbb{Q}}(\mathcal{B},r) \in \Pi^1_n(\mathsf{T})$$

In particular, we have $\mathrm{Acc}^\star_{\mathbb{P},\mathbb{Q}}(\mathcal{B},r) \in \Pi^1_0$ *in case of* $B \in \Pi^1_0$.

(d) $\mathbb{P},\mathbb{Q} \in \mathrm{Ty}{\restriction} \implies \big(\mathrm{Cl}_{\mathbb{P},\mathbb{Q}}(X)^\star \in \Pi^1_0 \ \& \ (t \in \mathsf{I}_{\mathbb{P},\mathbb{Q}})^\star \in \Pi^1_1\big)$.

(e) $A \in \mathrm{For}^+ \implies A^\star \in \Pi^1_1(\Sigma^1_1\text{-}\mathsf{AC}_0)$.

(f) $\mathbb{F} \in \mathrm{FT} \implies (t \in \mathbb{F})^\star \in \Pi^1_2(\Sigma^1_1\text{-}\mathsf{AC}_0)$.

Proof. For (a): This follows easily after inspecting the definition of $\mathrm{V}^\star_t(x)$. For (b): $(t \in X)^\star \in \Pi^1_0$ follows from (a). Given $\mathbb{P} \in \mathrm{Ty}{\restriction}$, we first note that then by definition, it can only be the case that $\mathbb{P}$ is N, $\overline{\mathsf{N}}$, or $\{x\colon A\}$ for some $A \in \mathrm{For}^+$ such that A does not contain any $\mathsf{I}_{\mathbb{P}',\mathbb{Q}'}$ expression or type variable. By (a) and Definition 7.38, one can easily verify that $(t \in \mathbb{P})^\star \in \Pi^1_0$ holds.

For (c): $\mathrm{Acc}^\star_{\mathbb{P},\mathbb{Q}}(\mathcal{B},r)$ translates to the formula

$$(r \in \mathbb{P})^\star \wedge \forall y((y \in \mathbb{P})^\star \to ((\langle y,x\rangle \in \mathbb{Q})^\star(r/x) \to y \in \mathcal{B})$$

and then the claim follows from Proposition 7.36 and (b), using the assumption $B \in \Pi^1_n(\mathsf{T})$ and that $\mathbb{P},\mathbb{Q} \in \mathrm{Ty}{\restriction}$ holds.

For (d): We have $\mathrm{Acc}^\star_{\mathbb{P},\mathbb{Q}}(X,x) \in \Pi^1_0$ by the second claim of (c), and further with (b) and after inspecting ($\star$-$\mathsf{I}_{\mathbb{P},\mathbb{Q}}$) on page 108 and ($\star$-$\mathrm{Cl}_{\mathbb{P},\mathbb{Q}}$) on page 109, the claim becomes clear.

For (e): We prove here a more general statement

$$\left.\begin{aligned} A \in \mathrm{For}^+ &\implies A^\star \in \Pi^1_1(\Sigma^1_1\text{-}\mathsf{AC}_0) \\ \neg A \in \mathrm{For}^+ &\implies \neg A^\star \in \Pi^1_1(\Sigma^1_1\text{-}\mathsf{AC}_0) \end{aligned}\right\} \tag{$*$}$$

and by induction on the build-up of the $\mathcal{L}_{\mathsf{FIT}}$ formula A. Now, let $A \in \mathrm{For}^+$ or $\neg A \in \mathrm{For}^+$ be given. Note that A cannot be of the form $\forall X A_0$ or $\exists X A_0$ because of the definition of For^+.

1. *Base case:* If A is of the form $t \in \mathsf{U}$, $t{\downarrow}$, or $s = t$, we have $A^\star \in \Pi^1_0$ and are done.
2. *Step case* $t \in \mathbb{P}$*:* If A is $t \in \mathbb{P}$ with $\mathbb{P} \in \mathrm{Ty}$, then $A \in \mathrm{For}^+$ must hold. Because of (b), we also only need to consider the case where $\mathbb{P} \notin \mathrm{Ty}{\restriction}$ and $\mathbb{P}$ is not a type variable. Hence, $\mathbb{P}$ is either of the form $\mathsf{I}_{\mathbb{P}',\mathbb{Q}'}$ with $\mathbb{P}',\mathbb{Q}' \in \mathrm{Ty}{\restriction}$ or $\mathbb{P}$ is of the form $\{z\colon B\}$ for some $B \in \mathrm{For}^+$.

In the first case, we get $A^\star \in \Pi^1_1(\Sigma^1_1\text{-}\mathsf{AC}_0)$ from (d). For the second case, recall that $(t \in \{z\colon B\})^\star$ equals

$$\exists x(\mathrm{V}^\star_t(x) \wedge B^\star(x/z)) \tag{7.19}$$

and note that by the induction hypothesis for $(*)$ with $B(x/z)$, we get $A_0(U,x) \in \Pi^1_0$ for some set variable U such that $B^\star(x/z)$ is equivalent to $\forall X A_0(X,x)$ over $\Sigma^1_1\text{-}\mathsf{AC}_0$. Hence (7.19) is equivalent to

$$\exists x \forall X(\mathrm{V}^\star_t(x) \wedge A_0(X,x)) \tag{7.20}$$

Letting $A_0'(W) := \exists x(\mathrm{V}_t^\star(x) \wedge A_0((W)_x, x))$, we get $\forall X A_0'(X) \in \Pi_1^1$ and it only remains to show that (7.20) and $\forall X A_0'(X)$ are equivalent over $\Sigma_1^1\text{-}\mathsf{AC}_0$, i.e.,

$$\Sigma_1^1\text{-}\mathsf{AC}_0 \vdash \exists x \forall X(\mathrm{V}_t^\star(x) \wedge A_0(X,x)) \leftrightarrow \forall X \exists x(\mathrm{V}_t^\star(x) \wedge A_0((X)_x, x)) \quad (**)$$

The "$\rightarrow$"-direction holds already over ACA_0: In order to show $A_0((X)_y, y)$ for some y for any given set X, take x that is given from the left-hand side of $(**)$. Then use (ACA) to get Z such that $z \in Z \leftrightarrow z \in (X)_x$ holds, then the left-hand side of $(**)$ yields $\mathrm{V}_t^\star(x) \wedge A_0(Z,x)$, i.e., $\mathrm{V}_t^\star(x) \wedge A_0((X)_x, x)$. For the "$\leftarrow$"-direction, we can work with the contraposition of $(**)$ and apply $(\Sigma_1^1\text{-}\mathsf{AC})$.
<u>**3.**</u> *Step case* $\forall, \exists$*:* If $A = \forall x A_0 \in \mathrm{For}^+$ holds, then $A^\star \in \Pi_1^1(\Sigma_1^1\text{-}\mathsf{AC}_0)$ is immediate from the induction hypothesis and Proposition 7.36. If $A = \exists x A_0 \in \mathrm{For}^+$ holds, then also $A_0 \in \mathrm{For}^+$ holds, and the induction hypothesis for $(*)$ with A_0 yields $A_0'(U,x) \in \Pi_0^1$ such that $A_0^\star$ is equivalent to $\forall X A_0'(X,x)$ over $\Sigma_1^1\text{-}\mathsf{AC}_0$. By letting $B(W) := \exists x A_0'((W)_x)$, we get

$$\Sigma_1^1\text{-}\mathsf{AC}_0 \vdash (\exists x A_0)^\star \leftrightarrow \exists x \forall X A_0'(X,x) \leftrightarrow \forall X B(X,x)$$

using a similar argument as before, and we have $\forall X B(X) \in \Pi_1^1$. In case that we have $\neg A \in \mathrm{For}^+$, the argument is analog to the case $A \in \mathrm{For}^+$.
<u>**4.**</u> *Step cases* $\neg, \rightarrow$*:* If A is $\neg A_0$, then we can use the induction hypothesis for $(*)$ with A_0. Similarly, this holds also for the case that A is $A_0 \rightarrow A_1$: We can work with $\neg A_0 \vee A_1$ and use that for instance in case of $A \in \mathrm{For}^+$, we have $\neg A_0, A_1 \in \mathrm{For}^+$, hence $\neg A_0^\star, A_1^\star \in \Pi_1^1(\Sigma_1^1\text{-}\mathsf{AC}_0)$. So by Proposition 7.36 also $\neg A_0^\star \vee A_1^\star \in \Pi_1^1(\Sigma_1^1\text{-}\mathsf{AC}_0)$ holds.
<u>**5.**</u> *Step cases* $\wedge, \vee$*:* If $A = A_0 \circ A_1 \in \mathrm{For}^+$ with $\circ \in \{\wedge, \vee\}$, then $A^\star \in \Pi_1^1(\Sigma_1^1\text{-}\mathsf{AC}_0)$ follows immediately from the induction hypothesis and Proposition 7.36. This holds analogously for the case $\neg A \in \mathrm{For}^+$.

For (f): We prove this for $\mathbb{F} \in \mathrm{FT}$ with $\mathbb{F} = \mathbb{P}_0 \rightarrow \ldots \rightarrow \mathbb{P}_n$ by induction on $n \in \mathbb{N}$: If $n = 0$ holds, then we have $\mathbb{F} \in \mathrm{Ty}$ and $(t \in \mathbb{F}) \in \mathrm{For}^+$, so we can use (e). If $n > 0$ holds, then let $\mathbb{F}' := \mathbb{P}_1 \rightarrow \ldots \rightarrow \mathbb{P}_n$. Now, $(t \in \mathbb{F})^\star$ translates to $\forall x((x \in \mathbb{P})^\star \rightarrow (tx \in \mathbb{F}')^\star)$. By (e) and the induction hypothesis, we get $(x \in \mathbb{P})^\star \in \Pi_1^1(\Sigma_1^1\text{-}\mathsf{AC}_0)$ and $(tx \in \mathbb{F}')^\star \in \Pi_2^1(\Sigma_1^1\text{-}\mathsf{AC}_0)$. By Corollary 7.37, we get $(t \in \mathbb{F})^\star \in \Pi_2^1(\Sigma_1^1\text{-}\mathsf{AC}_0)$. □

Theorem 7.42. Π^1_3-RFN_0 *proves* $A^\star$ *for every instance* A *of* (FT-ID).

Proof. Let A be an instance of (FT-ID), say

$$\mathrm{Cl}_{\mathbb{P},\mathbb{Q}}(\Lambda z.tz \in \mathbb{F}) \to t \in (\mathsf{I}_{\mathbb{P},\mathbb{Q}} \twoheadrightarrow \mathbb{F})$$

with $\mathbb{F} \in \mathrm{FT}$. Similar as in ($\star$-$\mathrm{Cl}_{\mathbb{P},\mathbb{Q}}$) on page 109, we have with $\mathcal{A} := \Lambda z.(tz \in \mathbb{F})^\star$ that $A^\star$ translates to

$$\forall x\big(\mathrm{Acc}^\star_{\mathbb{P},\mathbb{Q}}(\mathcal{A}, x) \to \mathcal{A}(x)\big) \to \forall x\big((x \in \mathsf{I}_{\mathbb{P},\mathbb{Q}})^\star \to \mathcal{A}(x)\big)$$

and therefore we assume (with a slight renaming of bound variables to make the following more readable) that

$$\forall y\big(\mathrm{Acc}^\star_{\mathbb{P},\mathbb{Q}}(\mathcal{A}, y) \to \mathcal{A}(y)\big) \tag{7.21}$$

holds. Due to Lemma 7.41.(f), we know that a formula $B \in \Pi^1_2$ exists such that

$$\Sigma^1_1\text{-}\mathsf{AC}_0 \vdash B \leftrightarrow \mathcal{A}(y)$$

holds. For $\mathcal{B} := \Lambda y.B$, we get from Corollary 7.37 and Lemma 7.41.(c) a formula $C \in \Pi^1_3$ such that

$$\mathsf{ACA}_0 \vdash C \leftrightarrow \forall y(\mathrm{Acc}^\star_{\mathbb{P},\mathbb{Q}}(\mathcal{B}, y) \to \mathcal{B}(y)) \tag{7.22}$$

holds. Note that this holds over ACA_0 since we work with $B \in \Pi^1_2$ instead of $(ty \in \mathbb{F})^\star$. Moreover, we have over Σ^1_1-AC_0 that (7.21) is equivalent to $\forall y(\mathrm{Acc}^\star_{\mathbb{P},\mathbb{Q}}(\mathcal{B}, y) \to \mathcal{B}(y))$ and we proceed now by assuming that the conclusion in $A^\star$ is false and will derive a contradiction from this. So, let a_0 be such that

$$(x \in \mathsf{I}_{\mathbb{P},\mathbb{Q}})^\star(a_0/x) \wedge \neg\mathcal{A}(a_0) \tag{7.23}$$

holds and note that the formula $\neg\mathcal{A}(a_0)$ (which is $\neg(tz \in \mathbb{F})^\star(a_0/z)$) is equivalent over Σ^1_1-AC_0 to $\neg B(a_0/y)$. Note that $\neg B(a_0/y)$ is equivalent to a Π^1_3 formula, and since we have $C \in \Pi^1_3$, there exists by Proposition 7.36 some $D \in \Pi^1_3$ that is provably equivalent over ACA_0 to $C \wedge \neg B(a_0/y)$. Then due to Corollary 7.31, we can work with Π^1_3-RFN_0 to apply (Π^1_3-RFN) to D and thus obtain an ω-model M of ACA_0 such that the following holds:

$$\forall y(\mathrm{Acc}^\star_{\mathbb{P},\mathbb{Q}}(\mathcal{B},y)^M \to \mathcal{B}(y)^M) \tag{7.24}$$

$$\neg B^M(a_0/y) \tag{7.25}$$

Relativization to M in (7.24) holds essentially because of the equivalence in (7.22) being provable over ACA_0. Now, (7.24) unfolds by Definition 7.21 and the build-up of $\mathrm{Acc}^\star_{\mathbb{P},\mathbb{Q}}(\mathcal{B},y)$ to

$$\forall y(\mathrm{Acc}^\star_{\mathbb{P},\mathbb{Q}}(\Lambda y.B^M,y) \to B^M) \tag{7.26}$$

Since B^M is arithmetical, (ACA) provides a set X_0 such that we have

$$\forall y(y \in X_0 \leftrightarrow B^M) \tag{7.27}$$

$$\forall y(\mathrm{Acc}^\star_{\mathbb{P},\mathbb{Q}}(X_0,y) \to y \in X_0) \tag{7.28}$$

Now, after recalling ($\star$-$\mathsf{I}_{\mathbb{P},\mathbb{Q}}$) on page 108, we instantiate $(x \in \mathsf{I}_{\mathbb{P},\mathbb{Q}})^\star(a_0/x)$ from (7.23) with X_0 and (7.28). We obtain then $(x \in X_0)^\star(a_0/x)$, i.e., $\exists z(\mathrm{V}^\star_x(z) \wedge z \in X_0)(a_0/x)$ which is equivalent to $a_0 \in X_0$ since $\mathrm{V}^\star_x(z)$ is just $x = z$. But then we get $B^M(a_0/y)$ by (7.27) which is a contradiction to (7.25) and we have proven the lemma. □

Remark 7.43. In the previous proof, we considered (7.26) as the pivotal property for the used proof method because it allowed us to internalize an argument withing the ω-model M. In particular, we needed that the positive operator form $\mathrm{Acc}^\star_{\mathbb{P},\mathbb{Q}}$ has the property described by Lemma 7.41.(c) with T being ACA_0. A conceptually similar proof in the setting of Π^1_2-RFN_0 and using similar standard results from the area of subsystems of second order arithmetic can be found in [AR10], treating the embedding of the theory ID^*_1 of positive induction into Π^1_2-RFN_0.

Now, turning to the question if our proof method would also work for arbitrary positive operator forms $\mathfrak{A}$, we point out that a direct embedding of TID into Π^1_3-RFN_0 can be carried out almost literally as the embedding of FIT into Π^1_3-RFN_0. More precisely, the previous lemmas can be reformulated in a very similar way so that they work for TID as well. The pivotal property to make the proof work would again correspond to (7.26), and essentially because Acc in the setting of TID has a similar bounded complexity as $\mathrm{Acc}^\star_{\mathbb{P},\mathbb{Q}}$ here. The latter means that for (7.22) in the proof of Theorem 7.42, we used that we had the property $\mathrm{Acc}^\star_{\mathbb{P},\mathbb{Q}}(\Lambda y.B,x) \in \Pi^1_2(\mathsf{ACA}_0)$ at hand for $B \in \Pi^1_2$, namely as provided by Lemma 7.41.(c).

Continuing from the perspective of TID, we shall consider for a moment its natural generalization $\mathsf{TID}^{\mathbf{f}}$ (where $\mathbf{f}$ stands for *full*) that allows for arbitrary arithmetical operator forms $\mathfrak{A}$. So, having $\mathfrak{A}$ instead of $\mathrm{Acc}^{\star}_{\mathbb{P},\mathbb{Q}}$ or Acc in (7.22), it would not always be possible to obtain a property such as $\mathfrak{A}(\mathcal{B}, x) \in \Pi^1_2(\mathsf{ACA}_0)$, nor can we expect that $G' \in \Pi^1_2$ exists that is equivalent over $\Sigma^1_1\text{-}\mathsf{AC}_0$ or $\Pi^1_3\text{-}\mathsf{RFN}_0$ to $\mathfrak{A}(\mathcal{B}, x)$. Comparing this with the mentioned embedding of ID^*_1 into $\Pi^1_2\text{-}\mathsf{RFN}_0$ from [AR10], we note that essentially only Π^1_1 formulas B needed to be considered there, and since a formula such as $\mathfrak{A}(\Lambda z.B, t)$ can be proven to be equivalent over $\Sigma^1_1\text{-}\mathsf{AC}_0$ to a Π^1_1 formula G', one can continue the proof with this G'.

For an embedding of $\mathsf{TID}^{\mathbf{f}}$ into $\Pi^1_3\text{-}\mathsf{RFN}_0$ where we cannot control anymore the syntactical complexity of the positive operator forms $\mathfrak{A}$, we apparently cannot directly apply the method of this section. As we shall describe in the conclusion of Chapter 7 (see Section 7.4), we remark here that the desired upper bound for $\mathsf{TID}^{\mathbf{f}}$ can be obtained by turning to the setting of set-theory.

Theorem 7.44. *Over* $\Pi^1_3\text{-}\mathsf{RFN}_0$*, the following holds.*

(a) $A^\star$ *holds for every formula* A *from axiom group* ***I.*** *of* FIT.

(b) $A^\star$ *holds for every instance* A *of the* N*-induction scheme* (FT-Ind) *of* FIT.

(c) $A^\star$ *holds for every instance* A *of the comprehension scheme* (CA^+) *of* FIT.

(d) $A^\star$ *holds for every instance* A *of the closure axiom* (FT-Cl) *of* FIT.

Proof. For (a): Note that according to Definition 7.38, the type N has no special role in the translation $A^\star$ of any of the formulas A given in the axiom group **I.** of FIT. As mentioned in Definition 7.38, we assume a standard interpretation of the constants k and s with the properties that we need for such a translation to be adequate. It is well-known that the combinators are available as partial recursive functions in the sense given here. Moreover, it is also more or less obvious that the interpretation of the remaining constants has the properties needed to make the translation of the remaining formulas in axiom group **I.** go through.

For (b): Over ACA_0, we have that (Π^1_3-RFN) implies transfinite induction for Π^1_2 formulas, and thus complete induction along the natural numbers for Π^1_2 formulas. For this, see in [Sim09] Theorem VIII.5.12 and in particular Exercise VIII.5.15, while noting there that Σ^1_4-RFN_0 is equivalent to Π^1_3-RFN_0. Now, let A be an instance $t0 \in \mathbb{F} \wedge (\forall x \in \mathsf{N})(tx \in \mathbb{F} \rightarrow tx' \in \mathbb{F}) \rightarrow t \in (\mathsf{N} \twoheadrightarrow \mathbb{F})$ of the N-induction scheme (FT-Ind) of FIT, where $\mathbb{F} \in \mathrm{FT}$ holds. By setting $\mathcal{B} := \Lambda z.(tz \in \mathbb{F})^\star$, we have that $A^\star$ is equivalent over ACA_0 to

$$\mathcal{B}(0) \wedge \forall x(\mathcal{B}(x) \rightarrow \mathcal{B}(x+1)) \rightarrow \forall x(\exists y(\mathrm{V}^\star_x(y)) \rightarrow \mathcal{B}(x)) \tag{7.29}$$

since $\mathcal{B}(x+1)$ is equivalent to $(t(\mathsf{s_N}x) \in \mathbb{F})^\star$. For the latter, note that $(t(\mathsf{s_N}x) \in \mathbb{F})^\star$ is $\exists y(\mathrm{V}^\star_{t(\mathsf{s_N}x)}(y) \wedge (y \in \mathbb{F})^\star)$ and that this is equivalent to

$$\exists y, z_1, z_2(\mathrm{V}^\star_t(z_1) \wedge \{\mathsf{s}^\star_\mathsf{N}\}(x) \simeq z_2 \wedge \{z_1\}(z_2) \simeq y \wedge (y \in \mathbb{F})^\star)$$

which again simplifies to

$$\exists y, z_1(\mathrm{V}^\star_t(z_1) \wedge \{z_1\}(x+1) \simeq y \wedge (y \in \mathbb{F})^\star)$$

and this is equivalent to $\mathcal{B}(x+1)$. Now arguing over Π^1_3-RFN_0, we have that (7.29) is equivalent to an instance of complete induction along the natural numbers for a Π^1_2 formula (use Lemma 7.41.(f)) and hence we are done.

For (c): Let A be an instance of (CA^+), say $y \in \{x\colon B\} \leftrightarrow B(y/x)$ with $B \in \mathrm{For}^+$. Then, $A^\star$ yields

$$\exists x(\mathrm{V}^\star_y(x) \wedge B^\star) \leftrightarrow (B(y/x))^\star$$

which is equivalent to $(B(y/x))^\star \leftrightarrow (B(y/x))^\star$ and hence a tautology.

For (d): Let $A := \mathrm{Cl}_{\mathbb{P},\mathbb{Q}}(\Lambda z.z \in \mathsf{I}_{\mathbb{P},\mathbb{Q}})$ be an instance of (FT-Cl). Following ($\star$-$\mathrm{Cl}_{\mathbb{P},\mathbb{Q}}$) on page 109 and in order to show $A^\star$, assume for $\mathcal{A} := \Lambda z.(z \in \mathsf{I}_{\mathbb{P},\mathbb{Q}})^\star$ that we have $\mathrm{Acc}^\star_{\mathbb{P},\mathbb{Q}}(\mathcal{A}, z_0)$ for some z_0, and we aim to prove $\mathcal{A}(z_0)$, i.e.,

$$\big(\forall X(\forall x(\mathrm{Acc}^\star_{\mathbb{P},\mathbb{Q}}(X,x) \rightarrow x \in X) \rightarrow (z \in X)^\star)\big)(z_0/z)$$

and in order to prove this, let X_0 be given such that

$$\forall x(\mathrm{Acc}^\star_{\mathbb{P},\mathbb{Q}}(X_0,x) \rightarrow x \in X_0) \tag{7.30}$$

holds and show $z_0 \in X_0$. We have $\forall z((z \in \mathsf{I}_{\mathbb{P},\mathbb{Q}})^\star \to z \in X_0)$ due to (7.30) and the definition of $(z \in \mathsf{I}_{\mathbb{P},\mathbb{Q}})^\star$, i.e., we have $\forall z(\mathcal{A}(z) \to z \in X_0)$. So, the latter yields

$$\mathrm{Acc}^\star_{\mathbb{P},\mathbb{Q}}(\mathcal{A}, z_0) \to \mathrm{Acc}^\star_{\mathbb{P},\mathbb{Q}}(X_0, z_0)$$

because $\mathrm{Acc}^\star_{\mathbb{P},\mathbb{Q}}$ is a *positive* operator form. We hence get $\mathrm{Acc}^\star_{\mathbb{P},\mathbb{Q}}(X_0, z_0)$ from our assumption $\mathrm{Acc}^\star_{\mathbb{P},\mathbb{Q}}(\mathcal{A}, z_0)$, and with (7.30) we are done. □

Corollary 7.45 (Embedding FIT into Π^1_3-RFN_0). *Let $A \in \mathcal{L}_{\mathsf{FIT}}$. Then we have*

$$\mathsf{FIT} \vdash A \implies \Pi^1_3\text{-}\mathsf{RFN}_0 \vdash A^\star$$

Proof. Let A be any $\mathcal{L}_{\mathsf{FIT}}$ formula. Due to Theorems 7.42 and 7.44, it remains only to show that the logical part of FIT embeds into Π^1_3-RFN_0 in the following sense:

$$\mathsf{LPT} \vdash A \implies \Pi^1_3\text{-}\mathsf{RFN}_0 \vdash A^\star$$

Assume $\mathsf{LPT} \vdash A$ with respect to any sound Hilbert calculus that may have been chosen in Definition 5.11. We prove Π^1_3-$\mathsf{RFN}_0 \vdash A^\star$ by induction on the definition of the derivability notion $\mathsf{LPT} \vdash A$. It is clear from Definition 7.38 that the translation of the propositional axioms and rules are derivable in the setting of $\mathcal{L}^2_{\mathsf{PA}}$. Similarly, the equality axioms and the translation of the quantificational axioms and rules for individual variables is stable, while the definedness axioms become trivial.

Now, we consider the remaining quantificational axioms and rules for type variables, we have the following cases (and given $\mathcal{L}_{\mathsf{FIT}}$ formulas A, B):
1. For axiom $A := \forall X B \to B(\mathbb{P}/X)$: Then $A^\star$ is

$$\forall z(B^\star((\Lambda a.\sqcap^1_1(z,a))/X)) \to B^\star(\Lambda a.(a \in \mathbb{P})^\star/X)$$

and the claim follows due to $(a \in \mathbb{P})^\star \in \Pi^1_1(\Sigma^1_1\text{-}\mathsf{AC}_0)$ from Lemma 7.41.(e) and since $\sqcap^1_1(x,y)$ denotes a universal Π^1_1 formula.
2. For axiom $A := B(\mathbb{P}/X) \to \exists X B$: Use the contraposition of A and argue as in the previous case.

3. For the logical rule

$$\frac{A \to B}{A \to \forall X B}$$

with X not occurring free in A, we get $\Pi^1_3\text{-}\mathsf{RFN}_0 \vdash A^\star \to B^\star$ form the induction hypothesis. Since the underlying calculus for $\Pi^1_3\text{-}\mathsf{RFN}_0$ from Definition 1.9 is closed under substitution and X does not occurring in A, we obtain $\Pi^1_3\text{-}\mathsf{RFN}_0 \vdash A^\star \to B^\star\big((\Lambda a.\sqcap^1_1(z,a))/X\big)$. If we further let $z \in \mathrm{FV}(A^\star)$, we eventually get $A^\star \to \forall z(B^\star\big((\Lambda a.\sqcap^1_1(z,a))/X\big))$.
4. For the logical rule

$$\frac{B \to A}{\exists X B \to A}$$

with X not occurring free in A, this holds similarly. □

7.3. Considering $\mathsf{TID^f}$ for General Positive Operator Forms

With regard to the upper-bound results, we embedded FIT into a subsystem of second order arithmetic, while exploiting the Π^1_1 definability of a least fixed-point in such a setting. However, it is more or less apparent that we can embed TID analogously via ω-model reflection[5], this approach seems to fail if we extend TID to a theory $\mathsf{TID^f}$ for general typed inductive definitions with the *full* range of positive arithmetical operator forms (as described in Remark 7.43). A way to avoid this obstacle is to shift the setting to set-theory rather than subsystems of second order arithmetic, namely by exploiting the Σ_1 definability of a least fixed-point. Working then in $\mathsf{KP}\omega^- + \Pi_2\text{-}\mathsf{Found}$ from [Rat92] (i.e., Kripke-Platek set-theory with a restricted axiom scheme for foundation) shall suffice to get an analog result as for FIT which we can apply to the theory $\mathsf{TID^f}$. Summing up, what we gain from these embeddings is that extending TID to the theory $\mathsf{TID^f}$ retains the proof-theoretic upper bound $\vartheta\Omega^\omega$ because $\mathsf{KP}\omega^- + \Pi_2\text{-}\mathsf{Found}$ has the same proof-theoretic strength as $\Pi^1_2\text{-}\mathsf{BI}_0$ according to [Rat92]. Since TID trivially embeds into $\mathsf{TID^f}$ and as depicted in figure 2, we get that $\mathsf{TID^f}$

[5] Instead of taking the detour via an intermediate embedding into FIT, see also Sections 8.3 and Chapter 9.

has the same proof-theoretic strength as TID (in a similar way as ID_1 corresponds to $\mathsf{ID}_1(\mathrm{Acc})$, i.e., to its restriction to accessible part arithmetical operator forms, see also [BFPS81]).

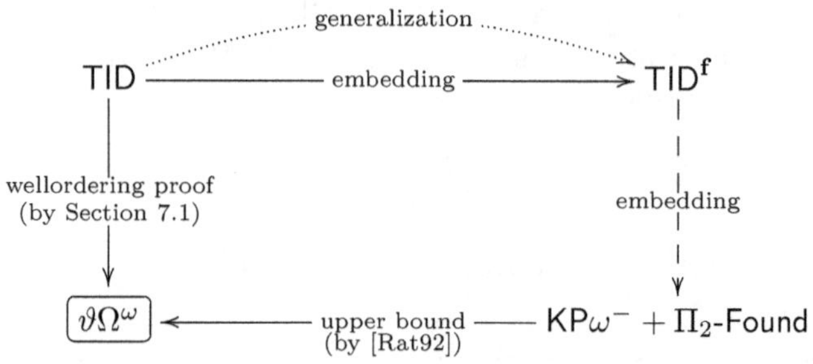

Figure 2.: Generalization of TID to the full theory $\mathsf{TID}^{\mathbf{f}}$

We finish with some conjectures on how to extend the proof-methods from sections 7.1 and 7.2 in order to analyze stronger systems: First, the collections of formulas Pos_0 and Pos_1 already suggest a generalization to collections Pos_n for any $n \geq 2$ in the sense that the correspondence of Pos_1 to *function* types of the form $\mathbb{P}_1 \twoheadrightarrow \ldots \twoheadrightarrow \mathbb{P}_k$ for each $k \in \mathbb{N}$ (i.e., "*level-1-functional* types") passes over to Pos_2 being in correspondence to *level-2-functional* types $\mathbb{F}_1 \twoheadrightarrow \ldots \twoheadrightarrow \mathbb{F}_k$ for each $k \in \mathbb{N}$, and similarly for $n > 2$. Accompanied by this and in particular for Pos_2, the transition from using Klammersymbols instead of finitary Veblen functions and the use of a higher-type functional for iterating the fixed-point construction on Klammersymbols allows to extend the ordinal notation system. Endowed with stronger induction principles (e.g., extending (Ind) and (TID) to induction formulas from Pos_2 instead of Pos_1), this may lead towards higher ordinals via wellordering proofs based on the accessible part of the primitive recursive ordering of the new ordinal notation system.

7.4. Notes

In short, we obtained theories FIT and TID that both have the small Veblen ordinal $\vartheta\Omega^\omega$ as their proof-theoretic ordinal, while FIT is a natural extension of Feferman's two-sorted theory $\mathrm{QL}(\mathsf{F}_0\text{-}\mathsf{IR}_N)$ from [Fef92] and TID becomes from this perspective a natural subsystem of ID_1. Moreover, we used techniques from the realm of predicative proof-theory in order to obtain a wellordering proof for TID (and hence for FIT). Th. Strahm gave the first ideas towards a suitable way of carrying out wellordering proofs, in particular the idea to consider [Fef92] stems from him. He also drew our attention to working with $\Pi^1_3\text{-}\mathsf{RFN}_0$ for the treatment of the upper bound of FIT.

8. TID_n and TID_n^+ as Generalizations of TID

Aiming for an internalization of the wellordering proof for the system TID from Chapter 7 that reaches up to the small Veblen ordinal, we shall introduce in this chapter a theory TID_1^+ which in Chapter 11 will turn out to be a very natural framework for carrying out wellordering proofs in the context of Klammersymbols and hence reaching up to the large Veblen ordinal $\vartheta\Omega^\Omega$. This shall lead to the following generic definition of families of theories TID_n and TID_n^+ for each $n \in \mathbb{N}$ where TID_1 essentially corresponds to TID. Furthermore and motivated by Corollary 7.37, we shall adapt the notion Pos_1 to $\mathrm{Pos}_1^{\rightarrow}$ and in general to $\mathrm{Pos}_n^{\rightarrow}$ for $n \in \mathbb{N}$.

8.1. The Arithmetical Theories TID_n and TID_n^+

Definition 8.1.

(a) $\mathrm{Pos}_0^{\rightarrow}$ denotes the collection of $\mathcal{L}_{\mathsf{TID}}$ formulas that contain each $P_\triangleleft$ at most positively.

(b) $\mathrm{Pos}_n^{\rightarrow}$ for each $n \geq 1$ is inductively defined as follows:

$$A \in \mathrm{Pos}_{n-1}^{\rightarrow} \implies A \in \mathrm{Pos}_n^{\rightarrow} \qquad (\mathrm{Pos}^{\rightarrow}\text{-Base})$$

$$\left.\begin{array}{l} A_0, \ldots, A_k \in \mathrm{Pos}_{n-1}^{\rightarrow} \,\&\, B \in \mathrm{Pos}_n^{\rightarrow} \\ \quad \implies \forall \vec{x}(A_0 \to \ldots \to A_k \to B) \in \mathrm{Pos}_n^{\rightarrow} \end{array}\right\} \qquad (\mathrm{Pos}^{\rightarrow}\text{-Cons})$$

for all $k \in \mathbb{N}$ and all (possibly empty) lists of variables $\vec{x}$.

For $n \in \mathbb{N}$, we write $\Lambda a.A \in \mathrm{Pos}_n^{\rightarrow}$ in order to denote $A \in \mathrm{Pos}_n^{\rightarrow}$, respectively.

Definition 8.2. For each $n \in \mathbb{N}$, we define the following:

(a) TID_n is the theory that arises from the axioms of Peano arithmetic PA without complete induction by adding the following axioms and axiom schemes

$$
\begin{array}{rl}
(\mathsf{Ind}_n) & \mathcal{B}(0) \wedge \forall x(\mathcal{B}(x) \to \mathcal{B}(\mathbf{S}x)) \to \forall x \mathcal{B}(x) \\
& \text{for } \mathcal{B} \in \mathrm{Pos}_n^{\rightarrow} \\
(\mathsf{Cl}) & \mathrm{Prog}_{\lhd}(P_{\lhd}) \qquad (\text{i.e., } \forall x(\mathrm{Acc}_{\lhd}(P_{\lhd}, x) \to P_{\lhd}x)) \\
& \text{for } \lhd \text{ being a binary relation symbol in } \mathcal{L}_{\mathsf{PA}} \\
(\mathsf{TID}_n) & \mathrm{Prog}_{\lhd}(\mathcal{B}) \to \forall x(P_{\lhd}x \to \mathcal{B}(x)) \\
& \text{for } \mathcal{B} \in \mathrm{Pos}_n^{\rightarrow} \text{ and } \lhd \text{ a binary relation symbol in } \mathcal{L}_{\mathsf{PA}}
\end{array}
$$

where (Cl) is called *closure* and (TID_n) is called *n-typed inductive definition.*

(b) $\mathsf{TID}_n + (\mathsf{Ind}_k)$ for $k > n$ is obtained from TID_n by exchanging the axiom scheme (Ind_n) by (Ind_k).

Definition 8.3.

(a) $\mathsf{TID}_\bullet^+$ is obtained from Peano arithmetic PA by adding the axioms

$$
\begin{array}{rl}
(\mathsf{Nat}) & \forall x(P_{<_{\mathbb{N}}}x) \\
(\mathsf{Cl}) & \mathrm{Prog}_{\lhd}(P_{\lhd}) \\
& \text{for each binary relation symbol } \lhd \text{ in } \mathcal{L}_{\mathsf{PA}}
\end{array}
$$

and the following rule of inference:

$$
(\mathsf{TID}^+)\ \frac{P_{\lhd}t}{\mathrm{Prog}_{\lhd}(\mathcal{B}) \to \mathcal{B}(t)}
$$

for each $\mathcal{B} \in \mathcal{L}_{\mathsf{TID}}$ (i.e., for *arbitrary* $\mathcal{L}_{\mathsf{TID}}$ class terms), each binary relation symbol $\lhd$ in $\mathcal{L}_{\mathsf{PA}}$, and each term t.

(b) $\mathsf{TID}_n^+ := \mathsf{TID}_\bullet^+ + (\mathsf{TID}_n)$ is obtained from $\mathsf{TID}_\bullet^+$ by adding the axiom scheme (TID_n).

Remark 8.4. The axiom (Nat) axiomatizes that the accessible part $P_{<_{\mathbb{N}}}$ of the $<_{\mathbb{N}}$-relation consists of all the natural numbers.

Lemma 8.5. *For each* $\mathcal{B} \in \mathcal{L}_{\mathsf{TID}}$*, we have*

$$\mathsf{TID}_\bullet^+ \vdash \mathcal{B}(0) \wedge \forall x(\mathcal{B}(x) \to \mathcal{B}(\mathbf{S}x)) \to \forall x(\mathcal{B}(x))$$

Proof. Note first that we have $\mathsf{TID}_\bullet^+ \vdash \forall x(P_{<_\mathbb{N}} x)$ because of (Nat), so we get $P_{<_\mathbb{N}} x$ for any x and can then use (TID^+) to get $\mathrm{Prog}_{<_\mathbb{N}}(\mathcal{B}) \to \mathcal{B}(x)$ for each $\mathcal{B} \in \mathcal{L}_{\mathsf{TID}}$. Now, ($\forall$-intro) from Definition 1.9 yields $\mathrm{Prog}_{<_\mathbb{N}}(\mathcal{B}) \to \forall x(\mathcal{B}(x))$ which is equivalent to $\mathcal{B}(0) \wedge \forall x(\mathcal{B}(x) \to \mathcal{B}(\mathbf{S}x)) \to \forall x(\mathcal{B}(x))$. Note for the latter that $\mathsf{TID}_\bullet^+$ includes PA, so we have in particular $\forall x(x = 0 \vee \exists y(x = \mathbf{S}y))$. □

Theorem 8.6. *For each* $A \in \mathcal{L}_{\mathsf{TID}}$ *and* $n \in \mathbb{N}$*, we have the following:*

$$\mathsf{TID}_n \vdash A \quad \Longrightarrow \quad \mathsf{TID}_n^+ \vdash A$$

Proof. This follows from Lemma 8.5. □

Remark 8.7. As for TID in Remark 6.7, it is clear that the following properties hold over TID_n and TID_n^+ for all $n \in \mathbb{N}$ (while note that (TID_0) is always available in TID_n and TID_n^+):

- For any binary relation symbol $\lhd$ in $\mathcal{L}_{\mathsf{PA}}$, we may identify (CI) with a fixed-point principle

$$(\mathsf{FP}) \qquad \forall x(P_\lhd x \leftrightarrow \mathrm{Acc}_\lhd(P_\lhd, x))$$

  and therefore we will sometimes use (CI) to ambiguously mean (FP).

- We can use instead of the formula from Lemma 8.5 also the following course-of-value variant of complete induction for $\mathcal{L}_{\mathsf{TID}}$ formulas, i.e., we have

$$\forall x(\forall x_0 <_\mathbb{N} x\mathcal{B}(x_0) \to \mathcal{B}(x)) \to \forall x\mathcal{B}(x)$$

  as an induction principle for all $\mathcal{B} \in \mathcal{L}_{\mathsf{TID}}$.

Convention 8.8. We may use (Ind_n) in $\mathsf{TID}_\bullet^+$ for all $n \in \mathbb{N}$ or its course-of-value variant without always mentioning Lemma 8.5.

8.2. Alternative Definition of TID_n

Let TID_n^- be the theory that is obtained from PA by adding the axioms (Nat) and (Cl) from $\mathsf{TID}_\bullet^+$ and the axiom scheme (TID_n) from TID_n, i.e.,

$$\mathsf{TID}_n^- := \mathsf{PA} + (\mathsf{Nat}) + (\mathsf{Cl}) + (\mathsf{TID}_n)$$

Then we can derive (Ind_n) in TID_n^- from (TID_n) and (Nat) in a similar way as in the proof of Lemma 8.5. Hence, we get that TID_n^- and TID_n are equivalent. We decided not to use TID_n^-, leaving the definition of TID_n as it is, because we wanted to keep the resemblance of TID_n to the theory $\mathsf{ID}_1^* \restriction$ from the introduction of this thesis as it is.

We shall see in Chapter 9, when determining the upper bound of $|\mathsf{TID}_n^+|$, that the interpretation of (TID^+) into the language $\mathcal{L}^2_{\mathsf{PA}}$ and the setting of subsystems of second order arithmetic corresponds to a form of bar rule[1] which allows to use set induction (from Definition 7.24) to derive complete induction for all $\mathcal{L}^2_{\mathsf{PA}}$ formulas, so this fits to the result of Lemma 8.5 (see also Section 9.3). Moreover, the upper bound result of Chapter 9 suggests that the strength of TID_n^+ is essentially given by adding (TID_n) to $\mathsf{TID}_\bullet^+$.

With respect to the wellordering proof of TID_1^+ in Chapter 11, we shall actually only use (Ind_2) and not the full strength of Lemma 8.5. We shall also only need such instances of (TID^+) where $\mathcal{B} \in \mathrm{Pos}_2^{\rightarrow}$ holds (instead of arbitrary $\mathcal{B} \in \mathcal{L}_{\mathsf{TID}}$), and we remark here that we included the rule (TID^+) for arbitrary $\mathcal{B} \in \mathcal{L}_{\mathsf{TID}}$ because on the one hand, the definition of TID_1^+ (and TID_n^+ in general) becomes simpler and more perspicuous, and on the other hand because of the upper bound result in Chapter 9.

8.3. Comparison of TID with the Theory TID_1

The applicative theory FIT that was introduced in Chapter 7 has the small Veblen ordinal $\vartheta\Omega^\omega$ as its proof-theoretic ordinal, and it influenced the definition of an arithmetical theory TID based on accessible part inductive definitions of primitive recursive binary relations. TID_1 is essentially the theory TID from Chapter 7.

[1] See for instance [FJ83] for a definition of the bar rule.

For the one direction, recall that we get for Pos_1 in Chapter 7 that $\mathcal{B} \in \mathrm{Pos}_1$ implies $\mathcal{B} \in \mathrm{Pos}_1^{\rightarrow}$. Note in particular the situation where we have

$$\mathcal{B} = \Lambda a.\forall\vec{x}(A_1 \rightarrow A_2) \;\;\&\;\; a \notin \mathrm{FV}(A_2) \;\;\&\;\; A_1, A_2 \in \mathrm{Pos}_0$$

and note that $A_1, A_2 \in \mathrm{Pos}_0$ is equivalent to $A_1, A_2 \in \mathrm{Pos}_0^{\rightarrow}$.

For the other direction, we get for each $\Lambda a.B \in \mathrm{Pos}_1^{\rightarrow}$ that some formula B' exists that is logically equivalent to B and such that $\Lambda a.B' \in \mathrm{Pos}_1$ holds. This is due to the following observation regarding Definition 8.1 and arguing by induction on the built-up $\Lambda a.B$:

- If $\Lambda a.B \in \mathrm{Pos}_1^{\rightarrow}$ is due to ($\mathrm{Pos}^{\rightarrow}$-Base), this is clear because Pos_0 and $\mathrm{Pos}_0^{\rightarrow}$ consist of the same formulas.

- If $\Lambda a.B \in \mathrm{Pos}_1^{\rightarrow}$ is due to ($\mathrm{Pos}^{\rightarrow}$-Cons), then B is

  $$\forall\vec{x}(A_0 \rightarrow \ldots \rightarrow A_k \rightarrow C)$$

  and we can use the induction hypothesis to get C'' with $\Lambda a.C'' \in \mathrm{Pos}_1$ and that is logically equivalent to C. Moreover, we have $A_0, \ldots, A_k \in \mathrm{Pos}_0$.

  In case of $C'' \in \mathrm{Pos}_0$, we can set $A'' := A_0 \wedge \ldots \wedge A_k$ and $B'' := \forall\vec{x}(A'' \rightarrow C'')$ which is logically equivalent to B due to an *uncurrying* argument. If the variable condition $a \notin \mathrm{FV}(A'')$ does not already hold, then let y be some fresh variable, set $A' := A''(y/a)$ and $C' := (y = a \rightarrow C'')$ and note that $A', C' \in \mathrm{Pos}_0$ holds with $a \notin \mathrm{FV}(A')$. It is now easy to see that $B' := \forall y\forall\vec{x}(A' \rightarrow C')$ is logically equivalent to B'' (hence also to B) and that $B' \in \mathrm{Pos}_1$ holds.

  In case of $C'' \notin \mathrm{Pos}_0$, we have that C'' is $\forall\vec{y}(C''_0 \rightarrow C''_1)$ such that $a \notin \mathrm{FV}(C''_0)$ and $C''_0, C''_1 \in \mathrm{Pos}_0$ hold. By setting $A'' := C''_0 \wedge A_0 \wedge \ldots \wedge A_k$ and $B'' := \forall\vec{x}\forall\vec{y}(A'' \rightarrow C''_1)$, we can argue as in the case $C'' \in \mathrm{Pos}_0$.

We used in Chapter 7 the variant with $\mathcal{B} \in \mathrm{Pos}_1$ (instead of $\mathcal{B} \in \mathrm{Pos}_1^{\rightarrow}$) in order have a more natural correspondence of TID to the applicative theory FIT, and also because this simplified the embedding of TID into FIT from Chapter 6.

8.4. Notes

The first idea of extending the theory TID was to strengthen the induction axiom (Ind). This emerged directly after observing the wellordering proof for TID, and this seemed necessary in particular for being able to internalize the proofs in Chapter 7 (note also Remark 7.19). The internalization of the wellordering proof of TID seemed to provide a local combinatorial property which can be generalized in a canonical way, and where the induction axiom (Ind_2) seemed strong enough to carry this. Though, in order to exploit this generalized combinatorial property and being able to push it forward in the framework of Klammersymbols, we needed to enhance (TID) by (TID_2) but it seemed a bit too strong. Now, by considering (TID_2) as a *rule*, we obtain in Chapter 11 a desired result for the ordinal notation system based on Klammersymbols, i.e., the *large Veblen ordinal* $\vartheta\Omega^\Omega$. The idea for this came from Th. Strahm. He also pointed towards a formulation of the rule (TID^+) where arbitrary $\mathcal{B} \in \mathcal{L}_{\mathsf{TID}}$ may occur in its formulation, hence allowing for an interpretation in $\mathcal{L}^2_{\mathsf{PA}}$ as a kind of bar rule. The theories TID_n and TID_n^+ then emerged naturally from the definitions of TID_1^+ and TID_2.

9. Embedding for TID_n and Derivability for TID_n^+

In this chapter, we shall determine upper bounds for the proof-theoretic ordinals of the theories TID_n and TID_n^+ for each $n \in \mathbb{N}$.

Definition 9.1 (Π^1_1 interpretation of $P_\triangleleft$)**.** For every $A \in \mathcal{L}_{\mathsf{TID}}$, we define $A^\star$ as the *interpretation of A in $\mathcal{L}^2_{\mathsf{PA}}$* by exchanging in A any occurrence of atomic formulas of the form $P_\triangleleft t$ for some $\triangleleft$ by

$$\begin{aligned}(P_\triangleleft t)^\star &:= \forall X(\mathrm{Prog}_\triangleleft(X) \to t \in X)\\ &= \forall X(\forall x(\mathrm{Acc}_\triangleleft(X,x) \to x \in X) \to t \in X)\\ &= \forall X(\forall x(\forall y(y \triangleleft x \to y \in X) \to x \in X) \to t \in X)\end{aligned}$$

and leaving everything else unchanged.

Notation 9.2. For each $\mathcal{A} := \Lambda a.A$ with $A \in \mathcal{L}_{\mathsf{TID}}$ and each $P_\triangleleft \in \mathcal{L}_{\mathsf{TID}}$, we use the following notation:

$$\begin{aligned}\mathcal{A}^\star &:= \Lambda a.A^\star\\ P^\star_\triangleleft(t) &:= (P_\triangleleft t)^\star\end{aligned}$$

Remark 9.3.

(a) For each $\mathcal{B} \in \mathcal{L}_{\mathsf{TID}}$, we have that $(\mathrm{Acc}_\triangleleft(\mathcal{B},t))^\star$ equals

$$\mathrm{Acc}_\triangleleft(\mathcal{B}^\star, t)$$

because of the definition of $\mathrm{Acc}_\triangleleft$.

(b) For each $\mathcal{B} \in \mathcal{L}^2_{\mathsf{PA}}$, we have that $\mathcal{B}^\star$ equals $\mathcal{B}$.

Lemma 9.4. *Let $n \in \mathbb{N}$ and $\mathsf{T} \in \{\mathsf{ACA}_0, \Sigma^1_1\text{-}\mathsf{AC}_0\}$. Then we have the following:*

(a) $(P_{\lhd}t)^\star \in \Pi^1_1$.

(b) $B \in \Pi^1_n(\mathsf{T}) \implies \mathrm{Acc}_{\lhd}(\Lambda a.B, t) \in \Pi^1_n(\mathsf{T})$.

(c) $B \in \mathrm{Pos}^{\rightarrow}_n \implies B^\star \in \Pi^1_{n+1}(\Sigma^1_1\text{-}\mathsf{AC}_0)$.

Proof. For (a): Immediate from Definition 9.1 and since $\mathrm{Acc}_{\lhd}(X, x)$ has no second order quantifiers.

For (b): Let $B \in \Pi^1_n(\mathsf{T}) \subseteq \mathcal{L}^2_{\mathsf{PA}}$ be given. Since $\mathrm{Acc}(\mathcal{B}, t)$ is the formula

$$\forall y(y \lhd t \rightarrow \mathcal{B}(y))$$

and we have $(y \lhd t) \in \Pi^1_0$, we get $\mathrm{Acc}(\mathcal{B}, t) \in \Pi^1_n(\mathsf{T})$ by Corollary 7.37.

For (c): By induction on n.

1. $n = 0$: This is proven almost literally as for Lemma 7.41.(e), while noting that $\mathrm{Pos}^{\rightarrow}_0$ corresponds in current consideration to For^+ from the applicative setting of FIT.

2. $n \geq 1$: We prove this by a side induction on the build-up of B and the definition of $B \in \mathrm{Pos}^{\rightarrow}_n$. This is similar to the proof of Lemma 7.41.(e).

2.1. If $B \in \mathrm{Pos}^{\rightarrow}_n$ is due to ($\mathrm{Pos}^{\rightarrow}$-Base) in Definition 8.1: Then we have $B \in \mathrm{Pos}^{\rightarrow}_{n-1}$ and the claim follows from the main induction hypothesis (while noting Lemma 7.36.(a)).

2.2. If $B \in \mathrm{Pos}^{\rightarrow}_n$ is due to ($\mathrm{Pos}^{\rightarrow}$-Cons) in Definition 8.1: Then we have that B equals

$$\forall \vec{x}(A_0 \rightarrow \ldots \rightarrow A_k \rightarrow B_0)$$

for some $A_0, \ldots, A_k \in \mathrm{Pos}^{\rightarrow}_{n-1}$, $B_0 \in \mathrm{Pos}^{\rightarrow}_n$, and some (possibly empty) list of variables $\vec{x}$. The side induction hypothesis yields $B_0^\star \in \Pi^1_{n+1}(\Sigma^1_1\text{-}\mathsf{AC}_0)$ and the main induction hypothesis yields $A_0, \ldots, A_k \in \Pi^1_n(\Sigma^1_1\text{-}\mathsf{AC}_0)$, hence the claim follows immediately from Corollary 7.37. □

9.1. Embedding TID_n into Π^1_{n+2}-RFN_0

Theorem 9.5. $\Pi^1_{n+2}\text{-}\mathsf{RFN}_0$ *proves $A^\star$ for every instance A of (TID_n) and for every $n \in \mathbb{N}$.*

Proof. We adapt now the proof of Theorem 7.42 for the current setting. Let A be an instance of (TID_n), say

$$\forall x(\mathrm{Acc}_{\lhd}(\mathcal{B}, x) \to \mathcal{B}(x)) \to \forall x(P_{\lhd}x \to \mathcal{B}(x))$$

with $\mathcal{B} := \Lambda a.B$ and $B \in \mathrm{Pos}_n^{\to}$. Then by definition and Remark 9.3, $A^\star$ is

$$\forall x(\mathrm{Acc}_{\lhd}(\mathcal{B}^\star, x) \to \mathcal{B}^\star(x)) \to \forall x(P^\star_{\lhd}(x) \to \mathcal{B}^\star(x))$$

where $\mathcal{B}^\star$ is $\Lambda a.B^\star$. Further assume

$$\forall x(\mathrm{Acc}_{\lhd}(\mathcal{B}^\star, x) \to \mathcal{B}^\star(x)) \tag{9.1}$$

Due to Lemma 9.4, we know that $D(a) \in \Pi^1_{n+1}$ exists such that

$$\Sigma^1_1\text{-}\mathsf{AC}_0 \vdash D(a) \leftrightarrow \mathcal{B}^\star(a) \tag{9.2}$$

holds. Letting $\mathcal{D} := \Lambda y.D(y)$ and noting that $D \in \Pi^1_{n+1}$ holds, we get by Corollary 7.37 and Lemma 9.4.(b) (with $\mathsf{T} := \mathsf{ACA}_0$) some $E \in \Pi^1_{n+2}$ with

$$\mathsf{ACA}_0 \vdash E \leftrightarrow \forall x(\mathrm{Acc}_{\lhd}(\mathcal{D}, x) \to \mathcal{D}(x)) \tag{9.3}$$

Moreover, we have that (9.1) is equivalent over Σ^1_1-AC_0 to

$$\forall x(\mathrm{Acc}_{\lhd}(\mathcal{D}, x) \to \mathcal{D}(x))$$

We proceed now by assuming that the conclusion in $A^\star$ is false and will derive a contradiction from this. Let a_0 be such that

$$P^\star_{\lhd}(a_0) \land \neg\mathcal{B}^\star(a_0) \tag{9.4}$$

holds and note that $\neg\mathcal{B}^\star(a_0)$ is equivalent over Σ^1_1-AC_0 to $\neg D(a_0)$ by (9.2) and that $\neg D(a_0) \in \Pi^1_{n+2}$ holds. Due to Theorem 7.30, we can apply $(\Pi^1_{n+2}$-$\mathsf{RFN})$ to the conjunction of E and $\neg D(a_0)$ in order to obtain an ω model M of ACA_0 such that we obtain (in particular due to (9.3)) that

$$\forall x(\mathrm{Acc}_{\lhd}(\mathcal{D}, x)^M \to \mathcal{D}(x)^M) \tag{9.5}$$

$$\neg D^M(a_0) \tag{9.6}$$

hold within the theory Π^1_{n+2}-RFN_0. Now, (9.5) unfolds by definition to

$$\forall x(\mathrm{Acc}_\lhd(\Lambda y.D^M(y), x) \to D^M(x)) \tag{9.7}$$

and hence, we obtain that (9.7) holds over $\Pi^1_{n+2}\text{-}\mathsf{RFN}_0$. As $D^M(x)$ is arithmetical, (ACA) provides a set X such that $\forall x(x \in X \leftrightarrow D^M(x))$ and $\forall x(\mathrm{Acc}_\lhd(X, x) \to x \in X)$ holds. This can be used with $P^\star_\lhd(a_0)$ from (9.4) to get $a_0 \in X$, i.e., $D^M(a_0)$ which is a contradiction to (9.6). □

Theorem 9.6. *For each* $n \in \mathbb{N}$*, the following holds over* $\Pi^1_{n+2}\text{-}\mathsf{RFN}_0$*:*

(a) $A^\star$ *holds for every formula* A *that is an axiom of* PA *without complete induction.*

(b) $A^\star$ *holds for every instance* A *of axiom* (Ind_n) *of* TID_n*.*

(c) $A^\star$ *holds for every instance* A *of the closure axiom* (Cl) *of* TID_n*.*

Proof. For (a), this is obvious. For (b), note that we have over ACA_0 that ($\Pi^1_{n+2}\text{-}\mathsf{RFN}$) implies transfinite induction for Π^1_{n+1} formulas, and thus complete induction along the natural numbers for Π^1_{n+1} formulas. For this, see in [Sim09] Theorem VIII.5.12 and in particular Exercise VIII.5.15, while noting there that $\Sigma^1_{n+2}\text{-}\mathsf{RFN}_0$ is equivalent to $\Pi^1_{n+2}\text{-}\mathsf{RFN}_0$. Then the claim follows, noting that $A^\star$ translates by Lemma 9.4.(c) to complete induction along the natural numbers for Π^1_{n+1} formulas. Note also Theorem 7.30.

For (c), we have to show

$$\forall x(\mathrm{Acc}_\lhd(\Lambda a.P^\star_\lhd(a), x) \to P^\star_\lhd(x))$$

So, assume x_0 with

$$\mathrm{Acc}_\lhd(\Lambda a.P^\star_\lhd(a), x_0) \tag{9.8}$$

and show $P^\star_\lhd(x_0)$, i.e.,

$$\forall X(\forall x(\mathrm{Acc}_\lhd(X, x) \to x \in X) \to x_0 \in X)$$

So, assume X_0 with

$$\forall x(\mathrm{Acc}_\lhd(X_0, x) \to x \in X_0) \tag{9.9}$$

and show $x_0 \in X_0$. We have $\forall z(P^\star_\lhd(z) \to z \in X_0)$ due to (9.9) and the definition of $P^\star_\lhd(z)$. Then this yields $\forall z(\mathrm{Acc}_\lhd(\Lambda a.P^\star_\lhd, z) \to \mathrm{Acc}_\lhd(X_0, z)))$

since $\mathrm{Acc}_\lhd$ is a *positive* operator form. Now, we first get $\mathrm{Acc}_\lhd(X_0, x_0)$ by (9.8) and then the claim $x_0 \in X_0$ by (9.9). □

Corollary 9.7 (Embedding TID_n into Π^1_{n+2}-RFN_0). *For each $A \in \mathcal{L}_{\mathsf{TID}}$ and $n \in \mathbb{N}$, we have*

$$\mathsf{TID}_n \vdash A \implies \Pi^1_{n+2}\text{-}\mathsf{RFN}_0 \vdash A^\star$$

Proof. This follows directly from the previous results. □

9.2. Arithmetical Derivability in TID_n^+

9.2.1. The Reference System Tow_n

Notation 9.8. For each $n \in \mathbb{N}$ and each set variable X, we denote by

$$X \models \Pi^1_{n+2}\text{-}\mathsf{RFN}_0$$

ambiguously to Notation 7.22 that X *is a model of* Π^1_{n+2}-RFN_0, i.e., this shall denote

$$(\mathrm{F}_{\Pi^1_{n+2}\text{-}\mathsf{RFN}})^X$$

where $\mathrm{F}_{\Pi^1_{n+2}\text{-}\mathsf{RFN}}$ is any Π^1_{n+2}-sentence that is a finite axiomatization[1] of Π^1_{n+2}-RFN_0.

Definition 9.9. For each $n \in \mathbb{N}$, we define

$$\mathsf{Tow}_n := \begin{cases} \mathsf{ACA}_0 \\ + \forall X \exists Y (X \mathrel{\dot\in} Y \land Y \models \Pi^1_{n+2}\text{-}\mathsf{RFN}_0) \end{cases}$$

We call Tow_n a theory for *towers*[2] of models over Π^1_{n+2}-RFN_0.

Remark 9.10. The theories Tow_n for $n \in \mathbb{N}$ are essentially the theories $\mathsf{p}_1\mathsf{p}_{n+2}(\mathsf{ACA}_0)$ from [Pro15].

[1] By means of $\mathrm{F}_{\mathsf{ACA}}$ from Proposition 7.25 and making use of a universal Π^1_{n+2} formula for Π^1_{n+2} formulas. See also [Hin78] and [Sim09].

[2] We can use the main axiom of Tow_n for each $k \geq 2$ iteratively in order to get sets $X_1, \ldots, X_k$ with $X_i \models \Pi^1_{n+2}$-RFN_0 for each $1 \leq i \leq k$ and such that $X_1 \mathrel{\dot\in} \ldots \mathrel{\dot\in} X_k$ holds.

9.2.2. Arithmetical Derivability

Theorem 9.11. *For each $n \in \mathbb{N}$, we have*

$$\mathsf{TID}_n^+ \vdash A \implies \mathsf{Tow}_n \vdash \forall Y(Y \models \Pi^1_{n+2}\text{-}\mathsf{RFN}_0 \to Y \models A^\star)$$

Proof. By induction on the derivation-length of $\mathsf{TID}_n^+ \vdash A$. In the following case distinction, we assume Y with

$$Y \models \Pi^1_{n+2}\text{-}\mathsf{RFN}_0 \tag{9.10}$$

and have to show $Y \models A^\star$.

1. *Arithmetical Axioms:* This is clear since Y is in particular a model of ACA_0 by (9.10).

2. *Axiom* (Nat)*:* We have to show $\forall x(Y \models P^\star_{<_\mathbb{N}}(x))$, i.e.,

$$\forall x(\forall X \dot{\in} Y(\mathrm{Prog}(X) \to x \in X))$$

which is $\forall x(\forall y(\mathrm{Prog}((Y)_y) \to x \in (Y)_y))$. So, we can derive this from set induction and (ACA) which both are available in Tow_n.

3. *Axiom* (TID_n)*:* Let A be an instance

$$\mathrm{Prog}_\lhd(\mathcal{B}) \to \forall x(P_\lhd x \to \mathcal{B}(x))$$

of (TID_n) with $\mathcal{B} \in \mathrm{Pos}_n^\to$. We have that $\mathcal{B}$ is of the form $\Lambda a.B$ and that $B^\star$ is equivalent over Σ^1_1-AC_0 to some $B' \in \Pi^1_{n+1}$ by Lemma 9.4. Hence, this equivalence holds also in the model Y since Y is a model of Π^1_{n+2}-RFN_0 by (9.10). Further, and as in Section 9.1, we get that $\mathrm{Prog}(\mathcal{B}^\star)$ is equivalent to some $C \in \Pi^1_{n+2}$ and we can argue within Y as we did in Section 9.1 when we were working externally in Π^1_{n+2}-RFN_0.

4. *Axiom* (Cl)*:* As for the treatment of (Cl) for TID_n in Section 9.1 but working now within Y.

5. *Rule modus ponens, ($\forall$-intro), and ($\exists$-intro):* This follows easily from the induction hypothesis. For instance for ($\forall$-intro), let A be $A_0 \to \forall x B_0$ with $x \notin \mathrm{FV}(A_0)$. So, the induction hypothesis for the premiss $A_0 \to B_0$ of ($\forall$-intro) yields $Y \models A_0^\star \to B_0^\star$, i.e., ${A_0^\star}^Y \to {B_0^\star}^Y$, hence ($\forall$-intro) yields ${A_0^\star}^Y \to \forall x({B_0^\star}^Y)$, i.e., $Y \models A^\star$.

6. *Rule* (TID^+)*:* Let A be the conclusion $\mathrm{Prog}_\lhd(\mathcal{B}) \to \mathcal{B}(t)$ of the rule (TID^+) with $\mathcal{B} \in \mathcal{L}_\mathsf{TID}$, and we remark that the *-translation of (TID^+)

into $\mathcal{L}^2_{\mathsf{PA}}$ yields a kind of bar rule, i.e., a rule of the form

$$(\mathsf{BR}^+)\ \frac{\forall X(\mathrm{Prog}_\lhd(X) \to t \in X)}{\mathrm{Prog}_\lhd(\mathcal{B}^\star) \to \mathcal{B}^\star(t)}$$

while recalling that the *-translation of the premiss $P_\lhd t$ of TID^+ becomes $\forall X(\mathrm{Prog}_\lhd(X) \to t \in X)$ and that $\mathcal{B}^\star$ is $\Lambda a.B^\star$ given that $\mathcal{B}$ is $\Lambda a.B$. Now, we have to show

$$Y \models (\mathrm{Prog}_\lhd(\mathcal{B}^\star) \to \mathcal{B}^\star(t)) \tag{$*$}$$

and therefore assume $Y \models \mathrm{Prog}_\lhd(\mathcal{B}^\star)$, i.e.,

$$\mathrm{Prog}_\lhd(\Lambda x.\mathcal{B}^\star(x)^Y) \tag{9.11}$$

where x is some fresh variable. In order to get $(*)$, we have to show $Y \models \mathcal{B}^\star(t)$, i.e.,

$$\mathcal{B}^\star(t)^Y \tag{$**$}$$

Arguing within Tow_n, we get Z such that $Y \mathrel{\dot\in} Z$ and $Z \models \Pi^1_{n+2}\text{-}\mathsf{RFN}_0$ hold. Now, note that $\mathcal{B}^\star(x)^Y \in \Pi^1_0$ holds, so we get

$$\exists X_0 \mathrel{\dot\in} Z \forall x(x \in X_0 \leftrightarrow \mathcal{B}^\star(x)^Y) \tag{9.12}$$

because each instance of (ACA) holds relativized to Z and we have $Y \mathrel{\dot\in} Z$. On the other hand, we have $\mathsf{TID}_1^+ \vdash P_\lhd t$ and hence

$$\mathsf{Tow}_n \vdash \forall Y_0 \begin{pmatrix} Y_0 \models \Pi^1_{n+2}\text{-}\mathsf{RFN}_0 \\ \to Y_0 \models \forall X(\mathrm{Prog}_\lhd(X) \to t \in X) \end{pmatrix} \tag{9.13}$$

by the induction hypothesis, i.e., we get $\forall X \mathrel{\dot\in} Z(\mathrm{Prog}_\lhd(X) \to t \in X)$ and hence $\mathrm{Prog}_\lhd(X_0) \to t \in X_0$ by making use of X_0 from (9.12). By showing $\mathrm{Prog}_\lhd(X_0)$, we are done because $t \in X_0$ and (9.12) imply $(**)$. For $\mathrm{Prog}_\lhd(X_0)$, we can use (9.11) and again (9.12). □

Corollary 9.12. *For each $A \in \mathcal{L}_{\mathsf{PA}}$ and each $n \in \mathbb{N}$, the following holds:*

$$\mathsf{TID}_n^+ \vdash A \implies \mathsf{Tow}_n \vdash A$$

Proof. Follows immediately from Theorem 9.11 and since $(A^\star)^Y$ equals A for all set variables Y and all $\mathcal{L}_{\mathsf{PA}}$ formulas A. □

9.3. Comparison with a Bar Rule

We motivated the treatment of the rule (TID^+) in the proof of Theorem 9.11 by depicting the *-translation of this rule's premiss and conclusion with an informal indication of a bar rule

$$(\mathsf{BR}^+)\ \frac{\forall X(\mathrm{Prog}_\lhd(X) \to t \in X)}{\mathrm{Prog}_\lhd(\mathcal{B}) \to \mathcal{B}(t)}$$

for arbitrary $\mathcal{B} \in \mathcal{L}^2_{\mathsf{PA}}$ and which we named (BR^+) so that it bears analogy to (TID^+). This rule (BR^+) is a special case of a (parameter-free) *substitution rule* (SUB), i.e.,

$$(\mathsf{SUB})\ \frac{\forall X(A)}{A(\mathcal{B}/X)}$$

where $A \in \mathcal{L}^2_{\mathsf{PA}}$ is *arithmetical* and $\forall X(A)$ contains no set parameters (i.e., no free set variables), while $\mathcal{B} \in \mathcal{L}^2_{\mathsf{PA}}$ can be arbitrary. On the other hand, one of the common definitions of the *bar rule* (BR) is

$$(\mathsf{BR})\ \frac{\forall X(\mathrm{Prog}_\lhd(X) \to \forall x(x \in X))}{\mathrm{Prog}_\lhd(\mathcal{B}) \to \forall x(\mathcal{B}(x))}$$

which is given for arbitrary $\mathcal{B} \in \mathcal{L}^2_{\mathsf{PA}}$ and which is treated for instance in [FJ83]. Clearly, (BR) is a special case of (SUB), and we know from the literature that adding (BR) to a theory T that comprises ACA_0 (and is a subsystem of second order arithmetic as described in Section 7.2) is strong enough to derive (SUB), see [Rat91, Lemma 1.4.(iii)] or [Fef70] for this.[3]

These observations yield

$$|\Pi^1_{n+2}\text{-}\mathsf{RFN}_0 + (\mathsf{BR})| = |\Pi^1_{n+2}\text{-}\mathsf{RFN}_0 + (\mathsf{SUB})|$$

and under the assumption $|\mathsf{TID}_n| = |\Pi^1_{n+2}\text{-}\mathsf{RFN}_0|$, we hence get immedi-

[3] In fact, (BR^+) follows from (BR) over ACA_0 if we use (BR) for the restriction $\lhd\restriction t$ of any given $\lhd$ and t that is given in (BR^+). Obviously, (BR^+) implies also (BR).

ately that $|\mathsf{TID}_n^+| \leq |\Pi^1_{n+2}\text{-}\mathsf{RFN}_0 + (\mathsf{BR})|$ holds because the *-translation of the rule (TID^+) yields a special case (BR^+) of (SUB) and because TID_n is by Lemma 8.5 essentially included in TID_n^+. Further, the proof-method for showing Theorem 9.11 can be used to show that the arithmetical formulas that are derivable in $\Pi^1_{n+2}\text{-}\mathsf{RFN}_0$ + (BR) are also derivable in Tow_n, This yields $|\Pi^1_{n+2}\text{-}\mathsf{RFN}_0 + (\mathsf{BR})| \leq |\mathsf{Tow}_n| = \vartheta\Omega(n, \Omega)$ since $|\mathsf{Tow}_n| = \vartheta\Omega(n, \Omega)$ follows from [Pro15] (while noting that Tow_n appears in [Pro15] as the theory $\mathsf{p}_1\mathsf{p}_{n+2}(\mathsf{ACA}_0)$).

In case of $n = 1$, we know already $|\mathsf{TID}_1| = |\Pi^1_3\text{-}\mathsf{RFN}_0|$ by Chapter 7 and Section 8.3, i.e., that $|\mathsf{TID}_1|$ is the small Veblen ordinal. From the wellordering proof of TID_1^+ in Chapter 11, we hence get that $\Pi^1_3\text{-}\mathsf{RFN}_0$ + (BR) corresponds to the large Veblen ordinal, i.e., adding (BR) yields the step from the small to the large Veblen ordinal. This gives rise to the conjectures on $|\mathsf{TID}_n^+|$ that are depicted by (?) in Table 1 on page 8.

As in Section 8.2, we note that the result of Lemma 8.5 corresponds here to the provability of complete induction for the full language $\mathcal{L}^2_{\mathsf{PA}}$. This follows from the substitution rule (SUB), and hence from (BR^+), by essentially applying (SUB) to the axiom of set induction.

9.4. Upper Bounds for TID_n and TID_n^+

Theorem 9.13. *$|\mathsf{TID}_n| \leq \vartheta\Omega(n, \omega)$ holds for all $n \in \mathbb{N}$.*

Proof. This is a direct consequence from Corollary 9.7 and Corollary 7.33. □

Theorem 9.14. *$|\mathsf{TID}_n^+| \leq \vartheta\Omega(n, \Omega)$ holds for all $n \in \mathbb{N}$.*

Proof (Sketch). This is a consequence of Corollary 9.12 and the results of [Pro15] on $\mathsf{p}_1\mathsf{p}_{n+2}(\mathsf{ACA}_0)$, i.e., Tow_n. □

9.5. Notes

The results of Chapter 9 concerning TID_n for $n \in \mathbb{N}$ are inspired by the upper bound results for FIT in Chapter 7, though the idea to work with $\Pi^1_3\text{-}\mathsf{RFN}_0$ at all in Chapter 7 is due to Th. Strahm. The treatment of TID_n^+ via Tow_n, i.e., "towers" of models for ω-model reflection for Π^1_{n+2}

formulas, was motivated by Th. Strahm and D. Probst. In particular, D. Probst uses in [Pro15] essentially the same systems Tow_n which are however based on *operators* p_1 and p_{n+2} that take theories (that can be coded as sentences) and output new theories in a modular way that allows for a powerful and flexible treatment of proof-theoretic investigations. In particular, $\mathsf{p}_{n+2}(\mathsf{ACA}_0)$ corresponds to Π^1_{n+2}-RFN_0 and $\mathsf{p}_1\mathsf{p}_{n+2}(\mathsf{ACA}_0)$, i.e., $\mathsf{p}_1(\mathsf{p}_{n+2}(\mathsf{ACA}_0))$, corresponds to Tow_n.

10. Special Considerations for TID_0 and TID_0^+

10.1. Calibrating TID_0 with Σ^1_1-DC_0 and $\vartheta\Omega(0,\omega)$

Recall that TID_0 is $\mathsf{ID}_1^*\!\restriction$ from [Pro06] with the restriction to accessible part operator forms, so $|\mathsf{TID}_0| = \varphi(\omega, 0)$ holds.[1] Due to $\vartheta\Omega(0,\omega) = \vartheta(\Omega \cdot \omega) = \varphi(\omega, 0)$ from Section 2.4 and due to Theorem 7.32, the following holds:

$$|\mathsf{TID}_0| = \vartheta\Omega(0,\omega) = \varphi(\omega,0) = |\Sigma^1_1\text{-}\mathsf{DC}_0|$$

10.2. Calibrating TID_0^+ with ATR_0 and $\vartheta\Omega(0,\Omega)$

Arithmetical formulas that are provable in TID_0^+ are also provable in a theory Tow_0 that formalizes over ACA_0 models of Π^1_2-RFN_0. Using that Σ^1_1-DC_0 is equivalent to Π^1_2-RFN_0 by Theorem 7.30 and using [Sim09, Theorem VIII.4.20, Lemma VIII.4.19], we get that Tow_0 can be embedded into the theory ATR_0, a theory for *arithmetical transfinite recursion*, see [Sim09] for a definition of ATR_0. After inspection of the proof of Lemma 7.6 in Subsection 7.1.1, one can see that the rule (TID^+) in TID_0^+ allows to get a wellordering proof for ordinals below Γ_0, using the following usual approximations $\mathfrak{g}_n$ of Γ_0 that are defined for each $n \in \mathbb{N}$ by

$$\mathfrak{g}_0 := \varepsilon_0 \qquad\qquad \mathfrak{g}_{n+1} := \varphi(\mathfrak{g}_n, 0)$$

and yielding $\sup_{n\in\mathbb{N}}(\mathfrak{g}_n) = \Gamma_0$. Altogether, we obtain

$$|\mathsf{TID}_0^+| = \vartheta\Omega(0,\Omega) = \Gamma_0 = |\mathsf{ATR}_0|$$

while $\vartheta(\Omega \cdot \Omega) = \vartheta\Omega^2 = \Gamma_0$ is due to [Sch92], see also Section 2.4.

[1] This follows actually from the considerations of Corollary 7.7 and Remark 7.8.

11. The Large Veblen Ordinal $\vartheta\Omega^\Omega$ measures TID_1^+

In this chapter, we shall show that TID_1^+ is a natural theory for carrying out wellordering proofs in the context of Klammersymbols and hence reaching up to the large Veblen ordinal $\vartheta\Omega^\Omega$. In order to be able to work more efficiently with Klammersymbols, we shall use the notions from Chapter 4 that allow to manipulate the represented ordinals in a natural and suitable way for predicative investigations. Bear in mind that our aim to internalize the concepts from Section 7.1 within the arithmetical theory TID_1^+ is the main difficulty of the following content.

11.1. Generalization of Concepts from Chapter 7

Convention 11.1.

(a) $(\mathrm{OT}, \prec)$ and all associated notions shall refer to the ordinal notation system $(\mathrm{OT}(\boldsymbol{L}_0), \prec)$ that was circumscribed in Chapter 4.

(b) In order to increase readability, we shall use the following abbreviations for denoting *quantification over (labeled) Klammersymbols*:

- $\forall\alpha(\ldots)$ abbreviates $\forall x(x \in \boldsymbol{L}_0 \to \ldots)$ and
- $\exists\alpha(\ldots)$ abbreviates $\exists x(x \in \boldsymbol{L}_0 \wedge \ldots)$.

(c) For more readability, we shall prefer now the notation

$$t \in P_\lhd$$

rather than $P_\lhd t$ (since we do not work any more in the setting of FIT, so there is no clash of notations). In particular, we shall make more use of expressions of the form $\forall x \in P_\lhd(\ldots)$ or $\exists x \in P_\lhd(\ldots)$. Compare this with the notational framework introduced in Chapter 1.

(d) Moreover and similar to Chapter 7, we let

- P denote $P_\prec$,
- Acc denote $\mathrm{Acc}_\prec$, and
- Prog denote $\mathrm{Prog}_\prec$.

Definition 11.2.

(a) In order to formally express that for any Klammersymbol $\left(\begin{smallmatrix} a_0 & \dots & a_n \\ b_0 & \dots & b_n \end{smallmatrix}\right)$, we have $a_i \in P$ for each $i \leq n$, we introduce the following formula:

$$x \mathrel{\dot\in} P :\Leftrightarrow \forall y \leq \mathsf{lh}_{\boldsymbol{L}}(x)\big(\forall z \leq \mathsf{lh}_{\boldsymbol{S}}(\mathsf{p}(x,y))\big(\mathsf{c}(\mathsf{p}(x,y),z) \in P\big)\big)$$

If it is clear from the context, we also write $\alpha \in P$ instead of $\alpha \mathrel{\dot\in} P$. Clearly, $x \mathrel{\dot\in} P$ is in $\mathrm{Pos}_0^{\rightarrow}$.

(b) Let $\alpha \in \boldsymbol{L} \cap P$ abbreviate $\alpha \in \boldsymbol{L} \wedge \alpha \mathrel{\dot\in} P$, and clearly $\alpha \in \boldsymbol{L} \cap P$ is in $\mathrm{Pos}_0^{\rightarrow}$. This notation shall be tacitly used analogously for similar expressions such as $\alpha \in \boldsymbol{S} \cap P$.

Remark 11.3. The wellordering proof crucially depends on the following notions which are generalizations of concepts from Chapter 7 and adapted for the current treatment *without* fundamental sequences.

Definition 11.4.

- $\mathrm{Fun}(\alpha)$ is called *functionality* and defined as

$$\forall x \in P(\{\alpha\}x \in P)$$

- $\mathrm{Small}(s,\alpha,a)$ is called the *(generic) small Veblen jump* and defined as

$$\forall \rho,\sigma\left(\begin{pmatrix} \mathsf{c}(\sigma,s) \prec a \\ \wedge\, \mathsf{lh}_{\boldsymbol{S}}(\sigma) \leq s \leq \mathsf{lh}_{\boldsymbol{S}}(\alpha) \\ \wedge\, \sigma \in \boldsymbol{S}_0^{\mathsf{e}(\alpha)} \cap P \\ \wedge\, \rho \in \boldsymbol{L}_0^{\prec \mathsf{e}(\alpha)} \cap P \end{pmatrix} \rightarrow \mathrm{Fun}(\rho * \sigma * \alpha|_s^{\boldsymbol{S}})\right)$$

Definition 11.5.

- $\mathrm{HypBase}(\alpha)$ is called the *base hypothesis* and defined as

$$\alpha \neq \tfrac{0}{0} \rightarrow \mathrm{Fun}(\alpha\Downarrow)$$

- $\mathrm{HypFull}(\alpha)$ is called the *full hypothesis* and defined as

$$\forall s \leq \mathsf{lh}_{\boldsymbol{S}}(\alpha)(\mathrm{Small}(s, \alpha, \mathsf{c}(\alpha, s)))$$

- $\mathrm{HypPart}(s, \alpha)$ is called the *part hypothesis* and defined as

$$\forall s_0 (s < s_0 \leq \mathsf{lh}_{\boldsymbol{S}}(\alpha) \rightarrow \mathrm{Small}(s_0, \alpha, \mathsf{c}(\alpha, s_0)))$$

Definition 11.6.

- $\mathrm{Full}(\alpha)$ is defined as

$$\mathrm{Prog}(\Lambda a.(a \in P \rightarrow \{\alpha\}a \in P))$$

- $\mathrm{Part}(s, \alpha)$ is defined as

$$\mathrm{Prog}(\Lambda a.(a \in P \rightarrow \mathrm{Small}(s, \alpha, a)))$$

- $\mathrm{Large}(a, b)$ is called the *large Veblen jump* and defined as

$$\forall \alpha \mathrel{\dot{\in}} \boldsymbol{L}_{\bar{0}}^{\prec b} \cap P(\mathsf{e}(\alpha) \preceq a \rightarrow \mathrm{HypBase}(\alpha))$$

11.1.1. Syntactical Properties

Lemma 11.7. *The following properties hold for all terms t_1, t_2, t_3:*

(a) $\mathrm{Fun}(t_1) \in \mathrm{Pos}_{\bar{1}}^{\rightarrow}$.

(b) $\mathrm{Small}(t_1, t_2, t_3) \in \mathrm{Pos}_{\bar{1}}^{\rightarrow}$.

(c) $\mathrm{HypBase}(t_1), \mathrm{HypFull}(t_1), \mathrm{HypPart}(t_1, t_2) \in \mathrm{Pos}_{\bar{1}}^{\rightarrow}$.

(d) $\mathrm{Large}(t_1, t_2) \in \mathrm{Pos}_{\bar{1}}^{\rightarrow}$.

Proof. This follows easily from the definitions. □

Lemma 11.8. *The following properties hold for all terms t_1, t_2:*

(a) $\mathrm{Part}(t_1, t_2) \in \mathrm{Pos}_2^{\rightarrow}$.

(b) $\mathrm{Full}(t_1) \in \mathrm{Pos}_2^{\rightarrow}$.

Proof. Use Lemma 11.7. Note for (a) that $\mathrm{Part}(t_1, t_2)$ is

$$\forall a(\forall a_0 \prec a(a_0 \in P \to \mathrm{Small}(t_1, t_2, a_0)) \to (a \in P \to \mathrm{Small}(t_1, t_2, a)))$$

and that we have

$$\forall a_0 \prec a(a_0 \in P \to \mathrm{Small}(t_1, t_2, a_0)) \in \mathrm{Pos}_1^{\rightarrow}$$

This is similar for (b). □

11.1.2. Motivation and Comparison with Chapter 7

For a motivation on the intuition behind $\mathrm{Small}(s, \alpha, a)$, we compare it with the approach in Chapter 7 and consider the following situation

$$\alpha \equiv \frac{a_0, \ldots, a_n}{0}$$
$$\rho \equiv \frac{0}{0}$$
$$\sigma \equiv \frac{y_1, \ldots, y_s, x}{0}$$

for arbitrary $a_0, \ldots, a_n$ and $y_1, \ldots, y_s, x$ with $0 \le s \le n$. Note that the list $y_1, \ldots, y_s$ starts with index 1 and that $s = 0$ means $\sigma \equiv \frac{x}{0} \equiv \binom{x}{0}$.

Now, informally speaking, these objects are suitable to be translated to *arguments of the finitary Veblen function φ*. In this sense, we can translate the instantiation of $\mathrm{Small}(s, \alpha, a)$ with ρ and σ essentially to

$$\left.\begin{array}{l} x \prec a \wedge x \in P \wedge y_1 \in P \wedge \ldots \wedge y_s \in P \\ \to \forall y_0 \in P(\varphi(a_n, \ldots, a_{s+1}, x, y_s, \ldots, y_0) \in P) \end{array}\right\} \qquad (*)$$

because of $\mathsf{c}(\sigma, s) = x$, $\mathsf{c}(\alpha, s) = a_s$, $\mathsf{lh}_{\boldsymbol{S}}(\sigma) \le s \le n = \mathsf{lh}_{\boldsymbol{S}}(\alpha)$, $\mathsf{e}(\alpha) = \mathsf{e}(\sigma) = 0$, and $\alpha|_s^{\boldsymbol{S}} = \frac{\bar{0}^{(s)}, a_{s+1}, \ldots, a_n}{0}$. Note that $\mathsf{lh}_{\boldsymbol{S}}(\sigma) \le s$ holds because we have $y_1, \ldots, y_s$ and not $y_0, \ldots, y_s$ in σ. In case of $x = 0$, we get $\mathsf{lh}_{\boldsymbol{S}}(\sigma) < s$ and hence $\mathsf{c}(\sigma, s) = 0$ by the definition of $\mathsf{c}(\sigma, s)$. In other words and with respect to the expression $\varphi(a_n, \ldots, a_{s+1}, x, y_s, \ldots, y_0)$, we have the following:

$\alpha\|_s^L$	corresponds to the list	$a_n, \ldots, a_{s+1}$.
σ	corresponds to the list	$x, y_s, \ldots, y_1$.
ρ	does not exist.	

Next, and since $y_1, \ldots, y_s, x$ are arbitrary, we add universal quantifiers to $(*)$ and rewrite the result to

$$\forall y_0, \ldots, y_s \left(\begin{array}{l} y_0 \in P \wedge y_1 \in P \wedge \ldots \wedge y_s \in P \\ \to \forall x \prec a\big(x \in P \to \varphi(a_n, \ldots, a_{s+1}, x, y_s, \ldots, y_0) \in P\big) \end{array} \right)$$

Now, compare this with "Small_n^k" from Chapter 7 in Definition 7.10:

1. "a_k" in Definition 7.10 corresponds here to a.

2. "x" in Definition 7.10 corresponds here to x, and note that the condition $x \in P$ does not occur in Definition 7.10. We use this extra condition in order to make later proofs technically simpler. In Chapter 7, the situation was conceptually simpler because we worked there with *fundamental sequences.*

3. "y" in Definition 7.10 corresponds here to y_s. In case of $s > 0$, we further have that $y_0, \ldots, y_{s-1}$ are treated as "0" in Definition 7.10.

Note that we introduced the notion of a *fundamental sequence* in Chapter 3 in the setting of the ordinal notation system for the small Veblen ordinal (and we verified its properties in the appendix). This allowed us to work in Chapter 7 with these fundamental sequences, while here, in Chapter 11, we work *without fundamental sequences.* The cost of not having to introduce such objects (and not having to verify their adequacy) is that we have to work with a more general list

$$y_0, \ldots, y_s, x$$

instead of a list of the form

$$\text{“}0, \ldots, 0, y, x\text{”}$$

Recall that a list of the form "$0, \ldots, 0, y, x$" appears essentially in Definition 7.10.[1] Having $(*)$ from above in mind and its initiated comparison to Chapter 7, we can motivate Definition 11.5 and Definition 11.6 as follows:

- HypFull(α) corresponds essentially to (an internalization of) the *hypothesis* of the main implication given in Theorem 7.12.
- HypPart(s, α) corresponds essentially to the *hypothesis* of the main implication given in Theorem 7.15.
- Full(α) corresponds essentially to the *conclusion* of Theorem 7.12.
- Part(s, α) corresponds essentially to the *conclusion* of Theorem 7.15.

With these observations, the theorems of Section 11.3 include essentially the main results of Section 7.1. In particular, we remark the following:

- Theorem 7.12 is generalized to Theorem 11.15, i.e., it *internalizes* the list of universal quantifiers

  $$\text{“}\forall \bar{a}^{(n-1)}\text{”}$$

  from Theorem 7.12 by *encoding* it using *one* universal quantification

  $$\text{“}\forall \alpha\text{”}$$

  i.e., by quantifying over a (labeled) Klammersymbol.

  We account for this generalized situation by adding for instance HypBase(α) to the premiss in Theorem 11.15 and as a kind of generic hook which allows us to extract the essential statement of Theorem 7.12 in a general form.

[1]The ordinal notation system for the *large* Veblen ordinal has been described in Chapter 4, but we did not introduce and verify its properties in full detail. This would be necessary for a proper definition and verification of fundamental sequences (since it is sensitive to the exact definition of the underlying ordinal notion system). Moreover, the introduction of fundamental sequences did not seem to be as straight-forward as for ordinals below the small Veblen ordinal and by means of finitary Veblen functions. On the contrary, it seemed to make the situation rather more complicated. Since the current setting already is technically advanced, we decided to work without fundamental sequences (and to base the ordinal notation system on the so-called *fixed-point free value* of Klammersymbols, see also Definition 2.7).

Comparing Theorem 11.15 to Theorem 7.12, we always have $\rho \equiv \frac{0}{0}$ in the formulation of Theorem 11.15 because we have here $\mathsf{e}(\alpha) = 0$ and hence that $\rho \in \boldsymbol{L}_0^{\prec \mathsf{e}(\alpha)}$ implies $\rho \equiv \frac{0}{0}$.

- Theorem 7.15 is generalized to Theorem 11.22 analogously. More precisely, the auxiliary statement (•) in the proof of Theorem 11.22 corresponds to Theorem 7.15.

11.2. Basic Results

11.2.1. Basic Wellordering Results

We have the following results that are analogs of the results from Chapter 7.

Lemma 11.9. $\mathsf{TID}_0 \vdash \forall x(\underline{x} \in P)$.

Proof. Recall that $\underline{x} \in \mathrm{OT}$ is used to encode finite ordinals, so in particular $y \prec \underline{0}$ does not hold for each y. By (Cl), it suffices to show $\forall y \prec \underline{x}(y \in P)$ for which we can use (Ind_0). □

Lemma 11.10. $\mathsf{TID}_0 \vdash \forall x, y(x \in P \wedge y \in P \to x \tilde{+} y \in P)$.

Proof. As in Chapter 7. Note $\mathcal{B} \in \mathrm{Pos}_0^{\rightarrow}$ for $\mathcal{B} := \Lambda b.(x \tilde{+} b \in P)$. □

Proposition 11.11.

(a) $\mathsf{TID}_0 \vdash \forall x(x \notin \mathrm{OT} \to x \in P)$.

(b) $\mathsf{TID}_0 \vdash \forall x(x \in P \to \mathrm{TI}(\mathcal{A}, x))$ *for all* $\mathcal{A} \in \mathcal{L}_{\mathsf{PA}}$.

(c) $\mathsf{TID}_0 \vdash \mathrm{TI}(\mathcal{A}, \mathfrak{a})$ *holds for each (externally given) term* $\mathfrak{a} \prec \omega$ *and* $\mathcal{A} \in \mathcal{L}_{\mathsf{TID}}$.

Proof. As in Chapter 7. In particular note for (b) that $\mathcal{A} \in \mathcal{L}_{\mathsf{PA}}$ implies $\mathcal{A} \in \mathrm{Pos}_0^{\rightarrow}$. □

Convention 11.12. Due to Proposition 11.11.(a), we can assume from now on without loss of generality that $a \in \mathrm{OT}$ holds whenever we try to show $a \in P$ for some a within TID_0 or any extension. For instance, if we aim to prove $a \tilde{+} b \in P$ for some a, b, we shall tacitly assume that $a \tilde{+} b \in \mathrm{OT}$ holds.

11.2.2. Basic Results for the New Notions

Lemma 11.13.

(a) $\mathsf{TID}_0 \vdash \text{HypBase}(\frac{1}{0}) \to \text{HypFull}(\frac{1}{0})$.

(b) $\mathsf{TID}_0 \vdash \forall\alpha(\mathsf{e}(\alpha) \neq 0 \to \text{HypBase}(\frac{1}{0} * \alpha) \to \text{HypFull}(\frac{1}{0} * \alpha))$.

Proof. For (b), assume α with $\mathsf{e}(\alpha) \neq 0$ and $\text{HypBase}(\frac{1}{0} * \alpha)$ and note that this yields

$$\text{Fun}(\alpha) \tag{11.1}$$

by $\frac{1}{0} * \alpha \neq \frac{0}{0}$ and $(\frac{1}{0} * \alpha){\Downarrow} \equiv \mathsf{tl}_{\boldsymbol{L}}(\frac{1}{0} * \alpha) \equiv \alpha$. For the claim $\text{HypFull}(\frac{1}{0} * \alpha)$, we have to show

$$\forall s \leq \mathsf{lh}_{\boldsymbol{S}}(\tfrac{1}{0} * \alpha)\big(\text{Small}(s, \tfrac{1}{0} * \alpha, \mathsf{c}(\tfrac{1}{0} * \alpha, s))\big)$$

i.e., we have to show

$$\text{Small}(0, \tfrac{1}{0} * \alpha, 1) \tag{$*$}$$

due to $\mathsf{lh}_{\boldsymbol{S}}(\frac{1}{0} * \alpha) = 0$ and $\mathsf{c}(\frac{1}{0} * \alpha, 0) = 1$. Moreover, we have $\mathsf{e}(\frac{1}{0} * \alpha) = 0$ and $(\frac{1}{0} * \alpha)|_0^{\boldsymbol{S}} = \mathsf{tl}_{\boldsymbol{L}}(\frac{1}{0} * \alpha) = \alpha$, so the goal $(*)$ becomes

$$\forall \rho, \sigma\left(\begin{pmatrix} \mathsf{c}(\sigma, 0) \prec 1 \\ \wedge\, \mathsf{lh}_{\boldsymbol{S}}(\sigma) = 0 \\ \wedge\, \sigma \in \boldsymbol{S}_0^0 \cap P \\ \wedge\, \rho \in \boldsymbol{L}_0^{\prec 0} \cap P \end{pmatrix} \to \text{Fun}(\rho * \sigma * \alpha)\right) \tag{$**$}$$

and note that for all $\sigma \in \boldsymbol{S}_0$ with $\mathsf{lh}_{\boldsymbol{S}}(\sigma) = 0$, we have that $\mathsf{c}(\sigma, 0) \prec 1$ implies $\sigma \equiv \frac{0}{0}$, and that $\rho \in \boldsymbol{L}_0^{\prec 0}$ implies $\rho \equiv \frac{0}{0}$.

So, the goal $(**)$ becomes to show $\text{Fun}(\alpha)$ which we get from (11.1). Now, for showing (a), we can apply the same argument and (11.1) becomes $\text{Fun}(\frac{0}{0})$ due to $\frac{1}{0}{\Downarrow} \equiv \frac{0}{0}$. □

Lemma 11.14.

(a) $\mathsf{TID}_0 \vdash \forall \alpha, \rho(\mathrm{Fun}(\alpha) \land \rho \preceq_{\mathbf{lex}} \alpha \land \rho \,\dot{\in}\, P \to \mathrm{Fun}(\rho))$

(b) $\mathsf{TID}_0 \vdash \forall \alpha, \rho, a, c \begin{pmatrix} \alpha \,\dot{\in}\, P \land a \in P \\ \to \alpha \prec_{\mathbf{lex}} \rho \\ \to \{\rho\}c \prec \{\alpha\}a \\ \to \{\rho\}c \in P \end{pmatrix}$

Proof. For (a) let α, ρ be given and note that the case $\alpha \equiv \rho$ is trivial. So, we assume now

$$\alpha \neq \rho$$

and let c be given such that we have

$$\mathrm{Fun}(\alpha) \tag{11.2}$$
$$\rho \prec_{\mathbf{lex}} \alpha \tag{11.3}$$
$$\rho \,\dot{\in}\, P \tag{11.4}$$
$$c \in P \tag{11.5}$$

Then we have to show $\{\rho\}c \in P$. Let $a_0, \ldots, a_n, b_0, \ldots, b_n$ be given with

$$\rho \equiv \left(\begin{smallmatrix} a_0 & \ldots & a_n \\ b_0 & \ldots & b_n \end{smallmatrix}\right)$$

and let $\hat{c} := \max_{\prec}(\{c\} \cup \{a_0, \ldots, a_n\})$. We get $\hat{c} \in P$ from (11.5) and (11.4), and hence $\{\alpha\}\hat{c} \in P$ from (11.2). Now, $\{\rho\}c \in P$ follows with (FP) from $\{\rho\}c \prec \{\alpha\}\hat{c}$ which holds because of (11.3), $c, a_0, \ldots, a_n \preceq \hat{c} \prec \{\alpha\}\hat{c}$, and the definition of $\prec$ (see Chapter 4 and also Corollary 2.25), while $\hat{c} \prec \{\alpha\}\hat{c}$ holds due to Section 4.3. Hence, we get $\mathrm{Fun}(\rho)$ since $c \in P$ was arbitrary.

For (b), let $e_0, \ldots, e_l$ and $f_0, \ldots, f_l$ be given such that $\alpha \equiv \left(\begin{smallmatrix} f_0 & \ldots & f_l \\ e_0 & \ldots & e_l \end{smallmatrix}\right)$ holds and let $d := \{\rho\}c$. Then we get by the definition of $\prec$ and due to $\alpha \prec_{\mathbf{lex}} \rho$ that $d \prec \{\alpha\}a$ implies $d \preceq a$ or $d \preceq f_j$ for some $j \leq l$. Given $\alpha \,\dot{\in}\, P$ and $a \in P$, we can then use (FP) to get $d \in P$. Note that (b) formulated with $\alpha \preceq_{\mathbf{lex}} \rho$ does not hold in general. □

11.3. Core Results

11.3.1. Core Result for Full

Theorem 11.15.

$$\mathsf{TID}_0 \vdash \forall \alpha \mathrel{\dot{\in}} P(\mathrm{HypBase}(\alpha) \to \mathrm{HypFull}(\alpha) \to \mathrm{Full}(\alpha))$$

Proof. Assume α with

$$\alpha \mathrel{\dot{\in}} P \tag{11.6}$$
$$\mathrm{HypBase}(\alpha) \tag{11.7}$$
$$\mathrm{HypFull}(\alpha) \tag{11.8}$$

and a with

$$\forall x \prec a\big(x \in P \to \{\alpha\}x \in P\big) \tag{11.9}$$
$$a \in P \tag{11.10}$$

We have to prove

$$\{\alpha\}a \in P \tag{$*$}$$

From (11.6) and (11.10), we get in particular

$$a \in P \wedge \alpha \mathrel{\dot{\in}} P \tag{11.11}$$

We can use (CI) to show $(*)$, i.e., it suffices to assume

$$d \prec \{\alpha\}a \tag{11.12}$$

and show $d \in P$ by induction on d, i.e., we use (Ind_0) on $\Lambda d.(d \prec \{\alpha\}a \to d \in P)$. By Convention 11.12, it suffices to consider the following cases.
1. $d = \underline{x}$ for some x: The claim follows from Lemma 11.9.
2. $d = d_0 \oplus \ldots \oplus d_{m+1} \in \mathrm{OT}$: Then $d_0, \ldots, d_{m+1} <_{\mathbb{N}} d$ holds by Section 4.3, and we have $d = d_0 \mathbin{\tilde{+}} \ldots \mathbin{\tilde{+}} d_{m+1}$. Now, the induction hypothesis yields $d_0, \ldots, d_{m+1} \in P$ and hence by Lemma 11.10 that $d \in P$ holds.
3. $d = \{\alpha\}c$: This implies $c \prec a$, so we can use (11.9) to get $d \in P$ since $c \prec a$ and (11.11) imply $c \in P$ by (FP).

4. $d = \{\gamma\}c$ with $\alpha \prec_{\mathbf{lex}} \gamma$: Use Lemma 11.14.(b) because we have (11.11).
5. Otherwise: We have $d = \{\gamma\}c$ with

$$\gamma \prec_{\mathbf{lex}} \alpha \tag{11.13}$$

and this implies in particular

$$\alpha \neq \tfrac{0}{0} \tag{11.14}$$

Let $e_1, \ldots, e_{p+1}, c_1, \ldots, c_{p+1}$ be such that we have $\gamma \equiv \left(\begin{smallmatrix} c_1 & \cdots & c_{p+1} \\ e_1 & \cdots & e_{p+1} \end{smallmatrix}\right)$. We get $c, c_1, \ldots, c_{p+1} <_{\mathbb{N}} \{\gamma\}c$ and $c, c_1, \ldots, c_{p+1} \prec \{\gamma\}c$ by Section 4.3. Hence, $c, c_1, \ldots, c_{p+1} \prec \{\rho * \alpha\}a$ also holds and the induction hypothesis implies $c, c_1, \ldots, c_{p+1} \in P$, i.e.,

$$c \in P \wedge \gamma \mathrel{\dot{\in}} P \tag{11.15}$$

5.1. $\gamma \preceq_{\mathbf{lex}} \mathsf{tl}_{\boldsymbol{L}}(\alpha)$: Then we also have $\gamma \preceq_{\mathbf{lex}} \alpha\Downarrow$. Since $\alpha \neq \frac{0}{0}$ holds by (11.14), we get $\mathrm{Fun}(\alpha\Downarrow)$ from (11.7) and therefore Lemma 11.14.(a) and (11.15) yield $d = \{\gamma\}c \in P$.
5.2. $\mathsf{tl}_{\boldsymbol{L}}(\alpha) \prec_{\mathbf{lex}} \gamma$: With $\gamma \prec_{\mathbf{lex}} \alpha \equiv \mathsf{hd}_{\boldsymbol{L}}(\alpha) * \mathsf{tl}_{\boldsymbol{L}}(\alpha)$ from (11.13), we get

$$\gamma \equiv \delta * \sigma * \mathsf{tl}_{\boldsymbol{L}}(\alpha) \tag{11.16}$$

for some $\delta \in \boldsymbol{L}_0^{\prec \mathsf{e}(\alpha)} \cap P$ and $\sigma \in \boldsymbol{S}_0^{\mathsf{e}(\alpha)} \cap P$, while note here (11.15). Moreover, we have

$$\sigma \prec_{\mathbf{lex}} \mathsf{hd}_{\boldsymbol{L}}(\alpha) \tag{11.17}$$

and note here that (11.14) implies $\mathsf{hd}_{\boldsymbol{L}}(\alpha) \neq \frac{0}{0}$. Now, we get

$$\forall s \leq \mathsf{lh}_{\boldsymbol{S}}(\alpha)\big(\mathrm{Small}(s, \alpha, \mathsf{c}(\alpha, s))\big) \tag{11.18}$$

from (11.8). Next, we let

$$\begin{aligned} b &:= \mathsf{e}(\alpha) \\ n &:= \mathsf{lh}_{\boldsymbol{S}}(\alpha) \\ a_i &:= \mathsf{c}(\alpha, i) \quad \text{(for all } i \leq n) \\ b_i &:= \mathsf{c}(\sigma, i) \quad \text{(for all } i \leq n) \end{aligned}$$

and get

$$\mathsf{hd}_{\boldsymbol{L}}(\alpha) \equiv \frac{a_0,\ldots,a_n}{b} \quad \& \quad a_n \neq 0 \tag{11.19}$$

since $\alpha \neq \frac{0}{0}$ holds by (11.14). With respect to b_i for $i \leq n$, we note that $b_i = 0$ is possible (while recalling that we have for each i with $\mathsf{lh}_{\boldsymbol{S}}(\sigma) < i$ that $\mathsf{c}(\sigma, i) = 0$ holds by the definition of $\mathsf{c}(\sigma, i)$, and that also $\sigma \equiv \frac{0}{0}$ may hold).[2] Now, from (11.17) and $\sigma, \mathsf{hd}_{\boldsymbol{L}}(\alpha) \in \boldsymbol{S}_0$, we get

$$\mathsf{lh}_{\boldsymbol{S}}(\sigma) \leq \mathsf{lh}_{\boldsymbol{S}}(\alpha) = n \tag{11.20}$$

and some $s \leq n$ such that we have

$$\sigma \equiv \frac{b_0,\ldots,b_s,a_{s+1},\ldots a_n}{b} \tag{11.21}$$

$$b_s \prec a_s \tag{11.22}$$

This includes the special situation if $\sigma \equiv \frac{b_0,\ldots,b_{s_0}}{b}$ holds with $s_0 < n$ because we can then just take $s := n$ and $b_{s_0+1} := \ldots := b_s := 0$ due to $a_n \neq 0$ from (11.19). Noting (11.18) and the definition of $\mathrm{Small}(s, \alpha, \mathsf{c}(\alpha, s))$, let

$$\sigma' := \frac{b_0,\ldots,b_s}{b} \tag{11.23}$$

and get $\sigma' \in \boldsymbol{S}_0^b \cap P$ (note that $\sigma' \equiv \frac{0}{0}$ holds in case of $b_0 = \ldots = b_s = 0$). So, we get from (11.18) and with $s \leq n = \mathsf{lh}_{\boldsymbol{S}}(\alpha)$ the following:

$$\begin{pmatrix} \mathsf{c}(\sigma', s) \prec \mathsf{c}(\alpha, s) \\ \wedge\, \mathsf{lh}_{\boldsymbol{S}}(\sigma') \leq s \leq \mathsf{lh}_{\boldsymbol{S}}(\alpha) \\ \wedge\, \sigma' \in \boldsymbol{S}_0^{\mathsf{e}(\alpha)} \cap P \\ \wedge\, \delta \in \boldsymbol{L}_0^{\prec \mathsf{e}(\alpha)} \cap P \end{pmatrix} \to \mathrm{Fun}(\delta * \sigma' * \alpha|_s^{\boldsymbol{S}})$$

This yields

$$\mathrm{Fun}(\delta * \sigma' * \alpha|_s^{\boldsymbol{S}}) \tag{11.24}$$

because (11.22) yields $\mathsf{c}(\sigma', s) = b_s \prec a_s = \mathsf{c}(\alpha, s)$ and because (11.20)

[2] Furthermore and as a technical remark, we recall that in case of $b_0 = \ldots = b_n = 0$, we get $\frac{b_0,\ldots,b_n}{b} \equiv \frac{0}{0}$ by the definition of $\frac{b_0,\ldots,b_n}{b}$ even if $b \neq 0$ holds.

yields $\mathsf{lh}_{\boldsymbol{S}}(\sigma') \leq s \leq n = \mathsf{lh}_{\boldsymbol{S}}(\alpha)$. Note in (11.24) that $\delta * \sigma' * \alpha|_s^{\boldsymbol{S}} \equiv \gamma$ holds because of the following:

$$\begin{aligned} \gamma &\equiv \delta * \sigma * \mathsf{tl}_{\boldsymbol{L}}(\alpha) && \text{[by (11.16)]} \\ &\equiv \delta * \sigma' * \mathsf{hd}_{\boldsymbol{L}}(\alpha)|_s^{\boldsymbol{S}} * \mathsf{tl}_{\boldsymbol{L}}(\alpha) \\ &\equiv \delta * \sigma' * \alpha|_s^{\boldsymbol{S}} \end{aligned}$$

Hence, (11.24) implies $\{\gamma\}c \in P$ by (11.15). □

Corollary 11.16.

$$\mathsf{TID}_1 \vdash \forall \alpha \mathrel{\dot{\in}} P\big(\mathrm{HypBase}(\alpha) \to \mathrm{HypFull}(\alpha) \to \mathrm{Fun}(\alpha)\big)$$

Proof. This follows from Theorem 11.15 and by making use of (TID_1), while note that $\mathrm{Full}(\alpha) \in \mathrm{Pos}_1^{\rightarrow}$ holds. □

11.3.2. Advanced Wellordering Results

Corollary 11.17 (Closure under the ω-function).

$$\mathsf{TID}_1 \vdash \mathrm{Fun}(\tfrac{0}{0})$$

Proof. We have $\frac{0}{0} \mathrel{\dot{\in}} P$ and $\frac{1}{0} \mathrel{\dot{\in}} P$ due to $0, 1 \in P$ from Lemma 11.9. Further, $\mathrm{HypBase}(\frac{0}{0})$ and $\mathrm{HypFull}(\frac{0}{0})$ hold trivially (while note here that $\mathrm{Small}(0, \frac{0}{0}, \mathsf{c}(\frac{0}{0}, 0))$ is trivial). Hence $\mathrm{Fun}(\frac{0}{0})$ holds by Corollary 11.16. □

Corollary 11.18 (Closure under the ε-function).

$$\mathsf{TID}_1 \vdash \mathrm{Fun}(\tfrac{1}{0})$$

Proof. From Corollary 11.17 and $\frac{1}{0}{\Downarrow}{\equiv}\mathsf{tl}_{\boldsymbol{L}}(\frac{1}{0}){\equiv}\frac{0}{0}$, we get $\mathrm{HypBase}(\frac{1}{0})$. So, Lemma 11.13 yields $\mathrm{HypFull}(\frac{1}{0})$ and Corollary 11.16 yields $\mathrm{Fun}(\frac{1}{0})$. □

Corollary 11.19 (Closure under the binary Veblen function).

$$\mathsf{TID}_1 \vdash \forall a \in P(\mathrm{Fun}(\tfrac{a}{0}))$$

i.e., we get $\mathsf{TID}_1 \vdash \forall a, x(a \in P \wedge x \in P \to \{\frac{a}{0}\}x \in P)$.

Proof. It suffices to show $\mathrm{Prog}(\Lambda a.\mathrm{Fun}(\frac{a}{0}))$ because then, the claim follows by (TID_1). So let a, x be given and assume

$$\forall a_0 \prec a(\mathrm{Fun}(\tfrac{a_0}{0})) \tag{11.25}$$

For $\alpha := \frac{a}{0}$, we shall show $\mathrm{Fun}(\alpha)$. By Corollary 11.16, it suffices to show

$$\mathrm{HypBase}(\alpha) \tag{$*$}$$
$$\mathrm{HypFull}(\alpha) \tag{$**$}$$

By $\frac{a}{0}{\Downarrow}\equiv\frac{0}{0}$, we get $(*)$ from Corollary 11.17. Showing $(**)$ means to show $\mathrm{Small}(0, \alpha, a)$ due to $\mathsf{lh}_{\boldsymbol{S}}(\alpha) = 0$ and $\mathsf{c}(\alpha) = a$. From $\mathsf{e}(\alpha) = 0$, we get in the definition of $\mathrm{Small}(0, \alpha, a)$ for each $\sigma \in \boldsymbol{S}_0^{\mathsf{e}(\alpha)} \cap P$ with $\mathsf{lh}_{\boldsymbol{S}}(\sigma) \leq 0$ that

$$\sigma \equiv \tfrac{b}{0}$$

holds for some b and that $\mathsf{c}(\sigma, 0) \prec a$ yields $b \prec a$. So (11.25) yields

$$\mathrm{Fun}(\sigma) \tag{11.26}$$

for such σ. By the definition of $\mathrm{Small}(0, \alpha, a)$, we are done now because of $\alpha|_0^{\boldsymbol{S}}\equiv\frac{0}{0}$ and because $\mathsf{e}(\alpha) = 0$ implies $\rho\equiv\frac{0}{0}$ for each $\rho \in \boldsymbol{L}_0^{\prec\mathsf{e}(\alpha)} \cap P$. Hence, we can use (11.26) in order to get the conclusion of $\mathrm{Small}(0, \alpha, a)$. □

Remark 11.20.

- Corollary 11.17 corresponds essentially to the closure of P under

  $$\text{“}x \mapsto \omega^x\text{”}$$

  i.e., the *ω-exponential function.* Recall that $\{\frac{x}{0}\}$ corresponds to “ω^{1+x}” in our setting and that we can use Lemma 11.9 for “ω^0”.

- Corollary 11.19 corresponds essentially to the closure of P under

  $$\text{“}x, y \mapsto \varphi_2(x, y)\text{”}$$

  i.e., the *binary Veblen function.* Compare this with Lemma 7.6.

Lemma 11.21.

$$\mathsf{TID}_1 \vdash \forall \alpha \begin{pmatrix} \mathsf{tl}_{\boldsymbol{L}}(\alpha) \mathrel{\dot{\in}} P \\ \quad \to \mathrm{Fun}(\mathsf{tl}_{\boldsymbol{L}}(\alpha)) \\ \quad \to \forall b \prec \mathsf{e}(\alpha)(\mathrm{Fun}(\frac{1}{b} * \mathsf{tl}_{\boldsymbol{L}}(\alpha))) \\ \quad \to \mathrm{Fun}(\frac{1}{\mathsf{e}(\alpha)} * \mathsf{tl}_{\boldsymbol{L}}(\alpha)) \end{pmatrix}$$

Proof. We assume α, d with

$$\mathsf{tl}_{\boldsymbol{L}}(\alpha) \mathrel{\dot{\in}} P \tag{11.27}$$

$$\mathrm{Fun}(\mathsf{tl}_{\boldsymbol{L}}(\alpha)) \tag{11.28}$$

$$\forall b \prec \mathsf{e}(\alpha)(\mathrm{Fun}(\tfrac{1}{b} * \mathsf{tl}_{\boldsymbol{L}}(\alpha))) \tag{11.29}$$

and show

$$\mathrm{Fun}(\tfrac{1}{\mathsf{e}(\alpha)} * \mathsf{tl}_{\boldsymbol{L}}(\alpha)) \tag{$*$}$$

<u>1.</u> $\mathsf{e}(\alpha) = 0$: We get $(*)$, i.e., $\mathrm{Fun}(\frac{1}{0} * \mathsf{tl}_{\boldsymbol{L}}(\alpha))$, from Corollary 11.16 because of the following observations: We have that $\frac{1}{0} * \mathsf{tl}_{\boldsymbol{L}}(\alpha) \mathrel{\dot{\in}} P$ holds due to (11.27) and $1 \in P$ by Lemma 11.9. Then, $\mathrm{HypBase}((\frac{1}{0} * \mathsf{tl}_{\boldsymbol{L}}(\alpha))\Downarrow)$ holds due to $(\frac{1}{0} * \mathsf{tl}_{\boldsymbol{L}}(\alpha))\Downarrow \equiv \mathsf{tl}_{\boldsymbol{L}}(\alpha)$ and (11.28). Finally, we get also $\mathrm{HypFull}(\frac{1}{0} * \mathsf{tl}_{\boldsymbol{L}}(\alpha))$ by Lemma 11.13. So, we can use Corollary 11.16.
<u>2.</u> $\mathsf{e}(\alpha) \neq 0$: We shall show

$$\mathrm{Prog}(\Lambda a.a \in P \to \{\tfrac{1}{\mathsf{e}(\alpha)} * \mathsf{tl}_{\boldsymbol{L}}(\alpha)\}a \in P) \tag{$**$}$$

because then $(**)$ and (TID_1) yield the claim $\mathrm{Fun}(\frac{1}{\mathsf{e}(\alpha)} * \alpha)$. For $(**)$, assume a, d with

$$\forall a_0 \prec a(a_0 \in P \to \{\tfrac{1}{\mathsf{e}(\alpha)} * \mathsf{tl}_{\boldsymbol{L}}(\alpha)\}a_0 \in P) \tag{11.30}$$

$$a \in P \tag{11.31}$$

$$d \prec \{\tfrac{1}{\mathsf{e}(\alpha)} * \mathsf{tl}_{\boldsymbol{L}}(\alpha)\}a \tag{11.32}$$

and show

$$d \in P \tag{\#}$$

Then (FP) yields the remaining claim $\{\frac{1}{\mathsf{e}(\alpha)} * \mathsf{tl}_{\boldsymbol{L}}(\alpha)\}a \in P$. The current case $\mathsf{e}(\alpha) \neq 0$ implies in particular

$$\alpha \neq \tfrac{0}{0} \tag{11.33}$$

$$\alpha{\Downarrow} \equiv \tfrac{1}{\mathsf{e}(\alpha)} * \mathsf{tl}_{\boldsymbol{L}}(\alpha) \tag{11.34}$$

We show (#) by induction on d. More precisely, we shall use (Ind_0) on $\Lambda d.(d \prec \{\frac{1}{\mathsf{e}(\alpha)} * \mathsf{tl}_{\boldsymbol{L}}(\alpha)\}a \to d \in P)$. Since we assume tacitly and without loss of generality that $d \in \mathrm{OT}$ holds (see Convention 11.12), it suffices to consider the following case distinctions.

2.1. $d = \underline{x}$ for some x: The claim follows from Lemma 11.9.

2.2. $d = d_0 \oplus \ldots \oplus d_{m+1} \in \mathrm{OT}$: Then $d_0, \ldots, d_{m+1} <_{\mathbb{N}} d$ holds by Section 4.3, and we have $d = d_0 \tilde{+} \ldots \tilde{+} d_{m+1}$. Now, the induction hypothesis yields $d_0, \ldots, d_{m+1} \in P$ and hence by Lemma 11.10 that $d \in P$ holds.

2.3. $d = \{\frac{1}{\mathsf{e}(\alpha)} * \mathsf{tl}_{\boldsymbol{L}}(\alpha)\}c$: This implies $c \prec a$, so we use (11.30) to get $d \in P$ since $c \prec a$ and (11.31) imply $c \in P$ by (FP).

2.4. $d = \{\gamma\}c$ with $\frac{1}{\mathsf{e}(\alpha)} * \mathsf{tl}_{\boldsymbol{L}}(\alpha) \prec_{\mathbf{lex}} \gamma$: Use Lemma 11.14.(b) because we have $a \in P$ by (11.31), $\frac{1}{\mathsf{e}(\alpha)} * \mathsf{tl}_{\boldsymbol{L}}(\alpha) \,\dot{\in}\, P$ by (11.27) and $1 \in P$.

2.5. Otherwise: We have $d = \{\gamma\}c$ with

$$\gamma \prec_{\mathbf{lex}} \tfrac{1}{\mathsf{e}(\alpha)} * \mathsf{tl}_{\boldsymbol{L}}(\alpha) \tag{11.35}$$

Let $e_1, \ldots, e_{p+1}, c_1, \ldots, c_{p+1}$ be such that we have $\gamma \equiv \left(\begin{smallmatrix} c_1 & \cdots & c_{p+1} \\ e_1 & \cdots & e_{p+1}\end{smallmatrix}\right)$. We get $c, c_1, \ldots, c_{p+1} <_{\mathbb{N}} \{\gamma\}c$ and $c, c_1, \ldots, c_{p+1} \prec \{\gamma\}c$ by Section 4.3. Hence, $c, c_1, \ldots, c_{p+1} \prec \{\frac{1}{\mathsf{e}(\alpha)} * \mathsf{tl}_{\boldsymbol{L}}(\alpha)\}a$ also holds and the induction hypothesis implies $c, c_1, \ldots, c_{p+1} \in P$, i.e.,

$$c \in P \wedge \gamma \,\dot{\in}\, P \tag{11.36}$$

2.5.1. $\gamma \preceq_{\mathbf{lex}} \mathsf{tl}_{\boldsymbol{L}}(\alpha)$: Use Lemma 11.14.(a), (11.36), and (11.28).

2.5.2. $\mathsf{tl}_{\boldsymbol{L}}(\alpha) \prec_{\mathbf{lex}} \gamma$: With $\gamma \prec_{\mathbf{lex}} \frac{1}{\mathsf{e}(\alpha)} * \mathsf{tl}_{\boldsymbol{L}}(\alpha)$ from (11.35), we get

$$\gamma \equiv \rho * \sigma * \mathsf{tl}_{\boldsymbol{L}}(\alpha)$$

for some $\sigma \in \boldsymbol{S}^{\prec \mathsf{e}(\alpha)}$ and $\rho \in \boldsymbol{L}_0^{\prec \mathsf{e}(\sigma)}$. Let

$$b := \mathsf{e}(\sigma) \,\tilde{+}\, \mathsf{lh}_{\boldsymbol{S}}(\sigma) \,\tilde{+}\, 1$$

In other words, we have $\frac{1}{b} \equiv \frac{\bar{0}^{(\mathsf{lh}_S(\sigma)+1)},1}{\mathsf{e}(\sigma)}$. Now, because of $\mathsf{e}(\sigma) \prec \mathsf{e}(\alpha)$ and $\mathsf{e}(\alpha) \in \mathrm{Lim}$, we get $b \prec \mathsf{e}(\alpha)$ and therefore $\mathrm{Fun}(\frac{1}{b} * \mathsf{tl}_L(\alpha))$ by (11.29). We get now $\mathrm{Fun}(\gamma)$ by Lemma 11.14.(a) with $\gamma \prec_{\mathsf{lex}} \frac{1}{b} * \mathsf{tl}_L(\alpha)$ and $\gamma \dot{\in} P$ from (11.36). With $c \in P$ from (11.36), we hence get $d = \{\gamma\}c \in P$. □

11.3.3. Core Result for HypFull

Theorem 11.22.

$$\mathsf{TID}_1 + (\mathsf{Ind}_2) \vdash \mathrm{Prog}\big(\Lambda c.\forall\alpha_0 \dot{\in} P \begin{pmatrix} \mathsf{e}(\alpha_0) \preceq c \wedge c \in P \\ \to \mathrm{HypBase}(\alpha_0) \\ \to \mathrm{HypFull}(\alpha_0) \end{pmatrix}\big)$$

Proof. We assume

$$\forall c_0 \prec c \forall\alpha_0 \dot{\in} P \begin{pmatrix} \mathsf{e}(\alpha_0) \preceq c_0 \wedge c_0 \in P \\ \to \mathrm{HypBase}(\alpha_0) \\ \to \mathrm{HypFull}(\alpha_0) \end{pmatrix} \tag{Prog-Hyp}$$

and c with

$$c \in P \tag{11.37}$$

Furthermore, we assume α_0 with

$$\alpha_0 \dot{\in} P \tag{11.38}$$

$$\mathsf{e}(\alpha_0) \preceq c \tag{11.39}$$

$$\mathrm{HypBase}(\alpha_0) \tag{11.40}$$

and have to show $\mathrm{HypFull}(\alpha_0)$. We get this by first showing the following auxiliary statement

$$\mathsf{TID}_1 + (\mathsf{Ind}_2) \vdash \forall s \forall\alpha \dot{\in} P \begin{pmatrix} \mathsf{e}(\alpha) \preceq c \\ \to \mathrm{HypBase}(\alpha) \\ \to \mathrm{HypPart}(s,\alpha) \\ \to \mathrm{Part}(s,\alpha) \end{pmatrix} \tag{$\bullet$}$$

from which we get for all $s \leq \mathsf{lh}_{\boldsymbol{S}}(\alpha_0)$ that

$$\mathrm{Small}(s, \alpha_0, \mathsf{c}(\alpha_0, s)) \tag{$\circ$}$$

holds, i.e., the claim $\mathrm{HypFull}(\alpha_0)$. More precisely, we get ($\circ$) by an induction on $\mathsf{lh}_{\boldsymbol{S}}(\alpha)_0 \dot{-} s$ for $s \leq \mathsf{lh}_{\boldsymbol{S}}(\alpha_0)$ as follows:

- In case of $\mathsf{lh}_{\boldsymbol{S}}(\alpha_0) \dot{-} s = 0$, we have $s = \mathsf{lh}_{\boldsymbol{S}}(\alpha_0)$ and so $\mathrm{HypPart}(s, \alpha_0)$ is trivial. Therefore $\mathrm{Part}(s, \alpha)$ follows from ($\bullet$) with (11.38), (11.39), and (11.40). We then get ($\circ$) from $\mathrm{Part}(s, \alpha)$ by making use of (TID_1) and that $\mathsf{c}(\alpha_0, s) \in P$ holds by $\alpha_0 \mathrel{\dot{\in}} P$ from (11.38). Note hereby that $\mathsf{c}(\alpha_0, s) \in P \to \mathrm{Small}(s, \alpha_0, \mathsf{c}(\alpha_0, s))$ is in $\mathrm{Pos}_1^{\rightarrow}$.

- If we have on the other hand $\mathsf{lh}_{\boldsymbol{S}}(\alpha_0) \dot{-} s \neq 0$, then the induction hypothesis yields $\mathrm{Small}(s_0, \alpha_0, \mathsf{c}(\alpha_0, s_0))$ for all s_0 with $s_0 \leq \mathsf{lh}_{\boldsymbol{S}}(\alpha_0)$ and $\mathsf{lh}_{\boldsymbol{S}}(\alpha_0) \dot{-} s_0 < \mathsf{lh}_{\boldsymbol{S}}(\alpha_0) \dot{-} s$, i.e., for all s_0 with $s < s_0 \leq \mathsf{lh}_{\boldsymbol{S}}(\alpha_0)$. This yields $\mathrm{HypPart}(s, \alpha_0)$ and hence, ($\circ$) follows again from ($\bullet$) by making use of (TID_1) and that $\mathsf{c}(\alpha_0, s) \in P$ holds.

It remains to show the auxiliary statement ($\bullet$) which we do by induction on s. Note that (Ind_2) can be applied here because

$$\Lambda s.\forall\alpha \begin{pmatrix} \alpha \mathrel{\dot{\in}} P \\ \quad \to \mathrm{HypBase}(\alpha) \\ \quad \to \mathrm{HypPart}(s, \alpha) \\ \quad \to \mathrm{Part}(s, \alpha) \end{pmatrix} \in \mathrm{Pos}_2^{\rightarrow}$$

holds by the definition of $\mathrm{Pos}_2^{\rightarrow}$, while we use here that $\mathrm{Part}(s, \alpha) \in \mathrm{Pos}_2^{\rightarrow}$ holds by Lemma 11.8.(a), that $\mathrm{HypBase}(\alpha), \mathrm{HypPart}(s, \alpha) \in \mathrm{Pos}_1^{\rightarrow}$ holds by Lemma 11.7, and that $\alpha \mathrel{\dot{\in}} P$ is in $\mathrm{Pos}_0^{\rightarrow}$ (and hence in $\mathrm{Pos}_1^{\rightarrow}$). Before we distinguish the cases on s, let s, α, a be given, set

$$\begin{aligned} n &:= \mathsf{lh}_{\boldsymbol{S}}(\alpha) \\ b &:= \mathsf{e}(\alpha) \\ \gamma &:= \mathsf{tl}_{\boldsymbol{L}}(\alpha) \end{aligned}$$

and assume

$$\alpha \mathrel{\dot\in} P \tag{11.41}$$
$$\mathsf{e}(\alpha) \preceq c \tag{11.42}$$
$$\mathrm{HypBase}(\alpha) \tag{11.43}$$
$$\mathrm{HypPart}(s, \alpha) \tag{11.44}$$
$$\forall x \prec a(x \in P \to \mathrm{Small}(s, \alpha, x)) \tag{11.45}$$
$$a \in P \tag{11.46}$$

while (11.44) is

$$\forall s_0(s < s_0 \leq n \to \mathrm{Small}(s_0, \alpha, \mathsf{c}(\alpha, s_0))) \tag{11.47}$$

Then we have to show $\mathrm{Small}(s, \alpha, a)$, i.e.,

$$\forall \rho, \sigma\left(\begin{pmatrix} \mathsf{c}(\sigma, s) \prec a \\ \wedge\, \mathsf{lh}_{\boldsymbol{S}}(\sigma) \leq s \leq n \\ \wedge\, \sigma \in \boldsymbol{S}_0^b \cap P \\ \wedge\, \rho \in \boldsymbol{L}_0^{\prec b} \cap P \end{pmatrix} \to \mathrm{Fun}(\rho * \sigma * \alpha|_s^{\boldsymbol{S}})\right) \tag{*-1}$$

In case of $\alpha \equiv \frac{0}{0}$, we have $b = 0$, so for ρ in (*-1), we have $\rho \equiv \frac{0}{0}$. Since we also have $n = 0$ in case of $\alpha \equiv \frac{0}{0}$, we get $\sigma \equiv \frac{x}{0}$ with $x \prec a$ for σ in (*-1), i.e., the conclusion of (*-1) becomes $\mathrm{Fun}(\frac{x}{0})$. Then, we can use Corollary 11.19 because $x \prec a$ and (11.46) imply $x \in P$. Therefore, we shall assume from now on

$$\alpha \neq \tfrac{0}{0} \tag{11.48}$$

and in order to show (*-1), we further assume ρ, σ, y with

$$\mathsf{c}(\sigma, s) \prec a \tag{11.49}$$
$$\mathsf{lh}_{\boldsymbol{S}}(\sigma) \leq s \leq n \tag{11.50}$$
$$\sigma \in \boldsymbol{S}_0^b \cap P \tag{11.51}$$
$$\rho \in \boldsymbol{L}_0^{\prec b} \cap P \tag{11.52}$$
$$y \in P \tag{11.53}$$

and show

$$\{\rho * \sigma * \alpha|_s^{\boldsymbol{S}}\}y \in P \tag{*-2}$$

Note that (11.48) with (11.43) implies

$$\mathrm{Fun}(\alpha\Downarrow) \tag{11.54}$$

Next, we set

$$\tau := \sigma * \mathsf{hd}_{\boldsymbol{L}}(\alpha)|_s^{\boldsymbol{S}}$$
$$\beta_s := \tau * \gamma$$

and get

$$\beta_s \equiv \sigma * \alpha|_s^{\boldsymbol{S}} \tag{11.55}$$
$$\tau \in \boldsymbol{S}_0^b \cap P \tag{11.56}$$

while we can use for (11.56) that (11.51) and (11.41) hold. So the goal (*-2) becomes to show

$$\{\rho * \beta_s\}y \in P \tag{*-3}$$

Moreover, we get $\tau * \gamma \mathrel{\dot\in} P$ because of $\sigma \mathrel{\dot\in} P$ from (11.51) and $\alpha \mathrel{\dot\in} P$ from (11.41), i.e., we have

$$\beta_s \mathrel{\dot\in} P \tag{11.57}$$

__1.__ $\tau \equiv \frac{0}{0}$: We now have $\beta_s \equiv \gamma$. So for showing (*-3), we now have to show $\{\rho * \gamma\}y \in P$ and we shall consider the following cases on b.

__1.1.__ $b = 0$, i.e., $\mathsf{e}(\alpha) = 0$: Then $\rho \equiv \frac{0}{0}$ must hold (due to (11.52)) and we get $\alpha\Downarrow \equiv \gamma$. Now, (11.54) yields $\mathrm{Fun}(\gamma)$ and hence $\{\gamma\}y \in P$ together with (11.53) and we are done.
__1.2.__ Otherwise: Note that $\rho * \gamma \prec_{\mathbf{lex}} \frac{1}{b} * \gamma \equiv \alpha\Downarrow$ holds due to $\rho \in \boldsymbol{L}_0^{\prec b}$ from (11.52). Then use Lemma 11.14.(a) with $\mathrm{Fun}(\alpha\Downarrow)$ from (11.54) and $\rho * \gamma \mathrel{\dot\in} P$ from (11.57) and (11.52). We thus have $\mathrm{Fun}(\rho * \gamma)$ and so (*-3) follows with (11.53).

2. $\tau \neq \frac{0}{0}$: This implies

$$\left.\begin{array}{lll} \mathsf{lh}_{\boldsymbol{S}}(\beta_s) \leq n & \mathsf{hd}_{\boldsymbol{L}}(\beta_s) \equiv \tau & \beta_s \neq \frac{0}{0} \\ \quad = \mathsf{lh}_{\boldsymbol{S}}(\alpha) & & \\ & & \\ \mathsf{e}(\beta_s) = b & \mathsf{tl}_{\boldsymbol{L}}(\beta_s) \equiv \gamma & \beta_s{\Downarrow} \equiv \alpha{\Downarrow} \\ \quad = \mathsf{e}(\alpha) & \quad \equiv \mathsf{tl}_{\boldsymbol{L}}(\alpha) & \end{array}\right\} \tag{11.58}$$

where the situation $\mathsf{lh}_{\boldsymbol{S}}(\beta_s) < n$ in (11.58) is only possible in case of $s = n$ because we have $\mathsf{hd}_{\boldsymbol{S}}(\alpha) = \mathsf{hd}_{\boldsymbol{S}}(\mathsf{tl}_{\boldsymbol{L}}(\alpha)) \neq 0$ due to $\alpha \neq \frac{0}{0}$ from (11.48). With (11.54) and (11.58), we get $\mathrm{Fun}(\beta_s{\Downarrow})$ and hence

$$\mathrm{HypBase}(\beta_s) \tag{11.59}$$

2.1. $\rho \equiv \frac{0}{0}$: In this case, we shall show

$$\mathrm{HypFull}(\beta_s) \tag{\#-1}$$

and then get by Corollary 11.16 with (#-1), (11.59), and (11.57) that $\mathrm{Fun}(\beta_s)$ holds. The claim (*-3) follows then by (11.53). For showing the remaining goal (#-1), we note first that the following holds (using the current case $\tau \neq \frac{0}{0}$, while $\mathsf{c}(\sigma, s) = 0$ may hold):

$$\mathsf{c}(\beta_s, s) = \mathsf{c}(\tau, s) = \mathsf{c}(\sigma, s) \in P \tag{11.60}$$
$$\forall s_0 (s < s_0 \leq n \rightarrow \mathsf{c}(\beta_s, s_0) = \mathsf{c}(\alpha, s_0)) \tag{11.61}$$

This implies

$$\forall s_0 (s \leq s_0 \leq n \rightarrow \alpha|_{s_0}^{\boldsymbol{S}} \equiv \beta_s|_{s_0}^{\boldsymbol{S}}) \tag{11.62}$$

and further, we get

$$\mathrm{Small}(s, \beta_s, \mathsf{c}(\beta_s, s)) \tag{11.63}$$

because of the following: First, we have that $\mathrm{Small}(s, \alpha, \mathsf{c}(\sigma, s))$ holds due to (11.45) with (11.49) and since we have $\mathsf{c}(\sigma, s) \in P$ by (11.51). Next, we have that $\mathrm{Small}(s,\alpha,\mathsf{c}(\sigma,s))$ is

$$\forall\rho',\sigma'\left(\begin{pmatrix}\mathsf{c}(\sigma',s)\prec\mathsf{c}(\sigma,s)\\ \wedge\,\mathsf{lh}_{\boldsymbol{S}}(\sigma')\le s\le\mathsf{lh}_{\boldsymbol{S}}(\alpha)\\ \wedge\,\sigma'\in\boldsymbol{S}_0^{\mathsf{e}(\alpha)}\cap P\\ \wedge\,\rho'\in\boldsymbol{L}_0^{\prec\mathsf{e}(\alpha)}\cap P\end{pmatrix}\to\mathrm{Fun}(\rho'*\sigma'*\alpha|_s^{\boldsymbol{S}})\right)$$

and so by using (11.58), (11.60), and (11.62), this implies (11.63). Note in case of $\mathsf{lh}_{\boldsymbol{S}}(b_s)<\mathsf{lh}_{\boldsymbol{S}}(\alpha)=n$ that we have $s=n$, hence (11.63) is trivial then because $\mathsf{lh}_{\boldsymbol{S}}(\sigma')\le s\le\mathsf{lh}_{\boldsymbol{S}}(\beta_s)$ is impossible in the definition of $\mathrm{Small}(s,\beta_s,\mathsf{c}(\beta_s,s))$. So, we have shown (11.63). Furthermore, we get

$$\forall s_0(s<s_0\le n\to\mathrm{Small}(s_0,\beta_s,\mathsf{c}(\beta_s,s_0))) \tag{11.64}$$

because $\mathrm{Small}(s_0,\alpha,\mathsf{c}(\alpha,s_0))$ holds for each s_0 with $s<s_0\le n$ by (11.47), and this yields (11.64) because of (11.61), (11.62), and the definition of $\mathrm{Small}(s_0,\alpha,\mathsf{c}(\alpha,s_0))$. So, (11.64) with (11.63) yields

$$\forall s_0(s\le s_0\le n\to\mathrm{Small}(s_0,\beta_s,\mathsf{c}(\beta_s,s_0))) \tag{11.65}$$

If we can also show

$$\forall s_1(s_1<s\to\mathrm{Small}(s_1,\beta_s,\mathsf{c}(\beta_s,s_1))) \tag{\#-2}$$

then (#-2) and (11.65) yield (#-1) and we are done. For the remaining goal (#-2), we can assume $s\neq 0$ and do a *side* induction on $s\dot{-}s_1$.

Formally, this means that we shall apply (Ind_1) in order to show

$$\forall s_2,l(0<l\le s_2\le s\to\mathrm{Small}(s\dot{-}l,\beta_s,\mathsf{c}(\beta_s,s\dot{-}l))) \tag{\#-3}$$

while noting that

$$\Lambda s_2.\forall l(0<l\le s_2\le s\to\mathrm{Small}(s\dot{-}l,\beta_s,\mathsf{c}(\beta_s,s\dot{-}l)))\in\mathrm{Pos}_1^{\to}$$

holds by the definition of $\mathrm{Pos}_1^{\to}$, using that $\mathrm{Small}(s\dot{-}l,\beta_s,\mathsf{c}(\beta_s,s\dot{-}l))\in\mathrm{Pos}_1^{\to}$ holds by Lemma 11.7 and that $0<l\le s_2\le s$ is in $\mathrm{Pos}_0^{\to}$. For (#-3), we have nothing to show in case of $s_2=0$. So, assume now $s_2>0$: Since

$s_2 \dot{-} 1 < s_2$ holds, we get from the *side* induction hypothesis for (#-3):

$$\forall l(0 < l \leq s_2 \dot{-} 1 \leq s \to \text{Small}(s \dot{-} l, \beta_s, \mathsf{c}(\beta_s, s \dot{-} l))) \tag{11.66}$$

For (#-3), it remains to consider the case $l = s_2$ with $s_2 \leq s$ and to show

$$\text{Small}(s \dot{-} s_2, \beta_s, \mathsf{c}(\beta_s, s \dot{-} s_2)) \tag{\#-4}$$

Note that (11.66) and $s_2 \dot{-} 1 < s_2 \leq s$ yield

$$\forall s_0(s \dot{-} s_2 < s_0 < s \to \text{Small}(s_0, \beta_s, \mathsf{c}(\beta_s, s_0))) \tag{11.67}$$

so by using the *main* induction hypothesis for (•), i.e.,

$$\forall \alpha' \dot{\in} P \begin{pmatrix} \mathsf{e}(\alpha') \preceq c \\ \to \text{HypBase}(\alpha') \\ \to \text{HypPart}(s \dot{-} s_2, \alpha') \\ \to \text{Part}(s \dot{-} s_2, \alpha') \end{pmatrix}$$

Note that $\mathsf{e}(\beta_s) = \mathsf{e}(\alpha) \preceq c$ holds by (11.58) and (11.42). So, we get for $\alpha' := \beta_s$ from (11.57), (11.59), (11.67), and (11.65) that $\text{Part}(s \dot{-} s_2, \beta_s)$ holds, i.e., $\text{Prog}(\mathcal{C})$ for

$$\mathcal{C} := \Lambda a_0.(a_0 \in P \to \text{Small}(s \dot{-} s_2, \beta_s, a_0))$$

Since $\mathcal{C} \in \text{Pos}_1^{\to}$ holds and since we have

$$\mathsf{c}(\beta_s, s \dot{-} s_2) = \mathsf{c}(\tau, s \dot{-} s_2) = \mathsf{c}(\sigma, s \dot{-} s_2)$$

due to $s_2 < s$, we get with (TID_1) and $\mathsf{c}(\sigma, s \dot{-} s_2) \in P$ from (11.51) that (#-4) holds and we are done.

2.2. $\rho \neq \frac{0}{0}$: In this case, we shall show

$$\text{Fun}(\rho * \beta_s) \tag{†-1}$$

by a *side* induction on $\mathsf{lh}_{\mathcal{L}}(\rho)$. Note that the claim (∗-3) follows from (†-1) and (11.53). For showing (†-1), let now

$$\beta' := \mathsf{tl}_{\boldsymbol{L}}(\rho) * \beta_s$$
$$\rho' := \mathsf{hd}_{\boldsymbol{L}}(\rho)$$

and note that $\mathsf{hd}_{\boldsymbol{L}}(\rho') \in \boldsymbol{S}^{\prec b}$ holds due to $\rho \neq \frac{0}{0}$. We first get that

$$\mathrm{Fun}(\beta') \tag{11.68}$$

holds due to the following observation: In case of $\mathsf{lh}_{\boldsymbol{L}}(\rho) = 0$, we have $\beta' \equiv \beta_s$ and get $\mathrm{Fun}(\beta_s)$ in (11.68) due to $\mathrm{HypFull}(\beta_s)$, i.e., (#-1), from case **2.1.** and $\mathrm{HypBase}(\beta_s)$ from (11.59). Then we can apply Corollary 11.16 to get $\mathrm{Fun}(\beta_s)$. If otherwise $\mathsf{lh}_{\boldsymbol{L}}(\rho) \neq 0$ holds, then we get (11.68) immediately by the *side* induction hypothesis for (†-1) due to $\beta' \equiv \mathsf{tl}_{\boldsymbol{L}}(\rho) * \beta_s$. Note that

$$\mathsf{e}(\rho') \preceq \mathsf{e}(\rho) \prec \mathsf{e}(\alpha) \preceq c \tag{11.69}$$

holds by $\mathsf{e}(\rho') = \mathsf{e}(\rho) \prec \mathsf{e}(\beta_s) = \mathsf{e}(\alpha)$ and $\mathsf{e}(\alpha) \preceq c$ from (11.42).

2.2.1. $\mathsf{e}(\rho') = 0$: Then we have $(\rho * \beta_s){\Downarrow} \equiv (\rho' * \beta'){\Downarrow} \equiv \beta'$ because of $\rho * \beta_s \equiv \rho' * \beta'$ and so, (11.68) yields

$$\mathrm{HypBase}(\rho * \beta_s) \tag{11.70}$$

Recall that $\rho \neq \frac{0}{0}$ holds, so we have $\mathsf{e}(\rho * \beta_s) = \mathsf{e}(\rho) \prec c \in P$ from (11.69) and (11.37), so we can use (Prog-Hyp) with (11.70) and with $\rho * \beta_s \mathrel{\dot{\in}} P$ from (11.57) and (11.52) in order to get $\mathrm{HypFull}(\rho * \beta_s)$. So, the claim (†-1) follows by Corollary 11.16.

2.2.2. $\mathsf{e}(\rho') \neq 0$: We shall show now

$$\mathrm{Prog}(\Lambda d.d \prec \mathsf{e}(\rho') \to \mathrm{Fun}(\tfrac{1}{d} * \beta')) \tag{†-2}$$

Then (†-2) implies the claim (†-1) due to the following observation. First, we get from (†-2) that

$$\forall d \prec \mathsf{e}(\rho')(\mathrm{Fun}(\tfrac{1}{d} * \beta')) \tag{11.71}$$

holds because we can apply (TID_1) to (†-2) and because we have that $d \in P$ holds for all $d \prec \mathsf{e}(\rho')$ due to $\mathsf{e}(\rho') \prec c$ from (11.69) and $c \in P$ from (11.37). Next, note that we have $\mathsf{tl}_{\boldsymbol{L}}(\frac{1}{\mathsf{e}(\rho')} * \beta') \equiv \beta' \mathrel{\dot{\in}} P$ by (11.57), (11.52), and the definition of β'. So, Lemma 11.21 applied to $\frac{1}{\mathsf{e}(\rho')} * \beta'$ yields $\mathrm{Fun}(\frac{1}{\mathsf{e}(\rho')} * \beta')$ because we have (11.68) and (11.71). Now, this is just

$$\mathrm{HypBase}(\rho * \beta_s) \tag{11.72}$$

because we have $(\rho * \beta_s)\Downarrow \equiv (\rho' * \beta')\Downarrow \equiv \frac{1}{\mathsf{e}(\rho')} * \beta'$. Now, $\rho \neq \frac{0}{0}$ yields $\mathsf{e}(\rho{*}\beta_s) = \mathsf{e}(\rho) \prec c \in P$ from (11.69) and (11.37), so we can use (Prog-Hyp) with (11.72) and with $\rho * \beta_s \mathrel{\dot\in} P$ from (11.57) and (11.52) in order to get $\mathrm{HypFull}(\rho * \beta_s)$. So, the claim (†-1) follows by Corollary 11.16.

Now, it remains to show (†-2) and for this, we let d be given with

$$d \prec \mathsf{e}(\rho') \tag{11.73}$$

$$\forall d_0 \prec d(d_0 \prec \mathsf{e}(\rho') \to \mathrm{Fun}(\tfrac{1}{d_0} * \beta')) \tag{11.74}$$

and show

$$\mathrm{Fun}(\tfrac{1}{d} * \beta') \tag{†-3}$$

2.2.2.1. $d \in \mathbb{L}$: By Lemma 11.21, (11.68), (11.74) and $\mathsf{e}(\frac{1}{d} * \beta') = d\Downarrow = d$.
2.2.2.2. Otherwise: We have $d \in \mathrm{Suc}$ and hence $d\Downarrow \prec d$. Recall $\mathsf{e}(\rho') \prec \mathsf{e}(\alpha) \prec c$ from (11.69), so we have $\mathsf{e}(\frac{1}{d} * \beta') \prec c$ due to $\mathsf{e}(\frac{1}{d} * \beta') = d\Downarrow \prec d \prec \mathsf{e}(\alpha) \preceq c \in P$ from (11.37) and $d \in \mathrm{Suc}$. Therefore, we get from (Prog-Hyp) that the following holds:

$$\mathrm{HypBase}(\tfrac{1}{d} * \beta') \to \mathrm{HypFull}(\tfrac{1}{d} * \beta') \tag{11.75}$$

In particular due to $d\Downarrow \prec d$, we get $\mathrm{Fun}(\frac{1}{d\Downarrow} * \beta')$ due to (11.74). This and (11.68), respectively, yield

$$\mathrm{HypBase}(\tfrac{1}{d} * \beta') \tag{11.76}$$

by the definition of $\mathrm{HypBase}(\frac{1}{d} * \beta')$. We therefore get $\mathrm{HypFull}(\frac{1}{d} * \beta')$ by (11.75) and (11.76). So, Corollary 11.16 yields $\mathrm{Fun}(\frac{1}{d} * \beta')$ and hence the claim (†-3). □

Corollary 11.23. *For all terms t, the following holds:*

(a) $\mathsf{TID}_1^+ \vdash t \in P$ *implies* $\mathsf{TID}_1^+ \vdash \forall \alpha \mathrel{\dot{\in}} P \begin{pmatrix} \mathsf{e}(\alpha) \preceq t \\ \to \mathrm{HypBase}(\alpha) \\ \to \mathrm{Fun}(\alpha) \end{pmatrix}$

(b) $\mathsf{TID}_2 \vdash t \in P \to \forall \alpha \mathrel{\dot{\in}} P \begin{pmatrix} \mathsf{e}(\alpha) \preceq t \\ \to \mathrm{HypBase}(\alpha) \\ \to \mathrm{Fun}(\alpha) \end{pmatrix}$

Hence, $\mathsf{TID}_2 \vdash \forall x \in P \forall \alpha \mathrel{\dot{\in}} P(\mathsf{e}(\alpha) \preceq x \to \mathrm{HypBase}(\alpha) \to \mathrm{Fun}(\alpha))$.

Proof. Assume $t \in P$, while we can also assume $\mathsf{TID}_1^+ \vdash t \in P$ if showing (a). Further assume α with

$$\alpha \mathrel{\dot{\in}} P \tag{11.77}$$
$$\mathrm{HypBase}(\alpha) \tag{11.78}$$

Now, by (TID^+) and TID_2, respectively, we get by Theorem 11.22 that

$$\forall \alpha_0 \mathrel{\dot{\in}} P(\mathsf{e}(\alpha_0) \preceq t \wedge t \in P \to \mathrm{HypBase}(\alpha_0) \to \mathrm{HypFull}(\alpha_0))$$

holds. Hence, we get also $\mathrm{HypFull}(\alpha)$ from which the claim $\mathrm{Fun}(\alpha)$ follows due to Corollary 11.16 with (11.78) and (11.77) . □

11.4. Towards the Large Veblen Ordinal in TID_1^+ and TID_2

11.4.1. Wellordering Results Getting Beyond $\vartheta\Omega^\omega$

Corollary 11.24 (Closure under the finitary Veblen functions)**.** *For all* $n \in \mathbb{N}$, *the following holds:*

$$\mathsf{TID}_1 + (\mathsf{Ind}_2) \vdash \forall a_0 \in P \ldots \forall a_n \in P(\{\tfrac{a_1,\ldots,a_n}{0}\}a_0 \in P)$$

Proof. Let $n \in \mathbb{N}$ and $a_0, \ldots, a_n \in P$ be given and set $\sigma := \frac{a_1,\ldots,a_n}{0}$. We have to show $\mathrm{Fun}(\sigma)$. Note that Theorem 11.22 (for $c := \mathsf{e}(\sigma) := 0$) trivially yields

$$\mathrm{HypBase}(\sigma) \to \mathrm{HypFull}(\sigma)$$

and so, we show $\mathrm{HypBase}(\sigma)$ and get then $\mathrm{HypFull}(\sigma)$ which yields with Corollary 11.16 the claim $\mathrm{Fun}(\sigma)$. For $\mathrm{HypBase}(\sigma)$, note that we get $\mathrm{Fun}(\sigma{\Downarrow})$ by Corollary 11.17 and due to $\sigma{\Downarrow} \equiv \frac{0}{0}$. □

Corollary 11.25 (Closure under weak Veblen ordinals[3]).

(a) $\mathsf{TID}_1 + (\mathsf{Ind}_2) \vdash \forall \sigma \,\dot{\in}\, \boldsymbol{S}_0^0 \cap P(\mathrm{Fun}(\sigma))$

(b) $\mathsf{TID}_1 + (\mathsf{Ind}_2) \vdash \mathrm{Fun}(\frac{1}{\omega})$.

Proof. For (a), we can argue as in Corollary 11.24. For (b), we shall use Lemma 11.21 with

$$\alpha := \frac{1}{\omega}$$

For this note that $\mathsf{tl}_{\boldsymbol{L}}(\alpha) \equiv \frac{0}{0}$ and $\mathsf{e}(\alpha) = \omega$ hold. So, we get $\mathrm{Fun}(\frac{0}{0})$ due to Corollary 11.17 and

$$\forall b \prec \mathsf{e}(\alpha)(\mathrm{Fun}(\tfrac{1}{b} * \mathsf{tl}_{\boldsymbol{L}}(\alpha)))$$

due to (a). For the latter, note that $b \prec \mathsf{e}(\alpha) = \omega$ implies $\frac{1}{b} * \mathsf{tl}_{\boldsymbol{L}}(\alpha) \equiv \frac{1}{b} \in \boldsymbol{S}^0$. Hence, we get $\mathrm{Fun}(\frac{1}{\mathsf{e}(\alpha)} * \mathsf{tl}_{\boldsymbol{L}}(\alpha))$ from Lemma 11.21, i.e., $\mathrm{Fun}(\frac{1}{\omega})$. □

11.4.2. Weak and Strong Veblen Ordinals

Turning in this subsection to an informal standpoint and in the setting of $(\mathrm{On}, <)$ from Chapter 2, we remark that ordinals that are enumerated by the function $\{\frac{1}{\omega}\}\colon \mathrm{On} \to \mathrm{On},\ x \mapsto \{\frac{1}{\omega}\}x$ are sometimes called *weak Veblen ordinals*. These are ordinals $d \in \mathrm{On}$ that can not be approximated by the value $\overline{\varphi_\bullet}\left(\begin{smallmatrix} a_0 & \cdots & a_n \\ b_0 & \cdots & b_n \end{smallmatrix}\right)$ of a Klammersymbol $\left(\begin{smallmatrix} a_0 & \cdots & a_n \\ b_0 & \cdots & b_n \end{smallmatrix}\right)$ for any $b_n < \omega$ and $a_0, \ldots, a_n < d$.

[3]See Subsection 11.4.2.

Hence, Corollary 11.25.(b) corresponds to the statement that the theory $\mathsf{TID}_1 + (\mathsf{Ind}_2)$ proves the closure under weak Veblen ordinals. In particular, note that the *small Veblen ordinal* is the *first* weak Veblen ordinal.

Similarly, we can define an ordinal $d \in \mathrm{On}$ to be a *strong Veblen ordinal* in case d cannot be approximated by the value $\overline{\varphi_\bullet}\left(\begin{smallmatrix} a_0 & \dots & a_n \\ b_0 & \dots & b_n \end{smallmatrix}\right)$ of a Klammersymbol $\left(\begin{smallmatrix} a_0 & \dots & a_n \\ b_0 & \dots & b_n \end{smallmatrix}\right)$ for any $b_n, a_0, \dots, a_n < d$. Hence, the *large Veblen ordinal* is the *first* strong Veblen ordinal.

11.4.3. The Large Veblen Jump in TID_1^+ and TID_2

Theorem 11.26. *For all terms t, the following holds:*

(a) $\mathsf{TID}_1^+ \vdash t \in P$ *implies* $\mathsf{TID}_1^+ \vdash \mathrm{Prog}(\Lambda b.\mathrm{Large}(b,t))$.

(b) $\mathsf{TID}_2 \vdash t \in P \to \mathrm{Prog}(\Lambda b.\mathrm{Large}(b,t))$.

Proof. Let t, b, α, a be given with

$$t \in P \qquad \left[\mathsf{TID}_1^+ \vdash t \in P \text{ if showing (a)}\right] \tag{11.79}$$

$$\forall b_0 \prec b(\mathrm{Large}(b_0, t)) \tag{Prog-Hyp}$$

$$\alpha \mathrel{\dot{\in}} \boldsymbol{L}_{\bar{0}}^{\prec t} \cap P \tag{11.80}$$

$$\mathsf{e}(\alpha) \preceq b \tag{11.81}$$

and we show by a *main* induction on $\mathsf{lh}_{\boldsymbol{L}}(\alpha)$ the claim

$$\mathrm{HypBase}(\alpha) \tag{$*$}$$

Then we can assume $\mathsf{e}(\alpha) \neq 0$ because otherwise $\alpha\Downarrow \equiv \mathsf{tl}_{\boldsymbol{L}}(\alpha)$ holds and we get the claim $(*)$ in case of $\mathsf{tl}_{\boldsymbol{L}}(\alpha) \equiv \frac{0}{0}$ by Corollary 11.17 or otherwise, we get $\mathrm{HypBase}(\mathsf{tl}_{\boldsymbol{L}}(\alpha)\Downarrow)$ from $(*)$ and the *main* induction hypothesis. We can then use Corollary 11.23 with (11.79) in order to get $\mathrm{Fun}(\mathsf{tl}_{\boldsymbol{L}}(\alpha))$. So, we shall assume from now on

$$\mathsf{e}(\alpha) \neq 0 \tag{11.82}$$

and we therefore have $\alpha\Downarrow \equiv \frac{1}{\mathsf{e}(\alpha)} * \mathsf{tl}_{\boldsymbol{L}}(\alpha)$. Now, for showing $(*)$, we assume

$$\alpha \neq \tfrac{0}{0} \tag{11.83}$$

and have to show $\mathrm{Fun}(\frac{1}{\mathsf{e}(\alpha)} * \mathsf{tl}_{\boldsymbol{L}}(\alpha))$. For this and due to (TID_1), it suffices to show

$$\mathrm{Prog}(\Lambda a.a \in P \to \{\tfrac{1}{\mathsf{e}(\alpha)} * \mathsf{tl}_{\boldsymbol{L}}(\alpha)\}a) \tag{\#}$$

So, we assume further a with

$$a \in P \tag{11.84}$$

$$\forall a_0 \prec a(a_0 \in P \to \{\tfrac{1}{\mathsf{e}(\alpha)} * \mathsf{tl}_{\boldsymbol{L}}(\alpha)\}a_0) \tag{11.85}$$

and proceed by showing $d \in P$ by a *side* induction on the build-up d for each $d \prec \{\frac{1}{\mathsf{e}(\alpha)} * \mathsf{tl}_{\boldsymbol{L}}(\alpha)\}a$ and by considering the following case distinction. This yields the claim $\{\frac{1}{\mathsf{e}(\alpha)} * \mathsf{tl}_{\boldsymbol{L}}(\alpha)\}a \in P$ due to (FP).

<u>1.</u> $d = \underline{x}$ for some x: The claim follows from Lemma 11.9.
<u>2.</u> $d = d_0 \oplus \ldots \oplus d_{m+1} \in \mathrm{OT}$: Then $d_0, \ldots, d_{m+1} <_{\mathbb{N}} d$ holds by Section 4.3, and we have $d = d_0 \tilde{+} \ldots \tilde{+} d_{m+1}$. Now, the *side* induction hypothesis yields $d_0, \ldots, d_{m+1} \in P$ and hence by Lemma 11.10 that $d \in P$ holds.
<u>3.</u> $d = \{\frac{0}{0}\}d_0$ for some d_0: Then $d_0 <_{\mathbb{N}} d$ and $d_0 \prec d$ hold by Section 4.3, so $d_0 \in P$ by the *side* induction hypothesis. Then use Corollary 11.17.
<u>4.</u> $d = \{\frac{1}{\mathsf{e}(\alpha)} * \mathsf{tl}_{\boldsymbol{L}}(\alpha)\}a_0$ for some $a_0 \prec a$: By (11.85) and $a_0 \prec a \in P$.
<u>5.</u> $d = \{\gamma\}d_0$ with $\frac{1}{\mathsf{e}(\alpha)} * \mathsf{tl}_{\boldsymbol{L}}(\alpha) \prec_{\mathbf{lex}} \gamma$: Use Lemma 11.14.(b). Note that we have $\frac{1}{\mathsf{e}(\alpha)} * \mathsf{tl}_{\boldsymbol{L}}(\alpha) \mathrel{\dot\in} P$ by (11.80) and $1 \in P$, that we have $a \in P$ by (11.84), and that $\{\gamma\}d_0 = d \prec \{\frac{1}{\mathsf{e}(\alpha)} * \mathsf{tl}_{\boldsymbol{L}}(\alpha)\}a$ holds.
<u>6.</u> Otherwise: We have $d = \{\gamma\}d_0$ for some d_0 and γ with

$$\gamma \neq \tfrac{0}{0} \tag{11.86}$$

$$\gamma \prec_{\mathbf{lex}} \tfrac{1}{\mathsf{e}(\alpha)} * \mathsf{tl}_{\boldsymbol{L}}(\alpha) \tag{11.87}$$

Note that the *side* induction hypothesis gives us

$$d_0 \in P \tag{11.88}$$

$$\gamma \mathrel{\dot\in} P \tag{11.89}$$

From (11.87) and (11.80), we obtain

$$\gamma \in \boldsymbol{L}_{\bar{0}}^{\preceq t} \cap P \tag{11.90}$$

6.1. $\gamma \equiv \rho * \mathsf{tl}_{\boldsymbol{L}}(\alpha)$ for some $\rho \in \boldsymbol{L}^{\prec \mathsf{e}(\alpha)}$: This means that $\rho \neq \frac{0}{0}$ holds[4] and hence we have $\mathsf{e}(\gamma) \equiv \mathsf{e}(\rho) \prec \mathsf{e}(\alpha) \preceq b$. So, by (Prog-Hyp) we get $\mathrm{Large}(\mathsf{e}(\gamma), t)$, i.e.,

$$\forall \alpha' \dot{\in} \boldsymbol{L}_{\bar{0}}^{\preceq t} \cap P(\mathsf{e}(\alpha') \preceq \mathsf{e}(\gamma) \to \mathrm{HypBase}(\alpha')) \tag{11.91}$$

and by (11.90) and (11.91), we get

$$\mathrm{HypBase}(\gamma) \tag{11.92}$$

Now, we use $t \in P$ from (11.79), while we can even assume $\mathsf{TID}_1^+ \vdash t \in P$ in case we show (a), and get from Corollary 11.23 by (TID^+) or (TID_2), respectively, that $\mathrm{Fun}(\gamma)$ holds and hence the claim $d = \{\gamma\}d_0 \in P$ by (11.88).
6.2. Otherwise: Due to (11.87) we must have

$$\gamma \preceq_{\mathbf{lex}} \mathsf{tl}_{\boldsymbol{L}}(\alpha) \tag{11.93}$$

Then (11.86) yields $\mathsf{tl}_{\boldsymbol{L}}(\alpha) \neq \frac{0}{0}$, so we can use the *main* induction hypothesis for $(*)$ to obtain $\mathrm{Fun}(\mathsf{tl}_{\boldsymbol{L}}(\alpha){\Downarrow})$, i.e.,

$$\mathrm{HypBase}(\mathsf{tl}_{\boldsymbol{L}}(\alpha)) \tag{11.94}$$

From (11.94) and since we have $\mathsf{tl}_{\boldsymbol{L}}(\alpha) \dot{\in} P$ by (11.80), we can use as before $t \in P$ from (11.79) with Corollary 11.23 in order to get

$$\mathrm{Fun}(\mathsf{tl}_{\boldsymbol{L}}(\alpha)) \tag{11.95}$$

by Corollary 11.16. In case we show (a), we can use $\mathsf{TID}_1^+ \vdash t \in P$. From (11.95), (11.93), and (11.89), we get $\mathrm{Fun}(\gamma)$ by Lemma 11.14.(a). Hence $d = \{\gamma\}d_0 \in P$ follows due to (11.88) and we are done. □

---

[4]Note that we assumed in this case $\rho \in \boldsymbol{L}^{\prec \mathsf{e}(\alpha)}$ and not $\rho \in \boldsymbol{L}_{0}^{\prec \mathsf{e}(\alpha)}$.

Corollary 11.27. *For all terms t, the following holds:*

(a) $\mathsf{TID}_1^+ \vdash t \in P$ *implies* $\mathsf{TID}_1^+ \vdash \mathrm{Fun}(\frac{1}{t})$.

(b) $\mathsf{TID}_2 \vdash t \in P \rightarrow \mathrm{Fun}(\frac{1}{t})$.
Hence $\mathsf{TID}_2 \vdash \forall x(\mathrm{Fun}(\frac{1}{x}))$.

Proof. Assume $t \in P$, while we can assume $\mathsf{TID}_1^+ \vdash t \in P$ if showing (a). From Theorem 11.26 and (TID_1), we get $\mathrm{Large}(t,t)$ and hence $\mathrm{HypBase}(\frac{1}{t})$. Then Corollary 11.23 yields $\mathrm{Fun}(\frac{1}{t})$. □

11.5. Remark on Complete Induction for TID_1

Let $\mathsf{TID}_1 + (\mathsf{Ind}_{\mathcal{L}_{\mathsf{TID}}})$ be the system obtained from TID_1 by allowing complete induction for the *full* language $\mathcal{L}_{\mathsf{TID}}$ instead of having (Ind_1) with its restriction to $\mathrm{Pos}_1^{\rightarrow}$.[5] As a variant of Proposition 11.11.(c), we get

$$\mathsf{TID}_1 + (\mathsf{Ind}_{\mathcal{L}_{\mathsf{TID}}}) \vdash \mathcal{L}_{\mathsf{TID}}\text{-}\mathrm{TI}(\prec\varepsilon_0)$$

i.e., $\mathsf{TID}_1 + (\mathsf{Ind}_{\mathcal{L}_{\mathsf{TID}}}) \vdash \mathrm{TI}(\mathcal{A},\mathfrak{a})$ for each $\mathfrak{a} \prec \varepsilon_0$ and $\mathcal{A} \in \mathcal{L}_{\mathsf{TID}}$. So, for

$$\mathcal{A} := \Lambda c.\Big(c \in P \rightarrow \forall \alpha \mathbin{\dot{\in}} P \begin{pmatrix} \mathsf{e}(\alpha) \preceq c \wedge c \in P \\ \rightarrow \mathrm{HypBase}(\alpha) \\ \rightarrow \mathrm{HypFull}(\alpha) \end{pmatrix}\Big)$$

and in the presence of Theorem 11.22, we therefore get for each $\mathfrak{a} \prec \varepsilon_0$ that

$$\mathsf{TID}_1 + (\mathsf{Ind}_{\mathcal{L}_{\mathsf{TID}}}) \vdash \forall \alpha \mathbin{\dot{\in}} P \begin{pmatrix} \mathsf{e}(\alpha) \preceq \mathfrak{a} \wedge \mathfrak{a} \in P \\ \rightarrow \mathrm{HypBase}(\alpha) \\ \rightarrow \mathrm{HypFull}(\alpha) \end{pmatrix} \tag{11.96}$$

holds. Next, the proof of Theorem 11.26.(a) can be adapted in the sense that we use (11.96) instead of applying (TID^+) to $\mathsf{TID}_1^+ \vdash t \in P$ and Theorem 11.22. With this, we get for all $\mathfrak{a} \prec \varepsilon_0$ that

$$\mathsf{TID}_1 + (\mathsf{Ind}_{\mathcal{L}_{\mathsf{TID}}}) \vdash \mathrm{Prog}(\Lambda b.\mathrm{Large}(b,\mathfrak{a})) \tag{11.97}$$

[5] Compare this with Remark 7.3.

holds. Then similar to the proof of Corollary 11.27.(a) but using (11.97) instead of Theorem 11.26, we get $\mathsf{TID}_1+(\mathsf{Ind}_{\mathcal{L}_{\mathsf{TID}}}) \vdash \mathrm{Fun}(\frac{1}{\mathfrak{a}})$ for each $\mathfrak{a} \prec \varepsilon_0$. Comparing this with the bound for TID (and hence of TID_1), we have:

$$\mathsf{TID}_1 \vdash \mathcal{L}_{\mathsf{PA}}\text{-TI}(\prec\vartheta\Omega^\omega)$$
$$\mathsf{TID}_1 + (\mathsf{Ind}_{\mathcal{L}_{\mathsf{TID}}}) \vdash \mathcal{L}_{\mathsf{PA}}\text{-TI}(\prec\vartheta\Omega^{\varepsilon_0})$$

11.6. Wellordering Proof for TID_1^+ and TID_2

Definition 11.28. We define $\mathfrak{v}_n$ for each $n \in \mathbb{N}$ as follows:

$$\mathfrak{v}_0 := 0$$
$$\mathfrak{v}_{n+1} := \{\tfrac{1}{\mathfrak{v}_n}\}0$$

Theorem 11.29. *For each $n \in \mathbb{N}$, the following holds:*

(a) $\mathsf{TID}_1^+ \vdash \mathfrak{v}_n \in P$.

(b) $\mathsf{TID}_2 \vdash \mathfrak{v}_n \in P$.

Proof. We prove this by meta-induction on n.
1. $n = 0$: Use Lemma 11.9.
2. $n = n_0+1$: We have $\mathfrak{v}_n = \{\frac{1}{\mathfrak{v}_{n_0}}\}0$ and can use the induction hypothesis $\mathfrak{v}_{n_0} \in P$ together with Corollary 11.27 to get $\mathrm{Fun}(\frac{1}{\mathfrak{v}_{n_0}})$. Hence, we get that $\mathfrak{v}_n = \{\frac{1}{\mathfrak{v}_{n_0}}\}0 \in P$ holds by (TID_1) and Lemma 11.9. □

Corollary 11.30. $|\mathsf{TID}_1^+| = \vartheta\Omega^\Omega \leq |\mathsf{TID}_2|$.

Proof. By Section 9.4, we have $|\mathsf{TID}_1^+| \leq \vartheta\Omega^\Omega$. Moreover, $\sup_{n\in\mathbb{N}}(\mathfrak{v}_n) = \vartheta\Omega^\Omega$ follows from [Sch92], so we get $\vartheta\Omega^\Omega \leq |\mathsf{TID}_1^+|$ and $\vartheta\Omega^\Omega \leq |\mathsf{TID}_2|$ from Theorem 11.29. □

12. Concluding Remarks on Typed Induction

In Part II, we investigated a concept of *typed induction* that originated in considerations on S. Feferman's applicative theory $\mathrm{QL}(\mathsf{F}_0\text{-}\mathsf{IR}_N)$ from [Fef92] and whose concept of *function types* cumulated into our type system FIT from Chapter 5 with strength of the *small Veblen ordinal*, i.e.,

$$|\mathsf{FIT}| = \vartheta\Omega^\omega$$

Further comparisons with the arithmetical theory $\mathsf{ID}_1^* \restriction$ led in Chapter 6 to the theory TID as a natural implementation of FIT as a subsystem of ID_1. We further generalized TID in Chapter 8 to hierarchies $\{\mathsf{TID}_n\}_{n\in\mathbb{N}}$ and $\{\mathsf{TID}_n^+\}_{n\in\mathbb{N}}$ of subsystems of ID_1, establishing hereby

$$|\mathsf{TID}| = |\mathsf{TID}_1| = \vartheta\Omega^\omega \qquad\qquad |\mathsf{TID}_1^+| = \vartheta\Omega^\Omega$$

i.e., we obtained a theory TID_1^+ with strength of the *large Veblen ordinal.*

In particular with respect to the involved *wellordering proofs* for obtaining a lower bound, we started for FIT with the theory TID and extracted in Chapter 7 a generalized scheme from the common wellordering proof in the setting of $\mathsf{ID}_1^* \restriction$ or ID_1^*. More precisely, our approach generalized common methods from the realm of *predicative proof-theory* by using the *finitary Veblen functions* (see Subsection 7.1.2) instead of the *binary Veblen function* (see Subsection 7.1.1). In this setting, we reached beyond the Feferman-Schütte ordinal Γ_0 and hence into the realm of *metapredicative proof-theory.*

After having obtained these new results, we continued (in the spirit of predicativity) to further generalize our methods in order to exceed the small Veblen ordinal. For this, we used *Klammersymbols* as a means to generalize the finitary Veblen functions to the transfinite (while we chose to work with Klammersymbols because the literature provided well-established results on ordinal notations based on such a concept). See Section 12.1 below for ideas on another representation of ordinals that may be technically more amenable (in comparison with Klammersymbols).

It turned out in Chapter 11 that our methods almost literally translate to the transfinite. The key observation was to consider a so-called *partitioning of Klammersymbols* in Chapter 4 where we introduced and refined ordinal notations based on Klammersymbols. In other words, we considered for ordinals $a < \Omega^\Omega$ their Cantor normal form (with base Ω), say $\Omega^{b_1} a_1 + \ldots + \Omega^{b_n} a_n$, and labeled the exponents b_i by the "nearest" limit or by zero (which we called "label", see also the corresponding notion $b_i{\Downarrow}$ from Section 4.4). Having such a *partitioning by labels* at hand, we identified the method for the wellordering proof of Chapter 7 as the base case for steps that reach towards the large Veblen ordinal, i.e., Chapter 7 deals with the label 0. By an *internalizing* method (which typically comes along with greater technical difficulties), we showed in Chapter 11 that our methods from Chapter 7 have a canonical generalization in the setting of Klammersymbols, allowing us to deal with arbitrary *labels* (i.e., with limit ordinals instead of only the zero ordinal).

12.1. Higher Type Functionals

In order to get beyond the large Veblen ordinal $\vartheta\Omega^\Omega$ and following our metapredicative standpoint of generalizing the wellordering proofs of Chapter 11 further, we would need a more expressive ordinal notation system.

We suggest the concept of *higher type functionals* for a representation of ordinals which is on the one hand suitable for reaching to the Bachmann-Howard ordinal $\vartheta\varepsilon_{\Omega+1}$ and that seems on the other hand to be technically more amenable than the representation based on Klammersymbols.

Having Corollary 11.27.(b) at hand, we already have a strong conjecture that

$$\vartheta\Omega^\Omega < |\mathsf{TID}_2|$$

holds. The idea for showing this is (again) to internalize the argument of the proof of Theorem 11.29, namely by internalizing the meta-induction on $n \in \mathbb{N}$. According to Corollary 11.30, TID_1^+ is not strong enough to prove this internalization. For TID_2 on the other hand, we are not restricted to Corollary 11.27.(a) in the proof of Theorem 11.29 because we can use Corollary 11.27.(b) instead.

Unfortunately, in order to show this, we would need an ordinal notation system that goes beyond notations that are describable by *Klammersymbols* (and that are adequate from a metapredicative standpoint). One possible solution would be to work with *higher type functionals* (in the spirit of [Wey76] and [Buc15]), and we tried to indicate this by using the representation $\{\alpha\}a$ and notions such as *functionality* $\mathrm{Fun}(\alpha)$. In this context, we have the following open questions:

(I) Do the conjectures hold which we depicted in Table 1 on page 8?

(II) Can the methods from Chapter 7 and Chapter 11 be generalized and used for answering (I)?

12.2. Generalizations of FIT

Another question that comes up naturally is:

(III) Can we set up hierarchies $\{\mathsf{FIT}_n\}_{n\in\mathbb{N}}$ and $\{\mathsf{FIT}_n^+\}_{n\in\mathbb{N}}$ that are analogs in the setting of applicative theories of the hierarchies $\{\mathsf{TID}_n\}_{n\in\mathbb{N}}$ and $\{\mathsf{TID}_n^+\}_{n\in\mathbb{N}}$?

This seems quite straight-forward due to the way the embedding of TID into FIT from Chapter 6 was done, while having in mind the result from Section 8.3. Furthermore, there is the question:

(IV) What would happen if we allow arbitrary types $\mathbb{P}, \mathbb{Q}$ to occur in $\mathsf{I}_{\mathbb{P},\mathbb{Q}}$?

We conjecture that this corresponds to having *iterated inductive definitions*, and that this corresponds to FIT in a similar way as the theories ID_n for any $n \geq 2$ correspond to ID_1. Similarly, we ask:

(V) What is the relation of FIT to the extension of FIT where we have apart from $\mathsf{I}_{\mathbb{P},\mathbb{Q}}$ also types for *general inductive definitions*?

Part III.

Stratified Induction

13. The Theory $\mathsf{SID}_{<\omega}$ of Stratified Induction

13.1. Adaptations of Syntax from Chapter 1

Before introducing and investigating the concept of stratified induction, we shall slightly adapt our general notational framework. This will allow for a more simplified proof-theoretic approach in the setting of Tait-style proof systems. Let $\mathcal{L}$ be a fixed language with $\mathcal{L}_{\mathsf{PA}} \subseteq \mathcal{L}$.

Definition 13.1 (Dropping implication $\rightarrow$). The *basic logical symbols (with equation)* shall be restricted to the symbols $\neg, \wedge, \vee, \forall, \exists, =$.

Definition 13.2 (Adaptation of formulas). We define $\mathcal{L}$ *formulas* as usual inductively from $\mathcal{L}$ and the basic symbols but *with the restriction* that the negation symbol $\neg$ is only allowed to occur in front of an atomic formula. We still use A, B, C, D as syntactic variables for $\mathcal{L}$ formulas. A *literal* is either an atomic formula or its negated version. In case of a compound formula A, its *negation*

$$\neg A$$

now stands for the translation of A according to De Morgan's laws and the law of double negation. Moreover, we introduce the abbreviation

$$A \rightarrow B := \neg A \vee B$$

and we call a formula A *arithmetical* in case of $A \in \mathcal{L}^2_{\mathsf{PA}}$. If P is a unary relation symbol of $\mathcal{L}$ and A an $\mathcal{L}$ formula, then we say that P occurs *positively* in A if A does not contain the negated formula $\neg P(t)$ for any term t. This corresponds to the definition of positive from Part II. Moreover, we now prefer the notation $t \in P$ instead of $P(t)$ and $t \notin P$ instead of $\neg P(t)$.

Definition 13.3 (Sequents). We use capital Greek letters Γ, Δ, Σ as syntactic variables for $\mathcal{L}$ *sequents*, i.e., finite (possibly empty) lists of $\mathcal{L}$ formulas (e.g., $A_0, \ldots, A_k$) that are identified with finite sets (i.e., $\{A_0, \ldots, A_k\}$). Therefore, Γ, A is understood as $\Gamma \cup \{A\}$ and accordingly Γ, Δ is identified with $\Gamma \cup \Delta$.

Definition 13.4 (Ordinals from Part I). By *ordinals* we now mean ordinals smaller than the first strongly-critical ordinal Γ_0, in particular we will work with the binary Veblen-function φ. In fact, we will need only ordinals below $\varphi(\varepsilon_0, 0)$ and for most of the results even ordinals below ε_0 will suffice.

Notation 13.5. Unlike in Part II on typed induction, we do not need Klammersymbols, so we shall drop the convention of using small Greek letters as syntactic variables for Klammersymbols. Instead, small Greek letters

$$\alpha, \beta, \gamma, \delta, \xi, \pi, \nu, \tau, \ldots$$

shall be used as syntactic variables for ordinals. Furthermore, we shall work with ordinals from an informal, set-theoretic standpoint. In particular, we use $<$ instead of $\prec$ and we identify $\mathbb{N}$ with ω.

13.2. Definition of $\mathsf{SID}_{<\omega}$ and SID_n

Definition 13.6. For each $\mathfrak{A}$ and $1 \leq n < \omega$ let $P_n^{\mathfrak{A}}$ denote a new and distinguished unary relation symbol. Furthermore, define for each $n < \omega$:

$$\mathcal{L}_0 := \mathcal{L}_{\mathsf{PA}} \qquad \mathcal{L}_{n+1} := \mathcal{L}_n \cup \{\, P_{n+1}^{\mathfrak{A}} : \mathfrak{A} \text{ is a positive operator form} \,\}$$

From now on, let A, B, C, D range over formulas of the language

$$\mathcal{L}_{<\omega} := \bigcup\nolimits_{n<\omega} \mathcal{L}_n$$

Definition 13.7. For each $n < \omega$, the theory SID_n with language $\mathcal{L}_n$ consists of the following axioms.

I. Number-theoretic and logical axioms:

Axioms of PA with the scheme of complete induction for all $\mathcal{L}_n$ formulas.

II. Stratified induction axioms for $1 \leq m \leq n$ and $\mathcal{B} \in \mathcal{L}_{m-1}$:

$$\forall x(\mathfrak{A}(\mathcal{B}, x) \to \mathcal{B}(x)) \to \forall x(x \in P^{\mathfrak{A}}_m \to \mathcal{B}(x))$$

III. Fixed-point axioms for $1 \leq m \leq n$:

$$\forall x(\mathfrak{A}(P^{\mathfrak{A}}_m, x) \leftrightarrow x \in P^{\mathfrak{A}}_m)$$

Finally, we define

$$\mathsf{SID}_{<\omega} := \bigcup_{n<\omega} \mathsf{SID}_n$$

over the language $\mathcal{L}_{<\omega}$. We also presume that a derivability notion $\mathsf{SID}_n \vdash A$ is given for each $n < \omega$ and $A \in \mathcal{L}_n$ as indicated in Chapter 1. Accordingly, $\mathsf{SID}_{<\omega} \vdash A$ for $A \in \mathcal{L}_{<\omega}$ just means that $A \in \mathcal{L}_n$ and $\mathsf{SID}_n \vdash A$ hold for some $n < \omega$.

13.3. The Lower Bound of $\mathsf{SID}_{<\omega}$

Theorem 13.8.

$$\widehat{\mathsf{ID}}_1 \vdash A \implies \mathsf{SID}_1 \vdash A$$

holds for each $A \in \mathcal{L}_{\mathsf{PA}}$. Therefore, we have $\varphi(\varepsilon_0, 0) \leq |\mathsf{SID}_{<\omega}|$.

Proof. Recall that $|\widehat{\mathsf{ID}}_1| = \varphi(\varepsilon_0, 0)$ holds and note that $\widehat{\mathsf{ID}}_1$ is essentially SID_1 without **II.** from its definition. □

13.4. Strategy for the Upper Bound of $\mathsf{SID}_{<\omega}$.

We will work with infinitary proof systems SID_n^∞ with $n < \omega$ that are suitable for partial cut-elimination, asymmetric interpretation, and in case of $n = 0$ full predicative cut-elimination. The steps to reach the main result of Chapter 14 will be the following:

1. Add unary relation symbols $Q_{\mathfrak{A}}^{<\xi}$ for each $\mathfrak{A}$ and ξ to the language.

2. Set up an infinitary proof-system SID_n^∞ for each $n < \omega$. For $n > 0$, we obtain a useful result on *partial cut elimination (p.c.e.)*, while for the case $n = 0$, we can even achieve *full predicative cut-elimination (f.c.e.)*.

3. Establish the connection between the systems $\mathsf{SID}_{n+1}^\infty$ and SID_n^∞ for any $n < \omega$ by making use of *asymmetric interpretation (a.i.)*, given that we deal with derivations where we partially removed cuts first. In particular, the symbols $P_{n+1}^{\mathfrak{A}}$ are interpreted by $Q_{\mathfrak{A}}^{<\xi}$ for suitable ξ.

4. The theme is to start with a formal derivation in SID_{n+1} of an *arithmetical* formula A, embed it into $\mathsf{SID}_{n+1}^\infty$ such that the proof complexity stays below ε_0, combine a p.c.e. followed by an a.i. iteratively, and end up with a derivation in SID_0^∞ with proof complexity still below ε_0. Then f.c.e. yields the desired sharp bound $\varphi(\varepsilon_0, 0)$ for $|\mathsf{SID}_{<\omega}|$ via a standard boundedness argument:

$$\mathsf{SID}_{n+1} \overset{\text{embed}}{\rightsquigarrow} \mathsf{SID}_{n+1}^\infty \overset{\text{p.c.e.}}{\rightsquigarrow} \mathsf{SID}_{n+1}^\infty \overset{\text{a.i.}}{\rightsquigarrow} \mathsf{SID}_n^\infty \rightsquigarrow \cdots \rightsquigarrow \mathsf{SID}_0^\infty \overset{\text{f.c.e.}}{\rightsquigarrow} \mathsf{SID}_0^\infty$$

Besides the care needed to maintain a proof-complexity below ε_0, we also have to cope with the fact that in general an infinitary proof system may yield derivations whose cuts cannot be globally bounded. In particular for our iterative use of p.c.e. that started with embedding a formal derivation (e.g., from SID_{n+1} into $\mathsf{SID}_{n+1}^\infty$), we depend on the method of a.i. to provide always a derivation whose cut-formulas are bounded by a finite ordinal. To guarantee this, we shall fix a finite ordinal ℓ and restrict the derivability relation for SID_n^∞ with $n > 0$ such that the cut-formulas have to be globally bounded by ℓ.

14. Proof-Theoretic Results for the Theory $\mathsf{SID}_{<\omega}$

Convention 14.1. Fix some finite ordinal ℓ for the rest of this chapter. In particular, we will define the derivability relation for the proof systems SID_n^∞ such that ℓ globally bounds the length of the cut-formulas that are allowed in an application of a cut-rule if $n > 0$ holds. Compare the proof of Lemma 14.13 to see why this bound should not hold for the case $n = 0$.

14.1. The Infinitary Proof System SID_n^∞

Definition 14.2. Let $Q_{\mathfrak{A}}^{<\xi}$ be a fresh unary relation symbol for each $\mathfrak{A}$ and ξ. For each $n < \omega$, let

$$\mathcal{L}_n^\infty := \mathcal{L}_n \cup \{ Q_{\mathfrak{A}}^{<\xi} : \xi < \Gamma_0 \ \ \& \ \ \mathfrak{A} \text{ is a positive operator form} \}$$

In the following, let A, B, C, D range over formulas of the language

$$\mathcal{L}_{<\omega}^\infty := \bigcup_{n<\omega} \mathcal{L}_n^\infty$$

Definition 14.3. The *length* $\mathrm{lh}(A)$ of a formula A is defined as the number of basic logical symbols that occur in A. In particular, $\mathrm{lh}(A) = \mathrm{lh}(A_x(t))$ holds for all terms t.

Definition 14.4. Let $\mathrm{rk}_0(A) := 0$ for each $A \in \mathcal{L}_0^\infty$. For $1 \leq n < \omega$, we say that $A \in \mathcal{L}_n^\infty$ is *n-atomic* if $A \in \mathcal{L}_{n-1}^\infty$ or if it is a literal of the form $t \in P_n^{\mathfrak{A}}$ or $t \notin P_n^{\mathfrak{A}}$. We define two new rank-notions as follows:

- The *n-rank* $\mathrm{rk}_n(A) < \omega$ is defined for $1 \leq n < \omega$ and formulas $A \in \mathcal{L}_n^\infty$ by

$$\mathrm{rk}_n(A) := \begin{cases} 0 & \text{if } A \text{ is } n\text{-atomic, or otherwise} \\ \max(\mathrm{rk}_n(B), \mathrm{rk}_n(C)) + 1 & \text{if } A = B \wedge C \text{ or } A = B \vee C \\ \mathrm{rk}_n(B) + 1 & \text{if } A = \forall x B \text{ or } A = \exists x B \end{cases}$$

- The *ordinal-rank* $\mathrm{rk}(A) < \Gamma_0$ is defined for formulas $A \in \mathcal{L}_{<\omega}^\infty$ by

$$\mathrm{rk}(A) := \begin{cases} 0 & \text{if } A \text{ is a literal and } A \in \mathcal{L}_{<\omega} \\ \omega \cdot \xi & \text{if } A = t \in Q_{\mathfrak{A}}^{<\xi} \text{ or } A = t \notin Q_{\mathfrak{A}}^{<\xi} \\ \max(\mathrm{rk}(B), \mathrm{rk}(C)) + 1 & \text{if } A = B \wedge C \text{ or } A = B \vee C \\ \mathrm{rk}(B) + 1 & \text{if } A = \forall x B \text{ or } A = \exists x B \end{cases}$$

Furthermore for $1 \leq n < \omega$ and $A \in \mathcal{L}_n^\infty$, we write $A \in \mathrm{Pos}_n^\uparrow$ to denote that $P_n^{\mathfrak{A}}$ occurs at most positively in A for every $\mathfrak{A}$, and we write $A \in \mathrm{Neg}_n^\uparrow$ to denote $\neg A \in \mathrm{Pos}_n^\uparrow$.

Notation 14.5. The n-rank and the ordinal rank are not defined for $\mathcal{L}_{\mathsf{PA}}^2$ formulas. Therefore, we introduce the following abbreviations for arithmetical operator forms $\mathfrak{A}$ and each $n \in \mathbb{N}$:

$$\mathrm{rk}_n(\mathfrak{A}) := \mathrm{rk}_n(\mathfrak{A}(\mathsf{U}, 0))$$
$$\mathrm{rk}(\mathfrak{A}) := \mathrm{rk}(\mathfrak{A}(\mathsf{U}, 0))$$

Remark 14.6. For $A \in \mathcal{L}_n^\infty$ and $1 \leq n < \omega$, we have that $\mathrm{lh}(A) < \ell$ implies $\mathrm{rk}_n(A) < \ell$, and that $\mathrm{rk}_n(A) \neq 0$ implies that A is not a literal.

Definition 14.7. For each $n < \omega$, the infinitary Tait-style proof system SID_n^∞ with language $\mathcal{L}_n^\infty$ is defined by means of the following inferences (i.e., axioms and inference rules). SID_n^∞ shall derive $\mathcal{L}_n^\infty$ sequents that consist of *closed* formulas only, therefore we assume in this definition that the sequents of the axioms and the sequents that occur in the premiss of a rule consist of closed $\mathcal{L}_n^\infty$ formulas only. Note that the inference rules $(\bigwedge_{\forall x A})$ and $(\bigwedge_{t \notin Q_{\mathfrak{A}}^{<\tau}})$ have infinitely many premisses.

I. Number-theoretic and logical axioms:

Γ, A	if A is a true $\mathcal{L}_{\mathsf{PA}}$ literal
$\Gamma, \mathcal{A}(s), \neg\mathcal{A}(t)$	if $s^{\mathbb{N}} = t^{\mathbb{N}}$ holds and $\mathcal{A}$ is $\Lambda a.A$ for an atomic $A \in \mathcal{L}_n$

II. Stratified induction axioms for $1 \leq m \leq n$ and $\mathcal{B} \in \mathcal{L}_{m-1}$:

$$\Gamma, \exists x(\mathfrak{A}(\mathcal{B}, x) \wedge \neg\mathcal{B}(x)), t \notin P_m^{\mathfrak{A}}, \mathcal{B}(t)$$

III. Fixed-point rules for $1 \leq m \leq n$:

$$\frac{\Gamma, \mathfrak{A}(P_m^{\mathfrak{A}}, t)}{\Gamma, t \in P_m^{\mathfrak{A}}}\ (\mathsf{Fix}_{t \in P_m^{\mathfrak{A}}}) \qquad \frac{\Gamma, \neg\mathfrak{A}(P_m^{\mathfrak{A}}, t)}{\Gamma, t \notin P_m^{\mathfrak{A}}}\ (\mathsf{Fix}_{t \notin P_m^{\mathfrak{A}}})$$

IV. Predicative rules:

$$\frac{\Gamma, A}{\Gamma, A \vee B}\ (\bigvee_{A \vee B}^{A}) \qquad \frac{\Gamma, B}{\Gamma, A \vee B}\ (\bigvee_{A \vee B}^{B}) \qquad \frac{\Gamma, A \qquad \Gamma, B}{\Gamma, A \wedge B}\ (\bigwedge_{A \wedge B})$$

$$\frac{\Gamma, A_x(t)}{\Gamma, \exists x A}\ (\bigvee_{\exists x A}^{t}) \text{ for } t \in \mathrm{Ter}_0 \qquad \frac{\Gamma, \mathfrak{A}(Q_{\mathfrak{A}}^{<\xi}, t)}{\Gamma, t \in Q_{\mathfrak{A}}^{<\tau}}\ (\bigvee_{t \in Q_{\mathfrak{A}}^{<\tau}}^{\xi}) \text{ for } \xi < \tau$$

$$\frac{\ldots\ \Gamma, A_x(t)\ \ldots\ (t \in \mathrm{Ter}_0)}{\Gamma, \forall x A}\ (\bigwedge_{\forall x A})$$

$$\frac{\ldots\ \Gamma, \neg\mathfrak{A}(Q_{\mathfrak{A}}^{<\xi}, t)\ \ldots\ (\xi < \tau)}{\Gamma, t \notin Q_{\mathfrak{A}}^{<\tau}}\ (\bigwedge_{t \notin Q_{\mathfrak{A}}^{<\tau}})$$

V. Cut rule:

$$\frac{\Gamma, C \qquad \Gamma, \neg C}{\Gamma}\ (\mathsf{Cut}_C)$$

For each of the above mentioned inferences, we define the notions *side formula, minor formula,* and *main formula* as usual. In particular, (Cut_C)

has no main formulas, the axioms in **I** and **II** do not have minor formulas, and for every inference the formulas in the sequent Γ are the side formulas.

Definition 14.8. The derivability notion $\mathsf{SID}_n^\infty \vdash_{\rho,r}^{\alpha} \Gamma$ for $n, r < \omega$ is defined inductively on α:

- $\mathsf{SID}_n^\infty \vdash_{\rho,r}^{\alpha} \Gamma$ holds for all α, ρ, and $r < \omega$ if Γ is an axiom of SID_n^∞.
- $\mathsf{SID}_n^\infty \vdash_{\rho,r}^{\alpha} \Gamma$ holds if there is a rule of SID_n^∞ in **III** or **IV** such that Γ is its conclusion and $\mathsf{SID}_n^\infty \vdash_{\rho,r}^{\alpha_\iota} \Gamma_\iota$ holds for each of its premisses Γ_ι with some $\alpha_\iota < \alpha$.
- $\mathsf{SID}_n^\infty \vdash_{\rho,r}^{\alpha} \Gamma$ holds if $\mathsf{SID}_n^\infty \vdash_{\rho,r}^{\alpha_0} \Gamma, C$ and $\mathsf{SID}_n^\infty \vdash_{\rho,r}^{\alpha_1} \Gamma, \neg C$ hold for some $\alpha_0, \alpha_1 < \alpha$ and we have $\mathrm{rk}(C) < \rho$, $\mathrm{rk}_n(C) < r$, and in case of $n > 0$ also $\mathrm{lh}(C) < \ell$.

Moreover, $\mathsf{SID}_n^\infty \vdash_{\rho,r}^{<\alpha} \Gamma$ means that $\mathsf{SID}_n^\infty \vdash_{\rho,r}^{\alpha_0} \Gamma$ holds for some $\alpha_0 < \alpha$.

Remark 14.9. Recalling the end of Chapter 13 where we explained the strategy for investigating $\mathsf{SID}_{<\omega}$, we note here that for $n > 0$, the condition $\mathrm{lh}(C) < \ell$ in the third case of the above definition is needed in order to globally bound the occurring (cut-)formulas' syntactical complexity by a finite ordinal, namely ℓ. Having in mind the property of most derivability notions for infinitary proof systems that the underlying derivations may contain cut-formulas whose complexity cannot be globally bounded by a finite ordinal, we decided to add the condition $\mathrm{lh}(C) < \ell$ since otherwise it would have been more cumbersome to check and guarantee the well-behaviour of our iterative use of partial cut elimination and asymmetric interpretation that we are going to apply below. Furthermore, we put no extra effort in encoding such a property into rk_n because we wanted to keep rk_n as perspicuous as possible.

Lemma 14.10 (Weakening).

$$\mathsf{SID}_n^\infty \vdash_{\rho,r}^{\alpha} \Gamma \;\&\; \alpha \leq \beta \;\&\; \rho \leq \eta \;\&\; r \leq k \;\&\; \Gamma \subseteq \Delta \implies \mathsf{SID}_n^\infty \vdash_{\eta,k}^{\beta} \Delta$$

Proof. By a straight-forward induction on α. Note that the condition concerning ℓ can be preserved here. □

Remark 14.11. $\mathsf{SID}_n^\infty \vdash_{\rho,r}^{\alpha} \Gamma$ with $\rho = 0$ or $r = 0$ implies $\mathsf{SID}_n^\infty \vdash_{0,0}^{\alpha} \Gamma$. Note also that $\mathsf{SID}_0^\infty \vdash_{\rho,r}^{\alpha} \Gamma$ implies $\mathsf{SID}_0^\infty \vdash_{\rho,1}^{\alpha} \Gamma$ since $\mathrm{rk}_0(A) = 0$ for each

$A \in \mathcal{L}_0^\infty$. Furthermore, we note that in the following we will not mention every use of Lemma 14.10 explicitly.

14.2. Partial and Full Cut-Elimination

Lemma 14.12. *For each $1 \leq n < \omega$ and $C \in \mathcal{L}_n^\infty$ with $\mathrm{lh}(C) < \ell$, we have*

$$\left.\begin{array}{l}\mathrm{rk}_n(C) = 1 + r \\ \quad \& \ \mathsf{SID}_n^\infty \vdash^\alpha_{\rho,1+r} \Gamma, C \\ \quad \& \ \mathsf{SID}_n^\infty \vdash^\beta_{\rho,1+r} \Gamma, \neg C\end{array}\right\} \implies \mathsf{SID}_n^\infty \vdash^{\alpha\#\beta}_{\rho,1+r} \Gamma$$

Proof. By induction on $\alpha \# \beta$ and the following case distinction.
1. C or $\neg C$ is not among the main formulas of the last inference used for $\mathsf{SID}_n^\infty \vdash^\alpha_{\rho,1+r} \Gamma, C$ or $\mathsf{SID}_n^\infty \vdash^\beta_{\rho,1+r} \Gamma, \neg C$, respectively: The claim follows immediately from the induction hypothesis or, in case of an axiom, by reapplying the inference with suitable side formulas.
2. Otherwise, we note first that $\mathrm{rk}_n(C) \neq 0$ holds. Hence, C is not n-atomic and only the following cases are possible:
2.1. $C = C_0 \vee C_1$ and $\mathsf{SID}_n^\infty \vdash^{\alpha_0}_{\rho,1+r} \Gamma, C, C_0$ for some $\alpha_0 < \alpha$: Then we also get $\mathsf{SID}_n^\infty \vdash^{\beta_0}_{\rho,1+r} \Gamma, \neg C, \neg C_0$ for some $\beta_0 < \beta$, so by the induction hypothesis we get $\mathsf{SID}_n^\infty \vdash^{\alpha_0\#\beta}_{\rho,1+r} \Gamma, C_0$ and $\mathsf{SID}_n^\infty \vdash^{\alpha\#\beta_0}_{\rho,1+r} \Gamma, \neg C_0$. Since $\alpha_0 \# \beta, \alpha \# \beta_0 < \alpha \# \beta$, $\mathrm{rk}_n(C_0) < \mathrm{rk}_n(C) = 1 + r$, and also $\mathrm{lh}(C_0) < \mathrm{lh}(C)$ hold, we can apply (Cut_{C_0}) in order to obtain $\mathsf{SID}_n^\infty \vdash^{\alpha\#\beta}_{\rho,1+r} \Gamma$. The other cases where $\mathsf{SID}_n^\infty \vdash^{\alpha_0}_{\rho,1+r} \Gamma, C, C_1$ or $C = C_0 \wedge C_1$ holds are treated similarly.
2.2. $C = \exists x D$ or $C = \forall x D$: The claim follows similar to the previous case, noting that $\mathrm{lh}(D_x(t)) = \mathrm{lh}(D) < \mathrm{lh}(C)$ holds for any term t. □

Lemma 14.13. *For each $C \in \mathcal{L}_0^\infty$, we have*

$$\left.\begin{array}{l}\mathrm{rk}(C) = \rho \\ \quad \& \ \mathsf{SID}_0^\infty \vdash^\alpha_{\rho,r} \Gamma, C \\ \quad \& \ \mathsf{SID}_0^\infty \vdash^\beta_{\rho,r} \Gamma, \neg C\end{array}\right\} \implies \mathsf{SID}_0^\infty \vdash^{\alpha\#\beta}_{\rho,r} \Gamma$$

Proof. By induction on $\alpha \# \beta$ and almost literally as Lemma 14.12 because of a similar behaviour of the n-rank rk_n and the ordinal-rank rk in combination with the build-up of formulas. The following two special situations

illustrate the advantage of the ordinal-rank rk and why this does not work for SID_n^∞ with $n > 0$. Assume that both C and $\neg C$ are among the main formulas of the last inference.
1. C is the main formula of an axiom: Then it can only be due to an instance of **I**, so C and $\neg C$ are $\mathcal{L}_{\mathsf{PA}}$ literals. If C is $\mathsf{U}s$ for some term s, then we have $\neg\mathsf{U}t, \mathsf{U}t' \in \Gamma$ for some t, t' with $t^{\mathbb{N}} = s^{\mathbb{N}} = t'^{\mathbb{N}}$, and hence Γ is already an instance of **I**. Otherwise, the claim again follows easily from **I**.
2. $C = t \in Q_{\mathfrak{A}}^{<\tau}$ with $\mathsf{SID}_0^\infty \vdash_{\rho,r}^{\alpha_\xi} \Gamma, C, \mathfrak{A}(Q_{\mathfrak{A}}^{<\xi}, t)$ for some $\xi < \tau$ and $\alpha_\xi < \alpha$: Now $\rho = \omega \cdot \tau$ and $\neg C = t \notin Q_{\mathfrak{A}}^{<\tau}$ hold. Because of the definition of SID_0^∞, we do not have $\mathsf{SID}_0^\infty \vdash_{\rho,r}^{\beta} \Gamma, \neg C$ due to a logical axiom and hence $\neg C$ must be the main formula of $(\bigwedge_{t \notin Q_{\mathfrak{A}}^{<\tau}})$. Then we have $\mathsf{SID}_0^\infty \vdash_{\rho,r}^{\beta_\xi} \Gamma, \neg C, \neg\mathfrak{A}(Q_{\mathfrak{A}}^{<\xi}, t)$ available with $\beta_\xi < \beta$ for every $\xi < \tau$, so the claim follows very similar as in the proof of Lemma 14.12. Note that in the setting of SID_0^∞, we do not have to guarantee $\mathrm{lh}(\mathfrak{A}(Q_{\mathfrak{A}}^{<\xi}, t)) < \ell$, and that we have $\mathrm{rk}(\mathfrak{A}(Q_{\mathfrak{A}}^{<\xi}, t)) < \omega \cdot (\xi + 1) \leq \rho$ because of $\xi < \tau$. □

Theorem 14.14 (Cut-elimination).

(a) *Partial cut-elimination:*

$\mathsf{SID}_n^\infty \vdash_{\rho,1+r}^{\alpha} \Gamma$ *implies* $\mathsf{SID}_n^\infty \vdash_{\rho,1}^{\omega_r(\alpha)} \Gamma$ *for each* $1 \leq n < \omega$, *where we let* $\omega_0(\alpha) := \alpha$ *and* $\omega_{k+1}(\alpha) := \omega_k(\omega^\alpha)$.

(b) *Full predicative cut-elimination:*

$\mathsf{SID}_0^\infty \vdash_{\gamma+\omega^\delta,1}^{\alpha} \Gamma$ *implies* $\mathsf{SID}_0^\infty \vdash_{\gamma,1}^{\varphi(\delta,\alpha)} \Gamma$.

Proof. The theorem follows from the previous lemmas by a standard argument, and we refer to [Poh09] for details. □

14.3. Asymmetric Interpretation

Convention 14.15. We fix $n < \omega$ for this section and will only deal with the proof systems SID_n^∞ and $\mathsf{SID}_{n+1}^\infty$.

Definition 14.16. For $\mathcal{L}_{n+1}^\infty$ formulas A, $\mathcal{L}_{n+1}^\infty$ sequents Γ, and ordinals $\xi, \xi_1, \ldots, \xi_k$, we write the following:

A^ξ for the $\mathcal{L}_n^\infty$ formula obtained from A by substituting any $P_{n+1}^{\mathfrak{A}}$ in A with the corresponding symbol $Q_{\mathfrak{A}}^{<\xi}$,

$[\Gamma]^\xi$ for the $\mathcal{L}_n^\infty$ sequent obtained from Γ by substituting every occurring formula A with A^ξ,

and if Γ is explicitly given as a list $A_1, \dots, A_k$, we write

$[\Gamma]^{\xi_1,\dots,\xi_k}$ for the $\mathcal{L}_n^\infty$ sequent $A_1^{\xi_1}, \dots, A_k^{\xi_k}$.

Lemma 14.17.

(a) $\mathsf{SID}_n^\infty \vdash_{\rho,r}^{\alpha} \Gamma, \mathcal{B}(s_1), \neg\mathcal{B}'(s_2)$ *for each* s_1, s_2 *with* $s_1^{\mathbb{N}} = s_2^{\mathbb{N}}$ *implies that for each* t_1, t_2 *with* $t_1^{\mathbb{N}} = t_2^{\mathbb{N}}$ *also*

$$\mathsf{SID}_n^\infty \vdash_{\rho,r}^{\alpha+2\cdot\mathrm{rk}(\mathfrak{A})} \Gamma, \mathfrak{A}(\mathcal{B}, t_1), \neg\mathfrak{A}(\mathcal{B}', t_2)$$

holds.

(b) $s^{\mathbb{N}} = t^{\mathbb{N}}$ *and* $\nu \leq \pi$ *imply* $\mathsf{SID}_n^\infty \vdash_{0,0}^{\omega\cdot\nu} s \in Q_{\mathfrak{A}}^{<\pi}, t \notin Q_{\mathfrak{A}}^{<\nu}$.

(c) $s^{\mathbb{N}} = t^{\mathbb{N}}$ *and* $\mathcal{A} \in \mathcal{L}_n^\infty$ *imply* $\mathsf{SID}_n^\infty \vdash_{0,0}^{2\cdot\mathrm{rk}(A)} \mathcal{A}(s), \neg\mathcal{A}(t)$.

(d) $\mathcal{B} \in \mathcal{L}_n$ *implies* $\mathsf{SID}_n^\infty \vdash_{0,0}^{\omega\cdot\tau} \exists x(\mathfrak{A}(\mathcal{B}, x) \wedge \neg\mathcal{B}(x)), t \notin Q_{\mathfrak{A}}^{<\tau}, \mathcal{B}(t)$.

Proof. Statement (a) is proven by a straight-forward induction on $\mathrm{rk}(\mathfrak{A}) < \omega$ and we leave the proof to the reader. Statement (b) is proven by induction on ν: The case $\nu = 0$ follows from $(\bigwedge_{t\notin Q_{\mathfrak{A}}^{<0}})$. If $\nu > 0$ holds, then the induction hypothesis and (a) yield $\mathsf{SID}_n^\infty \vdash_0^{\omega\cdot\xi+2\cdot\mathrm{rk}(\mathfrak{A})} \mathfrak{A}(Q_{\mathfrak{A}}^{<\xi}, s), \neg\mathfrak{A}(Q_{\mathfrak{A}}^{<\xi}, t)$ for all $\xi < \nu$. Since $\nu \leq \pi$ holds, the claim follows from $(\bigvee_{t\in Q_{\mathfrak{A}}^{<\pi}}^{\xi})$ and $(\bigwedge_{s\notin Q_{\mathfrak{A}}^{<\nu}})$, and note that $\mathfrak{A} \in \mathcal{L}_{\mathsf{PA}}^2$ implies $\mathrm{rk}(\mathfrak{A}) < \omega$ and hence $\omega \cdot \xi + 2 \cdot \mathrm{rk}(\mathfrak{A}) + 1 < \omega \cdot (\xi + 1) \leq \omega \cdot \nu$ holds for all $\xi < \nu$. Statement (c) is proven by a straight-forward induction on $\mathrm{rk}(A)$, and we leave the proof to the reader, noting that (b) is used for the case that $\mathcal{A}$ is of the form $\Lambda a.(r \in Q_{\mathfrak{A}}^{<\xi})$. Finally, statement (d) is proven by induction on τ and we let $D := \exists x(\mathfrak{A}(\mathcal{B}, x) \wedge \neg\mathcal{B}(x))$. If $\tau = 0$, we immediately get $\mathsf{SID}_n^\infty \vdash_{0,0}^{0} D, \mathcal{B}(t), t \notin Q_{\mathfrak{A}}^{<0}$ from $(\bigwedge_{t\notin Q_{\mathfrak{A}}^{<0}})$. If $\tau > 0$, we get by the induction hypothesis that

$$\mathsf{SID}_n^\infty \vdash_{0,0}^{\omega\cdot\xi} D, \mathcal{B}(t), t \notin Q_{\mathfrak{A}}^{<\xi} \tag{14.1}$$

holds for all $\xi < \tau$ and all t. Using (a) with (14.1) and (c) with $\mathcal{B}(t)$ yields

$$\mathsf{SID}_n^\infty \vdash_{0,0}^{\omega\cdot\xi+2\cdot\mathrm{rk}(\mathfrak{A})} D, \mathfrak{A}(\mathcal{B}, t), \neg\mathfrak{A}(Q_{\mathfrak{A}}^{<\xi}, t)$$
$$\mathsf{SID}_n^\infty \vdash_{0,0}^{2\cdot\mathrm{rk}(\mathcal{B}(t))} D, \neg\mathfrak{A}(Q_{\mathfrak{A}}^{<\xi}, t), \mathcal{B}(t), \neg\mathcal{B}(t)$$

Since $\mathcal{B}(t) \in \mathcal{L}_n$, we have $\mathrm{rk}(\mathcal{B}(t)) < \omega$ and hence we get for some $m < \omega$

$$\mathsf{SID}_n^\infty \vdash_{0,0}^{\omega\cdot\xi+m} D, \mathfrak{A}(\mathcal{B}, t) \wedge \neg\mathcal{B}(t), \neg\mathfrak{A}(Q_{\mathfrak{A}}^{<\xi}, t), \mathcal{B}(t)$$

Using $(\bigvee_D^t)$ and that $\omega\cdot\xi+m+1 < \omega\cdot(\xi+1) \leq \omega\cdot\tau$ holds for each $\xi < \tau$, the claim follows with an $(\bigwedge_{t\notin Q_{\mathfrak{A}}^{<\tau}})$ inference. □

Lemma 14.18 (Persistence). *Let $\mathcal{L}_{n+1}^\infty$ sequents $\Delta^- := A_0, \dots, A_q$ and $\Delta^+ := B_0, \dots, B_r$ be given with $\Delta^- \subseteq \mathrm{Neg}_{n+1}^{\uparrow}$ and $\Delta^+ \subseteq \mathrm{Pos}_{n+1}^{\uparrow}$, then the following holds for all ordinals $\nu_0, \nu_0', \dots, \nu_q, \nu_q'$ with $(\forall i \leq q)(\nu_i' \leq \nu_i)$, all ordinals $\pi_0, \pi_0', \dots, \pi_p, \pi_p'$ with $(\forall i \leq p)(\pi_i \leq \pi_i')$, and each $\mathcal{L}_n^\infty$ sequent Γ:*

$$\mathsf{SID}_n^\infty \vdash_{\rho,r}^{\alpha} \Gamma, [\Delta^-]^{\nu_0,\dots,\nu_q}, [\Delta^+]^{\pi_0,\dots,\pi_p}$$
$$\Longrightarrow \mathsf{SID}_n^\infty \vdash_{\rho,r}^{\alpha} \Gamma, [\Delta^-]^{\nu_0',\dots,\nu_q'}, [\Delta^+]^{\pi_0',\dots,\pi_p'}$$

Proof. By induction on α. In case that all main formulas of the last inference are among Γ or if the last inference is an instance **I** or **II**, a fixed-point rule in **III**, or a cut-rule in **V**, then the proof is straight-forward. Otherwise the last inference is a rule in **IV** and we consider the following cases:
1. $(\bigvee_C^\xi)$ with $\xi < \pi_i$ and $C = t \in Q_{\mathfrak{A}}^{<\pi_i}$ for some $1 \leq i \leq p$: Then we have

$$\mathsf{SID}_n^\infty \vdash_{r,\rho}^{\alpha_0} \Gamma, [\Delta^-]^{\nu_0,\dots,\nu_q}, [\Delta^+]^{\pi_0,\dots,\pi_p}, \mathfrak{A}(Q_{\mathfrak{A}}^{<\xi}, t)$$

and $\alpha_0 < \alpha$. The induction hypothesis (keeping $\mathfrak{A}(Q_{\mathfrak{A}}^{<\xi}, t)$ unchanged) and $(\bigvee_{C'}^\xi)$ with $C' := t \in Q_{\mathfrak{A}}^{<\pi_i'}$ yield the claim since $\xi < \pi_i'$ holds by $\pi_i \leq \pi_i'$.
2. $(\bigwedge_C)$ with $C = t \notin Q_{\mathfrak{A}}^{<\nu_i}$ for $1 \leq i \leq q$: As the case above (use $\nu_i' \leq \nu_i$).
3. $(\bigwedge_C)$ with $C = C_0 \wedge C_1$ and w.l.o.g., let $C = A_0^{\nu_0}$: Then $C_0 = D_0^{\nu_0}$ and $C_1 = D_1^{\nu_0}$ for some $D_0, D_1 \in \mathrm{Neg}_{n+1}^{\uparrow}$: We can apply the induction hypothesis here as well but change C_0, C_1 now to $D_0^{\nu_0'}$ and $D_1^{\nu_0'}$, respectively. $(\bigwedge_{C'})$ with $C' := D_0^{\nu_0'} \wedge D_1^{\nu_0'}$ yields the claim.
4. Another rule of inference from **IV**: Similar as in the previous case. □

Theorem 14.19 (Asymmetric interpretation). *Assume that we have*

$$\mathsf{SID}^{\infty}_{n+1} \vdash^{\alpha}_{\rho,1} \Delta^-, \Delta^+$$

for some $\Delta^- \subseteq \mathrm{Neg}^{\uparrow}_{n+1}$ *and* $\Delta^+ \subseteq \mathrm{Pos}^{\uparrow}_{n+1}$. *Let* ν *and* π *be given such that* $\pi = \nu + 2^{\alpha}$ *and* $\rho \leq \omega \cdot \pi$ *hold, then we have*

$$\mathsf{SID}^{\infty}_{n} \vdash^{\omega\cdot\pi+\alpha}_{\omega\cdot\pi,\ell} [\Delta^-]^{\nu}, [\Delta^+]^{\pi}$$

Proof. By induction on α and a case distinction for the last inference.
1. Axioms in **I**: In case of $t \in P^{\mathfrak{A}}_{n+1} \in \Delta^+$ and $s \notin P^{\mathfrak{A}}_{n+1} \in \Delta^-$ with $s^{\mathbb{N}} = t^{\mathbb{N}}$, we can use (b) in Lemma 14.17 for $t \in Q^{<\pi}_{\mathfrak{A}}$ and $s \notin Q^{<\nu}_{\mathfrak{A}}$. The other cases are trivial by taking appropriate instances of the corresponding axiom schemes.
2. Axioms in **II**: If we have an instance for some $P^{\mathfrak{A}}_{m}$ with $1 \leq m \leq n$, the axiom can be reused immediately. Otherwise it is an instance for some $P^{\mathfrak{A}}_{n+1}$, and then the claim follows by using (d) in Lemma 14.17 for $Q^{<\nu}_{\mathfrak{A}}$.
3. (Cut_C) with $\mathrm{rk}(C) < \rho \leq \omega \cdot \pi$ and $\mathrm{rk}_{n+1}(C) = 0$ (and also $\mathrm{lh}(C) < \ell$):
3.1. If C is of the form $t \in P^{\mathfrak{A}}_{n+1}$ (or $t \notin P^{\mathfrak{A}}_{n+1}$): We have $\mathsf{SID}^{\infty}_{n+1} \vdash^{\alpha_0}_{\rho,1} \Delta^-, \Delta^+, t \in P^{\mathfrak{A}}_{n+1}$ and $\mathsf{SID}^{\infty}_{n+1} \vdash^{\alpha_1}_{\rho,1} \Delta^-, \Delta^+, t \notin P^{\mathfrak{A}}_{n+1}$ for some $\alpha_0, \alpha_1 < \alpha$. The induction hypothesis yields with ν and $\pi_0 := \nu + 2^{\alpha_0}$

$$\mathsf{SID}^{\infty}_{n} \vdash^{\omega\cdot\pi_0+\alpha_0}_{\omega\cdot\pi_0,\ell} [\Delta^-]^{\nu}, [\Delta^+]^{\pi_0}, t \in Q^{<\pi_0}_{\mathfrak{A}}$$

and it also yields with π_0 and $\pi_1 := \pi_0 + 2^{\alpha_1}$

$$\mathsf{SID}^{\infty}_{n} \vdash^{\omega\cdot\pi_1+\alpha_1}_{\omega\cdot\pi_1,\ell} [\Delta^-]^{\pi_0}, [\Delta^+]^{\pi_1}, t \notin Q^{<\pi_0}_{\mathfrak{A}}$$

After some weakening and applying Lemma 14.18 (using in particular $\nu < \pi_0$ and $\pi_1 = \pi_0 + 2^{\alpha_1} \leq \nu + 2^{\alpha} = \pi$), the claim follows by $(\mathsf{Cut}_{t\in Q^{<\pi_0}_{\mathfrak{A}}})$ since we have $\mathrm{rk}(t \in Q^{<\pi_0}_{\mathfrak{A}}) = \omega \cdot \pi_0 < \omega \cdot \pi$, $\mathrm{rk}_n(t \in Q^{<\pi_0}_{\mathfrak{A}}) = 0$, and in case of $n > 0$, we also have $\mathrm{lh}(t \in Q^{<\pi_0}_{\mathfrak{A}}) = \mathrm{lh}(C) < \ell$.
3.2. Otherwise $C \in \mathcal{L}^{\infty}_{n}$: First note that we have $\mathrm{rk}_n(C) \leq \mathrm{lh}(C) < \ell$, so we can use the induction hypothesis and then reuse (Cut_C) in $\mathsf{SID}^{\infty}_{n}$ to obtain the claim.
4. Fixed-point rules in **III**:
4.1. $(\mathsf{Fix}_{t\in P^{\mathfrak{A}}_{n+1}})$: We get $\mathsf{SID}^{\infty}_{n+1} \vdash^{\alpha_0}_{\rho,1} \Delta^-, \Delta^+, \mathfrak{A}(P^{\mathfrak{A}}_{n+1}, t)$ for some $\alpha_0 < \alpha$ with $\mathfrak{A}(P^{\mathfrak{A}}_{n+1}, t) \in \mathrm{Pos}^{\uparrow}_{n+1}$, and hence the induction hypothesis with ν and

$\pi_0 := \nu + 2^{\alpha_0} < \pi$ yields $\mathsf{SID}_n^\infty \vdash^{\omega\cdot\pi_0+\alpha_0}_{\omega\cdot\pi_0,\ell} [\Delta^-]^\nu, [\Delta^+]^{\pi_0}, \mathfrak{A}(Q_{\mathfrak{A}}^{<\pi_0}, t)$. Then the claim follows from $(\bigvee^{\pi_0}_{t\in Q_{\mathfrak{A}}^{<\pi}})$, Lemma 14.18, and some weakening.

4.2. $(\mathsf{Fix}_{t\notin P^{\mathfrak{A}}_{n+1}})$: We have now $\mathsf{SID}^\infty_{n+1} \vdash^{\alpha_0}_{\rho,1} \Delta^-, \Delta^+, \neg\mathfrak{A}(P^{\mathfrak{A}}_{n+1}, t)$ for some $\alpha_0 < \alpha$ with $\neg\mathfrak{A}(P^{\mathfrak{A}}_{n+1}, t) \in \mathrm{Neg}^{\uparrow}_{n+1}$, so we get with $\pi_0 := \nu + 2^{\alpha_0}$ by the induction hypothesis

$$\mathsf{SID}_n^\infty \vdash^{\omega\cdot\pi_0+\alpha_0}_{\omega\cdot\pi_0,\ell} [\Delta^-]^\nu, [\Delta^+]^{\pi_0}, \neg\mathfrak{A}(Q_{\mathfrak{A}}^{<\nu}, t)$$

and hence by Lemma 14.18 and some weakening, we get for each $\xi < \nu$

$$\mathsf{SID}_n^\infty \vdash^{\omega\cdot\pi+\alpha_0}_{\omega\cdot\pi,\ell} [\Delta^-]^\nu, [\Delta^+]^{\pi}, \neg\mathfrak{A}(Q_{\mathfrak{A}}^{<\xi}, t)$$

By using $(\bigwedge_{t\notin Q_{\mathfrak{A}}^{<\nu}})$, the claim follows.

4.3. $(\mathsf{Fix}_{t\in P^{\mathfrak{A}}_m})$ or $(\mathsf{Fix}_{t\notin P^{\mathfrak{A}}_m})$ for some $1 \le m \le n$: We can apply the induction hypothesis for the premiss and reuse the rule because it is available in SID_n^∞ and its minor formulas do not contain $P^{\mathfrak{A}}_{n+1}$.

5. Predicative rules in **IV**: Use the induction hypothesis and repeat the rule with an appropriate instance. □

Remark 14.20. An inspection of the proof of Theorem 14.19 yields that in case of $\rho = 0$, we even obtain $\mathsf{SID}_n^\infty \vdash^{\omega\cdot\pi+\alpha}_{0,0} [\Delta^-]^\nu, [\Delta^+]^\pi$ in the conclusion of Theorem 14.19. We do not need this stronger result, though.

14.4. Arithmetical Derivability

Theorem 14.21 (Arithmetical derivability). *Let $\Gamma \subseteq \mathcal{L}_{\mathsf{PA}}$ and $r, n < \omega$. If $\mathsf{SID}_n^\infty \vdash^{<\varepsilon_0}_{\rho,r} \Gamma$ holds for some $\rho < \varepsilon_0$, then $\mathsf{SID}_0^\infty \vdash^{<\varepsilon_0}_{\eta,1} \Gamma$ holds for some $\eta < \varepsilon_0$.*

Proof. By induction on n. The case $n = 0$ is clear (see Remark 14.11). We can also assume $r > 0$ w.l.o.g. and get $\mathsf{SID}_n^\infty \vdash^{<\varepsilon_0}_{\rho,1} \Gamma$ by Theorem 14.14.(a). Now Theorem 14.19 yields $\mathsf{SID}_{n-1}^\infty \vdash^{<\varepsilon_0}_{\eta,\ell} \Gamma$ for some $\eta < \varepsilon_0$ and hence the claim by the induction hypothesis. □

15. The Upper Bound of $\mathsf{SID}_{<\omega}$

Theorem 15.1. *If* $\mathsf{SID}_n \vdash A$ *for a closed* $\mathcal{L}_n$ *formula* A*, then there is an* $\ell < \omega$ *such that the derivability relation for* SID_n^∞ *and this* ℓ *yields* $\mathsf{SID}_n^\infty \vdash_{\ell,\ell}^{<\omega+\omega} A$.

Proof. As usual and inductively with respect to the underlying derivability notion $\mathsf{SID}_n \vdash A$. Note that complete induction can be proven by use of the infinitary inference rule $(\bigwedge_{\forall x B})$ and that no inferences are needed that involve symbols of the form $Q_{\mathfrak{A}}^{<\xi}$ when inductively translating from $\mathsf{SID}_n \vdash A$ to the proof-system SID_n^∞ (hence cuts of finite rank ℓ are sufficient). □

Corollary 15.2. $|\mathsf{SID}_{<\omega}| \leq \varphi(\varepsilon_0, 0)$.

Proof. For any closed arithmetical formula A with $\mathsf{SID}_n \vdash A$, we know from Theorem 15.1 that $\mathsf{SID}_n^\infty \vdash_{\ell,\ell}^{<\varepsilon_0} A$ holds for some $\ell < \omega$. According to Theorem 14.21, this means $\mathsf{SID}_0^\infty \vdash_{\rho,1}^{<\varepsilon_0} A$ for some $\rho < \varepsilon_0$. By weakening we have $\mathsf{SID}_0^\infty \vdash_{\omega^\rho,1}^{<\varepsilon_0} A$ since $\rho \leq \omega^\rho (< \varepsilon_0)$, so Theorem 14.14.(b) yields $\mathsf{SID}_0^\infty \vdash_{0,0}^{<\varphi(\varepsilon_0,0)} A$ because $\alpha, \rho < \varepsilon_0$ implies $\varphi(\rho, \alpha) < \varphi(\rho, \varphi(\varepsilon_0, 0)) = \varphi(\varepsilon_0, 0)$, using $\varepsilon_0 < \varphi(\varepsilon_0, 0)$. Finally, we get $|\mathsf{SID}_{<\omega}| \leq \varphi(\varepsilon_0, 0)$ by a standard boundedness argument. □

16. Concluding Remarks on Stratified Induction

We finish our investigations on the theory $\mathsf{SID}_{<\omega}$ of finitely stratified induction over fixed-points with some remarks on the proof-theoretic methods that we applied here and the generalization to transfinitely stratified induction. In this context, an immediate question is the relation of transfinite stratification to the *iteration of fixed-point definitions.* We established the connection of $\mathsf{SID}_{<\omega}$ to the non-iterated theory $\widehat{\mathsf{ID}}_1$ and will now briefly explain the concept of (finite) iteration of fixed-point definitions: Since $\widehat{\mathsf{ID}}_1$ is based on positive (arithmetical) operator forms $\mathfrak{A}_1$ that are formulated in the language $\mathcal{L}^2_{\mathsf{PA}}$, the theory $\widehat{\mathsf{ID}}_2$ is based on positive operator forms $\mathfrak{A}_2$ that are formulated in the language $\widehat{\mathcal{L}}_1$ (i.e., $\widehat{\mathsf{ID}}_2$ axiomatizes fixed-points of $\mathfrak{A}_2$ by means of new unary relation symbols $P^{\mathfrak{A}_2}$ for each such $\mathfrak{A}_2$, resulting in the language $\widehat{\mathcal{L}}_2$ of $\widehat{\mathsf{ID}}_2$). This is similarly defined for $\widehat{\mathsf{ID}}_n$ with arbitrary $2 < n < \omega$, and it further extends to transfinite iterations of fixed-point definitions $\widehat{\mathsf{ID}}_\alpha$. As remarked in the introduction, we know for instance that $|\mathsf{ID}^*_\beta| = |\widehat{\mathsf{ID}}_\beta|$ holds for any ordinal β, and we refer to [JKSS99] and [Pro06] for details on results and definitions.

16.1. Comparison with Proof-Theoretic Methods for $\widehat{\mathsf{ID}}_n$

Considering only the case $n = 2$ and the reduction of $\widehat{\mathsf{ID}}_2$ to $\widehat{\mathsf{ID}}_1$, we first note that similar methods (e.g., asymmetric interpretation) are used as in the reduction of SID_2 to SID_1 but with the difference that $|\widehat{\mathsf{ID}}_1| < |\widehat{\mathsf{ID}}_2|$ holds and that we actually established $|\mathsf{SID}_1| = |\mathsf{SID}_2|$ here. This is due to the following observation: Without going into too many details, let $\widehat{\mathsf{ID}}_2^\infty$ and $\widehat{\mathsf{ID}}_1^\infty$ be the infinitary proof-systems assigned to $\widehat{\mathsf{ID}}_2$ and $\widehat{\mathsf{ID}}_1$, respectively, which are defined in a similar way as the infinitary proof-systems in Section 14.1. The difference is that stratified induction axioms are missing and that for $\widehat{\mathsf{ID}}_2^\infty$, we have fixed-point rules

$$\frac{\Gamma, \mathfrak{A}_2(P^{\mathfrak{A}_2}, t)}{\Gamma, t \in P^{\mathfrak{A}_2}} \, (\mathsf{Fix}_{t \in P^{\mathfrak{A}_2}}) \qquad \frac{\Gamma, \neg\mathfrak{A}_2(P^{\mathfrak{A}_2}, t)}{\Gamma, t \notin P^{\mathfrak{A}_2}} \, (\mathsf{Fix}_{t \notin P^{\mathfrak{A}_2}})$$

for positive operator forms $\mathfrak{A}_2 \in \widehat{\mathcal{L}}_1$ that may contain symbols $P^{\mathfrak{A}_1}$ for positive operator forms $\mathfrak{A}_1 \in \widehat{\mathcal{L}}_0 (= \mathcal{L}_{\mathsf{PA}})$ in arbitrary position. This is not the case for SID_2 where the operator form is arithmetical. As remarked above, the reduction from $\widehat{\mathsf{ID}}_2$ to $\widehat{\mathsf{ID}}_1$ uses asymmetric interpretation of $\widehat{\mathsf{ID}}_2^\infty$ in $\widehat{\mathsf{ID}}_1^\infty$, therefore $\widehat{\mathsf{ID}}_1^\infty$ has for example predicative rules of the form

$$\frac{\Gamma, \mathfrak{A}_2(Q^{<\xi}_{\mathfrak{A}_2}, t)}{\Gamma, t \in Q^{<\tau}_{\mathfrak{A}_2}} \, (\mathsf{V}^{\xi}_{t \in Q^{<\tau}_{\mathfrak{A}_2}}) \text{ for } \xi < \tau \qquad (\#)$$

with $\mathfrak{A}_2$ being a positive operator form over the language $\widehat{\mathcal{L}}_2$ rather than $\widehat{\mathcal{L}}_1$. This is needed in order to be able to interpret a $(\mathsf{Fix}_{t \in P^{\mathfrak{A}_2}})$ inference, but it also makes it more difficult to remove cuts partially. Recall that in order to be able to use Theorem 14.19, we first had to partially remove cuts in SID_2^∞ before doing an asymmetric interpretation (this was needed to make the proof by induction of Theorem 14.19 work). Similarly, $\widehat{\mathsf{ID}}_2^\infty$ needs first to partially remove cuts, and because of the existence of rule of inferences such as (#) this is only possible by doing a partial cut-elimination that involves a cut-reduction for formulas of transfinite rank (compare Lemma 14.13). In contrast to this, we were able to avoid such cut-reductions for SID_2^∞ so that it was needed only once in the very end for SID_0^∞. We refer to the references for more details on the proof-theoretic analysis of $\widehat{\mathsf{ID}}_n$ for $n < \omega$ (yielding $|\widehat{\mathsf{ID}}_{<\omega}| = \Gamma_0$) and the generalization to the transfinite.

16.2. Transfinite Stratification

As described in the introduction, the equality $\varphi(\varepsilon_0, 0) = |\widehat{\mathsf{ID}}_1| = |\mathsf{SID}_n| = |\mathsf{SID}_{<\omega}|$ (with $n < \omega$) established here still leaves the question open concerning the relationship of stratification to iteration. For this, we refer to [JP15] where a generalization of stratification to the transfinite gives an answer to it. See also Table 2 on page 10.

A. Appendix: Remaining Proofs of Chapter 3

A.1. Theorem 3.6.

Proof. In order to show that $(\mathrm{OT}, \prec)$ is a strict total order, we need to show *irreflexivity*, *antisymmetry*, *totality*, and *transitivity* for $\prec$. For *irreflexivity*, we show that

$$a \not\prec a$$

holds for each $a \in \mathrm{OT}$ by induction on a, using the following case distinction. With this, we also get that $\prec_{\mathbf{lex}}$ is irreflexive.
1. $a = 0$ or $a = \tilde{1}$: Clearly, $a \not\prec a$.
2. $a = a_1 \oplus a_2$ and $a_2 \neq 0$: By the induction hypothesis, we have $a_1 \not\prec a_1$ and $a_2 \not\prec a_2$, hence by Definition 3.4 also $a \not\prec a$.
3. $a = \phi\bar{a}^{(m+1)}\bar{0}^{(k)}$ with $a_{m+1} \neq 0$: By the induction hypothesis, we have $a_i \not\prec a_i$ for all $1 \leq i \leq m+1$ and hence $a \not\prec_{\mathbf{lex}} a$. By Definition 3.4, this yields $a \not\prec a$.

For *antisymmetry*, we show that

$$a \prec b \implies b \not\prec a$$

holds for all $a, b \in \mathrm{OT}$ by induction on $a +_{\mathbb{N}} b$.

With this, we also get that $\prec_{\mathbf{lex}}$ is antisymmetric: For any $a, b \in \mathrm{PT}_{\mathrm{OT}}$ with $a \prec_{\mathbf{lex}} b$, this is clear if $\mathsf{lh}(a) < \mathsf{lh}(b)$ holds. If $a = \phi\bar{c}^{(n)}\bar{a}^{(k)}$ and $b = \phi\bar{c}^{(n)}\bar{b}^{(k)}$ hold with $a_1 \prec b_1$, then we have $b_1 \not\preceq a_1$ by irreflexivity ($b_1 = a_1$ would contradict $a_1 \prec b_1$) and antisymmetry of $\prec$, yielding $b \not\prec_{\mathbf{lex}} a$.

Now turning to the antisymmetry of $\prec$, assume $a \prec b$. Hence $a, b \in \mathrm{OT}$ holds with $b \neq 0$, and we consider the following cases.
1. $a = 0$ and $b \neq 0$: This is obvious.
2. $a = \tilde{1}$, $b \neq 0$, and $b \neq \tilde{1}$: This is also obvious.

3. $a \in \mathrm{PT}_+$ with $\phi\bar{a}^{(m+1)}\bar{0}^{(k)}$ and $a_{m+1} \neq 0$: Since $a \prec b$ holds, we must have $b = b'_1 \oplus b'_2$ with $b'_1 \in \mathrm{PT}_+$ where $b'_2 = 0$ may hold, and we consider the following two cases:
3.1. $b'_2 \neq 0$: If $a = b'_1$, we get $b = a \oplus b'_2 \not\prec a \oplus 0 = a$ due to $b'_2 \neq 0$. Otherwise $a \neq b'_1$ and $a \prec b'_1$ holds, so $b \not\prec a$ follows from the induction hypothesis $b'_1 \not\prec a$.
3.2. $b'_2 = 0$: Then $b'_1 = b \in \mathrm{PT}_+$ must hold, and we consider now $b = \phi\bar{b}^{(n+1)}\bar{0}^{(l)}$ with $b_{n+1} \neq 0$.
3.2.1. $a \prec_{\mathbf{lex}} b$ and $a_i \prec b$ for all $1 \leq i \leq m+1$: By the induction hypothesis, we have $b \not\prec a_i$ for all $1 \leq i \leq m+1$. If $b \prec a$ holds, then by Definition 3.4, we need either $b \preceq a_j$ for some $1 \leq j \leq m$ or $b \prec a_{m+1}$. Both is impossible due to $a_i \prec b$ for all $1 \leq i \leq m+1$, either by the induction hypothesis or by irreflexivity.
3.2.2. $b \prec_{\mathbf{lex}} a$ and $a \prec b_j$ for some $1 \leq j \leq n+1$: By the induction hypothesis, we have $b_j \not\prec a$ for this $1 \leq j \leq n+1$. If $b \prec a$ would hold, then $b \prec_{\mathbf{lex}} a$ would imply that $b_i \prec a$ holds for all $1 \leq i \leq n+1$ which is impossible.
3.2.3. $b \prec_{\mathbf{lex}} a$ and $a = b_j$ for some $1 \leq j \leq n$: Again $b \prec a$ is impossible since then $b_j \prec a$ would hold, yielding a contradiction to irreflexivity.
4. $a = a_1 \oplus a_2$ with $a_2 \neq 0$: Then $a \prec b$ means that $b = b_1 \oplus b_2$ holds for some $b_1, b_2 \in \mathrm{OT}$ with $b_1 \in \mathrm{PT}$ and we have the following cases:
4.1. $a_1 = b_1$ and $a_2 \prec b_2$: By the induction hypothesis, we have $b_2 \not\prec a_2$, hence $b \prec a$ is impossible.
4.2. $a_1 \prec b_1$: By the induction hypothesis, we have $b_1 \not\prec a_1$, hence for $b \prec a$ to hold, we need $b_1 = a_1$ and $b_2 \prec a_2$. But $b_1 = a_1$ and $a_1 \prec b_1$ contradicts irreflexivity.

For *totality*, we show that

$$a \prec b \text{ or } a = b \text{ or } b \prec a$$

holds for all $a, b \in \mathrm{OT}$ by induction on $a +_{\mathbb{N}} b$.

With this, we also get that $\prec_{\mathbf{lex}}$ is total: For any $a, b \in \mathrm{PT}_{\mathrm{OT}}$, if not already $\mathsf{lh}(a) < \mathsf{lh}(b)$ or $\mathsf{lh}(b) < \mathsf{lh}(a)$ holds, we get $a = \phi\bar{a}^{(n)}$ and $b = \phi\bar{b}^{(n)}$ with $a_1, \dots, a_n, b_1, \dots, b_n \in \mathrm{OT}$. So, we get the claim by totality of $\prec$.

Now turning to the totality of $\prec$, let $a, b \in \mathrm{OT}$ and consider the following cases.
1. $a = 0$: This is obvious.
2. $a = \tilde{1}$: Again, this is obvious. In case of $b = 0$, we get $b \prec a$, and in

case of $b = \tilde{1}$, we get $a = b$. Otherwise, we have $a \prec b$ by Definition 3.4.
<u>3.</u> $a \in \mathrm{PT}_+$ with $a = \phi\bar{a}^{(m+1)}\bar{0}^{(k)}$ and $a_{m+1} \neq 0$:
<u>3.1.</u> $b = 0$ or $b = \tilde{1}$: By definition, $b \prec a$ holds already due to $a \neq 0$ and $a \neq \tilde{1}$.
<u>3.2.</u> $b \in \mathrm{PT}_+$ with $b = \phi\bar{b}^{(n+1)}\bar{0}^{(l)}$ and $b_{n+1} \neq 0$: We have the following cases (and due to the induction hypothesis if necessary[1]):
<u>3.2.1.</u> $a \prec_{\mathbf{lex}} b$: Again due to the induction hypothesis, we can distinguish the following cases.
<u>3.2.1.1.</u> $a_i \prec b$ for all $1 \leq i \leq m+1$: Then we get $a \prec b$ by Definition 3.4.
<u>3.2.1.2.</u> $a_j = b$ for some $1 \leq j \leq m$: Then we get $b \prec a$ by Definition 3.4.
<u>3.2.1.3.</u> $a_{m+1} = b$ and $a_i \neq b$ for all $1 \leq i \leq m$: Then $a_{m+1} \in \mathrm{PT}_+$ and because of $a \prec_{\mathbf{lex}} b = a_{m+1}$ and $a \in \mathrm{OT}$, we have $b = a_{m+1} \preceq a_j$ for some $1 \leq j \leq m$, yielding $b \prec a$ by Definition 3.4.
<u>3.2.1.4.</u> $a_i \neq b$ for all $1 \leq i \leq m+1$ and $b \prec a_j$ for some $1 \leq j \leq m+1$: Since $a \prec_{\mathbf{lex}} b$ holds, we get immediately $b \prec a$.
<u>3.2.2.</u> $b \prec_{\mathbf{lex}} a$: Analogously as for the previous case.
<u>3.2.3.</u> Otherwise and since $a, b \in \mathrm{OT}$ holds, this implies that we have $m = n$, $k = l$, and $a_i = b_i$ for all $1 \leq i \leq m+1$, yielding $a = b$.
<u>3.3.</u> $b = b_1 \oplus b_2$ with $b_2 \neq 0$: By the induction hypothesis, we have $a \preceq b_1$ or $b_1 \prec a$. Then we obviously get $a \preceq b$ or $b \prec a$, while for the case $a_1 = b_2$, note that $b_2 \neq 0$ implies $0 \prec b_2$, hence $a = a \oplus 0 \prec b$.
<u>4.</u> $a = a_1 \oplus a_2$ with $a_2 \neq 0$: Analogously to the previous cases.

Finally for *transitivity*, the claims for $(\mathrm{OT}, \prec)$ and $(\mathrm{PT}_{\mathrm{OT}}, \prec_{\mathbf{lex}})$ are proven simultaneously, i.e., we show

$$a, b, c \in \mathrm{OT} \;\;\&\;\; a \prec b \;\;\&\;\; b \prec c \implies a \prec c \tag{$*$}$$

$$a, b, c \in \mathrm{PT}_{\mathrm{OT}} \;\;\&\;\; a \prec_{\mathbf{lex}} b \;\;\&\;\; b \prec_{\mathbf{lex}} c \implies a \prec_{\mathbf{lex}} c \tag{$**$}$$

by induction on $a +_{\mathbb{N}} b +_{\mathbb{N}} c$. Now, let $a, b, c \in \mathbb{N}$ be arbitrary.

For statement $(**)$, assume that $a, b, c \in \mathrm{PT}_{\mathrm{OT}}$ holds with $a \prec_{\mathbf{lex}} b$ and $b \prec_{\mathbf{lex}} c$. In particular, we have $(a)_0 = (b)_0 = (c)_0 = 1$. If $\mathsf{lh}(a) < \mathsf{lh}(b)$ or $\mathsf{lh}(b) < \mathsf{lh}(c)$ holds, then also $\mathsf{lh}(a) < \mathsf{lh}(c)$ and so $a \prec_{\mathbf{lex}} c$ holds by definition of $\prec_{\mathbf{lex}}$. Otherwise $\mathsf{lh}(a) = \mathsf{lh}(b) = \mathsf{lh}(c)$ and some $j_1, j_2 < \mathsf{lh}(a)$ exist with

[1] More precisely, if $\mathsf{lh}(a) \neq \mathsf{lh}(b)$ holds, then we have directly $a \prec_{\mathbf{lex}} b$ or $b \prec_{\mathbf{lex}} a$. If $\mathsf{lh}(a) = \mathsf{lh}(b)$ holds, then we use the induction hypothesis for $\bar{a}^{(m+1)}, \bar{0}^{(k)}$ and $\bar{b}^{(n+1)}, \bar{0}^{(l)}$.

- $a_{j_1} \prec b_{j_1}$ and $a_i = b_i$ for all $1 \leq i < j_1$, and
- $b_{j_2} \prec c_{j_2}$ and $b_i = c_i$ for all $1 \leq i < j_2$.

If $j_1 = j_2$ holds, then we get $a_{j_1} \prec b_{j_1}$ and $b_{j_1} \prec c_{j_1}$, so by the induction hypothesis on statement $(*)$, we have $a_{j_1} \prec c_{j_1}$ and hence $a \prec_{\mathbf{lex}} c$. If $j_1 < j_2$ holds, then we get $a_i = b_i = c_i$ for all $1 \leq i < j_1$ and $a_{j_1} \prec b_{j_1} = c_{j_1}$, hence again $a \prec_{\mathbf{lex}} c$ holds. If $j_1 > j_2$ holds, then we get $a_i = b_i = c_i$ for all $1 \leq i < j_2$ and $a_{j_2} = b_{j_2} \prec c_{j_2}$, hence $a \prec_{\mathbf{lex}} c$ by definition. This shows $(**)$.

Now turning to statement $(*)$ for the transitivity of $\prec$, assume that $a, b, c \in \mathrm{OT}$ holds with $a \prec b$ and $b \prec c$, hence $b \neq 0$ and $c \neq 0$ hold. Keeping in mind that we have shown $(**)$ for the given numbers $a, b, c \in \mathbb{N}$ (and that $(**)$ actually holds in all combinations of a, b, c), we consider the following case distinction.

<u>1.</u> $a = 0$: $b \prec c$ implies $c \neq 0$, hence $a \prec c$.

<u>2.</u> $a = \tilde{1}$: $a \prec b$ implies $b \neq 0$ and $b \neq \tilde{1}$, hence $b \prec c$ implies also $c \neq 0$ and $c \neq \tilde{1}$ (since otherwise we have $c \prec b$ which contradicts antisymmetry). This yields $a \prec c$.

<u>3.</u> $a \in \mathrm{PT}_+$ with $a = \phi\bar{a}^{(m+1)}\bar{0}^{(k)}$ and $a_{m+1} \neq 0$: Due to $a \prec b$, we have the following cases.

<u>3.1.</u> $b \in \mathrm{PT}_+$ with $b = \phi\bar{b}^{(n+1)}\bar{0}^{(l)}$ and $b_{n+1} \neq 0$: Due to $b \prec c$, we have further the following cases.

<u>3.1.1.</u> $c \in \mathrm{PT}_+$ with $c = \phi\bar{c}^{(p+1)}\bar{0}^{(q)}$ and $c_{p+1} \neq 0$: We distinguish the following situations.

<u>3.1.1.1.</u> $a \prec_{\mathbf{lex}} b$ and $b \prec_{\mathbf{lex}} c$: By $(**)$, we get $a \prec_{\mathbf{lex}} c$, hence since here $a_i \prec b$ holds for all $1 \leq i \leq m+1$, and since we have $b \prec c$, we get $a_i \prec c$ by the induction hypothesis on a_i, b, and c for all $1 \leq i \leq m+1$, yielding $a \prec c$.

<u>3.1.1.2.</u> $a \prec_{\mathbf{lex}} b$ and $c \prec_{\mathbf{lex}} b$: Due to antisymmetry, the case $a = c$ is impossible, since otherwise $c = a \prec b$ and $b \prec c$ would hold. Hence totality induces the following two situations:

(i) If $c \prec_{\mathbf{lex}} a$: With $b \prec c$ and $c \prec_{\mathbf{lex}} b$, we have $b \prec c_{p+1}$ or $b \preceq c_j$ for some $1 \leq j \leq p$. Hence $a \prec b$ and the induction hypothesis yields $a \prec c_j$ for some $1 \leq j \leq p+1$, and we get $a \prec c$ by the definition of $\prec$ and due to $c \prec_{\mathbf{lex}} a$.

(ii) If $a \prec_{\mathbf{lex}} c$: With $a \prec b$ and $a \prec_{\mathbf{lex}} b$, we have $a_i \prec b$ for all $1 \leq i \leq m+1$, hence by the induction hypothesis $a_i \prec c$ for all $1 \leq i \leq m+1$ and we get $a \prec c$ due to $a \prec_{\mathbf{lex}} c$.

3.1.1.3. $b \prec_{\mathbf{lex}} a$ and $b \prec_{\mathbf{lex}} c$: Due to $b \prec c$, we have $b_i \prec c$ for all $1 \leq i \leq n+1$, and due to $a \prec b$, we have the following two situations: If $a \prec b_j$ holds for some $1 \leq j \leq p+1$, then we get by the induction hypothesis $a \prec c$ since we have here $b_j \prec c$. Otherwise $a = b_j$ holds for some $1 \leq j \leq p$, and since $b_j \prec c$ holds, we immediately get $a \prec c$.
3.1.1.4. $b \prec_{\mathbf{lex}} a$ and $c \prec_{\mathbf{lex}} b$: By (**), we get $c \prec_{\mathbf{lex}} a$ and due to $b \prec c$, we have the following two situations: If $b \prec c_{p+1}$ holds, we get by the induction hypothesis $a \prec c_{p+1}$ since we have $a \prec b$. Hence with $c \prec_{\mathbf{lex}} a$ and Definition 3.4 also $a \prec c$ holds. Otherwise, we have $b = c_j$ for some $1 \leq j \leq p$, and then $a \prec b$ yields $a \prec c_j$ and with $c \prec_{\mathbf{lex}} a$, we are done.

3.1.2. $c = c_1 \oplus c_2$ with $c_2 \neq 0$: We get $b \preceq c_1$ from $b \prec c$ because of $b \in \mathrm{PT}_+$. So by the induction hypothesis (if necessary), $a \prec b$ yields $a \prec c_1$ and since $a \in \mathrm{PT}_+$ holds, we hence get $a \prec c$ by Definition 3.4.

3.2. $b = b_1 \oplus b_2$ with $b_2 \neq 0$: We get $a \preceq b_1$ from $a \prec b$ because of $a \in \mathrm{PT}_+$. We have $b_1 = b_1 \oplus 0 \prec b_1 \oplus b_2 = b$ since $b_2 \neq 0$ holds, hence $b_1 \prec b$, so by the induction hypothesis and with $b \prec c$, we get $b_1 \prec c$, and hence with $a \preceq b_1$ and using (if necessary) the induction hypothesis once more, we get $a \prec c$.

4. $a = a_1 \oplus a_2$ with $a_2 \neq 0$:

4.1. $b \in \mathrm{PT}$: Then $a \prec b$ implies $a_1 \prec b$, hence by the induction hypothesis and $b \prec c$, we get $a_1 \prec c$.

4.1.1. $c \in \mathrm{PT}$: Then also $a \prec c$ holds by definition.
4.1.2. $c \notin \mathrm{PT}$: Since $c \neq 0$ (due to $b \prec c$), we have $c = c_1 \oplus c_2$ with $c_2 \neq 0$. So we get $b \preceq c_1$ from $b \prec c$ and hence $a_1 \prec c_1$ from $a_1 \prec b$ by the induction hypothesis (if necessary). This yields $a \prec c$ by definition.

4.2. $b \notin \mathrm{PT}$: Since $b \neq 0$ (due to $a \prec b$), we have $b = b_1 \oplus b_2$ with $b_2 \neq 0$, so we get $a_1 \preceq b_1$.

4.2.1. $c \in \mathrm{PT}$: Then $b_1 \prec c$ because $b \prec c$ and $a_1 \preceq b$ yield $a_1 \prec c$ by the induction hypothesis (if necessary), hence $a \prec c$ by definition.
4.2.2. $c \notin \mathrm{PT}$: Again we have $c = c_1 \oplus c_2$ with $c_2 \neq 0$. If $b_1 \prec c_1$, the induction hypothesis (if necessary) and $a_1 \preceq b_1$ yield $a_1 \prec c_1$, hence $a \prec c$ by definition. If $b_1 = c_1$ and $a_1 \prec b_1$ hold, then also $a_1 \prec c_1$ by the induction hypothesis, hence $a \prec c$. If $a_1 = b_1 = c_1$, then $a_2 \prec b_2$ and $b_2 \prec c_2$ hold, yielding $a_2 \prec c_2$ by the induction hypothesis and hence again $a \prec c$. □

A.2. Lemma 3.15

Proof. We note first that the lemma follows easily if one of the ordinal notations involved is 0. Therefore, we assume $a \neq 0$, $b \neq 0$, and $c \neq 0$ and further that we have

$$a = a_1 \oplus a_2 \qquad b = b_1 \oplus b_2 \qquad c = c_1 \oplus c_2$$

with $a_1, b_1, c_1 \in \mathrm{PT}$. This will render the following computations more readable.

For (a), we assume $a \oplus b \in \mathrm{OT}$, hence we get $\mathsf{hd}(b) \preceq a$ and $a \in \mathrm{PT}$. Given $c \preceq b$, we get $\mathsf{hd}(c) \preceq \mathsf{hd}(b) \preceq a = \mathsf{hd}(a)$ and $a \tilde{+} c = \mathsf{hd}(a) \oplus (\mathsf{tl}(a) \tilde{+} c) = a \oplus (0 \tilde{+} c) = a \oplus c$ since we assumed $a, c \neq 0$.

For (b), we argue by induction on a and the following case distinction. Note that we have $a_2 <_{\mathbb{N}} a$ since we assumed $a \neq 0$.

1. $a_1 \prec b_1$: $a \tilde{+} b = b$ and $(a \tilde{+} b) \tilde{+} c = b \tilde{+} c$. Now, we have only the following cases (since $b, c \neq 0$):

1.1. $b_1 \prec c_1$: Then $b \tilde{+} c = c$ and with $a_1 \prec c_1$ also $a \tilde{+} c = c$, hence $a \tilde{+} (b \tilde{+} c) = a \tilde{+} c = c$ and we are done.

1.2. $c_1 \preceq b_1$: Then $b \tilde{+} c = b_1 \oplus (b_2 \tilde{+} c)$ holds. So we get $a \tilde{+} (b \tilde{+} c) = b \tilde{+} c$ and we are done.

2. $b_1 \preceq a_1$: We have $a \tilde{+} b = a_1 \oplus (a_2 \tilde{+} b)$ and consider the following cases.

2.1. $a_1 \prec c_1$: Then $a \tilde{+} c = c$ and also $b_1 \prec c_1$, hence $b \tilde{+} c = c$. So we have $a \tilde{+} (b \tilde{+} c) = a \tilde{+} c = c$. Moreover, $a \tilde{+} b = a_1 \oplus (a_2 \tilde{+} b)$, hence also $(a \tilde{+} b) \tilde{+} c = c$.

2.2. $c_1 \preceq a_1$: We have either $\mathsf{hd}(b \tilde{+} c) = b_1$ or $\mathsf{hd}(b \tilde{+} c) = c_1$, hence by $b_1 \preceq a_1$ and $c_1 \preceq a_1$ we get $a \tilde{+} (b \tilde{+} c) = a_1 \oplus (a_2 \tilde{+} (b \tilde{+} c))$ and $(a \tilde{+} b) \tilde{+} c = (a_1 \oplus (a_2 \tilde{+} b)) \tilde{+} c = a_1 \oplus ((a_2 \tilde{+} b) \tilde{+} c)$, using the induction hypothesis.

For (c), we argue again by induction on a. Let $b \prec c$, so we have $b_1 \preceq c_1$ by definition of $\prec$.

1. $a_1 \prec b_1$: Then $a_1 \prec c_1$ and $a \tilde{+} b = b \prec c = a \tilde{+} c$.

2. $b_1 \preceq a_1$:

2.1. $a_1 \prec c_1$: Then $a \tilde{+} b = a_1 \oplus (a_2 \tilde{+} b) \prec c_1 \oplus c_2 = c = a \tilde{+} c$.

2.2. $c_1 \preceq a_1$: By the induction hypothesis, we have $a_2 \tilde{+} b \prec a_2 \tilde{+} c$, hence $a \tilde{+} b = a_1 \oplus (a_2 \tilde{+} b) \prec a_1 \oplus (a_2 \tilde{+} c) = a \tilde{+} c$.

For (d), we argue again by induction on a. Let $a \preceq c$, hence $a_1 \preceq c_1$.

1. $a_1 \prec c_1$: $a \tilde{+} c = c$, so let $d := c$.

2. $a_1 = c_1$: Then we have $a_2 \preceq c_2$ and the induction hypothesis yields $a_2 \tilde{+} d = c_2$ for some $d \in \mathrm{OT}$. Hence with (b), we get $a \tilde{+} d = (a_1 \tilde{+} a_2) \tilde{+} d = a_1 \tilde{+} (a_2 \tilde{+} d) = a_1 \tilde{+} c_2 = c_1 \tilde{+} c_2 = c$.

For (e), let $a \preceq c$ and $c \prec a \tilde{+} b$. We have $c = a \tilde{+} d$ for some $d \in \mathrm{OT}$ by (d), hence $a \tilde{+} d = c \prec a \tilde{+} b$. This implies $d \neq b$ and due to (c) also $b \not\prec d$, hence $d \prec b$ by totality.

For (f), we recall first that we consider only the case $a, b \neq 0$ here. Then (c) implies $a = a \tilde{+} 0 \prec a \tilde{+} b$. Furthermore, if $a_1 \prec b_1$, then $a \tilde{+} b = b$, and if $b_1 \prec a_1$, then $b \prec a \prec a \tilde{+} b$. Now, for the remaining case $a_1 = b_1$, we have $b = a_1 \tilde{+} b_2 \prec a_1 \tilde{+} b$ with (c) by using $b_2 \prec b$ from Lemma 3.8.

For (g), let $a \preceq c$. We have $c = a \tilde{+} d$ for some $d \in \mathrm{OT}$ by (d), and by (f), we have, $b \preceq d \tilde{+} b$. Hence with (c) and (b), we get $a \tilde{+} b \preceq a \tilde{+} (d \tilde{+} b) = (a \tilde{+} d) \tilde{+} b = c \tilde{+} b$.

For (h), we have $a \tilde{+} b = a \neq 0$ if $b = 0$, and $a \tilde{+} b = b \neq 0$ if $a = 0$. Otherwise, $a \tilde{+} b = a_1 \oplus (a_2 \tilde{+} b) \neq 0$.

For (i), let $a \prec b \tilde{+} \tilde{1}$ and assume $a \npreceq b$. Then $b \prec a$ and $a = b \tilde{+} d$ for some $d \prec \tilde{1}$ by (e), hence $d = 0$ and $b = a$, a contradiction.

For (k), let $a \in \mathrm{Lim}$ and $b \prec a$. Assume $b \tilde{+} \tilde{1} \not\prec a$, so we have $a \preceq b \tilde{+} \tilde{1}$. Note that by the definition of $\tilde{+}$, we have that $\mathrm{last}(b \tilde{+} \tilde{1}) = \tilde{1}$ holds, so $a = b \tilde{+} \tilde{1}$ contradicts $a \in \mathrm{Lim}$. Further, $a \prec b \tilde{+} \tilde{1}$ implies $a \preceq b$ by (i), contradicting $b \prec a$.

For (l), we argue by induction on a. If $a_2 = 0$, then $a = \tilde{1} \notin \mathrm{PT}_+$, hence let $d := 0$. If $a_2 \neq 0$, then obviously $a \notin \mathrm{PT}_+$ holds and we have also $\mathrm{last}(a_2) = \tilde{1}$, so we get by the induction hypothesis that $a_2 \notin \mathrm{PT}_+$ and $a_2 = d_2 \tilde{+} \tilde{1}$ hold for some $d_2 \in \mathrm{OT}$. Hence with (b), we get $a = a_1 \tilde{+} (d_2 \tilde{+} \tilde{1}) = (a_1 \tilde{+} d_2) \tilde{+} \tilde{1}$ and we can set $d := a_1 \tilde{+} d_2$. □

A.3. Auxiliary Corollary A.3.1

Corollary A.3.1. *Let $k, m \in \mathbb{N}$ and $a_1, \ldots, a_m, b, c \in \mathrm{OT}$. Then we have:*

$$b \prec c \implies \tilde{\varphi}(\bar{a}^{(m)}, b, \bar{0}^{(k)}) \prec \tilde{\varphi}(\bar{a}^{(m)}, c, \bar{0}^{(k)})$$

Proof. Assume $b \prec c$ and consider the following cases. By Lemma 3.17, we can assume without loss of generality that $a_1 \neq 0$ holds.

1. If $\phi\bar{a}^{(m)}b\bar{0}^{(k)} \notin \mathrm{OT}$ and $\phi\bar{a}^{(m)}c\bar{0}^{(k)} \notin \mathrm{OT}$: From Lemma 3.17, we get

$$\tilde{\varphi}(\bar{a}^{(m)}, b, \bar{0}^{(k)}) = b \prec c = \tilde{\varphi}(\bar{a}^{(m)}, c, \bar{0}^{(k)})$$

2. If $\phi\bar{a}^{(m)}b\bar{0}^{(k)} \in \mathrm{OT}$ and $\phi\bar{a}^{(m)}c\bar{0}^{(k)} \in \mathrm{OT}$: From the definition of $\prec$, we get

$$\tilde{\varphi}(\bar{a}^{(m)}, b, \bar{0}^{(k)}) = \phi\bar{a}^{(m)}b\bar{0}^{(k)} \prec \phi\bar{a}^{(m)}c\bar{0}^{(k)} = \tilde{\varphi}(\bar{a}^{(m)}, c, \bar{0}^{(k)})$$

using $b \prec c$ from our assumption to get $\phi\bar{a}^{(m)}b\bar{0}^{(k)} \prec \phi\bar{a}^{(m)}c\bar{0}^{(k)}$ and $a_1, \ldots, a_m, c \prec \phi\bar{a}^{(m)}c\bar{0}^{(k)}$ from Lemma 3.8.

3. If $\phi\bar{a}^{(m)}b\bar{0}^{(k)} \notin \mathrm{OT}$ and $\phi\bar{a}^{(m)}c\bar{0}^{(k)} \in \mathrm{OT}$: Using Lemma 3.8, we get

$$\tilde{\varphi}(\bar{a}^{(m)}, b, \bar{0}^{(k)}) = b \prec c \prec \phi\bar{a}^{(m)}c\bar{0}^{(k)} = \tilde{\varphi}(\bar{a}^{(m)}, c, \bar{0}^{(k)})$$

4. If $\phi\bar{a}^{(m)}b\bar{0}^{(k)} \in \mathrm{OT}$ and $\phi\bar{a}^{(m)}c\bar{0}^{(k)} \notin \mathrm{OT}$: We have

$$\tilde{\varphi}(\bar{a}^{(m)}, b, \bar{0}^{(k)}) = \phi\bar{a}^{(m)}b\bar{0}^{(k)} \prec c = \tilde{\varphi}(\bar{a}^{(m)}, c, \bar{0}^{(k)})$$

because $\phi\bar{a}^{(m)}c\bar{0}^{(k)} \notin \mathrm{OT}$ implies $c \in \mathrm{PT}_+$ with $\phi\bar{a}^{(m)}c\bar{0}^{(k)} \prec_{\mathbf{lex}} c$ by Lemma 3.17. Hence, $b \prec c$ implies $\phi\bar{a}^{(m)}b\bar{0}^{(k)} \prec_{\mathbf{lex}} \phi\bar{a}^{(m)}c\bar{0}^{(k)} \prec_{\mathbf{lex}} c$, and we get $\phi\bar{a}^{(m)}b\bar{0}^{(k)} \prec c$ from the definition of $\prec$ since $a_1, \ldots, a_m \prec c$ holds by Lemma 3.8 and $b \prec c$ by assumption. □

A.4. Lemma 3.21

Proof. Let $a, b \in \mathrm{OT}$. For (a): Immediate by induction on a.

For (b): By induction on $a+b \in \mathrm{OT}$ and a case distinction on $b \in \mathrm{OT}$.

1. If $b = 0$: Then we have nothing to show.
2. If $b = \tilde{1}(= \phi 0)$: This is obvious because of $a = 0$ and $\mathrm{o}(b) = \varphi(0) = 1$.
3. If $b = b_1 \oplus b_2$ with $b_2 \neq 0$: Then let $a = a_1 \oplus a_2$ for some $a_1, a_2 \in \mathrm{OT}$. Now $a \prec b$ implies either $a_1 \prec b_1$ or $a_1 = b_1$ with $a_2 \prec b_2$. The induction hypothesis and the definition of $\mathrm{o}(a)$ and $\mathrm{o}(b)$ yield immediately the claim.
4. $b = \phi\bar{b}^{(n+1)}\bar{0}^{(l)}$ with $b_1, b_{n+1} \neq 0$:

4.1. If $a = 0$: The claim is trivial since here $\mathrm{o}(b) \neq 0$ holds due to $\mathrm{o}(b_1) \neq 0$ and the definition of $\mathrm{o}(b)$.

4.2. If $a = \phi\bar{a}^{(m+1)}\bar{0}^{(k)}$ with $a_1, a_{m+1} \neq 0$: Then we have

$$\mathrm{o}(a) = \varphi(\mathrm{o}(a_1), \ldots, \mathrm{o}(a_{m+1}), \bar{0}^{(k)})$$
$$\mathrm{o}(b) = \varphi(\mathrm{o}(b_1), \ldots, \mathrm{o}(b_{n+1}), \bar{0}^{(l)})$$

Assuming $a \prec b$, we show $\mathrm{o}(a) < \mathrm{o}(b)$ via the following two cases. (The reverse direction holds analogously.)

(i) If $a \prec_{\mathsf{lex}} b$ holds with $a_i \prec b$ for all $1 \leq i \leq m+1$: Let $p := \mathsf{lh}(b) - \mathsf{lh}(a)$, and so we get $\mathrm{o}(a) = \varphi(\bar{0}^{(p)}, \mathrm{o}(a_1), \ldots, \mathrm{o}(a_{m+1}), \bar{0}^{(k)})$. Moreover, the induction hypothesis yields for all $1 \leq i \leq m+1$

$$\mathrm{o}(a_i) < \mathrm{o}(b) \tag{A.1}$$

In case of $p \neq 0$, Corollary 2.18 directly yields the claim together with $0 < \mathrm{o}(b_1)$ and (A.1). If $p = 0$ holds, then we have $m \leq n$ and some $1 \leq r \leq m+1$ exists such that $a_i = b_i$ holds for all $1 \leq i < r$ and such that $a_r \prec b_r$ holds. The induction hypothesis and Corollary 2.18 yield then the claim, using again (A.1).

(ii) Otherwise, $b \prec_{\mathsf{lex}} a$ holds with $a \prec b_{n+1}$ or $a \preceq b_j$ for some $1 \leq j \leq n$: For $p := \mathsf{lh}(a) - \mathsf{lh}(b)$, we get $\mathrm{o}(b) = \varphi(\bar{0}^{(p)}, \mathrm{o}(b_1), \ldots, \mathrm{o}(b_{n+1}), \bar{0}^{(l)})$. Moreover, the induction hypothesis yields

$$\mathrm{o}(a) < \mathrm{o}(b_{n+1}) \text{ or } \big(\mathrm{o}(a) \leq \mathrm{o}(b_j) \text{ for some } 1 \leq j \leq n\big) \tag{A.2}$$

We can argue as for the previous case, using Corollary 2.18 and (A.2).

4.3. If $a = a_1 \oplus a_2$ with $a_2 \neq 0$: Note that $a \prec b$ implies $a_1 \prec b$ with $a_1 \in \mathrm{PT}$. We can then argue as in the previous case if $b \in \mathrm{PT}_+$.

For (c): By induction on a and the following case distinction.

1. If $b = 0$: Then $\mathrm{o}(a \tilde{+} b) = \mathrm{o}(a) = \mathrm{o}(a) + \mathrm{o}(b)$.

2. If $a = 0$ and $b \neq 0$: Then $\mathrm{o}(a \tilde{+} b) = \mathrm{o}(b) = \mathrm{o}(a) + \mathrm{o}(b)$.

3. If $a, b \neq 0$ and $\mathsf{hd}(b) \preceq \mathsf{hd}(a)$: Then $\mathrm{o}(a \tilde{+} b) = \mathrm{o}(\mathsf{hd}(a) \oplus (\mathsf{tl}(a) \tilde{+} b)) = \mathrm{o}(\mathsf{hd}(a)) + \mathrm{o}(\mathsf{tl}(a) \tilde{+} b)$. Since $a \neq 0$, we have $\mathsf{tl}(a) \prec a$, so with the induction hypothesis yielding $\mathrm{o}(\mathsf{tl}(a) \tilde{+} b) = \mathrm{o}(\mathsf{tl}(a)) + \mathrm{o}(b)$, we get $\mathrm{o}(a \tilde{+} b) = \mathrm{o}(\mathsf{hd}(a)) + \mathrm{o}(\mathsf{tl}(a)) + \mathrm{o}(b) = \mathrm{o}(\mathsf{hd}(a) \oplus \mathsf{tl}(a)) + \mathrm{o}(b) = \mathrm{o}(a) + \mathrm{o}(b)$.

4. Otherwise, we have $a, b \neq 0$ and $\mathsf{hd}(a) \prec \mathsf{hd}(b)$: Then $\mathrm{o}(a \tilde{+} b) = \mathrm{o}(b)$ and by (b), we have $\mathrm{o}(\mathsf{hd}(a)) < \mathrm{o}(\mathsf{hd}(b))$. We have by the definition of OT that $a = \mathsf{hd}(a) \oplus \mathsf{tl}(a)$ holds with $\mathsf{tl}(a) \preceq \mathsf{hd}(a)$. By (b), we get $\mathrm{o}(\mathsf{tl}(a)) \preceq \mathrm{o}(\mathsf{hd}(a))$. Since $\mathsf{hd}(b) \in \mathrm{PT}$ implies $\mathrm{o}(b) \in \mathbf{P}$ by (a), we now get

$o(a) + o(b) = o(b)$ and hence the claim.

For (d): By Lemma 3.19, it suffices to show that $o(a) < \nu_n$ holds for some $n \in \mathbb{N}$, and we shall prove this by induction on a.

1. If $a = 0$: Use $\nu_0 = f_\omega\binom{1}{0} = \omega^0 = 1$.
2. If $a = \tilde{1}(= \phi 0)$: Use $\nu_1 = f_\omega\binom{1}{1} = \omega^1 = \omega$.
3. If $a = a_1 \oplus a_2$ with $a_2 \neq 0$: Then $a_1, a_2 <_{\mathbb{N}} a$ holds and the induction hypothesis yields n_1, n_2 such that $o(a_1) < \nu_1$ and $o(a_2) < \nu_2$. Letting $n := \max\{n_1, n_2\}$ yields $o(a_1), o(a_2) < \nu_n$ by Lemma 3.19. Since $\nu_n = f_\omega\binom{1}{n} \in \mathrm{PT}$ holds, we get $o(a) < \nu_n$ by (c).
4. If $a = \phi\bar{a}^{(m+1)}\bar{0}^{(l)}$ with $a_1, a_{m+1} \neq 0$: We get by Lemma 2.16 that $o(a) = \varphi(o(a_1), \ldots, o(a_{m+1}), \bar{0}^{(l)}) = f_\omega\left(\begin{smallmatrix} a_{m+1} & \cdots & a_1 \\ 0 & \cdots & m \end{smallmatrix}\right)$ holds. The induction hypothesis yields $n_1, \ldots, n_m$ such that $o(a_i) < \nu_{n_i}$ holds for each $i \in \{n_1, \ldots, n_{m+1}\}$. By letting $n := \max\{n_1, \ldots, n_{m+1}\}$, we get that $o(a_1), \ldots, o(a_{m+1}) < \nu_n$ holds, and so $o(a) = f_\omega\left(\begin{smallmatrix} o(a_{m+1}) & \cdots & o(a_1) \\ 0 & \cdots & m \end{smallmatrix}\right) < \nu_n$ holds by Proposition 2.15.

For (e): By transfinite induction on $\gamma < \vartheta\Omega^\omega$. By Proposition 2.34, we have $\vartheta\Omega^\omega = f_\omega\binom{1}{\omega}$. Now, $\gamma < f_\omega\binom{1}{\omega}$ implies $\gamma < f_\omega\binom{1}{\gamma}$ because otherwise, we would have $f_\omega\binom{1}{\gamma} = \gamma < f_\omega\binom{1}{\omega}$ and hence $\gamma < \omega$ by Proposition 2.10, contradicting with $\omega = f_\omega\binom{1}{0} \leq f_\omega\binom{1}{\gamma} = \gamma$. With Lemma 2.28, we therefore get

$$\gamma = \gamma_1 + \ldots + \gamma_n$$

for some $n \geq 1$ and where $\gamma \geq \gamma_1 \geq \ldots \geq \gamma_n$ and

$$\gamma_i = f\left(\begin{smallmatrix} \alpha_{i,1} & \cdots & \alpha_{i,k_i} \\ \beta_{i,1} & \cdots & \beta_{i,k_i} \end{smallmatrix}\right)$$

holds for some $k_1, \ldots, k_n \in \mathbb{N}$ with $\alpha_{i,j}, \beta_{i,j} < \gamma_i$ for $1 \leq i \leq n$ and $1 \leq j \leq k_i$. Fix now $1 \leq i \leq n$, so the induction hypothesis yields $a_{i,j} \in \mathrm{OT}$ with

$$\alpha_{i,j} = o(a_{i,j})$$

for each $1 \leq j \leq k_i$. If $\alpha_{i,j} = 0$ holds for all $1 \leq j \leq k_i$, then $\gamma_i = f_\omega\binom{0}{0} = f_\omega(0)$ hold and we set $c_i := \tilde{1}$. Otherwise, $\alpha_{i,j} \neq 0$ holds for some

$1 \leq j \leq k_i$, so let

$$j_0 := \min(\{j\colon \alpha_{i,j} \neq 0\})$$
$$j_1 := \max(\{j\colon \alpha_{i,j} \neq 0\})$$

and we shall show that $\gamma_i = \mathrm{o}(c_i)$ holds for

$$c_i := \phi a_{i,j_1}\bar{0}^{(l_{j_1})} a_{i,j_1-1}\bar{0}^{(l_{j_1-1})} \ldots \phi a_{i,j_0}\bar{0}^{(l_{j_0})}$$

and some $l_{j_0}, \ldots, l_{j_1} \in \mathbb{N}$. We shall show in particular that $c_i \in \mathrm{OT}$ holds. Having done this for every $1 \leq i \leq n$, we get that

$$c := c_1 \oplus (\ldots(c_{n-1} \oplus c_n)\ldots)$$

implies $c \in \mathrm{OT}$ with $\gamma = \mathrm{o}(c)$ because $\mathrm{o}(c_i) = \gamma_i$ and $\gamma_1 \geq \ldots \geq \gamma_n$ yield $c_n \preceq \ldots \preceq c_1$ by (b), hence we can use the definition of OT. It rests now to show that $\mathrm{o}(c_i) = \gamma_i$ and $c_i \in \mathrm{OT}$ holds in case of $\alpha_{i,j} \neq 0$ for some $1 \leq j \leq k_i$: Note that

$$\alpha_{i,j} < \gamma_i \leq \gamma < f\left(\begin{smallmatrix}1\\ \omega\end{smallmatrix}\right) \qquad \text{(for all } 1 \leq j \leq k_i\text{)}$$

implies $\left(\begin{smallmatrix}\alpha_{i,1} & \ldots & \alpha_{i,k_i}\\ \beta_{i,1} & \ldots & \beta_{i,k_i}\end{smallmatrix}\right) < \left(\begin{smallmatrix}1\\ \omega\end{smallmatrix}\right)$ with respect to the lexicographic order on Klammersymbols (see Chapter 2) since otherwise our assumption that $\alpha_{i,j} < \left(\begin{smallmatrix}1\\ \omega\end{smallmatrix}\right)$ holds for all j would contradict Proposition 2.15. Now, as we have $\left(\begin{smallmatrix}\alpha_{i,1} & \ldots & \alpha_{i,k_i}\\ \beta_{i,1} & \ldots & \beta_{i,k_i}\end{smallmatrix}\right) < \left(\begin{smallmatrix}1\\ \omega\end{smallmatrix}\right)$ with respect to the lexicographic order on Klammersymbols and $\alpha_{i,j}$ for all $1 \leq j \leq k_i$, we get that

$$\beta_{i,j} < \omega$$

holds for all $1 \leq j \leq k_i$, and from this follows together with Lemma 2.16 that

$$\gamma_i = \varphi(\alpha_{i,j_1}, \bar{0}^{(l_{j_1})}, \alpha_{i,j_1-1}\bar{0}^{(l_{j_1-1})}, \ldots, \alpha_{i,j_0}, \bar{0}^{(l_{j_0})})$$

holds, hence we get immediately $\gamma_i = \mathrm{o}(c_i)$ if $c_i \in \mathrm{OT}$ holds. Now, to show the latter, we have due to $a_{i,j_1} \neq 0$ only to show:

$$(a_{i,j_0} \in \mathrm{PT}_+ \implies a_{i,j_0} \prec_{\mathbf{lex}} c_i)$$
$$\& \ \left(a_{i,j_0} \in \mathrm{PT}_+ \implies (c_i \prec_{\mathbf{lex}} a_{i,j_0} \ \& \ a_{i,j_0} \preceq a_j \text{ for some } j_0 < j \leq j_1)\right)$$

Note that this follows essentially from Lemma 2.20 and by making use of (b) since we have that $\alpha_{i,j} < \gamma_i$ holds for all j, i.e., we have $\gamma_i =_{\mathrm{NF}} \varphi(\alpha_{i,j_1}, \bar{0}^{(l_{j_1})}, \alpha_{i,j_1-1}\bar{0}^{(l_{j_1-1})}, \ldots, \alpha_{i,j_0}, \bar{0}^{(l_{j_0})})$. □

A.5. Theorem 3.25

Proof. (a) is obvious since $d \in \mathrm{Suc}$ implies $d = d_0 \tilde{+} 1$ for some $d_0 \in \mathrm{OT}$ and hence $d[x] = (d_0 + 1)[x] = d_0 \prec d$ by Lemma 3.15.

We show (b) by induction on $d \in \mathrm{Lim}$, i.e., using (Ind), and via the following case distinction (while note that Lemma 3.15 implies either $d \in \mathrm{PT}_+$ or $d = a \oplus b$ with $b \in \mathrm{Lim}$). In particular, we have to verify $d[x] \in \mathrm{OT}$ for each x.

1. $d = a \oplus b$ with $b \in \mathrm{Lim}$: By the induction hypothesis, we have $b[x] \in \mathrm{OT}$, $b[x] \neq 0$, $b[x] \prec b$, and $b[x] \prec b[x +_{\mathbb{N}} 1]$. Since $d[x] = a \tilde{+} (b[x])$, we hence get $d[x] \in \mathrm{OT}$, $d[x] \neq 0$, $d[x] \prec d[x +_{\mathbb{N}} 1]$ by Lemma 3.15.
2. $d = \phi a$ with $a \neq 0$:
2.1. $a \in \mathrm{Lim}$: The induction hypothesis yields $a[x] \in \mathrm{OT}$, hence $d[x] = \tilde{\varphi}(a[x]) \in \mathrm{OT}$ and clearly $d[x] \neq 0$. Now $a[x] \prec a[x +_{\mathbb{N}} 1]$ implies $d[x] = \tilde{\varphi}(a[x]) \prec \tilde{\varphi}(a[x +_{\mathbb{N}} 1]) = d[x +_{\mathbb{N}} 1]$.
2.2. $a = a_0 \tilde{+} \tilde{1}$: Since $\tilde{\varphi}(a_0) \in \mathrm{OT}$ holds, we have $d[x] = \tilde{\varphi}(a_0) \tilde{\cdot} (x +_{\mathbb{N}} 1) \in \mathrm{OT}$ and clearly $d[x] \neq 0$. We have $\tilde{\varphi}(a_0) \prec \tilde{\varphi}(a) = \phi a$ and $d[x] = \tilde{\varphi}(a_0) \oplus (\tilde{\varphi}(a_0) \tilde{\cdot} x)$, therefore $d[x] \prec \phi a = d$. Further, $\tilde{\varphi}(a_0) \oplus (\tilde{\varphi}(a_0) \tilde{\cdot} x) \prec \tilde{\varphi}(a_0) \oplus (\tilde{\varphi}(a_0) \tilde{\cdot} (x +_{\mathbb{N}} 1))$ holds via a side induction on x, noting that $\tilde{\varphi}(a_0) \prec \tilde{\varphi}(a_0) \oplus \tilde{\varphi}(a_0)$ holds because of $\tilde{\varphi}(a_0) \neq 0$, so this yields $d[x] \prec d[x +_{\mathbb{N}} 1]$.
3. $d = \phi \bar{a}^{(m)} b \bar{0}^{(k+1)}$ with $b \neq 0$:
3.1. If $b \in \mathrm{Lim}$: By the main induction hypothesis, we have $b[x] \in \mathrm{OT}$, $b[x] \neq 0$, $b[x] \prec b[x +_{\mathbb{N}} 1]$, and $b[x] \prec b$ for each x. Hence, $d[x] = \tilde{\varphi}(\bar{a}^{(m)}, b[x], \bar{0}^{(k+1)}) \in \mathrm{OT}$ holds by Lemma 3.13. Moreover, $d[x] \in \mathrm{PT}$ holds by Lemma 3.17, implying $d[x] \neq 0$, and Corollary A.3.1 yields $d[x] \prec d[x +_{\mathbb{N}} 1]$ and $d[x] \prec d$.
3.2. If $b \in \mathrm{Suc}$: We show the claim by a side induction on x.
3.2.1. If $x = 0$: We have $d[0] = \tilde{1} \in \mathrm{PT} \cap \mathrm{OT}$ and therefore $d[0] \neq 0$, and

$d[0] \prec d$ (since $d \neq 0$ and $d \neq \tilde{1}$ hold). Moreover, we have

$$d[1] = \begin{cases} \phi\tilde{1}\bar{0}^{(k)} & \text{if } m = 0 \text{ and } b = \tilde{1} \\ \phi\bar{a}^{(m)}(b[0])\tilde{1}\bar{0}^{(k)} & \text{otherwise} \end{cases}$$

using Lemma 3.17. Hence $d[1] \in \mathrm{OT}$ holds and $d[0] = \tilde{1} \prec d[1]$ is obvious.
3.2.2. If $x = x_0 +_{\mathbb{N}} 1$: We have

$$d[x] = \tilde{\varphi}(\bar{a}^{(m)}, b[x_0], d[x_0], \bar{0}^{(k)})$$
$$d[x +_{\mathbb{N}} 1] = \tilde{\varphi}(\bar{a}^{(m)}, b[x], d[x], \bar{0}^{(k)})$$

implying $d[x], d[x +_{\mathbb{N}} 1] \in \mathrm{OT}$ and $d[x], d[x +_{\mathbb{N}} 1] \neq 0$ by Lemma 3.13 and 3.17, using $d[x_0] \in \mathrm{OT}$ from the side induction hypothesis. Furthermore, we get $d[x_0] \prec d[x]$ and $b[x_0] = b[x]$, while recalling for the latter that $b \in \mathrm{Suc}$ holds. So, we get $d[x] \prec d[x +_{\mathbb{N}} 1]$ by Corollary A.3.1. In particular, we get

$$d[x] = \begin{cases} \phi d[x_0]\bar{0}^{(k)} & \text{if } m = 0 \text{ and } b = \tilde{1} \\ \phi\bar{a}^{(m)}(b[x_0])d[x_0]\bar{0}^{(k)} & \text{otherwise} \end{cases}$$

from $d[x_0] \neq 0$ and $d[x_0] \prec d[x]$ together with Lemma 3.17, yielding $d[x] \prec d$ from the definition of $\prec$, noting that we have $b[x_0] \prec b$ by (a) and $d[x_0] \prec d$ by the side induction hypothesis.

4. $d = \phi\bar{a}^{(m)}b\bar{0}^{(k)}c$ with $b \neq 0$ and $c \in \mathrm{Suc}$ with $c = c_0 \tilde{+} \tilde{1}$: Let

$$d' := \tilde{\varphi}(\bar{a}^{(m)}, b, \bar{0}^{(k)}, c_0)$$

Then we get $d' \in \mathrm{OT}$ and $d' \prec d$ due to Corollary A.3.1 because of $c_0 \prec c$. We show the claim by a side induction on x.

4.1. If $x = 0$: Note that we have

$$\begin{aligned} d[0] &= d' \tilde{+} \tilde{1} \\ d[1] &= \tilde{\varphi}(\bar{a}^{(m)}, b[0], d[0], \bar{0}^{(k)}) = \\ &= \begin{cases} \phi(d[0])\bar{0}^{(k)} & \text{if } m = 0 \text{ and } b = \tilde{1} \\ \phi\bar{a}^{(m)}(b[0])(d[0])\bar{0}^{(k)} & \text{otherwise} \end{cases} \end{aligned}$$

because we have $b[0] \in \mathrm{OT}$ and $d[0] \in \mathrm{Suc}$ and can use Lemma 3.17. In

particular, we get $d[0] \prec d[1]$ by Lemma 3.8. Moreover, $d \in \mathrm{Lim}$ and $d[0] \in \mathrm{Suc}$ imply $d[0] \prec d$ by Lemma 3.15.
4.2. For $x = x_0 +_{\mathbb{N}} 1$: We get

$$d[x] = \tilde{\varphi}(\bar{a}^{(m)}, b[x_0], d[x_0], \bar{0}^{(k)})$$

and in particular $d[x] \in \mathrm{OT}$ since $b[x_0], d[x_0] \in \mathrm{OT}$ holds by the main and side induction hypothesis. Also $d[x] \neq 0$ holds due to $d[x] \in \mathrm{PT}$ by Lemma 3.17. This implies

$$d[x] = \begin{cases} \phi(d[x_0])\bar{0}^{(k)} & \text{if } m = 0 \text{ and } b = \tilde{1} \\ \phi\bar{a}^{(m)}(b[x_0])(d[x_0])\bar{0}^{(k)} & \text{otherwise} \end{cases} \tag{A.3}$$

using Lemma 3.17 and $d[x_0] \prec d[x]$ from the side induction hypothesis. Now, $d[x] \prec_{\mathsf{lex}} d$ holds (while using $b[x_0] \prec b$ in case of $m \neq 0$ and $b \neq \tilde{1}$). With $d[x_0] \prec d$ from the side induction hypothesis, $a_1, \ldots, a_{n+1} \prec d$, and $0 \prec d$, we get $d[x] \prec d$ by the definition of $\prec$. Now, turning to $d[x] \prec d[x +_{\mathbb{N}} 1]$, we recall that

$$d[x +_{\mathbb{N}} 1] = \tilde{\varphi}(\bar{a}^{(m)}, b[x], d[x], \bar{0}^{(k)})$$

holds and we are now going to show that

$$d[x +_{\mathbb{N}} 1] = \begin{cases} \phi(d[x])\bar{0}^{(k)} & \text{if } m = 0 \text{ and } b = \tilde{1} \\ \phi\bar{a}^{(m)}(b[x])(d[x])\bar{0}^{(k)} & \text{otherwise} \end{cases} \tag{$*$}$$

holds. For this, note first that we have $d[x] \preceq d[x +_{\mathbb{N}} 1]$ by Lemma 3.17. Furthermore, we have $b[x_0] \preceq b[x]$ (using the main induction hypothesis in case of $b \in \mathrm{Lim}$) and $d[x_0] \prec d[x]$ from the side induction hypothesis. Hence with (A.3) and ($*$), this readily yields $d[x] \prec_{\mathsf{lex}} d[x +_{\mathbb{N}} 1]$. The definition of $\prec$ then yields $d[x] \prec d[x +_{\mathbb{N}} 1]$ because we have $a_1, \ldots, a_{n+1} \prec d[x +_{\mathbb{N}} 1]$, $b[x_0] \preceq b[x] \prec d[x +_{\mathbb{N}} 1]$, and $d[x_0] \prec d[x] \preceq d[x +_{\mathbb{N}} 1]$.

For ($*$), it suffices to show $\phi(d[x])\bar{0}^{(k)} \in \mathrm{OT}$ in case of $m = 0$ and $b = \tilde{1}$, and $\phi\bar{a}^{(m)}(b[x])(d[x])\bar{0}^{(k)} \in \mathrm{OT}$ otherwise. Therefore, we consider the following cases:

4.2.1. If $m = 0$ and $b = \tilde{1}$: Then $b[x] = 0$, hence $d[x +_{\mathbb{N}} 1] = \tilde{\varphi}((d[x]), \bar{0}^{(k)})$ holds by Lemma 3.17. We have $d[x] \in \mathrm{PT}_+$ by (A.3) and we have $d[x] = \phi d[x_0]\bar{0}^{(k)} \prec_{\mathsf{lex}} \phi d[x]\bar{0}^{(k)}$, so $\phi d[x]\bar{0}^{(k)} \in \mathrm{OT}$ holds by the definition of OT.

4.2.2. Otherwise: Then $b[x] \neq 0$ holds. By (A.3), we get that $d[x] = \phi\bar{a}^{(m)}(b[x_0])d[x_0]\bar{0}^{(k)} \in \mathrm{PT}_+$ and $d[x] \prec_{\mathbf{lex}} \phi\bar{a}^{(m)}(b[x])d[x]\bar{0}^{(k)}$ from $b[x_0] \preceq b[x]$ and $d[x_0] \prec d[x]$, hence we get $\phi\bar{a}^{(m)}(b[x])d[x]\bar{0}^{(k)} \in \mathrm{OT}$.
5. $d = \phi\bar{a}^{(m)}b\bar{0}^{(k)}c$ with $b \neq 0$ and $c \in \mathrm{Lim}$: By the main induction hypothesis, we have $c[x] \in \mathrm{OT}$, $c[x] \neq 0$, $c[x] \prec c[x +_{\mathbb{N}} 1]$, and $c[x] \prec c$ for each x. Then $d[x] \in \mathrm{OT}$ and $d[x] \neq 0$ hold by Lemma 3.13 and Lemma 3.17, respectively. Now, Corollary A.3.1 yields $d[x] \prec d[x +_{\mathbb{N}} 1]$ and $d[x] \prec d$. □

A.6. Theorem 3.27

Proof. Let $d \in \mathrm{Lim}$ and $d_0 \prec d$. We prove the theorem by induction on d and a side induction on d_0, i.e., using (Ind). Note that the case $d_0 = 0$ is clear, since $d[0] \neq 0$ holds by Theorem 3.25. Assuming now $d_0 \neq 0$, we can write

$$d_0 = d_1 \oplus d_2$$

with $d_1 \in \mathrm{PT}$ (and where $d_2 = 0$ may hold here). Then $d_1 \prec d$ must hold since we have either $d_1 = d_0 \prec d$ if $d_2 = 0$ holds, or $d_1 \prec d_0 \prec d$ by Lemma 3.8 if $d_2 \neq 0$ holds. Moreover, we can also write

$$d_1 = \phi\bar{f}^{(p+1)} \tag{A.4}$$

for some $f_1, \ldots, f_{p+1}$, and we get $f_1, \ldots, f_{p+1} \prec d_1$ by Lemma 3.8. We proceed by a case distinction on the build-up of d.
1. $d = a \oplus b$ with $b \in \mathrm{Lim}$: We have $d[x] = a \tilde{+} (b[x])$. Now, either $d_0 \prec a$ holds, which gives already $d_0 \prec d[0]$, or $a \preceq d_0$ holds and hence also $d_0 = a \tilde{+} b_0$ for some $b_0 \prec b$ by Lemma 3.15. Since $b_0 \prec b[x]$ holds for some x by the induction hypothesis, we get $d_0 \prec d[x]$.
2. $d = \phi a$ with $a \neq 0$:
2.1. $a \in \mathrm{Lim}$: Recall the build-up of d_1 from (A.4).
2.1.1. If $p = 0$: We get $d_1 = \phi f_1$ with $f_1 \prec a$ by the definition of $\prec$. Because of $a \in \mathrm{Lim}$ and the induction hypothesis, there is some x such that $f_1 \prec a[x]$ holds, i.e., we get $d_1 = \tilde{\varphi}(f_1) \prec \tilde{\varphi}(a[x]) = d[x]$ by Corollary A.3.1. $d_0 \prec \tilde{\varphi}(a[x])$ now holds by the definition of $\prec$ using that $\tilde{\varphi}(a[x]) \in \mathrm{PT}$ holds by Lemma 3.17.
2.1.2. If $p \neq 0$: We get $d = \phi a \prec_{\mathbf{lex}} \phi\bar{f}^{(p+1)} = d_1$, and hence $d_1 \prec a$ must hold by the definition of $\prec$. As before, there is some x such that $d_1 \prec a[x]$

holds, and we have $a[x] \preceq \tilde{\varphi}(a[x]) = d[x]$, using Lemma 3.17. This yields $d_1 \prec d[x]$ and hence $d_0 \prec d[x]$.

2.2. $a = a_0 \tilde{+} \tilde{1}$: We have $d[x] = \tilde{\varphi}(a_0)\tilde{\cdot}(x +_{\mathbb{N}} 1)$ and we show that $d_0 \prec d[x]$ holds for some x by a side induction on $d_0 \neq 0$. Note first that we have

$$d_2 \prec d[x_0]$$

for some x_0, namely: If $d_2 = 0$ holds, then we can use $x_0 = 0$. If $d_2 \neq 0$ holds, then we have $d_2 \prec d_0 \prec d$ by Lemma 3.8 and also $d_2 <_{\mathbb{N}} d_0$, so the side induction hypothesis on d_2 yields x_0 with $d_2 \prec d[x_0]$.

We shall show below that $d_1 \preceq \tilde{\varphi}(a_0)$ holds, and then we get

$$d_0 = d_1 \oplus d_2 \prec \tilde{\varphi}(a_0) \oplus (d[x_0])$$

i.e., $d_0 \prec d[x]$ for $x := x_0 +_{\mathbb{N}} 1$. In order to show $d_1 \preceq \tilde{\varphi}(a_0)$, recall from (A.4) that $d_1 = \phi \bar{f}^{(p+1)}$ holds and consider the following cases:

2.2.1. $p = 0$: Then $d_1 = \phi f_1$ holds, and we get $f_1 \prec a = a_0 \tilde{+} \tilde{1}$ from $d_1 \prec d = \phi a$, hence $f_1 \preceq a_0$ holds. This yields $d_1 = \tilde{\varphi}(f_1) \preceq \tilde{\varphi}(a_0)$ by Corollary A.3.1.
2.2.2. $p \neq 0$: We have then $d = \phi a \prec_{\mathsf{lex}} \phi \bar{f}^{(p+1)} = d_1$ and so by $d_1 \prec d$ and the definition of $\prec$, we must have $d_1 \prec a$. Hence, $d_1 \preceq a_0 \preceq \tilde{\varphi}(a_0)$.

3. $d = \phi \bar{a}^{(m)} b \bar{0}^{(k)} c$ with $b \neq 0$ and either $c \in \mathrm{Suc}$ or $c = 0$ with $b \in \mathrm{Suc}$: We show now that $d_0 \prec d[x]$ holds for some x by a side induction on $d_0 \neq 0$. We shall make the representation of d_1 from (A.4) more explicit, namely let $n, l \in \mathbb{N}$ be such that

$$d_1 = \phi \bar{f}^{(n+1)} \bar{0}^{(l)} \;\; \& \;\; f_{n+1} \neq 0$$

where we have in particular $f_1 \neq 0$. Since $d_0 \prec d$ implies $d_1 \prec d$, we distinguish the following cases:

3.1. $d_1 \prec_{\mathsf{lex}} d$: Then we have $\mathsf{lh}(d_1) \leq \mathsf{lh}(d)$. Moreover, $d_1 \prec d$ implies now $f_i \prec d$ for all $1 \leq i \leq n+1$, and the side induction hypothesis gives $x_1, \ldots, x_{n+1}$ such that $f_i \prec d[x_i]$ for all $1 \leq i \leq n+1$. Then let

$$\begin{aligned} x_0 &:= \max\{x_1, \ldots, x_{n+1}\} \\ x &:= x_0 +_{\mathbb{N}} 1 \end{aligned}$$

so together with Theorem 3.25, we have

$$f_i \prec d[x_0] \prec d[x] \text{ for all } 1 \leq i \leq n+1 \tag{A.5}$$

Note that we have $b \neq 0$ and that in case of $m \neq 0$, we also have $a_1 \neq 0$ because of $d = \phi\bar{a}^{(m)}b\bar{0}^{(k)}c$ and $d \in \mathrm{OT}$, and further note that we defined x such that $x \neq 0$ holds.

<u>**3.1.1.**</u> If $m = 0$ and $b = \tilde{1}$: Then we have $d = \phi\tilde{1}\bar{0}^{(k)}c$.

<u>**3.1.1.1.**</u> If $\mathsf{lh}(d_1) = \mathsf{lh}(d)$: We must have $d_1 = \phi\tilde{1}\bar{0}^{(k+1)}$ and hence $c \neq 0$ due to $d_1 \prec_{\mathbf{lex}} d$, i.e., we have $c \in \mathrm{Suc}$ and hence $c = c_0 \tilde{+} \tilde{1}$ for some c_0. Then clearly $d_1 = \tilde{\varphi}(\tilde{1}, \bar{0}^{(k)}, 0) \preceq \tilde{\varphi}(\tilde{1}, \bar{0}^{(k)}, c_0)$ holds and therefore $d_1 \prec \tilde{\varphi}(\tilde{1}, \bar{0}^{(k)}, c_0) \tilde{+} \tilde{1} = c[0]$.

<u>**3.1.1.2.**</u> If $\mathsf{lh}(d_1) < \mathsf{lh}(d)$: We have

$$d[x] = \phi d[x_0]\bar{0}^{(k)}$$

by Corollary 3.26 and hence $\mathsf{lh}(d[x]) = \mathsf{lh}(d) - 1 = k+1$. If $\mathsf{lh}(d_1) = k+1$ holds, then we get $d_1 \prec_{\mathbf{lex}} d[x]$ with $f_1 \prec d[x_0]$ from (A.5). Otherwise, we get $d_1 \prec_{\mathbf{lex}} d[x]$ immediately. Hence, together with (A.5) and the definition of $\prec$, we obtain $d_1 \prec d[x]$.

<u>**3.1.2.**</u> Otherwise, $m \neq 0$ or $\tilde{1} \prec b$: Then we get

$$d[x] = \phi\bar{a}^{(m)}b[x_0]d[x_0]\bar{0}^{(k)}$$

again by Corollary 3.26. If $\mathsf{lh}(d_1) < \mathsf{lh}(d)$ holds, then we have $d_1 \prec_{\mathbf{lex}} d[x]$ because of $\mathsf{lh}(d) = \mathsf{lh}(d[x])$, and again $d_1 \prec d[x]$ holds by (A.5). Otherwise, we have $\mathsf{lh}(d_1) = \mathsf{lh}(d) = \mathsf{lh}(d[x])$ and can consider the following cases that are induced by $d_1 \prec_{\mathbf{lex}} d$.

<u>**3.1.2.1.**</u> If $f_j \prec a_j$ holds for some $1 \leq j \leq \min\{m, n+1\}$: Then we have again $d_1 \prec_{\mathbf{lex}} d[x]$, hence $d_1 \prec d[x]$ by (A.5).

<u>**3.1.2.2.**</u> If $n \geq m$ holds and some $1 \leq j \leq n+1$ exists with $f_j \prec b$ with $f_i = a_i$ for all $1 \leq i < j$:

(i) If $b = b_0 \tilde{+} \tilde{1}$, then we have $f_j \preceq b_0 = b[x_0]$ and we get $d_1 \prec_{\mathbf{lex}} d[x]$ (where in case of $f_j = b_0$, we can use $0 \prec d[x_0]$ if $j = n+1$, or $f_{j+1} \prec d[x_0]$ otherwise), hence $d_1 \prec d[x]$ by (A.5).

(ii) If $b \in \mathrm{Lim}$, we get $f_j \prec b[y]$ for some y from the main induction hypothesis. Then take $z := \max\{x_0, y\}$, and so we get $f_j \prec b[z]$, hence $d_1 \prec_{\mathbf{lex}} d[z +_{\mathbb{N}} 1]$. Since $d[x_0] \preceq d[z] \prec d[z +_{\mathbb{N}} 1]$ holds by Theorem 3.25, we get by (A.5) also $f_i \prec d[z +_{\mathbb{N}} 1]$ for all $1 \leq i \leq n+1$, hence $d_1 \prec d[z +_{\mathbb{N}} 1]$.

3.1.2.3. Otherwise: We have $n+1 = m+k+2$ and $d_1 = \phi\bar{a}^{(m)}b\bar{0}^{(k)}f_{n+1}$, hence $f_{n+1} \prec c$ must hold, and so we have $c \in \mathrm{Suc}$ with $c = c_0 \tilde{+} \tilde{1}$ for some c_0 since we assumed $c \notin \mathrm{Lim}$. We get $f_{n+1} \preceq c_0$ and then $d_1 = \tilde{\varphi}(\bar{a}^{(m)}, b, \bar{0}^{(k)}, f_{m+1}) \preceq \tilde{\varphi}(\bar{a}^{(m)}, b, \bar{0}^{(k)}, c_0) \prec \tilde{\varphi}(\bar{a}^{(m)}, b, \bar{0}^{(k)}, c_0) \tilde{+} \tilde{1} = d[0]$, using Corollary A.3.1 (with Lemma 3.15 and Lemma 3.17).

3.2. $d \prec_{\mathbf{lex}} d_1$ with $m = 0$ and $b = \tilde{1}$: We have $d = \phi\tilde{1}\bar{0}^{(k)}c$. Then $d_1 \prec d$ and $d \prec_{\mathbf{lex}} d_1$ imply by the definition of $\prec$ that $d_1 \preceq \tilde{1}$ or $d_1 \prec c$ holds. The first is impossible (note that $d_1 \in \mathrm{PT}$ holds, so only the case $d_1 = \tilde{1} = \phi 0$ would make sense, but this would contradict $d \prec_{\mathbf{lex}} d_1$). So the latter must hold, and so we have $c \neq 0$ and hence $c \in \mathrm{Suc}$ with $c = c_0 \tilde{+} \tilde{1}$ for some c_0. Then we get $d_1 \prec d[0]$ because we have $d[0] = \tilde{\varphi}(\bar{a}^{(m)}, b, \bar{0}^{(k)}, c_0) \tilde{+} \tilde{1}$ and since $d_1 \preceq c_0 \preceq \tilde{\varphi}(\bar{a}^{(m)}, b, \bar{0}^{(k)}, c_0)$ holds by Lemma 3.17.

3.3. $d \prec_{\mathbf{lex}} d_1$ with $m \neq 0$ or $\tilde{1} \prec b$: This means that for every x, we have

$$d[x +_{\mathbb{N}} 1] = \phi\bar{a}^{(m)}b[x]d[x]\bar{0}^{(k)} \tag{A.6}$$

by Corollary 3.26. Moreover, we get $d[x +_{\mathbb{N}} 1] \prec_{\mathbf{lex}} d$ since $b[x] \prec b$ holds (using Theorem 3.25 in case of $b \in \mathrm{Lim}$). Together with $d \prec_{\mathbf{lex}} d_1$, this implies

$$d[x +_{\mathbb{N}} 1] \prec_{\mathbf{lex}} d_1$$

for every x, using that $\prec_{\mathbf{lex}}$ is transitive here (by Theorem 3.6). Now, $d_1 \prec d$ and $d \prec_{\mathbf{lex}} d_1$ imply the following cases.

3.3.1. $d_1 \prec c$: Then $c \notin \mathrm{Lim}$ implies $c \in \mathrm{Suc}$ with $c = c_0 \tilde{+} \tilde{1}$ for some c_0, and so $d_1 \preceq c_0$ holds. Hence $d_1 \prec d[0]$ holds because of $d_1 \preceq c_0 \preceq \tilde{\varphi}(\bar{a}^{(m)}, b, \bar{0}^{(k)}, c_0) \prec \tilde{\varphi}(\bar{a}^{(m)}, b, \bar{0}^{(k)}, c_0) \tilde{+} \tilde{1} = d[0]$.

3.3.2. $d_1 \preceq b$: We consider the following two situations.

3.3.2.1. $d_1 = b$: Due to $d_1 \prec d$ and the definition of $\prec$, this is only possible in case of $c \neq 0$. Hence we have $c \in \mathrm{Suc}$ with $c = c_0 \tilde{+} \tilde{1}$ for some c_0 since we assumed $c \notin \mathrm{Lim}$. Then we have $d_1 = b \preceq \tilde{\varphi}(\bar{a}^{(m)}, b, \bar{0}^{(k)}, c_0) \prec \tilde{\varphi}(\bar{a}^{(m)}, b, \bar{0}^{(k)}, c_0) \tilde{+} \tilde{1} = d[0]$, using Lemma 3.17.

3.3.2.2. $d_1 \prec b$: If $b = b_0 \tilde{+} \tilde{1}$ holds, then we get $d_1 \prec d[1]$ because we get $d_1 \preceq b_0 = b[0] \prec \phi\bar{a}^{(m)}b[0]\bar{0}^{(k)} = d[1]$ by Lemma 3.8 and (A.6). If on the other hand $b \in \mathrm{Lim}$ holds, then we get $d_1 \prec b[x]$ for some x by the main induction hypothesis, hence $d_1 \prec d[x +_{\mathbb{N}} 1]$.

3.3.3. $d_1 \preceq a_j$ for some $1 \leq j \leq m$: Then we get $d_1 \preceq a_j \prec \phi\bar{a}^{(m)}b[0]\bar{0}^{(k)} = d[1]$ by Lemma 3.8 and (A.6). Hence $d_1 \prec d[1]$ follows from $d[1] \prec_{\mathbf{lex}} d_1$.

4. Otherwise: Then we have either $d = \phi\bar{a}^{(m)}b\bar{0}^{(k+1)}$ with $b \in \mathrm{Lim}$ or $d = \phi\bar{a}^{(m)}b\bar{0}^{(k)}c$ with $b \neq 0$ and $c \in \mathrm{Lim}$. Now, we have

$$d[x] = \begin{cases} \tilde{\varphi}(\bar{a}^{(m)}, b[x], \bar{0}^{(k+1)}) & \text{if } c = 0 \text{ and } b \in \mathrm{Lim} \\ \tilde{\varphi}(\bar{a}^{(m)}, b, \bar{0}^{(k+1)}, c[x]) & \text{if } c \in \mathrm{Lim} \end{cases}$$

for every x. From $d_1 \prec d$, we get the following cases, recalling the build-up $\phi\bar{f}^{(p+1)}$ of d_1 from (A.4).

4.1. $d_1 \prec_{\mathsf{lex}} d$: Then $f_i \prec d$ holds for all $1 \leq i \leq p+1$, and as before (and using the side induction hypothesis) there is some x_0 such that $f_i \prec d[x_0]$ holds for all $1 \leq i \leq p+1$. Moreover, the main induction hypothesis yields some x_1 such that we have $f_i \prec b[x_1]$ or $f_i \prec c[x_1]$, respectively, and for all $1 \leq i \leq p+1$. Letting $x := \max\{x_0, x_1\}$, it suffices to show $d_1 \prec_{\mathsf{lex}} d[x]$ in order to get $d_1 \prec d[x]$. So, we have to show

$$d_1 \prec_{\mathsf{lex}} \begin{cases} \phi\bar{a}^{(m)}(b[x])\bar{0}^{(k+1)} & \text{if } c = 0 \text{ and } b \in \mathrm{Lim} \\ \phi\bar{a}^{(m)}b\bar{0}^{(k)}(c[x]) & \text{if } c \in \mathrm{Lim} \end{cases} \qquad (*)$$

while note that $\phi\bar{a}^{(m)}(b[x])\bar{0}^{(k+1)} \notin \mathrm{OT}$ or $\phi\bar{a}^{(m)}b\bar{0}^{(k)}(c[x]) \notin \mathrm{OT}$ might hold, respectively. Now, to show $(*)$ we note that $d_1 \prec_{\mathsf{lex}} d$ implies either $\mathsf{lh}(d_1) < \mathsf{lh}(d)$ which immediately gives us $(*)$, or we have $\mathsf{lh}(d_1) = \mathsf{lh}(d)$. For the latter, we can work with $d_1 \prec_{\mathsf{lex}} d$ and that

$$f_i \prec \begin{cases} b[x] & \text{if } c = 0 \text{ and } b \in \mathrm{Lim} \\ c[x] & \text{if } c \in \mathrm{Lim} \end{cases}$$

holds for all $1 \leq i \leq p+1$.

Finally, we show $d_1 \prec_{\mathsf{lex}} d[x]$: If we have $\phi\bar{a}^{(m)}(b[x])\bar{0}^{(k+1)} \in \mathrm{OT}$ or $\phi\bar{a}^{(m)}b\bar{0}^{(k)}(c[x]) \in \mathrm{OT}$, respectively, then $d[x] = \phi\bar{a}^{(m)}(b[x])\bar{0}^{(k+1)}$ or $d[x] = \phi\bar{a}^{(m)}b\bar{0}^{(k)}(c[x])$ also holds, respectively, and we use $(*)$. Otherwise,

$$d[x] = \begin{cases} b[x] & \text{if } c = 0 \text{ and } b \in \mathrm{Lim} \\ c[x] & \text{if } c \in \mathrm{Lim} \end{cases}$$

holds with $\phi\bar{a}^{(m)}(b[x])\bar{0}^{(k+1)} \prec_{\mathsf{lex}} b[x]$ or $\phi\bar{a}^{(m)}b\bar{0}^{(k)}(c[x]) \prec_{\mathsf{lex}} c[x]$, respectively, and by Lemma 3.17.(d). Then using $(*)$ and that $\prec_{\mathsf{lex}}$ is transitive here (by Theorem 3.6) yield

$$d_1 \prec_{\mathbf{lex}} \begin{cases} b[x] = d[x] & \text{if } c = 0 \text{ and } b \in \mathrm{Lim} \\ c[x] = d[x] & \text{if } c \in \mathrm{Lim} \end{cases}$$

and we are done.

<u>4.2.</u> $d \prec_{\mathbf{lex}} d_1$: We distinguish the following two situations.

<u>4.2.1.</u> If $c = 0$ and $b \in \mathrm{Lim}$: Now $d_1 \prec d$ induces the following cases.

(i) $d_1 \prec b$: Then $d_1 \prec b[x] \preceq \tilde{\varphi}(\bar{a}^{(m)}, b[x], \bar{0}^{(k+1)}) = d[x]$ holds for some x by the induction hypothesis and Lemma 3.17.

(ii) $d_1 \preceq a_j$ for some $1 \leq j \leq m$: We can use that $a_j \prec d[x]$ holds by Lemma 3.17.(g).

<u>4.2.2.</u> If $c \in \mathrm{Lim}$: Now $d_1 \prec d$ induces the following cases.

(i) $d_1 \prec c$: Then $d_1 \prec c[x] \preceq \tilde{\varphi}(\bar{a}^{(m)}, b, \bar{0}^{(k)}, c[x]) = d[x]$ holds for some x by the induction hypothesis and Lemma 3.17.

(ii) $d \preceq b$ or $d_1 \preceq a_j$ for some $1 \leq j \leq m$: We can use that $b, a_j \prec d[x]$ holds by Lemma 3.17.(g). □

Bibliography

[Acz77a] Peter Aczel. An introduction to inductive definitions. In Jon Barwise, editor, *Handbook of Mathematical Logic*, volume 90, pages 739–782. North-Holland, Amsterdam, 1977.

[Acz77b] Peter Aczel. The strength of Martin-Löf's type theory with one universe. Technical report, Dept. of Philosophy, University of Helsinki, 1977.

[AR10] Bahareh Afshari and Michael Rathjen. A note on the theory of positive induction, ID_1^*. *Archive for Mathematical Logic*, 49:275–281, 2010. 10.1007/s00153-009-0168-9.

[Bee85] Michael J. Beeson. *Foundations of Constructive Mathematics: Metamathematical studies.* Springer Verlag, Berlin, Heidelberg, New York, 1985.

[BFPS81] Wilfried Buchholz, Solomon Feferman, Wolfram Pohlers, and Wilfried Sieg. *Iterated Inductive Definitions and Subsystems of Analysis: Recent Proof-Theoretical Studies*, volume 897 of *Lecture Notes in Mathematics.* Springer Verlag, Berlin, Heidelberg, New York, 1981.

[Bri75] Jane Bridge. A simplification of the Bachmann method for generating large countable ordinals. *The Journal of Symbolic Logic*, 40(2):171–185, 1975.

[BS88] Wilfried Buchholz and Kurt Schütte. *Proof Theory of Impredicative Subsystems of Analysis*, volume 2 of *Studies in Proof Theory Monographs.* Bibliopolis, Napoli, 1988.

[Buc05] Wilfried Buchholz. Prädikative Beweistheorie (Predicative proof theory). Lecture notes, University of Munich, 2004–2005.

[Buc15] Wilfried Buchholz. A survey on ordinal notations around the Bachmann-Howard ordinal. In Reinhard Kahle, Thomas Strahm, and Thomas Studer, editors, *Advances in Proof Theory.* Birkhaeuser, Springer Basel, 2015.

[Can85] Andrea Cantini. A note on a predicatively reducible theory of iterated elementary induction. *Boll. Unione Mat. Ital., VI. Ser., B*, 4:413–430, 1985.

[Can86] Andrea Cantini. On the relation between choice and comprehension principles in second order arithmetic. *The Journal of Symbolic Logic*, 51(2):360–373, 1986.

[Fef70] Solomon Feferman. Formal theories of transfinite iterations of generalized inductive definitions and some subsystems of analysis. In R. E. Vesley A. Kino, J. Myhill, editor, *Intuitionism and Proof Theory*, pages 303—-326. North-Holland, Amsterdam, 1970. Proceedings of the summer conference at Buffalo, N.Y., 1968.

[Fef82] Solomon Feferman. Iterated inductive fixed-point theories: application to Hancock's conjecture. In George Metakides, editor, *Patras Logic Symposion*, volume 109 of *Studies in Logic and the Foundations of Mathematics*, pages 171–196. Elsevier, Amsterdam, 1982.

[Fef92] Solomon Feferman. Logics for termination and correctness of functional programs, II. Logics of strength PRA. In Peter Aczel, Harold Simmons, and Stanley S. Wainer, editors, *Proof Theory*, pages 195–225. Cambridge University Press, 1992.

[FJ83] Soloman Feferman and Gerhard Jäger. Choice principles, the bar rule and autonomously iterated comprehension schemes in analysis. *Association for Symbolic Logic*, 48(1):63–70, 1983.

[FJS] Solomon Feferman, Gerhard Jäger, and Thomas Strahm. *Foundations of Explicit Mathematics*. Book in preparation.

[Hin78] Peter G. Hinman. *Recursion-Theoretic Hierarchies*. Perspectives in Logic. Springer Verlag, Berlin, Heidelberg, New York, 1978.

[Jäg05] Gerhard Jäger. Metapredicative and explicit Mahlo: a proof-theoretic perspective. In Rene Cori, Alexander Razborov, Stevo Todorcevic, and Carol Wood, editors, *Proceedings of Logic Colloquium '00*, volume 19 of *Association of Symbolic Logic Lecture Notes in Logic*, pages 272–293. AK Peters, 2005.

[Jer14] Jeroen Van der Meeren and Michael Rathjen and Andreas Weiermann. An order-theoretic characterization of the howard-bachmann-hierarchy, 2014. Preprint, `http://arxiv.org/abs/1411.4481`.

[JKSS99] Gerhard Jäger, Reinhard Kahle, Anton Setzer, and Thomas Strahm. The proof-theoretic analysis of transfinitely iterated fixed point theories. *The Journal of Symbolic Logic*, 64(1):53–67, 1999.

[JP15] Gerhard Jäger and Dieter Probst. A proof-theoretic analysis of theories for stratified inductive definitions. In Reinhard Kahle and Michael Rathjen, editor, *Gentzen's Centenary: The Quest for Consistency*. Springer Verlag, Berlin, Heidelberg, New York, 2015.

[JS99] Gerhard Jäger and Thomas Strahm. Bar induction and ω model reflection. *Annals of Pure and Applied Logic*, 97(1–3):221–230, 1999.

[JS05] Gerhard Jäger and Thomas Strahm. Reflections on reflections in explicit mathematics. *Annals of Pure and Applied Logic*, 136(1–2):116–133, 2005. Festschrift on the occasion of Wolfram Pohlers' 60th birthday.

[Lei94] Daniel Leivant. Intrinsic theories and computational complexity. In Daniel Leivant, editor, *Logic and Computational Complexity*, volume 960 of *Lecture Notes in Computer Science*, pages 177–194. Springer Verlag, Berlin, Heidelberg, New York, 1994.

[Poh09] Wolfram Pohlers. *Proof Theory: The First Step into Impredicativity*. Universitext. Springer Verlag, Berlin, Heidelberg, New York, 2nd edition, 2009.

[Pro06] Dieter Probst. The proof-theoretic analysis of transfinitely iterated quasi least fixed points. *The Journal of Symbolic Logic*, 71(3):721–746, 2006.

[Pro15] Dieter Probst. *Modular Ordinal Analysis of Subsystems of Second-Order Arithmetic of Strength up to the Bachmann-Howard Ordinal.* Habilitation, Universität Bern, 2015. In preparation.

[Rat91] Michael Rathjen. The role of parameters in bar rule and bar induction. *The Journal of Symbolic Logic*, 56(2):715–730, 1991.

[Rat92] Michael Rathjen. Fragments of Kripke–Platek set theory with infinity. In P. Aczel, H. Simmons, and S.S. Wainer, editors, *Proof Theory. A selection of papers from the Leeds Proof Theory Programme 1990*, pages 251–273. Cambridge University Press, 1992.

[RS14] Florian Ranzi and Thomas Strahm. A note on the theory $\mathsf{SID}_{<\omega}$ of stratified induction. *Mathematical Logic Quarterly*, 60(6):487–497, 2014.

[RW93] Michael Rathjen and Andreas Weiermann. Proof-theoretic investigations on Kruskal's theorem. *Annals of Pure and Applied Logic*, 60:49–88, 1993.

[Sch54] Kurt Schütte. Kennzeichnung von Ordnungszahlen durch rekursiv erklärte Funktionen. *Mathematische Annalen*, 127:15–32, 1954. 10.1007/BF01361109.

[Sch92] Kurt Schütte. Beziehungen des Ordinalzahlensystems $\mathrm{OT}(\vartheta)$ zur Veblen-Hierarchie. Unpublished notes, 1992.

[Sim09] Stephen G. Simpson. *Subsystems of Second Order Arithmetic.* Cambridge University Press, second edition, 2009. Cambridge Books Online.

[Str99] Thomas Strahm. First steps into metapredicativity in explicit mathematics. In S. Barry Cooper and John K. Truss, editors, *Sets and Proofs*, volume 258 of *London Mathematical Society Lecture Notes*, pages 383–402. Cambridge University Press, 1999.

[Wey76] Richard Weyhrauch. *Relations Between Some Hierarchies of Ordinal Functions and Functionals.* PhD thesis, Stanford University, 1976.

Index

Erklärung

gemäss Art. 28 Abs. 2 RSL 05

Name/Vorname:	Ranzi Florian
Matrikelnummer:	11-118-569
Studiengang:	Informatik Bachelor ☐ Master ☐ Dissertation ☒
Titel der Arbeit:	From a Flexible Type System to Metapredicative Wellordering Proofs
Leiter der Arbeit:	Prof. Dr. G. Jäger und Prof. Dr. Th. Strahm

Ich erkläre hiermit, dass ich diese Arbeit selbständig verfasst und keine anderen als die angegebenen Quellen benutzt habe. Alle Stellen, die wörtlich oder sinngemäss aus Quellen entnommen wurden, habe ich als solche gekennzeichnet. Mir ist bekannt, dass andernfalls der Senat gemäss Artikel 36 Absatz 1 Buchstabe r des Gesetzes vom 5. September 1996 über die Universität zum Entzug des auf Grund dieser Arbeit verliehenen Titels berechtigt ist.

....

Ort/Datum Unterschrift

Lebenslauf

1983	Geboren am 7. März in München
1989–1993	Volksschule München Zielstattstraße 74
1993–2002	Erasmus-Grasser-Gymnasium München
2002–2005	Diplomstudiengang Wirtschaftsmathematik an der Ludwig-Maximilians-Universität München
	Wechsel des Diplomstudiengangs nach dem Vordiplom
2005–2008	Diplomstudiengang Mathematik an der Ludwig-Maximilians-Universität München mit Nebenfach Informatik
	Abschluss mit Diplom
2009–2010	Werkstudent bei der Abteilung Produktentwicklung der Lebensversicherung von 1871 a.G. München
2010–2011	Lehrassistent beim Mathematischen Institut der Ludwig-Maximilians-Universität München
2011–2015	Doktorand bei Prof. Dr. Gerhard Jäger Forschungsgruppe *Logic and Theory Group* an der Universität Bern

www.ingramcontent.com/pod-product-compliance
Lightning Source LLC
Chambersburg PA
CBHW071421050326
40689CB00010B/1924
9781326455200